CARL MARIA von WEBER

WRITINGS ON MUSIC

Lithograph of Weber by Gustav Feckert (1847)
after a portrait by C. Vogel von Vogelstein.
Dresden, Staatliche Kunstsammlungen

CARL MARIA von WEBER

WRITINGS ON MUSIC

Translated by
MARTIN COOPER

Edited and introduced by
JOHN WARRACK

CAMBRIDGE UNIVERSITY PRESS

Cambridge
London   New York   New Rochelle
Melbourne   Sydney

Published by the Press Syndicate of the University of Cambridge
The Pitt Building, Trumpington Street, Cambridge CB2 1RP
32 East 57th Street, New York, NY 10022, USA
296 Beaconsfield Parade, Middle Park, Melbourne 3206, Australia

First published 1981

Printed in Great Britain at the
University Press, Cambridge

Library of Congress catalogue card number: 81-10053

British Library Cataloguing in Publication Data
Weber, Carl Maria von
Writings on music
1. Music – German – History and criticism
I. Title   II. Warrack, John
781.7'43   ML275.4
ISBN 0 521 22892 1

CONTENTS

viii   Contents

MONEY VALUES

The commonest money denominations in general use in Germany in the early nineteenth century were pfennig, thaler, groschen and kreuzer. Thaler and groschen were in most general use in the north of Germany, gulden and kreuzer in the south.

Silver 4 pfennig = 1 kreuzer (about ½d)
        3 kreuzer = 1 groschen (about 1½d)
      60 kreuzer = 1 gulden (about 2s)
      90 kreuzer = 1 reichsthaler (about 3s)

Gold 3 reichsthaler = 1 ducat (about 9s)
     5 reichsthaler = 1 pistole (also known as Louis d'or, or similarly after the authorizing ruler; about 15s)
     6 reichsthaler = 1 carolin (about 18s)

This simplifies a very complex situation. Owing to the number of different mints, the value of the groschen and thaler varied from time to time and from place to place, but these stood in fixed relationship to each other. The contemporary English equivalents are only approximate, and no allowance has been made for the change in purchasing power since the early nineteenth century. Many things were relatively cheaper or dearer than today. Clothes and luxuries such as tea, coffee and sugar were expensive, though Weber could buy 150 oysters in Berlin for about £1; modest furnished rooms were relatively cheap. Weber suggests the top annual salary for a principal operatic soprano (the famous Therese Grünbaum) in Dresden in 1817 as 3400 thaler, or a little over £500, but a more usual range for principals was 1500–2000 thaler, or £225–£300. He himself was engaged as Kapellmeister for Dresden at 1500 thaler. His Diary, in which he kept meticulous accounts, sheds much light on the professional and domestic economy of the day.

ABBREVIATIONS

AdB	*Allgemeine deutsche Biographie* (56 vols., Leipzig, 1875–1912)
AMZ	*Allgemeine musikalische Zeitung* (Leipzig, 1798–1848)
Anh	Anhang
BKP	J. Branberger, *Konservatoř hudby v Praže*, trans. as *Das Konservatorium für Musik in Prag* (Prague, 1911)
DAZ	Dresden *Abend-Zeitung* (Dresden, 1805, 1817–57)
D-Bds	Deutsche Staatsbibliothek, Berlin
Diary	Weber's diary (unpublished: MS in Jähns Collection *Weberiana*, D-Bds)
DKB	G. Dlabacž, *Allgemeines historisches Künstler-Lexicon für Böhmen* (Prague, 1815)
D-Mbs	Bayerische Staatsbibliothek, Munich
EBL	L. Eisenberg, *Grosses biographisches Lexikon der deutschen Bühne im XIX Jahrhundert* (Leipzig, 1905)
FétisB	F. J. Fétis, *Biographie universelle des musiciens* (Paris, 1873)
HHS	T. Hell, *Hinterlassene Schriften von Carl Maria von Weber* (Dresden and Leipzig, 1828)
J	F. W. Jähns, *Carl Maria von Weber in seinen Werken* (Berlin, 1871)
KPZ	*Königliche kaiserliche privilegierte Prager Zeitung*
KSS	G. Kaiser, *Sämtliche Schriften von Carl Maria von Weber* (Berlin and Leipzig, 1908)
LKA	K. Laux, *Carl Maria von Weber: Kunstansichten* (Leipzig, 1975)
LTB	C. von Ledebur, *Tonkünstler-Lexicon Berlins* (Berlin, 1861)
MMW	M. M. von Weber, *Carl Maria von Weber: ein Lebensbild* (3 vols., Leipzig, 1864–6)
Notizen-Buch	Weber's Prague register of performances (MS in Rudolfinum, Archiv Státní konservatoře v Praže (Pk))
NZfM	*Neue Zeitschrift für Musik* (Leipzig, 1834–1920)
WGA	Weber Gesamtausgabe (Augsburg, 1926—)
*	see Biographical Glossary

INTRODUCTION

Into his short life – he was not yet forty when he died in London in 1826 – Weber fitted enough careers for five or six men. As one of the pioneering composers of Romanticism, he left a volume of work (over three hundred entries in Jähn's catalogue)[1] much of which survives in concert and opera repertories and which helped to open up new ways of thought to his successors. There is good reason to think that he had himself by no means fully explored his own novel ideas, that he had by no means reached his fullest potential as a creator. As a pianist he was admired as one of the most brilliant and most sensitive in an age of great virtuosos, an artist whose technique helped to pave the way for Chopin and Liszt; domestically, he was also an accomplished guitarist and, until an accident ruined his voice, a singer. As a conductor he brought new virtuosity to the direction of the orchestra, whose instruments he understood so well, giving it above all a central importance in the opera house, where his triumphs were acknowledged even by his opponents. Here, too, his belief in what Wagner was to call the *Gesamtkunstwerk* led him to undertake every task, however menial, that contributed to the unification of the theatrical arts and crafts into a new expressive medium: he concerned himself with décor, with the wardrobe, with lighting, with stage movement and production, with fidelity to the score, with the library, with new systems of rehearsal that demanded proper understanding of text and music by all concerned. As a child and young man, he liked to draw and paint. Not least, he was a writer.

In this field, too, his versatility was extraordinary. He reviewed concerts, operas, books and music. He planned and contributed to a projected guidebook for travelling virtuosos. He founded a so-called Harmonischer Verein of like-minded musicians and established its precepts and rules. He gave accounts of new instruments, of music shops, of singers, of educational establishments. He wrote some poetry, made some translations, and left incomplete a substantial amount of a full-length novel. As part of a systematic policy, he introduced the operas he gave in Prague and Dresden with articles to explain them and to encourage the public to give them a sympathetic hearing; and

[1]   F. W. Jähns, *Carl Maria von Weber in seinen Werken. Chronologisch-thematisches Verzeichniss seiner sämmtlichen Compositionen* (Berlin, 1871).

when challenged over this or any other policy, he was a quick-witted and formidable controversialist, one not without arrogance but also capable of behaving with dignity and generosity. Throughout his writing, whether critical, polemical or imaginative, runs a single thread – his resolve to establish by every means at his disposal German opera as a mature, independent genre. As much of his earlier writing, whether satirical or serious in tone, makes clear, he knew that the soil in Germany was thin and needed fertilization, especially by the tradition of French *opéra comique* which was beginning to find a strong following in Germany even before his decisive lead; and he resisted the charms of Italian opera with a ferocity born of profound respect. His criticism was the spearhead of an attack which he backed up with his elaborate administrative work, his interpretative energies, and his powerful creative achievements.

That Weber should have combined so many different gifts into a single-minded artistic enterprise was novel, and characteristic of Romanticism's tendency to develop liaisons between the arts; but he was not the first composer–critic to emerge in Germany, nor the first to break a lance for an independent German opera. Johann Mattheson's *Critica Musica* (Hamburg, 1722–5) gave a platform to what had become one of the major issues of the eighteenth century in German music, the rivalry between Italian opera, traditionally the art of the courts, and native German music. Coming after Mattheson, and in the footsteps of J. C. Gottsched's efforts in *Die vernünftigen Tadlerinnen* (Leipzig, 1725–7) to challenge Italian conventions and to kindle respect for French drama, J. A. Scheibe published *Der critischer Musikus* (Hamburg, 1737–40). Here the attack on Italian opera sharpened and began to specify its targets, with the feebleness of librettos, the impoverished standards of production and the absurdities of the castratos being singled out for particular abuse. The 'Siebentes Stück' (28 May 1737) attacks, in true Enlightenment vein, the 'unreason' of Italian opera, in which too many librettists write to the standard musical forms required of them rather than according to dramatic sense; and Gottsched is quoted in support of the view that composers make too little differentiation between characters: 'An avenger or someone enraged, trying to slay his adversary, will often indulge in so much coloratura that the adversary could escape him ten times over,' Scheibe asserts, adding tartly of one unfortunate composer's female chorus in an Alexander opera, 'Did Alexander really conquer the world with a crowd of women?'

Though various other critics joined in the arguments, with Scheibe's

Romantic theory of music as an expression of natural feeling finding an increasing number of supporters, the most significant voice for opera belonged to a composer, Johann Adam Hiller (1728–1804). As a founding father of *Singspiel*, he put into currency a number of features that were still potent with the Romantics (he was the first to make significant use of the Polonaise), and gave the casual forms of *Singspiel* a new unity. Further, in his *Wöchentliche Nachrichten und Anmerkungen die Musik betreffend* (Leipzig, 1766–70), he shed the apparatus of learned aesthetic enquiry which had been thought proper in most previous German criticism, and based his journal on news and reviews. His critical platform was against Italian opera; and he now addressed himself not to fellow professionals but to an emerging bourgeois audience whose tastes he did much to educate. He was a figure of crucial importance to the most influential of his immediate successors, Johann Friedrich Reichardt (1752–1814).

Reichardt's book *Über die deutsche comische Oper* (Hamburg, 1774) – it is scarcely more than a pamphlet of a hundred pages – is basically an analysis of Hiller's most famous work, *Die Jagd* (1770). It opens with a reproach familiar from, among other sources, Scheibe's *Critischer Musikus*: 'There is no more generally accepted opinion than this, that in the arts the Germans are merely imitators'; and continues, 'The whole artistic world now admires Italian and French stage music, and looks down its nose at the German version as something upstart.' Hiller's piece is taken as the example of how by cutting down on extensive arias, except in carefully chosen places, and by improving the quality of the orchestra's contribution, a more unified and truly dramatic work can be achieved. As a practical musician, Reichardt recognized the poverty of German theatrical resources, and campaigned for better theatres, better native singers and orchestras. His own works were prized in their day – among them, *Brenno* (1801) was praised for its vivid characterization and for an overture that was 'in itself an entire drama' (*AMZ* IV (1802), 313–20) – but he was no less admired as a critic. His ideas impressed his successors (including Mendelssohn and Schumann), and his methods were rapidly imitated. Taking a lead from Hiller, he published a series of musical letters and journals, including the *Musikalisches Kunstmagazin* (Berlin, 1782–91) and the *Berlinische musikalische Zeitung* (Berlin, 1805–6), into which he poured his reports and opinions of music he had heard on his travels. A characteristic essay, 'Über das deutsche Singeschauspiel', points to one perennial problem, that the cadences of Italian are already so musical that only the slightest harmonic indications are necessary to make it into recitative, whereas the sounds of German are totally different; and Weber's demands in *Euryanthe* are anticipated by a call for more exacting subjects and by the insistence that subtler verses than the usual four-square patterns are needed as a stimulus to interesting dramatic music (*Musikalisches Kunstmagazin* I, pt 4 (1782), 161–4). Reichardt was himself a man of wide interests, well read, and befriended by philosophers and men of letters (among them Goethe, whose *Singspiele* he set); as a gardener's son, he had a particular feeling for nature, and did some painting; he was an accomplished singer and guitarist, with an ear for folksong and an understanding of its importance as a source of German art; his politics were liberal, and his sympathy with the ideals of the French Revolution coloured his views and opened his mind to new intellectual stimuli on music.

However useful Reichardt's energetic writings are as a source for contemporary opinion, his journalism is completely overshadowed by the work of Friedrich Rochlitz (1769–1842). Himself a man of some versatility, who had composed, written stories and dramas, and published almanacs, Rochlitz earns his place in history as the editor of the first twenty years of the *Allgemeine musikalische Zeitung*, founded in Leipzig by Breitkopf and Härtel in 1798. Without a break, it appeared weekly until 1848 (and was subsequently revived, in a new form). In that year, G. W. Fink, Rochlitz's successor, declared that its work had evidently been done. In truth, Fink's stale attitudes and failure to respond to new trends had been partly responsible for the foundation, as a corrective, of Schumann's *Neue Zeitschrift für Musik* (Leipzig, 1834–1920).

The format which Rochlitz devised for the *AMZ* needed little modification throughout his editorship. The journal normally opened with a substantial essay, on some aesthetic topic or on some technical aspect of musical theory or describing some novel instrument, perhaps an historical study (such as Gerber on the Camerata, *AMZ* II (1800), 418ff), sometimes an article on a particular work, or even a piece of fiction: E. T. A. Hoffmann, who was with Weber the most important contributor Rochlitz had, wrote both his famous essay on Beethoven's Fifth Symphony and his story *Don Juan* for the *AMZ*. It would continue with reports from anonymous correspondents, a somewhat erratic network of whom Rochlitz managed to build up not only in Germany but as far afield as London, Paris and Moscow. Berlin, Breslau, Dresden, Frankfurt, Kassel, Königsberg and Munich, as well as Leipzig itself, were the sources of the best and fullest reports at various times; but naturally the standard was very uneven, given the absence of proper critical disciplines and the lack of control over local enthusiasms and rivalries. In certain cities, among them Hamburg, Rochlitz seems never to have found a regular correspondent of sufficient quality. There would also be reviews of books and music, and sometimes lighter anecdotes (including Rochlitz's own unreliable ones about Mozart). A monthly 'Intelligenz-Blatt' would normally carry news, announcements, details of forthcoming publications, etc.; and there were regular supplements of music, sometimes whole pieces, sometimes arias from forthcoming operas, and so forth. Most of the articles were anonymous: Rochlitz allowed only the more distinguished authors, such as Gerber and Apel, and later Hoffmann and Weber, to sign their names, though pseudonyms or initials were sometimes permitted; and – an index of the importance he gave to French music – the regular Paris reports were signed in full by his correspondent G. L. P. Sievers.

From the very first, Rochlitz associated himself with the campaign for German opera. His opening essay (*AMZ* I (1798)) was 'Gedanken über die Oper', in which he defines opera as 'a drama in which everything, elsewhere spoken, is sung'. He continues with the usual complaints about Italian practices, adding that the French have fallen into a state of confusion and the English only support the great of other nations, such as Handel. In the following year, Rochlitz issued an eloquent call to young composers to cultivate opera as a serious art in which greater realism, more vivid characters and stronger situations, together with more functional use of scenery, were to be combined: with emphasized print, he went on to declare, 'Opera is the art that results from the unification of all the arts' (*AMZ* II (1799), 161ff). These and other essays were the first salvoes in a sustained battle waged by Rochlitz on behalf of German opera. He was under no illusions; he did not underestimate the attractions of Italian opera, especially given its entrenched popularity in the courts, nor the poor resources of the average German theatre. The first five years of the campaign culminated in a project to use the *AMZ* as a central agency for commissioning new operas; and this only failed for want of the necessary practical support, enthusiastically as the idea was received. Even if he was discouraged, Rochlitz was undeterred: he continued his fight by all means open to him, publishing articles arguing the case aesthetically, offering practical recommendations, pleading for singing schools (an important step in freeing German opera from the tyranny of the Italian star and the general feebleness of its own artists), even drawing on satirical fiction as a weapon. Though he had retired from the editorship by 1818, Rochlitz reviewed *Der Freischütz* in 1821, and lived to see the first fruits of his campaign.

Rochlitz himself was not a major critic; and, despite his encouragement of the new, he belonged fundamentally to the *Goethezeit*. However, he was able to command the services of good writers, and he had a nose for seeking them out. Already in the first year of issue he published a favourable review of Six Fughettas by 'Karl Marin von Weber in Salzburg', signed 'Z***' (*AMZ* I (1798), 32): they are slim little exercises and it was discerning of the reviewer to see any imaginative quality in them (Weber himself later made use of the material, for example as the subject of two fugues in his E flat Mass (J224)). Before long Rochlitz had made Weber's acquaintance, and in 1809 launched him on his critical career with his first published review, an extremely sharp piece of work attacking J. B. Schaul's *Briefe über den Geschmack in der Musik* (below, No. 2). In all, Weber wrote twenty-five articles for the *AMZ*, including polemics, reviews, essays and miscellanea. He maintained a lifelong friendship with Rochlitz, even setting his words to music in *Der erste Ton* (J58) and *In seiner Ordnung schafft der Herr* (J154): Rochlitz had a good conceit of his own creative powers. The *AMZ*, as by far the most important musical journal of Germany, was the one Weber regularly read, and he maintained a steady, uninterruptedly cordial correspondence with Rochlitz for most of his life.

However, the existence in early-nineteenth-century Germany of scores of local journals devoted to the arts, to news, comment, reviews and belles-lettres provided Weber with ample further encouragement for critical writing; and with varying regularity he turned to a dozen of these. His tenure as director of the Operas in Prague and Dresden gave him the opportunity for the articles in which some of his best critical work appeared. These were his so-called Musico-Dramatic Articles; rather than critical analyses, they were introductions to works which many of his potential audience would barely have known even by name. It was a system he pioneered; and though the articles are aimed at drawing in the general public, they often contain shrewd observations on the nature of opera as well as giving a persuasive assessment of some now long-forgotten works. In Prague, the natural outlet was the journal of the educated German aristocracy and middle classes in the city, the *Königliche kaiserliche privilegierte Prager Zeitung*. Founded in 1744 as the *K.K. privilegierte Prager Ober-Postamts-Zeitung*, it had won a steadily increasing reputation throughout the eighteenth century. By 1813, when Weber came to know it, times were difficult as a result of the wartime censorship. However, it was still appearing daily, and under Adolf Gerle, a circumspect and knowledgeable man, it won important contributors; indeed, such was its reputation that writers were said to offer payment for the publication of their articles (unsuccessfully). It emphasized foreign news at the expense of home news, but had columns on economics and market prices, and also published news of important visitors and announced forthcoming operas: it printed opera reviews only occasionally, concert reviews not at all until Weber. Latterly, after Weber left Prague, it fell on harder times; and in 1819 the only serious political journal in Bohemia was reduced in size (to four small folio sheets) and in frequency (to four times weekly) and increased steeply in price (for further details see A. Przedak, *Geschichte des deutschen Zeitschriftwesens in Böhmen* (Heidelberg, 1904)).

A more influential journal, however, was the Dresden *Abend-Zeitung*. Founded in 1805, it was almost immediately forced by the war to suspend publication, and did not resume until 1817; it then survived until 1857, with Weber's friend Carl Winkler ('Theodor Hell') as editor until 1843. Its co-founder in 1817 was Friedrich Kind, a Dresden litterateur and the librettist of *Der Freischütz*. The journal was thus strongly disposed towards Weber and his reforms, and generally indulgent towards him, though not to the exclusion of attacks such as that by Therese aus dem Winkel. One of the most widely read literary journals of the day, it appeared at first twice a week, then six times, and was a simply printed four-page sheet that published stories (including the original of Weber's unfinished opera, *Die drei Pintos*), poems, satirical essays, book reviews and articles on all manner of subjects, including fashion. It regularly carried reviews of both Italian and German theatres: normally drama was reviewed by Therese aus dem Winkel ('C'), and concerts and operas by Friedrich Huber ('F'). Less powerful was the *Literarischer Merkur*, a rival Dresden journal that dissociated itself from the German party, and was indeed generally regarded as being more independent-minded in its criticism even if it could not command such a good team of contributors.

In other cities where he worked, Weber found periodicals happy to accept his writings. Though always loyal to the *AMZ*, he contributed a few reviews to a local Leipzig journal, the *Zeitung für die elegante Welt* (1801–59). Founded by the composer and essayist Johann Gottlieb Karl Spazier ('Karl Pilger'), this appeared three times weekly and covered literature, theatre, art, and scholarly subjects, placing an unusual emphasis on fashion and belles-lettres: its Romantic enthusiasms, which included a strong editorial line against Kotzebue, clearly had an appeal for Weber. In Munich, he wrote for two prominent local journals, the *Kritischer Anzeiger für Literatur und Kunst* and the *Gesellschaftsblatt für gebildete Stände*. Of the two, the latter was the more important. Founded in 1800 as the *Kurpfalzisches Wochenblatt*, it became the *Königlich baierisches Wochenblatt* in 1806, then after further changes in title emerged under its most familiar name in 1811. From 1800 to 1810 it appeared weekly, and was both literary and political under its editor, Lorenz Hübner; from 1811 it was exclusively literary, and appeared twice weekly. In Weimar Weber contributed to the *Journal des Luxus und der Moden* (1786–1827). Founded by the journalist, and later Councillor, Friedrich Justin Bertuch, this covered a wide range of subjects concerning the graces of life, including furniture, jewellery, travel, even cosmetics, as well as the arts. It was a monthly, of about seventy well-printed octavo pages per issue, with attractive pictures (some in colour), and was very popular, even being read abroad. During his stay in Mannheim and Darmstadt, Weber contributed to the *Rheinische Correspondenz*. Originally entitled the *Rheinische Bundeszeitung*, this was published in Mannheim by its editor, Ferdinand Kaufmann, and appeared daily from 1 January 1808 until 31 October 1810. It consisted of four pages, divided into home news, foreign news (including bulletins from as far afield as Constantinople and Irkutsk), reviews (including one of Weber's Darmstadt concert, in No. 70, 11 March 1810) and somewhat gossipy editorials. Freiberg, where Weber's first surviving opera, *Das Waldmädchen*, was produced, provided a forum for reviews and for the controversy almost certainly run by his father, Franz Anton, in a journal whose importance seems to have been in inverse proportion to the majesty of its title, the *Gnädigst bewilligte Freyberger gemeinnützigen Nachrichten für das chursächsische Erzegebirge*.

A far more significant journal, and one sympathetic to his aims, was the one he encountered soon afterwards in Stuttgart, the *Morgenblatt für gebildete Stände* (1807–65). This had been founded in Tübingen by Johann Friedrich Cotta, also the initiator of several other influential literary journals including *Flora*, *Die Horen* and *Propyläen*; but in 1810 it moved to Stuttgart, and its reputation began to grow. One of its staff, later to be editor, was Therese Huber (wife of the Augsburg editor Ludwig Huber), who was responsible for encouraging many women writers. The journal appeared six times a week, and included essays, poems, memoirs, travel articles and criticism; initially taking a stand for Classicism against Romanticism, and notable for the lively controversies it published, the *Morgenblatt* became a more balanced forum for discussion after 1815, when the staff was joined by some Romantics under a new editor, the poet Friedrich Rückert.

Finally – and despite the complaints of an English visitor in 1818 about the miserable state of the Berlin press – the number of papers in the country's intellectual capital would have given Weber an outlet during his several happy stays in the city; but he was usually passing through on a brief visit, and only rarely made use of them. The *Dramaturgisches Wochenblatt* reprinted the appreciation of Therese Grünbaum (below, No. 98) which had originally appeared in the *DAZ*. His review of a set of Gottfried Weber's songs (below, No. 37) appeared in the *Haude- und Spenersche Zeitung*, the popular name for the *Berlinische Nachrichten von Staats- und gelehrten Sachen* (1740–1874), founded by Ambrosius Haude and run by him and Johann Spener. By 1800 this had become a daily, carrying extended theatre and concert criticism, and had achieved a circulation of ten thousand. However, it was not so widely read as the *Vossische Zeitung* or *Königliche privilegierte Berlinische Zeitung*, founded in 1721 and run for many years by Christian Friedrich Voss. By 1815 this latter influential daily included a substantial section dealing with cultural matters, and a supplement containing further articles and announcements. It was here that Weber chose to publish his thanks after the triumphant reception of *Der Freischütz* (below, No. 119).

Already in the first years of the new century Weber had begun to show an interest in writing. Together with his Viennese friend Ignaz Susann, a young law student and amateur flautist, he formed in 1802–3 the idea of compiling a musical dictionary and founding a musical journal. The latter scheme came to nothing; the articles Weber wrote for the dictionary were eventually used in E. L. Gerber's *Neues historisch-biographisches Lexicon der Tonkünstler* (4 vols., Leipzig, 1812–14). The subjects include Andreas Brunmayer, Joachim Fuertsch, Oswald Bach, and his teacher Johann Peter Heuschkel; Kaiser considered that Weber also wrote, or at any rate provided material for, another ten at least, including Michael Haydn, Vogler, Gottfried Weber, Franz Edmond Weber, J. N. Kalcher, J. E. Valesi and Johann Gänsbacher.[2] Weber also intended to write a theatrical and concert history of Vienna, and seems to have felt that he had an ally for these enterprises in Susann: in 1804 he was writing to say, 'The Italians will have the upper hand with you, too. Oh, how heartily I agree with all you say – but don't let our courage fail, together we can do something good, and perhaps put a lot of things right' (letter of 2 April 1804). However, he did not begin writing seriously until 1809, and between then and 1812, before he

[2] G. Kaiser, *Beiträge zu einer Charakteristik Carl Maria von Webers als Musik-schriftsteller* (Berlin and Leipzig, 1910).

took up his Prague appointment, he published some three dozen articles. These impressed Rochlitz and Fink so much that they urged him to devote himself more fully to writing.

However, journalism was for Weber, as for other composer–critics before him, only one aspect of his work, which he viewed as a totality. The Harmonischer Verein (see below, No. 13), with its elaborate formality and its secrecy, was intended not as a mutual admiration society but to increase the impact of the new generation of Romantic musicians; though how much the two could ever be kept wholly apart is a moot point. The original plan provided for a musical journal, but this was once again abandoned (partly out of respect for the *AMZ*, Weber later told Rochlitz) before the intended appearance in May 1811 of the first issue, to be called *Zeitung für die musikalische Welt* or *Der harmonische Bund*. However, the essence of the enterprise was to further ideas held in common by members; and so close did they believe these to be that they felt free to speak with a corporate voice. They used pseudonyms more to associate themselves with the society than to disguise themselves; indeed, some of the pseudonyms were interchangeable, and doubtless an editorial hand was frequently at work. Thus, the review of Meyerbeer's *Gott und die Natur* (below, No. 19) was signed 'N': it was constructed out of factual material provided by Meyerbeer himself and worked into shape with critical observations by Weber, who knew the score but was in Munich at the time of the Berlin première. Probably it was also further edited by Gottfried Weber, who contributed articles on behalf of the society to various journals, especially the *Zeitung für die elegante Welt* and the *Morgenblatt für gebildete Stände*. Later, still in the spirit of the Harmonischer Verein, Weber felt free to give factual mention to his own concerts and their intentions, though there was normally no one to add critical comments, except when Rochlitz appended some editorial remarks. Latterly he came to dislike anonymity among critics, and only in exceptional circumstances and with reluctance had recourse to it. By then, he had won himself an influential name in Germany; no longer part of a campaign, he wrote with more mature and independent judgement, in such essays as the review of Fesca's work (below, No. 110) and in parts of *Tonkünstlers Leben* ('A Composer's Life', below, No. 125) developing his aesthetic theories by means of argument, of fictionalized discussion and of aphorisms.

For some three years, however, the Harmonischer Verein was a going concern, and the journals of the time are filled with articles by and about its members. Yet it proved impossible to maintain the initial enthusiasm, and indeed it is difficult to see how any such artistic collective could work when men of real and highly individual talent were involved. By 1813 it was more or less defunct. Gottfried Weber, probably the most painstaking and practical of them, did his best to maintain interest, especially from his namesake Carl Maria, but with Gänsbacher often otherwise distracted, Dusch apparently inactive, and Meyerbeer (in their eyes) a renegade to Italy, the impetus had gone out of the movement. Many years later, Gottfried Weber recalled those days nostalgically: 'Imbued with youthful ardour for the good and the beautiful in art and learning, we solemnly promised ourselves to further these ends by every possible word and deed and to fight low standards and the underhand devices of pseudo-artists, critical hacks and phrase-mongering aesthetes' (*Caecilia* xv (1833), 33). Like Schumann's fictitious Davidsbündler after them, they set out to do battle with the Philistines; and there can be little doubt that their association gave them some much-needed confidence and strength to carry out their reforming work.

Weber's style in these early essays has an infectious enthusiasm, though it can, as he admitted in one of the notes attached to *Tonkünstlers Leben*, become somewhat exaggerated.

I find my style highly coloured and – because its intention is to give an exhaustive account – slightly precious and bombastic. However, I cannot divorce myself from it, however much I may respect and be deeply devoted to the clarity of a Goethe, a Schlegel or a Tieck. Perhaps it may be my very musicality that accounts for it. The many descriptive adjectives in a language closely resemble the instrumentation of a musical idea. I am conscious of being able to reproduce such an idea with just as much clarity as I conceived it, though this is very seldom true of ideas which I wish to express in words.

Discounting the *Waldmädchen* controversy as being largely or entirely the work of his father, one may agree to the extent that Weber is capable of allowing his natural artistic exuberance to run away with him in his first critical forays. The ferocious savaging of Schaul's *Letters* (below, No. 2) is the work of a young and intransigent critic; and the early reviews reveal the determination to insist upon his ideas which he later found bombastic, even if the modern reader may be less embarrassed about this than the older and wiser author himself. Later, he refined his style and tautened his method of argument: the controversialist of the Dresden days, retorting to C and A.C.H., was a more deadly adversary than the youthful arbiter of taste putting Schaul smartly in his place. At its best, his writing has a grace and ease which contrast agreeably with the general standard of German musical journalism of the day. Rochlitz's somewhat lordly manner, involuted and self-conscious, infected many of his contributors; and Weber's own style in the *AMZ* tends to be more ornate, with long sentences often dense in construction, than when he was writing for the Prague or Dresden newspapers. In times when authority of utterance was too often associated with pomposity, his generous salting of wit must have been the more welcome.

By far the largest proportion of Weber's articles consists of either reviews or introductory notices to operas he believed important to the cause of German Romantic opera. And though he wrote on Spohr, Hoffmann, Winter, Mozart, Marschner and Poissl, among others, there is a striking emphasis on the French composers whose *opéras comiques* were a stronger imaginative source than the native *Singspiel* – Isouard, Gaveaux, Méhul, Cherubini, Boieldieu, Grétry, Catel and Dalayrac. This reflected the policy of the *AMZ* – for many years the only regular monthly foreign reports were Sievers's from Paris – and in turn reflected the realization of intelligent German musicians that it was from France that the real imaginative impetus would come. French opera was widely popular in Germany during the latter part of the eighteenth century, as is shown by study of the repertories, the number of publications and translations of one and the same opera, and the frequency with which a work was reviewed, let alone the enthusiastic tone of the reviews. Weber was not the first Kapellmeister to find a generous place in his repertories for French opera, but he brought new system into his choice; and he was the first to accompany his seasons with articles arguing his case. He resisted Italian 'Kling-Klang', though he was quick to insist that he was objecting not so much to Italian opera itself – he admired its strengths, and even made a respectful call on Rossini in Paris – but to its qualities as an example for Germans. Twice he referred, in one of his most famous observations, to the German ideal, 'a self-sufficient work of art in which every feature and every contribution of the related arts are moulded together in a certain way and dissolve, to form a new world' (below, Nos. 87, 125); and again in his opening remarks 'To the art-loving citizens of Dresden' (No. 88), he referred to the German demand for 'a self-sufficient work of art, in which all the parts make up a beautiful and unified whole'.

In this glimpse of the *Gesamtkunstwerk* he foreshadowed Wagner; and towards this ideal he worked by critical argument as well as creative example. The singers he praises are those of striking dramatic gifts, rather than merely skilled vocalists: as he wrote of Therese

Grünbaum, 'a voice by itself no more constitutes a good singer than a good figure makes a good dancer' (below, No. 98). The plan he drew up for the Dresden company was based not on the star system but on an ensemble of actor–singers. His defence of his orchestral reseating shows his concern for a proper tonal blend and for giving the orchestra its proper role in the drama; all reviews speak eloquently of his actual skill as a conductor in realizing this precept. His use of pictorial images ('tonal canvas', 'the basic colour of each section', 'broad brush-strokes') suggests the interest he is known to have taken in the actual décor; but at the back of it, as in his accounts of the musical stimulus he drew from travelling through a picturesque landscape, is a merging of sensuous impressions in characteristic Romantic synaesthesia. His abhorrence of inserted ornamentation was obsessive, deriving as it did from his insistence that such impressions should be direct and eloquent, unconfused by decorations whose real purpose was to distract attention on to the performer. Although he accepted operas with inserted arias, and indeed wrote a number of such arias himself, he did so with reservations that he made abundantly clear. Moreover, he struck some blows for the performance of original versions at a time when this was scarcely possible; as he admitted in his essay on Grétry's *Raoul Barbe-bleue* (below, No. 96), the priority was to win an audience, and to this end he could even argue the case for giving a work with sub-stantial cuts (as in the conversation with Diehl in *Tonkünstlers Leben*).

His concert reviews are, on the whole, less important, except for the glimpses they give of artists both famous, such as F. W. and J. P. Pixis and Moscheles (below, Nos. 57, 78, 79), and forgotten, such as the adventurous Bohrer brothers (No. 4). It is a matter for regret that he did not live to fulfil his plan for a work on aesthetics, and that his technical observations are so few. He was enlarging and consolidating his aesthetic ideas, no less than his musical achievements, when illness began to drag him low; but his technical observations were always sharply to the point. The comments defending his word-setting for a little song in Adolf Müllner's *König Yngurd* (below, No. 103) show how scrupulously he approached this task, even for so minor a work; and the occasional remarks about the value of motif as a structural force suggest that had his energies endured, he might have had more to say on the subject, certainly when he had himself been able to capitalize on the gains won in *Euryanthe*.

Particularly in the second period of his critical activity – from 1815 until 1820, when the decline in the German Opera at Dresden and the need to conserve his failing energies for composition made him give up criticism – he concentrated on pleading a cause, going over to the attack only in self-defence. The deadliest shafts in his satirical comments in *Tonkünstlers Leben* are reserved for German opera, whose weaknesses he knew only too well; and though a few minor composers such as Wenzel Müller and Ferdinand Kauer receive back-handed comments, he never failed in his respect for Beethoven. However, since he has repeatedly been accused of scornful comment on Beethoven, the case demands examination.[3]

As a young man, Weber found Beethoven as disturbing as did all his contemporaries. His most extensive published comments on individual works concern some of Beethoven's lesser achievements, *Christus am Ölberge* (below, No. 66), the Choral Fantasia (No. 67) and *Wellingtons Sieg* (No. 69) (his passing comments on other works are invariably admiring). The latter, he wrote, showed 'obvious traits of genius, such as are never absent from the work of this mighty composer'; he was cool about the other two pieces, and his difficulties in appreciating Beethoven arise from his own differing view, as a composer, of where a path forward for German music might be found. The whole nature of his own art bears witness to his belief that this must lie with dramatic forms – though not in the Italian manner – rather than with the symphony. It was to take Wagner's genius to appreciate how the two were not mutually incompatible, how the methods of development evolved by Beethoven to such an advanced state could, in his own hands, be transmuted into something with relevance for opera. Weber's profound if guarded admiration for Beethoven can be compared to that of those later musicians in whom admiration for Wagner was considerably chastened by fear of what they saw as a dangerous course for German music as a whole. His respect for Beethoven was expressed not only in the visit he paid to the great man in Baden at the time of the première of *Euryanthe*, but in the many admiring references throughout his writings. As a very young man, he shared with most of his contemporaries a difficulty in grasping the full scale of Beethoven's genius; but the nearest he came to taking part in the chorus of confused resistance to Beethoven was in a letter to the publisher Nägeli (who had echoed some of the fashionable comparisons between himself and Beethoven), where he is as ever insistent on Beethoven's imaginative superiority.

You seem to see me from my Quartet and the Caprice as an imitator of Beethoven, and flattered as many might be by this, I don't find it in the least

3   See also J. Warrack, *Carl Maria von Weber*, 2nd edn (Cambridge, 1976), pp. 98–104.

pleasant. Firstly, I hate everything bearing the mark of imitation; secondly, my views differ too much from Beethoven's for me to feel I could ever agree with him. The passionate, almost incredible inventive powers inspiring him are accompanied by such a chaotic arrangement of his ideas that only his earlier compositions appeal to me; the later ones seem to me hopeless chaos, an incomparable struggle for novelty, out of which break a few heavenly flashes of genius proving how great he could be if he would tame his rich fantasy. Though of course I cannot enjoy the gift of Beethoven's great genius, I do at least believe I can defend my own music from a logical and technical point of view, and produce in every piece a definite effect (letter of 1 May 1810).

Weber was twenty-three when he wrote this private comment to Nägeli, in the first flush of his ardour for Romantic ideals and the spirit of the Harmonischer Verein; and to the same period belong the passages in *Tonkünstlers Leben* about the modern symphony. There is only one specific reference to Beethoven. In a passage (below, pp. 330–3) anticipating Berlioz's *Les Soirées de l'orchestre*, the instruments of the orchestra have fallen to arguing about their individual superiority. The attack on 'our latest composers' symphonies' is led by 'a sour-faced double bass', and the passage is to be taken as a satire upon the reluctance of contemporary musicians, with performers well in the rearguard, to make any effort to accommodate themselves to new ideas. Their only concern is to assert their own importance, and to stick to the old, lazy conventions. On his arrival the conductor threatens them with the Eroica Symphony, 'and then I should like to see which of you can raise a limb or a key'. Horrified, they beg for a nice easy Italian opera, 'where one gets a nap now and then'. The implication, in fact, is of Beethoven's originality and of his exacting demands making the contemporary orchestra bestir itself to new ways – a subtle compliment.

The conductor proceeds, in the same breath, to describe in derisive terms 'the latest symphony I've just got from Vienna'.

First, we have a slow tempo, full of brief, disjointed ideas, none of them having any connexion with each other, three or four notes every quarter of an hour! That's exciting! Then a hollow drum-roll and mysterious viola passages, all decked out with the right amount of silences and general pauses; eventually, when the listener has given up all hope of surviving the tension as far as the Allegro, there comes a furious tempo in which the chief aim is to prevent any principal idea from appearing, and the listener has to try to find one on his own; there's no lack of modulations; that doesn't matter, all that matters, as in Paer's *Leonore*, is to make a chromatic run and stop on any note you like, and there's your modulation. Above all, one must shun rules, for they only cramp genius (p. 332–3).

This passage has always been taken, even by Kaiser,[4] to refer to Beethoven's Fourth Symphony. Presumably the grounds are that mention of it immediately follows reference to the Eroica (which is named, while the other symphony is not) and that the Fourth had appeared in Vienna in the March of 1807. However, the description does not fit. The complaints about lack of ideas and surfeit of modulations are vague; and there are no silences in the Introduction to the Fourth Symphony longer than a quaver until just before the Allegro, no 'hollow drum-roll' (dumpfer Paukenwirbel) but only a pair of fortissimo rolls supporting the transition bars to the Allegro, and no 'mysterious viola passages' (mysteriöse Bratschensätze), since the violas play only in a doubling or purely harmonic role. It seems certain that, especially since he was not afraid to name his adversaries, Weber was attacking a generalized target; and the point is clinched by a little-known Diary entry for 19 December 1816: 'In the evening to Eunicke, then to Wollank, wonderful (herrlich) Symphony in B flat by Beethoven played through.'

Still further in the realm of fiction is the story that Weber had once declared Beethoven to be 'ripe for the madhouse', a long-enduring tale despite Kaiser's painstaking exposure of it as unfounded. In his biography of Beethoven, Anton Schindler quoted a remark attributed to Weber, to the effect that 'the extravagances of this genius have now reached the non plus ultra, and Beethoven must be quite ripe for the madhouse'.[5] This was attributed to 1815, concerning a performance of the Seventh Symphony (1812), and Weber was further accused of having written a number of bitter reviews. On the appearance of Schindler's book – which like so much of his writing shows a possessive adulation of Beethoven – two reviews challenged his allegations, which had further included the story that Weber had asked Beethoven for corrections to Euryanthe and been refused. One observed that among the flaws in Schindler's book was 'an unworthy attack on C. M. v. Weber', especially unworthy since Weber was dead and could not reply (Blätter für literarische Unterhaltung, No. 319, 14 November 1840). The other was in the Neue Zeitschrift für Musik:

Schindler's book includes an attack of loathsome inaccuracy, which can be seen at a glance to be motivated by personal hatred... What can one say of a biographer who can forget himself so far as to invent such things and

[4] Kaiser, Beiträge, p. 48.
[5] A. Schindler, Biographie von Ludwig van Beethoven (Münster, 1840, 2nd edn 1845, 3rd edn 1860, 4th edn 1871, etc.), 3rd edn trans. C. Jolly and D. MacArdle, Beethoven as I knew him (London, 1966).

trumpet them as the truth in a work that has been so keenly awaited and will be so eagerly read? (*NZfM*, No. 48, 12 December 1840.)

Schindler replied in the former journal:

Perhaps it appears, after strenuous enquiry, that Weber was not the author of those bitter reviews of Beethoven's work which originally the well-known composer and writer living in Vienna, Baron [Eduard] von Lannoy, considered had come from C. M. von Weber's pen (he having received the information from Beethoven's friends). In this matter I was only a reporter (*Blätter für literarische Unterhaltung*, No. 366, 31 December 1840).

However, Schindler did not make any amendments when he published his *Beethoven in Paris: ein Nachtrag zur Beethovens Biographie* (Münster, 1842): this includes a chapter on Weber and Beethoven, and repeats the allegation about the madhouse, suggesting that Weber's comments against Beethoven could be found among his posthumous papers. Schindler here ignores the fact that all the writings known to Theodor Hell had been published in 1828 (HHS). Even in the third edition of his biography (1860) Schindler continued to repeat the madhouse story, saying that 'sooner or later it will be found'. It never has, though Caroline Weber carefully preserved everything for her son Max Maria to use in his biography and collection of his father's writings (MMW); nor was it ever discovered by the painstaking F. W. Jähns, nor by Kaiser, both of whom went methodically through all the family documents. Finally, Weber had at the time been showing much greater appreciation of Beethoven than in his younger days. In November 1814 he had staged *Fidelio*, in which, he told Gänsbacher, 'there are truly great things', and he had been enraged by the lack of interest on the part of the Prague public (letter of 1 December 1814); and reviewing two Prague concerts, he wrote of the 'magnificent, clear and solidly composed' *Prometheus* Overture (below, No. 59) and the 'magnificent, lucid and fiery C major Symphony' (No. 65). He found Beethoven sometimes difficult – a more intelligent response than superficial acceptance – and admired him as much as anyone in Germany.

Noting the completion of verses for a song, 'Künstlers Liebesforderung' (lost), Weber has a passage in his Diary describing the urge to write poetry: 'The devil of poetry had taken possession of me, dug me in the ribs; whether I wanted to or not, I *had* to make verses' (Diary, 24 September 1811). His verse is in fact inconsiderable, as well as being in most cases untranslatable because of its puns or other linguistic word-plays. It includes a poem in praise of fugue, the last quatrain

being an acrostic on the letters FUGE; a set of lines for an occasional
ode written by Vogler's pupils for his birthday; several doggerel
musical verse letters (to Danzi, Bärmann, Hiemer and Gottfried
Weber); some occasional lines for inscription on a glass tankard and
to accompany his gift of a punch ladle to Caroline; six short translations
from Italian for musical setting; and some sharp little epigrams. One
of the latter attacks Therese aus dem Winkel, and includes the jibe
about her being unable to hold her ink. Another couplet of 1810
lampoons 'the variation-smith G–K' – the Abbé Gelinek, the profusion
of whose variations was notorious:

> Kein Thema auf dem Welt verschonte dein Genie,
> Das simpelste allein – dich selbst – varierst du nie.

As a rough equivalent:

> Through themes of every kind, great genius, you range;
> The simplest one of all, yourself, you never change.

Several of these *jeux d'esprit* were written for the Liederkreis, the
Dresden literary circle whose liking for verbal games took the form of
requiring the members to contribute diversions of many kinds. Weber's
A bourgeois family story (below, No. 120) was merely a rapidly
sketched solution to the game of handing round eccentric trick
questions for literary answers; and a rather more elaborate version of
the English game of 'Consequences', whereby each man wrote a
chapter of a novel, taking as his subject words chosen at random by
the women, is the source of *The Mudfish* (No. 108). However, fiction
was also for Weber a tool of criticism. The essay on Baden-Baden
(below, No. 11) and the account of Cherubini's *Les Deux journées*
(No. 21) are semi-fictional in tone partly because of the nature of the
journals for which they were written, partly because this enabled him
to make some special points, and make them in a way that would not
have been possible in a factual account. The device was not unique:
the *AMZ* published occasional pieces of fiction for special purposes,
such as the account of opera in 'Krähwinkel' (*AMZ* VII (1804),
97–101), and E. T. A. Hoffmann's *Don Juan* story (*AMZ* XV (1813),
213ff). By far Weber's most extensive attempt at fiction was the novel
Tonkünstlers Leben (below, No. 125), which he first planned in 1804
and continued to tinker with, finally abandoning it in 1820 as a group
of more or less completed chapters and a number of disjointed
fragments.

Weber's prose style in his imaginative writing, as in the criticism into
which it continually shades, has a distinct grace and individuality.

Especially under the influence of Franz Danzi in Stuttgart, he read widely among contemporary philosophers and writers, and he was quick to respond to current ideas. He was much impressed with his contemporary, E. T. A. Hoffmann, though their acquaintance never ripened into real friendship; and in the *Phantasiestücke in Callots Manier* he found new stimulus, as he told Rochlitz:

Have you read Hoffmann's *Fantasiestücke*, in four parts? I find much that's excellent and lively, though often with a wildly exuberant fantasy and the whole, if I may say so, seems to me without a real purpose. I like the first part best. This has rearoused my wish to take up my *Tonkünstlers Leben* again, and I'm making the odd little sketch (letter of 4 February 1816).

He also read a good deal of Schiller, quoting from him and taking the sermon in *Wallensteins Lager* as matter for parody; Goethe, whom he found personally unsympathetic when they met, he seems to have admired with some awe and to have read in some detail, certainly to the extent of quoting from *Die Wahlverwandschaften* and *Wilhelm Meister*. The latter is one of the prime models for *Tonkünstlers Leben*, as indeed it was for many a *Bildungsroman* and *Künstlerroman*.

Tonkünstlers Leben is both: that is to say, it is a novel of the growth of an artist's mind. In view of its fragmentary state, we do not gather a very consistent impression of how the hero finds his way in the world and gains in depth and understanding; and from what survives, we may deduce that Weber was really most interested in the work as a receptacle for some artistic discussions and some pleasant Romantic adventures and fancies. We cannot tell how it would eventually have been moulded into shape: in kind, it has much in common with other artist novels of the day, such as, Weber admitted in his Chapter 3, had 'overheated his imagination'. From *Wilhelm Meisters Lehrjahre* (1795–6) came the universally admired examples of a young, in-genuous artist hero going in search of education and development (*Bildung*), his amorous intrigues, his contact with the world of artists. *Wilhelm Meister* not only includes the most graphic of all descriptions of a travelling opera and drama company such as that of Weber's parents, but is famous for its elaborate discussion of *Hamlet*. The general pattern, including the generous use of interpolated poems, found many imitators who could not match the work's lofty, if somewhat oppressive, stature. In *Godwi* (1801) Clemens Brentano composed a so-called *verwilderte Roman*, mixing narrative, meditation and verse, changing the narrative stance by means of letters, description and story-telling, introducing plenty of amorous adventure, and preserving an ironic tone through all its eccentric structure. Brentano makes a habit of mentioning by name many artists – Mozart, Goethe, Tischbein – in the course of the letters in which, in the first half of the book, the characters address each other. Weber introduces mention of Shakespeare, Calderón and Schiller, as well as various musicians; and the tone of some of the writing, especially the ironic tinge even to the accounts of erotic adventures, suggests knowledge of what was a very popular and widely read work among the Romantics, as do the loose structure and abrupt changes of narrative technique. Closer to hand was the example of Ludwig Tieck's '*altdeutsche Geschichte*', *Franz Sternbalds Wanderungen* (1798), which shares with *Tonkünstlers Leben* the device of an artist hero, in this case a pupil of Dürer who wanders across Europe to Italy out of the necessity (as reflected by Weber in his own opening words) for the artist to find his area of experience in the world. There is much here that Weber would have found sympathetic – the idea (taken from *Wilhelm Meister*) of the hero pursuing a girl once glimpsed and never forgotten, a passionately sentimental relationship with a fellow artist, the interpolated poems and sketches, the artistic discussions and ruminations, not least the gentle accounts of the natural world stimulating the imagination. As Franz lies in the sunlit forest, he finds its beauty working on his creative mind.

The artist's soul is often seized by wonderful dreams, for everything in nature, every nodding flower, each passing cloud is to him either a memory or a glimpse of the future. A myriad shadowy forms, meaning nothing to the rest of mankind, will wander through his mind; for the artist's mind is a restless stream whose murmuring melodies are never for an instant silent; every breath of wind stirs him and leaves not a trace, every glint of light plays within him...he clothes his images with moonlight and sunset, and woos unheard sounds from invisible harps...

Though Weber's style is closer to Brentano's irony than to Tieck's sentimentality, there is a similar feeling for the stimulus of nature and its direct translation into the forms of his own art.

Nature's open spaces always have an extraordinary effect upon me, and one unlike that aroused in other spirits. Call it talent, vocation, genius, what you will, the object towards which all your faculties converge envelops your powers of contemplation in a magic circle. It is not only the corporeal eye that has its field of vision, but the eye of the soul also...The colour in which an object appears is unwittingly determined by the tone of your life and feelings; and since I speak of tones, I will not deny that in my case everything falls into musical forms. To me, a landscape is a kind of musical performance (below, pp. 323–4).

This is from one of the more reflective passages of *Tonkünstlers Leben*, in which Weber is discoursing on the dangerously confusing stimulus which travel always works upon him. Elsewhere, his irony and a distinctly sardonic humour can dominate; while the discussions of art can suggest the almost priest-like devotion of Grillparzer's *Der arme Spielmann* (1848). His style can also resemble the fantasy of Hoffmann; and there is a similarity between the scene of the hero visiting Herr von Y. and his ghastly daughter (1809, below, pp. 319–21) and Kreisler's evening with Röderlein's daughters in Hoffmann's *Johannes Kreislers musikalische Leiden* (1810) (coincidentally; Hoffmann and Weber did not meet until 1811). More than once, Weber makes mention of Jean Paul; and he seems to have shared his contemporaries' intoxication with the untrammelled structure, the heady apostrophes to nature and to the unfettered soul of genius, the giddy stylistic flourishes of *Titan* (1800–3). In common with *Godwi, Franz Sternbald* and even *Wilhelm Meister* is the tendency to neglect real characterization of the hero, perhaps an inescapable consequence of the didactic strain in the *Bildungsroman* and certainly one which the part-time author Weber was not expert enough to overcome – at any rate, in what survives. There does remain enough in outline to show how a large portion of it would have gone, and enough in the completed sections that is witty, illuminating, characteristic and imaginative to suggest that had Weber completed his scheme in the manner he once intended, the German novel would have acquired not merely another Romantic fragment, but a *Künstlerroman* to set worthily beside more famous examples.

The first of Weber's contemporaries to appreciate that his writings might have permanent value was his friend Carl Winkler, the court official who wrote under the pseudonym Theodor Hell. Not only through their contacts at the Liederkreis and elsewhere, but as librettist of *Die drei Pintos*, Hell came to form a high regard for Weber's skill with words, from which he claimed himself to have learnt much. Immediately after Weber's death in 1826 he busied himself with the posthumous papers entrusted to him by Caroline, and two years later published his three-volume *Hinterlassene Schriften von Carl Maria von Weber* (Dresden and Leipzig, 1828) (HHS). The first volume consists of *Tonkünstlers Leben*, the remaining two of miscellaneous writings of 1809–16 and 1817–20, and to the first Hell added a long prefatory memoir of Weber that included some of the writings, such as the Autobiographical Sketch (below, No. 106). The text is incomplete and inaccurate, Hell's purpose being merely to publish what he could, as quickly as possible, in a spirit of affection and practicality: 'My work in publishing these pages is only to make available materials for a future biographer of this exceptionally versatile man.' Upon this collection, Max Maria von Weber based the third volume appended to his two-volume biography, *Carl Maria von Weber: ein Lebensbild* (Leipzig, 1864–6) (MMW). Though he was able to add a few more items, he depended entirely upon Hell's texts, reproducing the omissions and errors caused by Hell's failure to check them. It was Weber's practice to make a draft, then prepare a fair copy for despatch to the newspaper concerned: often he would considerably tidy up the prose or sharpen the comments in so doing. Not only was the handwriting in the drafts sometimes barely legible – Weber was notorious among his friends in this respect, and it remains a problem – but the abbreviations and other tricks of reference often defeated the musically untutored Hell and Max Maria. Hell was able to check with the *DAZ*, of which he was editor, and Max Maria seems to have had the *AMZ* to hand; but much was in considerable disarray, with Weber's words misread and his ideas in consequence often traduced through paraphrase and guesswork. Rudolf Kleinecke's *Ausgewählte Schriften von Carl Maria von Weber* (Leipzig, 1892) is an inadequate selection from these two works.

The first catalogue of Weber's writings was prepared by F. W. Jähns for vol. III of MMW, as part of a general work list; but even Jähns made some mistakes. Some of the writings are listed without printed sources; others have disappeared, including the plan for a new musical journal (1811) and accounts of a Spohr oratorio and of the citizens of Weimar (1812). The first scholar to investigate the whole matter with real thoroughness was Georg Kaiser (1883–1918), whose work on behalf of Weber included plans for a complete edition of the letters (he left only a single collection, *Webers Briefe an den Grafen Karl von Brühl* (Leipzig, 1911)). Kaiser went through all the materials, and searched all the journals in which Weber had published articles: he was thereby able not only to produce accurate texts for the first time, but to establish some two dozen anonymous articles as Weber's work from their style and content. His *Sämtliche Schriften von Carl Maria von Weber* (Berlin and Leipzig, 1908) (KSS) is a masterpiece of scholarship and organization that presents a version of the texts as authentic as can now, with the disappearance of so many manuscripts, be achieved. It was the basis of the most conveniently accessible modern selection, Karl Laux's *Carl Maria von Weber: Kunstansichten* (Leipzig, 1975) (LKA). It is also the basis of the present collection.

This is complete, apart from the verse and one or two letters which Kaiser included but which Weber never intended for publication: they have their place in a collection of his letters. The articles are presented in chronological order; the titles are not necessarily those under which they first appeared, since these were conditioned by the journalistic conventions of the newspaper concerned and do not normally identify the subject conveniently. Each article is headed with brief document- ation of dates, sources, and first and main subsequent printings. There follows an introduction designed to help reading of the text, which is also footnoted where necessary. Asterisks in the texts refer to the Biographical Glossary at the end; normally when a name occurs more than once it is glossed here rather than in a footnote. The original paragraphing has not necessarily been retained. In the absence of any general collection of Weber's letters, they are referred to by date only: many are still in manuscript, some have appeared in special collections or in journals, while others have been reprinted several times, at least in part.

I should like to thank the following libraries for hospitality and help: the British Library; the London Library; the Library of the Senate House, London; the Bodleian Library, Oxford; the University of Durham Library; the Library of Ampleforth Abbey; the Universitäts- bibliothek, Heidelberg; the Weber-Gedenkstätte, Hosterwitz, near Dresden; the Staatliches Institut für Musikforschung (Preussischer Kulturbesitz), Berlin. I owe a particular debt to the Music Department of the Deutsche Staatsbibliothek, Berlin, and to its former director, Dr Karl-Heinz Köhler: the Jähns Collection of Weberiana, housed there together with much other valuable material and manuscripts, was made freely available to me and every encouragement and help was given to me. In this connexion, I should like to thank Freiherr Hans-Jürgen von Weber, great-great-grandson of the composer, who went to much personal trouble to make available to me material relating to his family and to lend his name and encouragement to my researches in Germany. For other help and advice I should like to thank Mr Peter Alexander, Mr Peter Branscombe, Dr David Charlton (especially for his help in tracing publication details of the two open letters to Castil-Blaze), Dr Imogen Fellinger, Mr Philip Smiley, Fr Placid Spearritt, Miss Joanna Unwin and Mr William Waterhouse. A particular word of gratitude is due to Mr Ralf Steyer, whose knowledge of German literature and language was enthusiastically placed at my disposal. To Mrs Ruth Smith I am deeply indebted for her supervision of the typescript with a care and interest that went far beyond the call of subeditorial duty: naturally I am responsible for any surviving errors, but her eagle eye and scholarly techniques saved me from many more.

Lastly, I must thank my colleague in this enterprise, Mr Martin Cooper, for adding to his work as translator a wealth of help and advice on innumerable matters musical, literary and historical, and for his limitless tolerance of all my demands upon him.

JOHN WARRACK

Rievaulx, 1981

1. Answer to criticism of *Das Waldmädchen*

Written: Freiberg, February 1801.
Published: Gnädigst bewilligte Freyberger gemeinnützigen Nachrichten für das chursächsische Erzgebirge VII (1801), 69.   *Signed:* C. M. von Weber.
Reprinted: NZfM, No. 16, 22 August 1845 (partial); MMW (inaccurate and abbreviated); KSS; LKA.

Weber's first surviving opera, *Das Waldmädchen* (JAnh1), was written in the autumn of 1800 in Freiberg, whither he had been taken by his father Franz Anton with the intention of setting up a lithography business. The librettist was Carl von Steinsberg, director of a travelling theatre company from Carlsbad which arrived on 24 August. The opera was probably composed in October, and it was first performed in the Stadttheater on 24 November. It was not a success. Some six weeks later, in January 1801, an article appeared in the *Nachrichten,* 'On the local public theatre'. This included a reasonably sympathetic mention of Weber's opera: 'To be indulgent, the music did not have quite the success it deserved. Of course one must describe it as no more than a blossom that promises fairer and riper fruit. (In Chemnitz this opera had an exceptional success.)' (No. 2, p. 11). A reply was published in No. 3, p. 25, as follows:

> That my composition should have pleased, since cabals motivated by prejudiced, base and the most bitter envy and jealousy formed the atmosphere of the performance, was to be as much expected as that an out of tune instrument should sound well. Why then did the work succeed in Chemnitz? – because things were in tune. My own observation, and the most disinterested testimony of important men and contrapuntalists (which is indeed something distinctly rare here), reassure me; moreover, my blossoms have already, two years ago, in the first pages and in the second volume of the Leipzig [*Allgemeine*] *musikalische Zeitung,* been acknowledged as fair and ripe fruit. Furthermore, my original work is available for inspection, and my eternal gratitude will be due to anyone who can show me my mistakes and teach me how to mend one of them.   C. M. v. W., Compositeur.

This drew a retort from C. G. Siegert, the town musician and the conductor of the performance, in which he attacked Weber's incompetence as composer and orchestrator, while suggesting that too much blame should not attach to 'an allegedly thirteen-year-old boy'; and he invoked the expert opinion of the cantor, J. G. Fischer (No. 4, p. 39). Fischer duly came to his colleague's support in No. 5, pp. 49–50, with a vigorous attack on the composer's attempt 'to trumpet his opera' and on the muddles and mistakes in the score. An article in the *Chemnitzer Anzeiger* (No. 5, 31 January 1801), by its editor, C. G. Kretzschmar, denied the success of the performance in Chemnitz, and counselled greater discretion on the part of the young composer: this also appeared in the *Nachrichten.* It drew the full-scale article printed below. This

25

is generally accepted, as is the previous communication and indeed the entire controversy, as stemming from Franz Anton, whose pompous style and attitudes it suggests more closely than anything that would have been produced by a boy of fourteen. Siegert published a 'last word' in the journal (No. 9, p. 87), to which a final Weber retort came (No. 10, p. 95). Friedrich Brendel, who published an account of the controversy with some of its documents in the *NZfM*, added that he had been told that on a visit to Freiberg in 1822 Weber had apologized to Siegert for his youthful hastiness. For Weber's own mature view of *Das Waldmädchen*, see below, No. 106. The whole controversy is summarized, with quotations of many of the exchanges, in MMW I, pp. 56–64, and is reprinted in K. Knebel, 'Weber in Freiberg 1800–1', *Mitteilungen vom Freiberger Altertumsverein*, XXXVII (1900), 72–89.

My dear Stadtmusikus,

1. You are quite mistaken in thinking that I expected such a great success for my work. But after all every labourer is worthy of his hire and your performance was a disgraceful betrayal of my musical intentions. Why did the dress rehearsal go so well and the performance itself so appallingly? It was not the good members of the orchestra who were to blame, but their sluggish conductor, who neglected his chief duty – the proper tuning of the orchestra beforehand – and then proceeded to ignore all markings of *piano* and *forte*, *crescendo* and *decrescendo*, and all tempo markings. The result was a complete absence of the necessary light and shade and a performance that no one could have enjoyed. Your enmity and jealousy have thereby achieved their object. Adverse criticism is not enough in itself – the critic must show his superior understanding and mastery of what he criticizes. The composition of an opera is not quite the same as performing an English country dance! You have admitted that you are ignorant of musical theory, counterpoint etc., and I do not find that difficult to believe, as your arrogant criticisms of my music are often self-contradictory, and it really is better if a cobbler sticks to his last. My birth-certificate vouches for the fact that I was born on 18 December 1787 and your favourite 'ostensibly' is therefore quite uncalled for.[1] Any composer who is forced to hear his music murdered by such a performance as you gave is really worthy of pity! And now I must give a short answer to the close friend whom you have invited to write in No. 5, p. 49.

2. I must also confess that I was amazed by the assurance with which Cantor Fischer[2] set himself to denigrate my opera *Das Wald-*

---

[1]   Weber's baptismal date is registered in the Eutin Landeskirche as 20 November 1786, implying a birth-date of 18 or 19 November. A note in Franz Anton's writing gives 18 December as the date, but there was never any question of 1787.

[2]   Johann Gottfried Fischer (1751–1821) studied theology before taking up music. He worked in Eisleben from 1777, becoming cantor in Freiberg in

mädchen simply in order to curry favour with his devoted but jealous friend. For I confess that I can imagine no other motive, since I have never, Herr Cantor, given you reason for offence even by an unfriendly glance. How could you allow yourself to be made use of in a matter that in no way concerns you? If I liked to go into matters of detail with you, the echo of our conversation would be most unflattering to you, though such a thing is absolutely foreign to both my nature and the principles on which I was brought up. I have already dealt with the matter of my 'ostensible' age, and I can only add further that the date of my parents' wedding in Vienna was 20 August 1785. I have only my Maker to thank for my exceptional mental powers, and it is not difficult to show that in my short life I have seen and heard more than many men of fifty. Kapellmeisters of the highest standing, attached to the foremost courts and their orchestras, have unanimously agreed that I have made a correct and thorough study of counterpoint and consequently know how to handle the different instruments, literary texts, harmony and rhythm properly and correctly; and this sets my mind at rest and convinces me that it is only envy and jealousy that discover 'mistakes' in my music! Heaven knows I have no desire to become a cantor or a town musician and am well aware that for many reasons I lack the necessary knowledge and skill for both posts. In addition to this I am only human and no more infallible than any other human being. I am quite willing to be corrected and am grateful to anyone who undertakes to censure me if he does so with modesty and not in a proud or overbearing manner. In any case you, Herr Cantor, have not the competence to act as my judge, and I am as unwilling to learn from you as I am to harbour the culpable idea of teaching you anything. Furthermore I have absolutely nothing against the excellent members of the orchestra here, and cannot think that Stadtmusikus Siegert can produce any evidence to the contrary. In the case of this opera it is he who has unfortunately shown prejudice and thereby deprived me of the applause of a public which is usually generous and sympathetic and quite above any inclination to nipping any talent in the bud. I have a manifest proof of this in the unbounded respect and enthusiastic affection for this admirable Freiberg public which was shown by my father, when he decided to leave a large and famous capital[3] and bring his family on the long journey here in order to participate in the friendly, good-hearted and welcoming social life of

---

1799. He wrote piano pieces and church music, and conducted the first local performances of *The Creation*, Mozart's Requiem and Bach's B minor Mass; he was also a successful teacher.

[3] Munich.

this town and spend his few remaining years in so high-minded a circle of friends.

Even if my work were in fact marred by mistakes, it would hardly be surprising, considering the pressure to which I was subjected by the director of the theatre. I had to write the second act of the opera in four days,[4] as can be borne out by three of the orchestra's oboists,[5] who took the sheets from my hand to the copyist while they were still wet, and spent several nights at my lodging with me. Mme Seyfert,[6] too, was present most of the time while I rewrote several passages in her bravura aria to suit her, as my oboist friends can bear witness. Moreover, the text was such that at the end I had no choice but to make *Liebe* the last word. I should have preferred *amore* of course, and therefore small blame attaches to me on this count. Then I must add that I am well acquainted with many works of the masters and composers quoted, as well as a number of scores by the three brothers Joseph, Michael and Johann Haydn, Fuchs, Tuma, Padre Martini, Mozart, *Vogler, *Naumann, Wanhal, Albrechtsberger, Kotzeluch, Schulz, Wagenseil, Gatti, Jommelli and Händel, most of whose operas and oratorios are in my possession.[7] The Herr Cantor, being a man of honour, will also admit that an additional proof of my abilities is provided by the little Fughettas,[8] written almost three years before by me in Salzburg and presented to him (despite many misprints) last September with six of my Variations.[9]

[4]   In the Autobiographical Sketch (below No. 106), Weber amends this to ten days. He admitted that he was spurred on by the tales of other composers' feats of speed; and there is little doubt that Franz Anton, like Johann van Beethoven and other ambitious fathers, was anxious to present his son as a Mozartian *Wunderkind*.

[5]   This does not imply a very large woodwind section: in German theatre orchestras of the day there was much doubling and interchanging of players between instruments. The two surviving fragments of *Das Waldmädchen* (WGA, Reihe 2, Bd 1) show the scoring as for two each of flutes, oboes and clarinets in the woodwind.

[6]   Mme Seyfert (Seiffert, Sayfert) sang Mathilde, the heroine.

[7]   The list is clearly designed to impress by its mixture of great composers, famous pedagogues and successful Kapellmeisters. There is a suspicious confusion over the Haydns: the two brothers were (Franz) Joseph and (Johann) Michael. 'Fuchs' is J. J. Fux (1660–1741), the famous contrapuntalist. Franz Tuma (1704–74) was a composer of much church music, a pupil of Fux. J. G. Naumann (1741–1801) was a Dresden Kapellmeister and opera composer. J. A. P. Schulz (1747–1800) was a composer and critic. Luigi Gatti (1740–1817) was a Salzburg Kapellmeister and composer.

[8]   J1–6. They were dated on the published copy by Weber '1 September 1798', and reviewed *AMZ* I (1798), 32 by Z***.

[9]   Variations on an Original Theme (J7). The piece was reviewed *AMZ* II (1799), 896, and III (1800), 256.

Heavens above, how mistaken I was in you, Herr Cantor! It would never have entered my head that you, whom I valued so highly, could be so offensive! You can surely be no native of Freiberg? I can give you my solemn word of honour that I will not utter a single syllable more in my defence, as I have better things to occupy me.

> My enemies have no more power
> To hurt me than a passing shower
> That clouds the bright noontide;
> However vile the jealous schemer,
> He surely knows that the Redeemer
> Will ever be my guide.

P.S. If you should decide, Herr Cantor, to give up your grudge against me and behave honourably, I should be the first to offer you my hand in reconciliation. I should then be delighted to show you my whole work in its original form and play it to you. This would convince you that you have been mistaken in what you heard, and I should then be willing to forget all that had happened and remain with true respect your obedient servant

C. M. v. Weber

3. My answer to the unknown gentleman from Chemnitz is that I pay no attention to the barking of small dogs.

C.M.v.W.

2. Review of J. B. Schaul's *Briefe über den Geschmack in der Musik*

Written: Stuttgart, 8 June 1809.
Published: AMZ xi (1809), 793–8.   *Signed:* M (= Melos).
Reprinted: HHS, MMW (both abbreviated and inaccurate); KSS; LKA.

Johann Baptist Schaul (d. 1822) was a Stuttgart court musician, also well known as a professor of Italian. He published various works on Italian grammar and translated Tasso's *Gerusalemme liberata* in 1790; there is an example of his curious Italian script reproduced in *AMZ* xxiii (1821), 695. The *Briefe* were published by Macklots Hofbuchhandlung in Stuttgart in 1809.

Most writers publish with a clearly defined purpose and one to which the title of their work refers. This does not seem to be the case with Herr Schaul's *Letters*, which appear to constitute an example of 'art for art's sake', regardless of the end product. Only a few chapters seem to show any definite purpose, and we shall be returning to them later. Questions of style also seem to have little interest for Herr Schaul; so that the present opusculum may be said to be as unrewarding in the matter of original ideas, or original expressions of familiar propositions, as it is in general cultivation of mind. It reminds me of a rather narrow, provincial-minded man smugly grumbling to his friends about the corruption of the times, the insufficient importance attached to this and that, and showing at the same time a quite considerable arrogance on the subject of great men and their works.

The present writer means to concern himself only with the various headings of these *Letters* and would not dream of attempting any refutation, which is indeed provided by the facts – rather in the way that a man who has undertaken in the dark to prove that the sun does not exist is refuted by next morning's sunrise. The mere rehearsing of the contents of the *Letters* will show clearly that anyone wishing to persuade the world that he is competent to pass judgement on great men must at least show more knowledge of his subject and in general better judgement than the present author.

Letter 1 is an almost schoolboy-like essay on chamber music, in which he praises first Pleyel (a composer to whom justice should certainly be done) and then Boccherini, after which he exclaims, 'But what a difference there is between a Boccherini and a Mozart!' Yes, a great difference indeed, and one which Herr Schaul's ecstatic talk of Boccherini's 'flowery meadows and thick groves' will do nothing to lessen. Poor Mozart! since Herr Schaul has discovered 'the true and essential aim of art', and with your 'inheritance of a charitable poverty of invention', you run the risk of being put in the shade by Pleyel and Boccherini! But do not be too concerned, for Haydn too is only capable of 'producing the superficial and ephemeral pleasure of arbitrary construction' according to Herr Schaul. But then of course, 'in Boccherini philosophy rules', and 'his music must not be played in too large or well-lighted a room', rather 'in the silence of the family circle, where this charming composer will transport the listener to the days of innocence and righteousness'. Oh! how beautiful and noble it is to gather our wives and children together, to play this music and allow ourselves to be thus transported! It is something we all need to do, and never more than at the present time!

In Letter 2 we find some observations that are excellent, though familiar and often repeated. In them, Herr Schaul takes the opportunity to praise Clementi as 'the King of composers for the fortepiano'. No doubt Clementi occupies a high position, but to find his music 'divine' and in a class by itself is something that surely nobody will do without some qualification. Nor, I think would anyone else find a parallel between Young's *Night Thoughts*[1] and Clementi's Adagios, of which some are indeed excellent but others somewhat dry and perfunctory. What is relevant to the matter and should not be overlooked in such an appreciation is that Clementi was always accustomed to write without accompaniment and that when he adds accompanying parts his music shows a manifest weakness. We are reluctant to have to be obliged to say this of a really great and deserving composer, but Herr Schaul's almost idolatrous admiration at the expense of all other composers leaves us no alternative.

Letters 3 and 4 are the cream of the book. How Mozart catches it! It would be an insult to his shade to defend him against Herr Schaul. Nobody is going to say that everything written by Mozart was perfect and Herr Schaul admits the same of his idol Jommelli.[2] But according to Herr Schaul, Jommelli was never guilty to the same degree as Mozart – 'whose vocal lines are unnatural, his harmonies often harsh and arbitrary in the extreme, his finales overcrowded, while much of his writing is contrary to plain reason'. No mean accusations, you may think, but Schaul is ready to prove his point. For example, he finds it unreasonable for the music of the Three Boys in the Act 2 finale of *Die Zauberflöte* to be so difficult. Of course people realize that Mozart did not envisage these three characters as schoolboys but as important characters, closely integrated into the drama and therefore given music of the same style and quality as the rest, to be performed not by choirboys but by women singers, as is the practice in Vienna and Prague. But of what use is this argument or the fact that so many thousands of listeners have so profoundly enjoyed this very finale, provided it is well performed – if Herr Schaul has decided that it is contrary to good sense? Herr Schaul seriously admonishes the heedless Mozart to write music that can be performed not only in musical centres, but everywhere (including Krähwinkel?);[3] and if there are

---

[1]   *The Complaint, or Night Thoughts on Life, Death and Immortality* (1742–5) by Edward Young (1683–1765). This was the work that made Young famous. It was widely translated, in Germany spreading a fashion for melancholy and moonlight. Some Germans were led to rate Young above Milton, and *Kotzebue's wife declared that he should have been made Archbishop of Canterbury.

[2]   Niccolò Jommelli (1714–74) was court Kapellmeister to Duke Carl Eugen of Württemberg from 1753 to 1759. Despite the success of his other operas in Stuttgart, notably *Fetonte* (1768), *Olimpiade* (1761) was the only one of his operas of which a contemporary score was published (1783).

[3]   The fictitious little town of Krähwinkel first occurs in a story by Jean Paul, *Das heimliche Klaglied der jetzigen Männer* (1801). The idea was seized upon by Kotzebue, whose *Die deutschen Kleinstädter* (1803) had a great success in

indeed still some composers who model themselves on this irresponsible Mozart, Herr Schaul must not be held to blame. There is only one point that should perhaps be made – that Herr Schaul remarks of Jommelli, his 'god of harmony', that in order to make their full effect his works can only be performed 'in a large theatre and by an orchestra familiar with their character'.

There are many other instances of the same kind to be found in these *Letters*, including the general observation that Mozart was not successful with his arias. Jommelli he regards as in every way his superior, but particularly in recitatives. Now there is no doubt that Jommelli was indeed an inventive, impassioned artist with a high conception of his art; but it is equally beyond doubt that his obsession with the illustration of individual passages was often incredibly petty and unworthy, and prejudiced the general effect of his works. It is only necessary to look at a passage in Act 2 scene 7 of his *L'Olimpiade* and observe the progressions on the single word *passo* in the phrase 'ah! che sarem di nuovo a quest'orrido passo'. Jommelli's recitative is consistently full of character and expression; but has he written anything better than, say, Sextus's recitative in the Act 1 finale of *La clemenza di Tito* or Donna Anna's in Act 1 of *Don Giovanni*? Herr Schaul calls 'Dies Bildnis ist bezaubernd schön' a street-song and maintains that *La clemenza di Tito* contains only a few flashes of genius, enough to show what Mozart might have achieved with better advice; and he asserts that none of Mozart's overtures are comparable in effect to Jommelli's – that they are in fact no more than 'openers', designed, and indeed needed, to 'call a halt to the chatter of the audience'. In view of all this the reader must ask himself whether this is not either a joke on Herr Schaul's part or an attempt at satire; and he will be tempted to apply Herr Schaul's 'What a rogue!' to himself. Only one word more. According to Herr Schaul, the true critic's motto is that the best criticism consists in showing how something could have been better done. Herr Schaul most certainly wishes to appear as a true rather than a false critic; and so we are entitled to promise all connoisseurs and music-lovers in Germany the happy prospect of Herr Schaul writing us a better *Don Giovanni* and a better *Zauberflöte*. *Quod deus bene vertat!*

Enough has been said to acquaint readers with this little book and its contents. The present writer would only like to praise Herr Schaul's conscientiousness as a writer in pointing out that the biographical

Vienna and then throughout Germany, establishing Krähwinkel as the epitome of all that was backward, lifeless and stifling in provincial town life.

notes in his appendix are taken from Gerber's *Lexicon der Tonkünstler*.[4] It is, however, an odd coincidence that in the book itself the twenty pages of notes (on Farinelli, Carestini, Bernardi, Guarducci etc.) are all taken verbatim from the same dictionary. Herr Schaul himself observes that it would take too long to introduce all such musicians (and there the present writer is in complete agreement, as we are expecting a second edition of the dictionary from Herr Schaul himself), but he cannot refrain from adding twenty-six pages to the *Letters* by the simple process of copying.

The present writer would be more than pleased to add some words of praise to a review which contains so much adverse criticism. But as the author had provided plenty of this in the *Letters*, and the present writer is less accustomed to copying, the interested reader must be asked to turn for this praise to the book itself.

[4] Ernst Ludwig Gerber's *Historisch-biographisches Lexicon der Tonkünstler* (2 vols., Leipzig, 1790–2) replaced J. G. Walther's *Lexicon* of 1732 as the most important historical musical dictionary of its time. Weber laid plans for a musical dictionary of his own in 1803, but when this came to nothing he probably gave some of his articles on Salzburg musicians to Gerber for the much-extended second edition, *Neues historisch-biographisches Lexicon der Tonkünstler* (4 vols., Leipzig, 1812–14).

3. Art and literature in Stuttgart

Written: Stuttgart, December 1809 (MS: 'sent to the *Elegante* on 20 December').
Published: Zeitung für die elegante Welt, No. 53, 15 March 1810.   *Unsigned.*
Reprinted: HHS (greatly altered); KSS; LKA.
This was Weber's first article for the Leipzig *Zeitung für die elegante Welt*.

There is no doubt that few towns in Germany can boast of possessing so much talent and distinction within their walls as Stuttgart. Intellectual and artistic activity goes quietly forward there, the pursuit of knowledge is its own reward and there is little concern with prestige or exterior demonstration. The very absence of such a stimulus makes the recognition and fostering of individual gifts and personal idealism all the more praiseworthy. In every town of note in Germany there are informatively inclined persons only too anxious to tell the rest of the world about the circumstances in which they live. Stuttgart seems to be the only exception, and the present writer cannot remember ever having read any such report from there. It is of course not made any easier to point to Stuttgart's virtues by the fact that the town seems to have no public meeting-place where the stranger can make the acquaintance of the inhabitants. It must therefore not be held against him if he leaves the town with a bad impression, and only when enquiring about the author of some remarkable piece of work learns to his amazement that he lives in Stuttgart, though quite probably not known to his fellow citizens as a writer.

Of course a literary man can always console himself with his ability to get to know the world and its ways without leaving his study, and he therefore does not feel so keenly the absence of a wide circle of friends and acquaintances. Even he, however, is deprived of many opportunities to widen his horizons and his knowledge of humanity, for these are plainly only offered by social intercourse and the mutual exchange of ideas. True scholarship, so called, suffers less from such a deprivation than do the arts, which depend on human intercourse for their very existence. No picture is painted, no play written and no music composed without the instinctive desire to communicate with others. Some such external stimulus is absolutely essential to the artist, for whom the simple mastery of his art is only half the battle and the courage to persist depends on the encouragement of others.

The recent foundation of the Museum[1] seemed to promise well for the development of artistic taste; and in fact during the short time that has elapsed since then much new talent has shown itself, and the very existence of an institution through which public taste might be influenced promised well for the future. Since then, however, the Museum has been reduced to a Reading Society, leaving us with only the theatre which, despite the admirable work done by the director,[2] is for many reasons unable to pursue exclusively the Good and the Beautiful and must also – for financial and other reasons – pursue the Popular.

Stuttgart has no amateur dramatic or concert-giving societies. Visiting artists do not find a Stuttgart engagement profitable and are therefore increasingly rare, so that only local artists are heard. In these circumstances it is inevitable to find a certain provincialism appearing and a lowering of standards, both of which are particularly noticeable in the theatre. The public has lost the habit of making its own judgements and forming its own tastes, and no longer expresses an opinion on what it is offered in the way of the arts. Indifferent and content to be no more than amused, the Stuttgarters know only two

[1]   In contemporary usage, a club or meeting-place where professionals and amateurs of the arts would gather.
[2]   *Franz Danzi.

extremes (often expressed about the same work) – a play is either awful or marvellous.

In the world of letters the *Morgenblatt*[3] is one of the pleasantest and most interesting features of the town, with a large readership and a very considerable influence in cultural matters. The two editors (Herren Reinbeck[4] and Haug[5]) are well known as writers and as men of wit and penetration, and there is naturally solid work in any production for which they are responsible. Yet the general circumstances prevailing in the town seem to have an influence even on the *Morgenblatt* and to prevent it from exercising its full potential influence.

Despite all this, I must repeat that I find all the greater satisfaction in the existence of so much individual talent developing without any inhibitions from outside; and the present writer is glad to list a number of writers, poets, composers and artists who can justly claim a high reputation everywhere.

Abeille,[6] Konzertmeister, is the composer of *Amor und Psyche*, *Peter und Ännchen* and many songs. An attractive gift for melody, combined with scrupulous attention to unity of conception, make his work worthy of being more widely known.

Von Arand, Oberjustizrat. A brilliant and accomplished pianist, the finest in the town, and also a composer of several piano works.

Frl. Charlotte von Bauer[7] excels both as a pianist and as a painter, with a genuine artistic sensibility and a charming feminine style that adds a certain nobility to all her efforts.

Prof. Dannecker,[8] Ritter des königlichen Zivilverdienstordens, is a sculptor whose name is worthy to be placed beside that of Canova himself, as anyone must agree who knows his *Ariadne*, his *Schiller* (of

[3]   The *Morgenblatt für gebildete Stände*, founded in 1807 by Johann Friedrich Cotta.

[4]   See below, n. 19.   [5]   See below, n. 11.

[6]   Johann Christoph Ludwig Abeille (1761–1838), a German of Huguenot descent, was a member of the Stuttgart Court Orchestra from 1782 until his death. His two light *Singspiele* had some popularity in their day. *Amor und Psyche* (Stuttgart, 1800) was to a text by *F. K. Hiemer. *Peter und Ännchen* (Stuttgart, 1809) was based on Favart's *Annette et Lubin*.

[7]   Charlotte von Bauer's work included an unremarkable pencil drawing of Goethe.

[8]   Johann Heinrich von Dannecker (1758–1841). The son of a groom, he showed artistic talent early. He became a friend of Herder, Goethe and Schiller, and also of Canova, who greatly influenced him. His *Ariadne* (begun 1803) became very popular in miniature reproductions. The famous Schiller bust was finished in 1810.

which he has executed three busts, one of colossal size) and many other of his works.

F. Danzi, Kapellmeister, already enjoys a reputation as one of our finest living composers. The present writer's only wish is that he would give the public an opportunity to hear his larger works, such as *Iphigenia*[9] etc., and in general supply the want of original German operas by his own excellent works.

Mme Duttenhofer,[10] born Hummel, has made interesting experiments with vase designs by cutting out flowers and leaves to form patterns similar to those of the Greek and Etruscan artists. She has had the opportunity in Rome of making a number of observations which she believes justify her in saying that the artists of antiquity also borrowed their vase and urn designs from flowers and leaves. A volume of prints showing these designs will shortly be published.

Lieutenant Faber is a caricaturist, wit and connoisseur of the arts.

Grüneisen, General Secretary. A man of much intelligence, wit and learning. The creations which he shows to the small circle of his friends make one regret that none of them is given to the world.

F. C. Haug[11] is known and admired for his epigrams. He has published two volumes of poems and epigrams; *Herz und Geist*, a commonplace book; *Elbondokani*, an operetta; a sketch of Zumsteeg's life; an anthology of epigrams (with Weisser); and a number of other separate poems. A small volume of stories, a new volume of poems, *Glossen, Gnomen und Paradoxen* etc. are all forthcoming. He has a quite outstanding skill with words, and this enables him to clothe what is apparently the most prosaic statement in poetic form; and his verbal virtuosity is truly remarkable.

Prof. Hetsch,[12] gallery director and historical painter. His most recent

[9]   *Iphigenia in Aulis* (Munich, 1807). Tragic opera in three acts; music lost. It was hailed as an important work and made the text of an article on German opera and its problems in *AMZ* IX (1807), 365–72.

[10] Christiane Luise Duttenhofer (1776–1829), who married the engraver Christian Duttenhofer in 1804, was a miniaturist. She was famous for her silhouettes, and was a friend of Goethe and Schiller.

[11] Friedrich Haug (1761–1829). A friend of Schiller, he was Royal Librarian and editor of the *Morgenblatt*, 1807–17. Weber set his poem 'Rhapsodie' (J70), first published in the *Morgenblatt* in 1810. *Elbondokani*, from a French original, was set by Danzi (*El Bondokani, der Calif von Bagdad*, Munich, 1802; music lost) and Zumsteeg (Stuttgart, 1803).

[12] Philipp Freidrich von Hetsch (1758–1838) was professor at the Karlschule and director of the Gemäldegalerie from 1798. He was known as a sculptor. His most famous portrait was the *Abschied des Brutus von Porcia* that Weber mentions here. Goethe described his works as 'very good and lively'.

large picture, *Brutus*, has had a sensational success. He is also highly considered as a portrait painter.

F. K. Hiemer has done great service to the German theatre by his translations of French operas such as *Adolphe und Klara*,[13] *Uthal*,[14] *Vetter Jakob*[15] etc. There is a great dearth of librettists with a good understanding of both music and the theatre, and it would be an excellent thing if Herr Hiemer would occupy himself more with original work in this field. His dialogue is easy and natural, and his lyrics musical in themselves and not so devoid of poetic worth as many suppose to be inevitable in his class of writing. His present work on the opera *Silvana* will certainly confirm what I say here of his talents.

Countess von Jennison is responsible for a number of card almanacs in which she displays a wit and taste that deserves the highest praise.

Dr Lehr[16] is Reader and Private Librarian to His Majesty the King. For a long time modesty prevented him from publishing anything, and it was only the poems which appeared in Bagge's Almanac that revealed his charm and individuality as an artist, which must delight every reader. At present he is preparing a commonplace book, which will certainly provide further evidence of his sense and sensibility.

Johann Gotthard Müller[17] is recognized as an exceptionally fine engraver.

Franz Müller,[17] his son, has just returned from Italy and has shown his high qualities as an artist by his version of Domenichino's *St John the Evangelist*.

Müller.[18] A delightful landscape painter.

Prof. Reinbeck[19] has made a name for himself by his casual

[13] Dalayrac, *Adolphe et Clara* (Paris, 1799; Stuttgart, 1801).
[14] Méhul, *Uthal* (Paris, 1806; Stuttgart, 1806).
[15] Méhul, *Une Folie* (Paris, 1802; Stuttgart, 1803). Very popular in Germany in five different versions, usually as *Je toller, je besser* (trans. Herklots), *Die beiden Füchse* (trans. Seyfried) or *Wagen gewinnt*.
[16] Lehr, one of Weber's close Stuttgart friends, encouraged him to read Kant and Schelling and helped to influence his intellectual development. Weber set his poems 'Er an Sie' (J57), 'Meine Farben' (J62) and 'Trinklied' (J80).
[17] Johann Gotthard von Müller (1747–1830) was an important engraver and lithographer. His son Johann Friedrich (not Franz) (1782–1816) was a professor in Dresden, and also a gifted engraver. His Domenichino engraving was done when he was working in Paris in 1805.
[18] Probably Franz Xaver Müller (1773–1841). A Benedictine monk for ten years as Odo, 1793–1803, he became court painter.
[19] Georg Reinbeck (1766–1849) taught in St Petersburg from 1792, returning in 1805. He edited the *Morgenblatt*, and was a dramatist, story-teller, travel writer and aesthetician. His *Briefe aus Heidelberg* were published in 1808; his two-volume collection of stories, *Winterblüten*, appeared in 1810.

observations on a journey from St Petersburg to Germany, his *Briefe aus Heidelberg*, a number of dramatic works and a volume of stories which is expected to delight the cultivated reader. His writing is especially noteworthy for purity of diction and that easy, natural style which is unquestionably the story-teller's greatest asset. His German deserves to be called classical and is certainly unique in character; and the same may be said of the wit displayed in the captions which he had provided for the latest Card Almanac. These show a creative imagination, quite apart from the drawings to which they are attached, and cannot fail to delight the connoisseur.

Ludwig Schubart[20] is the translator of Ossian and a number of Shakespeare plays and is at present editing a series of *Characterzeichnungen* that sound both interesting and entertaining. He has a wide and thorough knowledge of modern languages and his translations are aptly annotated as well as natural in style.

Seele,[21] director of the Privat-Galerie, is an historical painter who specializes in battle pieces.

Sutor[22] directs the orchestra and is the composer of *Apollos Wettgesang*, an opera which has been much applauded in Stuttgart.

Thouret[23] is the court architect, and has been much praised for the taste and skill of his work as theatrical designer.

Baron von Thumb[24] is a young man of talent who has the highest ideals. His chief interest lies in the theatre, and some of the scenes of his *Alonzo*, which is soon to appear, deserve public notice for the piece and its author.

[20]   Ludwig Schubart (1765–1811), son of the writer and musician Christian Daniel Schubart, was a lawyer, journalist and translator. His *Characters* include a life of his father, *Schubart's Karakter von seinem Sohn Ludwig* (Erlangen, 1798).

[21]   Johann Baptist von Seele (1774–1814) also specialized in group portraits. He was director of the gallery from 1804.

[22]   Wilhelm Sutor (*c* 1774–1828) was in Stuttgart 1801–6. *Apollos Wettgesang* was to a text by Hiemer after Thomas d'Hèle's for Grétry's *Le Jugement de Midas*: it was produced in Stuttgart in 1808, when it had a success (see *AMZ* x (1808), 735) that was repeated in other German cities. He wrote four more operas for Stuttgart.

[23]   Nikolaus Friedrich von Thouret (1767–1845) was an architect and painter. His work as an architect was admired by Goethe, who met him when travelling to Italy in 1797 and recommended him to Weimar; here he rebuilt the Steinertheater.

[24]   Karl Konrad von Thumb-Neuburg (1785–1831) was a court chamberlain. He settled in Stuttgart in 1809, and wrote a number of stage pieces, most of them translations from the French, that were very popular in their day.

Eberhard Waechter[25] is unquestionably one of the most poetic of painters. The conception of his *Job*, his *Death of Socrates*, his *Sleeping Pindar* and his *Sleeping Horace* is truly beautiful.

President von Wangenheim,[26] Acting Privy Councillor for the nobility, deserves notice as a businessman, patron of the arts and writer. Anything that he undertakes bears the marks of his personality. He makes light of all difficulties and is ready to tackle with equal enthusiasm and energy the most abstract problems as well as matters of pure entertainment. At the present moment, for instance, he is an enthusiastic furtherer of the *Pestalozzi method of education. He has made a deep study of this, as of every other question to which he addresses himself, so much so that he is preparing a dissertation on the subject. We can only wish a long life and unimpaired energies to such a hearty champion of all that is noble and beautiful, a true friend and connoisseur of the arts.

[25] Eberhard Waechter (1762–1852) was an historical painter who worked in Stuttgart from 1808 and was made Inspector of the collection of engravings. Of gloomy disposition, he was noted for his paintings on sombre themes. The most famous was the *Job* mentioned by Weber, *Der trauernde Hiob und seine Freunde* (Rome, 1797, finished 1824).

[26] Karl August von Wangenheim (1773–1850) came to Stuttgart from Gotha as Minister of Culture, and was known as a political journalist.

4. Review of a concert by the Bohrer brothers

Written: Stuttgart, 31 January 1810.
Published: Morgenblatt für gebildete Stände, No. 31, 5 February 1810.
Signed: Carl Marie.

Reprinted: KSS.

Anton and Max Bohrer were the third and fourth sons of the Mannheim bass player Caspar Bohrer (1744–1809). Anton (1783–1852) studied composition with *Danzi and completed his violin studies in Paris with *Rodolphe Kreutzer. Max (1785–1867) was a cellist, by some accounts (e.g. FétisB) the more gifted of the two. They had played in the Munich Court Orchestra and travelled together before the important tour of 1810 on which Weber heard them. From Germany they went on to Holland, Hungary, Poland and then Russia. Here, in 1812, they fled before the French advance but were arrested and only saved from being sent to Siberia by the music-loving General Seblovsky, who despatched them to St Petersburg as government couriers. They eventually returned home by way of Scandinavia. They married the pianist daughters of the Munich piano-maker Johann Ludwig Dulken, Anton marrying Fanny (b. 1807) and Max marrying Louise (b. 1805). Anton was the composer of the music they played, which included several concertanti for violin and cello.

The name of the travelling virtuoso is legion. Strong fingers, plenty of assurance and a bundle of introductions, and off he goes to lay the public under contribution. This being the case, it is all the more pleasant to find a pair of artists like the Bohrer brothers from the Munich Orchestra, who combine solid technical capabilities with real feeling in performance, and in addition a modest and pleasant manner. The elder of the two is not only a fine violinist but a superior composer; and in the concert given yesterday in the King of England Room the writer particularly admired a well-written Concertante for violin and violoncello played by the two brothers. Also in the programme were Herr Krebs[1] and Mlle Graff,[2] who both sang arias by our Danzi. Mlle Graff's outstanding charm of manner and fine style of performance in particular won universal admiration. The Bohrers are going from here to Frankfurt and then to Hamburg, and will doubtless be received everywhere with the same well-deserved and universal appreciation that they encountered here.

[1] Johann Baptist Krebs (1774–1851) studied philosophy and theology before embarking on a successful career as a tenor. He sang in Stuttgart from 1795 to 1825, also working as producer until 1849. He translated various operas (including *Così fan tutte* as *Mädchen sind Mädchen*, 1819) and wrote some songs and theoretical works on aesthetics. His adoptive son Karl Krebs (1804–80) succeeded Wagner as Kapellmeister at Dresden in 1850.

[2] Charlotte Graff (1782–1831) was the daughter of the actor Joseph Michael Böheim. She made her début in Berlin in 1800, and worked in Stuttgart from 1805 to 1811. She married the cellist Graff (to whom Weber dedicated his Grand Potpourri, J64), and left the stage in 1818.

5. Review of Peter Ritter's *Der Zitherschläger*

Written: Darmstadt, April 1810.
Published: ?
Reprinted: HHS; MMW; KSS.
    Der Zitherschläger was first produced in Stuttgart in 1810. It was in one act, to a text by Seidel. The vocal score was published in 1813, when the *AMZ* reviewed it as 'small and insignificant' (*AMZ* xv (1813), 503–4).

It is not often in my goings to and fro that I come upon anything so worthy and delightful as the opera *Der Zitherschläger* by that excellent musician *Kapellmeister Ritter in Mannheim; and I therefore feel impelled to bring it, however belatedly (for it has already been described in *Der Freimütige*) to the notice of you and your readers. This is admirable, deeply felt music, true to life and genuinely dramatic, and the various situations are grasped and developed with such a warmth of feeling that the present writer can hardly remember any work that has made so strong an impression on him. This was naturally heightened by an outstanding performance. *Herr Berger brought to the title role a quite exceptional veracity and acted with an ardour of feeling which must have communicated itself to everyone in the audience. Particularly fine was his singing of the delightful Romance 'Ritter Arno ging zu kämpfen', which was further marked by his excellent guitar playing, full of virtuoso passages excellently suited to the nature of the instrument and by no means unsuited to the dramatic situation.

Madame Gervais's[1] Röschen showed her to be an excellent actress and the orchestral playing did full justice to a score which contains not a few difficult passages, especially for the wind. In fact our warmest thanks are due to Herr Ritter and his librettist for an original German opera which can stand comparison with any French opera of the same kind; and the writer will always remember 1 April with pleasure as the day of the first performance of this opera in Mannheim.

[1] Mme Gervais. Wife of Andreas Gervais, leader of the Mannheim Court Orchestra. Weber acknowledged that she sometimes sang out of tune and forced her tone, but insisted that these were occasional faults and that she had great talent and skill (letters to *Franz Danzi, 16 March and 24 May 1816).

6. Mannheim

Written: Darmstadt, 11 or 12 June 1810.
Published: AMZ xii (1810), 659–62.   *Signed:* Carl Marie von Weber.
Reprinted: HHS (inaccurate); KSS; LKA.

On his expulsion from Stuttgart in 1810, Weber found a friendly reception in Mannheim, especially from *Gottfried Weber. In this 'Stadt-Brief' for the *AMZ*, he does not mention his own works played in the concert on 26 May: these were the Adagio and Rondo of his First Piano Concerto, which he played himself, and the concert aria 'Il momento s'avvicina', written for Luise Frank.

Mannheim may no longer occupy the same position in the musical world as it did in the happy days of Duke Carl Theodor,[1] but the feeling

[1] Carl Theodor was Elector Palatine in Mannheim from 1743 to 1778, during which period the orchestra reached the peak of its brilliance and attracted the collaboration of the so-called Mannheim School of composers, including the Stamitzes, Cannabich, Toeschi, Ignaz Fränzl, Richter, Holzbauer, the Cramers and *Danzi.

for music is still in general quite strong enough to make a good impression on the visitor and, should he obtain a closer knowledge of musical life there, to make Mannheim a valuable and enjoyable port of call. A special role is played by the music-lovers who maintain and foster the musical institutions in the Museum, where much enthusiastic and devoted work is done on behalf of the art. Particularly worthy of mention are Herr von Weiler, Herr von Stengel[2] and Herr [Gottfried] Weber – especially the last, who has a good claim to be considered a solid and thoughtful composer, although composition is not his main concern.

The present writer had the opportunity of attending a number of concerts in the Museum, at one of which an enthusiastic reception was given to a Symphony[3] by *Herr J. Gänsbacher, a pupil of *Vogler's, from Prague. This showed a thorough knowledge of harmony and an excellent ability to present and develop a theme. The present writer especially admired the very original *presto* Minuet and the spirited final Allegro. The opening Allegro, on the other hand, seemed to be, as it were, too much of a good thing, as though the composer had been misled by his own skill as a composer, and had forgotten that a concise unity of design is the most essential feature of any work of art claiming to be judged by the highest standards. All the more welcome was the impression made by the same composer's Mass,[4] performed on 3 June for the jubilee celebrations of the Catholic Stadtkirche. This was marked throughout by a noble spirit of repose and a deep emotion, a religious devotion undisturbed by any secular feature; and Herr Gänsbacher most certainly deserves a high reputation as a profound composer of church music with a fine melodic gift. The present writer was most struck by a powerfully worked fugue at the end of the Gloria, by the Kyrie and most especially the *Dona nobis*, which is of exceptional charm. Herr Gänsbacher's works also include a number of songs and canzonettas[5] in which a flowing Italian style is combined with a German vigorousness, forming a truly delightful whole best appreciated in the composer's own performance. I append the smallest of these pieces as an example, and should like at the same time to praise the modest and amiable manner shown by the composer on all occasions.

[2]   Ernst von Stengel (d. 1851) was a Chancellor of the High Court in Mannheim.
[3]   Gänsbacher's D major Symphony was written in 1807.
[4]   Gänsbacher wrote some thirty Masses. This one may have been that in C major, first performed in Eisenstadt in 1806.
[5]   Weber himself translated Gänsbacher's Six Songs (Op. 9) from their original Italian. One of these, 'L'amerò, sarò costante', was appended to the original *AMZ* review and to subsequent reprints.

The performance of the Mass, mostly by members of the Museum, was excellent; and it was a pleasure to note the high quality of the sopranos and altos, all amateur singers. The Museum and the members of the orchestra – which includes *Herr Frey, Herr Ahl, *Herr Dickhut, Herr Arnold etc. – deserve the admiration of all music-lovers for their active interest in church and chamber music; and the present writer heartily hopes that this enthusiasm will never flag, maintaining the high reputation of Mannheim and providing many such delightful occasions as those which the present writer was fortunate enough to enjoy.

7. A word on Vogler

Written: Darmstadt, 12 June 1810.
Published: Morgenblatt für gebildete Stände, No. 147, 20 June 1810.
Signed: Melos.
Reprinted: HHS (misdated 1809 and inaccurate); MMW (inaccurate); KSS; LKA.

At the time of this article, Weber was planning a full-scale biography of *Vogler – that is, as he wrote to *Gottfried Weber, 'if the seat of my trousers holds out' (letter of 23 June 1810). He told *Gänsbacher he had begun work (letter of 9 October 1810), and even after Vogler's death in Darmstadt on 6 May 1814 he had still not abandoned the idea (letter to *Rochlitz, 16 May 1814). When *Joseph Fröhlich wrote his *Biographie des grossen Tonkünstlers Abt Georg Joseph Vogler* (Würzburg, 1845), he included a note saying that he had supposed material for Weber's biography of Vogler to exist among his papers. However, all that has survived is the present article and Nos. 8 and 77 below.

Great men are notoriously misunderstood in their lifetime. All too often they themselves die of hunger, only to be applauded after their death by hungry publishers. In fact human beings have a way of neglecting the genius on their doorsteps and appreciating only those who are dead. This in fact is Vogler's fate. Some admire him because they cannot fully fathom his personality, while others abuse him because they fail to understand him and resent his disrupting the infallibility of the old monopolistic counterpoint and the routine of the figured bass.

Vogler is actually the first totally systematic composer, and of course many of his opinions differ from those of other great men for that very reason. He has not yet found a completely satisfactory formulation of his system,[1] but has a single critic ever bothered to acquaint himself

[1]   Vogler made much of the system of composition which he had developed. He expounded it in his *Handbuch zur Harmonielehre und für den Generalbass* (Prague, 1802).

with it? or modestly enquired of Vogler himself, who shows his real greatness and singleness of mind by being always ready to share his knowledge and experience with others?

No, a hasty glance at Vogler's writings may well reveal a few apparently unusual expressions, and the reviewer will pick on these in order to raise a laugh and show his own wittiness, exaggerating anything that can be made fun of (and even the greatest works offer such opportunities) in order to have the laugh on his side – leaving the poor author no other consolation than a speedy demise. Misrepresentation of this kind has in fact reduced Vogler, in the eyes of most music-lovers, to little more than a learned eccentric, a dry-as-dust composer. And what an injustice this is in the case of the composer of such flowing melodies, who can obtain from what is apparently the most unpromising theme such superb effects, simply by his musical skill and inventiveness.

His most recent major work provides excellent evidence of this – a Requiem[2] composed for himself, which the present writer had the good fortune to hear. This work includes all that art and artifice can achieve, treated with such genius, taste and skill that the listener is less aware of them than of the feelings which they arouse. The present writer was told that on the death of the great Haydn, Vogler, forgetting the original purpose of his Requiem, wished to have it performed in Vienna for the funeral of the composer whom he so much admired. Unfortunately hostilities made this generous idea impracticable, and when Vogler wanted the work performed at Haydn's memorial Mass in Frankfurt, he was again frustrated by circumstances beyond his control. If only heaven might grant Vogler a publisher concerned not solely with his own profit, his music might enjoy a wider popularity. As it is, he feels no call to thrust himself on the world's attention, though there can be no denying how much pleasure and profit are thereby lost to music and music-lovers. Meanwhile Vogler's name is universally respected, though this is a matter of tradition, since little of his music – and that only the earliest – is in fact known.

The philosophical retirement in which he lives at Darmstadt, as Chaplain Extraordinary and Commander of the Hesse Ludwigorden at the Court of the Grand Duke of Hesse, entitles us to hope for many more works from his still active and industrious muse. May every music student experience an enjoyment equal to that of the present writer

---

[2]   Vogler's Requiem in E flat, for soloists, chorus and orchestra, was written in 1809 and published by Schott in 1822 (No. 202 in Schafhäutl's catalogue: see K. von Schafhäutl, *Abt G. J. Vogler* (Augsburg, 1868)).

from Vogler's works, in which any unprejudiced listener will discover the purest and most heavenly sentiments that music can arouse.

8. Abt Vogler's birthday

Written: Darmstadt, 16 June 1810.
Published: Rheinische Correspondenz, No. 171, 22 June 1810. *Signed:* M—s.
Reprinted: H. Becker, ed., *Giacomo Meyerbeer: Briefwechsel und Tagebücher* I (Berlin, 1960).

For their teacher *Abt Vogler's sixty-first birthday on 15 June 1810, Weber, *Meyerbeer and *Gänsbacher collaborated on a short celebratory cantata. No-one being keen to write the words, lots were cast: Weber lost. His text comprises a brief chorus of welcome (Meyerbeer), a solo praising Vogler's qualities and achievements (Gänsbacher), a Terzett praying that his pupils may live to reflect his fame (Meyerbeer), a solo of gratitude to him (Gänsbacher), and a return of the opening chorus (text reprinted as No. 10 in KSS; however, Kaiser overlooked the present article).

The simple and heartfelt celebration of a day that must be precious to every lover of art should be generally known, and for this reason the present writer takes up his pen to describe the little musical festivity that was held by the assembled students of the greatly honoured artist and pedagogue, Councillor Abt Vogler, to mark his birthday on 15 June 1810. The word 'festivity' is not really appropriate here, since everything arose from the natural overflowing of heartfelt devotion to one who, valued alike as man and artist, could be delighted by nothing more than the efforts of his pupils on such a day; and so what could have been better than a work undertaken by all of them equally? On the morning of the day of celebration his bust was decorated with the laurel wreath the world has long conceded him, and garlanded with roses; and on his entrance into the room where a small group of his friends was gathered, there was performed a short cantata composed by Herr Meyer Beer of Berlin and Herr Gänsbacher of Prague, to a text by Herr Karl Marie von Weber. The text had the merit of truth and feeling, and was set by the two composers to music worthy of the pupils of such a master. It did not fail to make its effect, as was shown by the friendly high spirits which reigned among the company all morning; and the occasion closed with the general wish that there might often be repeated a day of joy and of value to art.

9. Twelve Bach chorales, arranged by Vogler and analysed

Written: Darmstadt, 21 June 1810.
Published: Bureau de Musique (later C. F. Peters), Leipzig, 1810.
Reprinted: HHS, MMW (both inaccurate and without music examples); KSS.

Having completed this piece of work, Weber wrote to *Gottfried Weber about it in some apprehension: 'I must tell you, my dear Weber, that at *Vogler's request I've taken on a job that could make me a reputation but also set a whole damned pack of hounds at my heels' (letter of 28 June 1810). His fears had not diminished when, after some difficulties with Kühnel about publication, review copies were sent out: 'The Kühnel Chorales are going to be reviewed in the *Reichsanzeiger*: keep a look out for it, and sharpen your pen, as I expect the Bachians will flay me' (letter of 1 November 1810). Despite Gerber's description of this in his *Neues Lexicon der Tonkünstler* as an important work, it was really (like Weber's piano score of Vogler's opera *Samori*) a kind of advanced exercise that was also of benefit to the teacher: according to Kaiser, the MS shows corrections in Vogler's hand, and the notes to No. 7 are in Gottfried's writing. Only the first pair of chorales is reproduced here (below, p. 49). For Weber's mature view of Bach, see below, No. 118.

It is admittedly a bold undertaking to touch upon the reputation and knowledge of a man recognized by all the world as great, and these arrangements will be regarded by many with a jaundiced eye – even perhaps (for the number of those who consider themselves infallible is large) condemned without both sides of the question being gone into. Nevertheless I have sufficient confidence in the power of the truth, in my ability to prove what I say and in the open-mindedness of a number of thinkers not ready to dismiss a case unheard.

Vogler has been the object of much misunderstanding, and the malice shown by many of those who have attacked him has often compelled him to speak out strongly in an attempt to establish his own merits. It may therefore not be superfluous to observe that his arrangements of these chorales have not been motivated by mere vanity or the desire to prove his own superior powers. On the other hand he has made these arrangements of the twelve chorales published in 1784 by Breitkopf in response to urgent requests by a number of music-lovers who believed that a comparison of the two versions would furnish students of harmony with a most interesting and rewarding experience, practical as well as theoretical. At the same time, it would provide new evidence of Vogler's own aspirations and his desire to serve the cause of music. The understanding and appreciation of music has often suffered from the pitting of one authority against another (as in this case Vogler against Bach) and students observing such disagreement between masters of the art inevitably experience a feeling of uncertainty, unless they are strong enough to stand back from what they have learnt from their academic studies and go their own way guided by their own experience.

One famous writer on music has called Bach the greatest harmonist not only of his own, but of all time. Vogler, who is always ready to recognize the merits of other composers, regards Bach as an altogether exceptional genius and a master of harmony, certainly superior to all his contemporaries, despite the fact that he possessed no actual system of harmonic practice. It is quite another thing to maintain that Bach exhausted all the resources of harmony, and indeed Vogler's own works prove the contrary. Vogler is a systematic composer, who draws his liberal principles from the essential nature of music, as he has shown, thereby opening up a vastly wider variety of harmonic possibilities. He is in fact the first theorist who is not content with prohibitions and recommendations but provides proofs and philosophical arguments for his principles.

The rules governing music are inherent in the art, and in comparing the works of great men any unprejudiced observer will be able to discover the truth, as in the present instance. For this reason I consider it beneath the dignity of the art to attempt in the following pages anything more than the statement of a point of view calculated to facilitate the understanding of the two versions. The musical world must then make its own judgement and come to a decision.

Finally I should like to express my full awareness of how much better a more worthy writer than myself could treat the present subject and of how disapprovingly many will regard such an attempt as this by a young and unknown musician. I can only repeat that I rest my confidence in the power of the truth, in my belief in the existence of unprejudiced readers and in Vogler's own invitation.

ANALYSIS

In his chorale arrangements Vogler takes into consideration:

1. Form. An aesthetic whole is created only by tonal logic. In harmonizing a chorale it is essential to have a clear overall view of the

cadences at the end of each line. For this reason I shall preface each of my analyses of the two versions by a scheme of comparison.

2. Harmony – that is to say, in Vogler's terminology

Harmonia simultanea $\begin{cases} \text{(a) choice of harmonies, i.e. actual chords} \\ \text{(b) choice of their position and} \end{cases}$

Harmonia successiva   (c) choice of their succession

Harmonic purity is not simply a matter of avoiding the forbidden consecutive fifths and octaves. A failure in the choice of position is neither so important nor so culpable as the neglect of the poetic significance of chordal succession, the fundamental characteristics determining the logical development of ideas.

3. Independence and melodic character of the individual parts in relation both to each other and to the whole. It is not enough to ensure that each part has a truly melodic character; the essential thing is their mutual relationship – the avoidance of unpleasing clashes between passing notes in order to ensure the easy movement of each part.

Chorale 1   'Aus meines Herzens Grunde' ('From the bottom of my heart')

Scheme of comparison between the cadences

Bach D G D G D C D G
Vogler – – A – – – A –

(N.B. Bach always repeats the first half exactly, while Vogler provides a different harmonization the second time.)

In Bach's bar 3 the middle voices make an unpleasing clash with the bass – first D/B against a bass C, then E/C against a bass B. In Bach's bars 20–1 the leap in the melody caused by the harmonization is noticeably harsh. The B in the top line against the F that forms a dominant seventh on G is inevitably felt as the leading note of C (particularly if we take other systems into account). Vogler cleverly avoids this by harmonizing on B as the seventh degree of C, which enables him to proceed at will. He has even added a bar here to make the cadence perfectly clear, but this is justified partly by the fact that the sound is identical and partly because Vogler could just have well made his close in the one bar. Bach's bar 24 is full of passing notes which offend the ear, a thing which never occurs in Vogler's harmonizations. (In order to be brief I will in future refer only to those passing notes which fall on an emphasized beat or section of the bar and are, in general or particular, incompatible with the character of the chorale.)

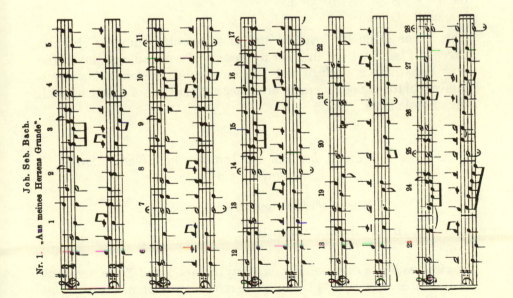

Chorale 2   'Ich dank' dir, lieber Herr' ('I thank thee, dear Lord')

Scheme of comparison between the cadences

Bach   E   E   E   E   E   B   E   A
Vogler   A   –   A   –   –   –   –   –

Bach's five cadences in E are monotonous and, particularly in bars 2 and 6, rather harsh. Vogler varies the harmonies each time with exceptionally rich harmonies. At bar 14 what the ear actually hears is consecutive fifths; provided that they were not visible to the eye from the score, as here, these were allowed. Bach's bar 16 is stiff compared with Vogler's and the dissonance B/A/G sharp is very unpleasing, whereas in Vogler's version each part moves smoothly and in perfect consonance with the others.

Chorale 3   'Ach Gott vom Himmel sieh darein' ('Consider, O God in Heaven')

Scheme of comparison between the cadences

Bach   E   A   E   A   B   A   E
Vogler   B   D   –   –   –   –   –

This is one of Bach's loveliest and most smoothly moving chorales except for bar 3 where, in order to preserve the melodic quality of the bass line, there is a clash of F/D/E on the last crotchet. The semiquavers in the melody seem an arbitrary addition out of character with the chorale form.

Chorale 4   'Es ist das Heil uns kommen her' ('Salvation is come down upon us')

Scheme of comparison between the cadences

Bach   A   B   A   B   B   C sharp   B
Vogler   –   –   D   E   –   –   –

It is impossible to overlook the fact that in bars 3 and 7 the harmony in the three upper parts is quite different from that which the bass would lead us to expect, and that Bach has apparently done this to preserve the character of the bass line. Such things are by no means rare in Bach, and I think we must draw the conclusion that, in general, he was prepared to sacrifice the harmonic effect of the whole to the quality of the individual part.

Vogler's harmonization of this chorale is a real triumph of skill and its noble, outstanding style cannot fail to delight every listener. Particularly elegant is the absolutely parallel movement of tenor and bass parts, as is the first bass entry on the fourth crotchet of the first bar (and the variation of this in bars 6–7).

Chorale 5 'An Wasserflüssen Babylons' ('By the waters of Babylon')

Scheme of comparison between the cadences

Bach	G	G	G	G	G	D	E	A	D	G
Vogler	B	–	E	C	–	–	B	–	G	–

Bach's version has five cadences in G, the first of them closing on the third, which is not in the chorale style. The second quaver in bar 2 is an example of the same phenomenon that we encountered in Chorale 4 – namely a contradiction between the bass and the harmony of the three upper parts. In bars 12–13 there are a number of harsh dissonances between tenor and bass, best observed by comparison with the pure harmonization of Vogler's version. His two last cadences are in G, a full close in bar 18 and a plagal cadence in bar 21.

Chorale 6 'Nun lob' meine Seel' den Herren' ('Come praise the Lord, my soul')

Scheme of comparison between the cadences

Bach	A		A		A	F sharp	E	D	B	D	E	E	A
Vogler	C sharp	–	F sharp	–		–	–	–	–	A	–	B	–

Bach's first cadence is again on the third. In bar 21 the second beat has only two parts. In bars 31–2 bass and tenor are uncomfortably close and in bar 43 the soprano part goes below the alto.

As in most of these examples, Vogler's harmonization is incomparably richer, but he never has recourse to enharmonic devices or the like in order to ensure a smooth flow. In his bar 14 the identification of G and F double sharp is worth noting.

Chorale 7   'Christus, der ist mein Leben' ('Christ is my life')

Scheme of comparison between the cadences

Bach   F   F   C   F
Vogler D   A   –   –

This is a beautifully written chorale, but in bar 5 crotchet 2 the alto part has two semiquavers designed to cover consecutive fifths, and these disturb the flow of the harmony. In bars 2–4 Vogler's harmonization avoids the cadences on the third, and in general his version offers more variety.

Chorale 8   'Freuet euch, ihr Christen' ('Christians, rejoice')

Scheme of comparison between the cadences

Bach	F	A flat	F	A flat	B flat	F	C	A flat	F
Vogler	–	–	–	C	–	–	–	D flat	–

In bars 2, 8, 14, 16 and 20 the last two crotchets are identical in harmony. This gives the whole harmonization a certain monotony which Vogler relieves by the use of dissonance. In bar 19 the bass and alto parts are as follows: B flat/A flat, A flat/B flat. The bass line in the four last bars of Vogler's version is magnificently firm and powerful, emphasizing the feeling of the approaching cadence (five-part, bar 20) by its parallel movement.

Chorale 9   'Ermuntre dich, mein schwacher Geist' ('Be of good cheer, poor drooping heart')

Scheme of comparison between the cadences

Bach   D   G   D   G   A   E   D   G
Vogler –   C   –   –   –   –   –   –

The part-writing in this chorale is frequently stiff and awkward. To ensure the flow of the melody Vogler allows himself consecutive (though dissimilar) fifths – D/G sharp, E/A. They could easily be avoided by changing A to E.

Chorale 10 'Aus tiefer Not schrei' ich zu dir' ('Out of the depths have I cried unto thee')

Scheme of comparison between the cadences

Bach E E E E A G E
Vogler – A B – D – –

The four cadences in E make a monotonous effect.

Chorale 11 'Puer natus in Bethlehem' ('A boy is born in Bethlehem')

Scheme of comparison between the cadences

Bach C C A A
Vogler G C – –

(N.B. In the printed edition this chorale is Bach's No. 12 and the following chorale is No. 11.)
This is a short chorale and two consecutive cadences in C make an undesirable impression.

Chorale 12 'Jesu, nun sei gepreiset' ('Jesus, now be praised')

Scheme of comparison between the cadences

Bach   B flat C F C B flat C F C A C C D G C
Vogler   G – – – D   – – – – C A E G – –

The tonic is C and Bach's first cadence is in B flat; and apart from this there are so many dissonant passing notes that the present writer feels obliged to mention only the most glaring – in bars 17, 19, 38 and 39.

This chorale shows Vogler at his very greatest. What nobility in his modulation! The five-part writing in bars 19–20 is both novel and arresting in its power. The close, powerful texture of the five-part final cadence is a perfect instance of genuine solemnity in church music. In fact a glance at the score will be enough to carry conviction, and the present writer closes with the well-founded hope that the world will confirm his judgement and thus perhaps persuade Vogler to give us more of these harmonizations as well as further large-scale works of his own.

10. Marianne Schönberger (1)

Written: Darmstadt, 28 June 1810.
Published: Rheinische Correspondenz, No. 179, 30 June 1810.   *Signed:* M—s.
Reprinted: here for the first time.

  *Marianne Schönberger had a great success on her visit to Frankfurt in the first half of 1810, as other reports testify. Towns she also visited included Carlsruhe, as well as Darmstadt, where Weber heard her. Though overlooked by Kaiser, who cannot have searched the short-lived *Rheinische Correspondenz*, and ignored by Weber himself when he came to review Mme Schönberger again two years later in Weimar (see below, No. 44), the article must be by him. No one else used the Harmonischer Verein pseudonym M—s (Melos), and he was in Darmstadt at the time.

We too have recently had the pleasure of becoming acquainted with the great talent of Mme Schönberger, born Marconi, for she has made three guest appearances at the Grossherzoglichestheater, as Belmonte in *Die Entführung aus dem Serail*, Loridan in *Camilla* and Murney in *Das unterbrochene Opferfest*. On each occasion she enjoyed a packed house and loud applause, and she was given an enthusiastic curtain call at the end of the first and third performances.

It would be superfluous to give an extensive description of her remarkable voice and of her singing in general after the full reports from Frankfurt published in several journals[1] (with which we are in complete agreement). We content ourselves with a few words on her simple yet noble acting, which by means of expressive mime and apt gesture, together with her majestically Junoesque presence and the picturesque beauty of her figure (which male clothing especially favoured), makes her one of the most interesting artists now on the stage. The orchestra and the rest of the company provided, with their ready and careful performance, a fine ensemble worthy of the excellent leadership of their guest artist. Grateful acknowledgement was due to their efforts, even when they did not always succeed.

[1] Including the *Rheinische Correspondenz* itself, e.g. unsigned reports in No. 56, 25 February 1810, and No. 143, 24 May 1810.

11. Baden-Baden

Written: 1 August 1810.
Published: Morgenblatt für gebildete Stände, No. 190, 9 August 1810.
Signed: Melos.

Reprinted: HHS (misdated 1809, abbreviated and inaccurate); MMW (abbreviated and inaccurate); KSS; LKA.

Weber noted on the MS of this 'Stadt-Brief' that it was written at the request of the Tübingen publisher Johann Friedrich Cotta (1764–1832). The son of the founder of the firm, which was responsible for publishing most of the German classics in the nineteenth century beginning with Goethe and Schiller, Cotta was also the owner of the *Morgenblatt*. Its social and literary nature accounts for the belle-lettristic tone Weber adopts.

I alighted from my carriage just as a friend of mine was entering his. 'Where are you off to?' I called to him. 'Baden', was the answer, and off he drove. I called on an old acqaintance and found him packing. 'Are you going away?' 'Yes.' 'Where?' 'To Baden.' In the street I ran into another, obviously preoccupied. 'Pity you come just as I must rush off to get a seat. You can't believe how full the coaches are,' he said. 'Everyone tells me that I mustn't lose a moment.' 'Where are you going then? what coaches?' 'Why, good heavens, to Baden, where else? Good-bye, I really must go.' And away he went.

Well, thought I, if the whole world is off to Baden, I had better turn my footsteps that way too – and I imagined all the pleasant excitement of a busy spa, with its gay social life. So in the hope of enjoying this sort of life at its best in Baden I entrusted my person to the tender mercies of postillions, who eventually deposited me safe and sound at the Badischer Hof.

There were certainly plenty of people, in fact so many that it was difficult to find a room. Often as many as fifteen or twenty people have to make do with a straw mattress until a room is free or a kind friend is ready to share his room. Even so, preliminary inconveniences of this kind only increase one's pleasure once one is installed, and make one look forward even more eagerly to the excitements of the next day. Unfortunately, though, I was disappointed. That free and easy social existence, in which one's neighbour at the table d'hôte soon becomes an old acquaintance and the conventions of everyday life are relaxed, was missing.

The number of visitors is so large that they inevitably split up into cliques, which are simply another form of closed societies, so that the newcomer finds himself alone until he can join one or another, and this may be a matter of days. Everyone I know complains of this, but nobody seems to have done anything about remedying it.

The chief trouble is the absence of any social rallying-point. Places where one takes the waters have this marked advantage – that they provide such a rallying-point by their very nature. At Baden the Promenadehaus is virtually the only place where everyone foregathers, and really its only attractions are a rouge-et-noir table for those who want to play, and a few newspapers for those with political interests, so that not many people meet there. There only remains the new casino in the Badischer Hof, an attractive and friendly place where one also finds the most popular newspapers. This is visited every evening by a group of select and pleasant guests, and one can only hope that an increasing number of people will go there to satisfy the visitors' need for mutual entertainment. The distance between the Promenadehaus and the Badischer Hof is the one great drawback and tells against the further development of either. The casino, on the other hand, can hardly fail to become more interesting and more popular.

Of course other forms of entertainment are not wanting. Herr Dengler's Theatre Company from Freiburg does its best to satisfy all tastes and contains some quite good members, who would doubtless provide a good evening's entertainment, if they were not mad enough to want to give *Don Giovanni*, *Opferfest* and *Lodoiska* with an orchestra of about three and a half players.[1] (For operas in these circumstances to be amusing one would need a worse company than Dengler's.)[2]

I must admit, too, that I never enter this particular theatre without a certain nervousness on the score of danger from fire or water. I simply cannot understand the negligence of a town that provides its guests with a wretched little theatre consisting of a few boards roughly hammered together, with gaps that let in the light and a single door which, in case of fire, would make escape more than problematical. As the foundations of the little building seem to have been designed to last, I can only console myself with the hope that it will be moved to a more suitable site and rebuilt more solidly and with a greater concern for the requirements of such an establishment. Those who are fond of dancing are well catered for in Baden, though space is poor,

---

[1]   Dengler's company was one of the smaller of the many *Wandertheater* upon which much of Germany depended for its entertainment. The standards of these were very variable, and not many would have attempted the works by Mozart, Winter and *Cherubini which Weber cites. *Don Giovanni* had previously been given in Freiburg without trumpets, trombones or timpani.
[2]   The bracketed sentence occurs only in the MS.

by weekly balls given at the Sun, the Salm and the Badischer Hof as
well as a number of other hotels. In fact there was even a fancy-dress
ball recently at the Badischer Hof, celebrated in the following poems
by one of our leading poets. You must know that the Badischer Hof
is built on the site of an old Capuchin monastery and that the ballroom
occupies what was once the chapel. At the fancy-dress ball one of the
guests came as a Capuchin, who expressed no little indignation at the
proceedings.

> For shame! here where we worshipped once, and loud
> The organ sounded in our festal throng,
> Where many a soul sloughed off its sinful shroud
> And winged its way toward heaven's eternal song!
> Here in this holy place wild passions reign
> Rude, wilful pleasure and unbridled glances!
> Shall the quiet church with flambeaux blaze amain
> And music raise her voice for jigging dances?

Another mask gave the following answer:

> ### Answer to the Capuchin
>
> My friend, God does not blame a life of ease
> Nor spurn man's longing to forget his pain –
> Happy is he whom every day can please,
> For whom each hour is sweet, each moment gain!
> He may to heaven raise a joyful heart,
> His faith so steel'd against misfortune's spell,
> That where the innocent meet to impart
> Mutual delight, there God returns to dwell!

I can certainly reassure all those concerned with the 'inner man'
as to the quality of the food and drink and the comfort, prices and
service in the hotels. The best of these are the Badischer Hof, the Salm
and the Sun. The food is equally good in all of these, but the Badischer
Hof is infinitely superior to the others in its appointments. The
dining-room is a high, handsome room with ceiling lighting, and the
Kasinosaal is most tastefully arranged. The baths, which in the other
hotels are wooden and tucked away in poky attics, are here made of
stone. All these considerations ensure the growing popularity of this
hotel, which is also adding a large number of rooms to the existing
sixty, so that future visitors will be sure of a booking.

More important than all other considerations is the unique natural
beauty of the surrounding countryside, which will always ensure
Baden a high place among spas and an unceasing flow of visitors. I
am familiar with many watering-places, but none combines so many

and varied natural attractions. Noble and delightful views, mountains and cliffs on the one hand, smiling plains on the other, the nearness of the magnificent Murgthal etc. – all these are permanent advantages, such as made Baden delightful even to the Romans and will continue always to endear it both to the Germans and to their Gallic neighbours.

Expeditions to the surrounding countryside therefore naturally form a regular feature of social life there; and those who take part in them never fail to come back cheered and refreshed, to return to their homes with happy memories and a strong desire to repeat their visit.

12. Review of the score of Ludwig Berger's *Colma*

Written: Frankfurt, 23 October 1810.
Published: AMZ XII (1810), 997–9.   *Signed:* Carl Maria von Weber.
Reprinted: HHS, MMW (both inaccurate); KSS.

Ludwig Berger (1777–1839) was a pupil of Clementi and the teacher of Mendelssohn, on whose *Songs without Words* his piano pieces had some influence. His many songs include the first settings of Wilhelm Müller's *Die schöne Müllerin* poems in a *Liederspiel* (1816). The Ossianic subject of Colma was also the source of Peter von Winter's opera *Colmal* (Munich, 1809).

'Colma', Ossianic Scene, composed with pianoforte accompaniment and dedicated to Her Imperial Highness the Princess Stephanie Napoleon, Hereditary Grand Duchess of Baden, by Louis Berger. Published by André of Offenbach.

Herr Berger is already known to the public by his affecting vocal compositions, and the present work will doubtless find many admirers. Melancholy seems to be Herr Berger's favourite mood, and the present writer therefore expected to find him particularly well suited by an Ossianic theme.

The poem offers a number of difficulties to any composer – in the first place length, and then the unrelievedly gloomy character of the whole piece, which makes it hard to achieve the variety indispensable to a musical composition of any length. In reading a poem, impressions succeed each other swiftly, and only a few words are needed to denote and achieve a change of mood. The composer's task is more arduous, for his language needs longer accents and the transition from one feeling to another cannot be achieved without surmounting a number of obstacles. Herr Berger has been outstandingly successful in meeting the majority of a critic's demands, more especially in passages of a markedly lyrical nature. The passage 'O Salgar, mon héros; mon ami, mon amant' etc. is excellently conceived, and the profound emotion and anxiety are strikingly expressed by a declamation unfailingly true to life. The same is true of the recitative which follows, with its impassioned *crescendo* ('L'echo seul me répond...' to 'mes cris doulour-eux' etc.). Equally admirable is the passage where Colma is exhausted by her trials and her anxieties and feels her strength failing her as her hopes fade. Gradually she yields to a growing lethargy at 'Zéphyr parfume l'air en caressant les fleurs, quand la Nature se ranime, je me sens défaillir.' Here the quickening of Nature is represented by the really charming accompaniment (E flat major) and Colma's surround-ings are shown in sharp contrast to the fragmentary monosyllabic phrases that betray her emotional state. No sensitive listener could fail to be charmed by this whole scene, played on a good fortepiano with the *son céleste*. The transition from this to F minor is somewhat brusque, despite the *adagio* marking, and the rather frequent modula-tions both here and elsewhere are open to question, despite the fact that they are prompted by the frequent changes of mood in the text.

The recitative 'De sa valeur, Salgar est la victime' is excellent in its reflective manner, up to the words 'Il n'a pu m'oublier', when an F major melody expresses relief at her assurance of Salgar's love. The emotional colouring of the music now becomes increasingly dark, Colma's phrases become shorter and shorter, and it is only the accompaniment that keeps up a semblance of life. Finally this too begins to die away, and the end comes on a long *ritardando* leading to the words 'Je meurs, du moins ce soir cache mon ombre errante.' For this scene to make its full effect an experienced player, a good instrument (on which Berger seems to have counted) and a singer to encompass Berger's exceptional vocal range are all needed. This is perhaps the only objection that can justly be made to the composer of this amiable piece.

13. The statutes of the Harmonischer Verein

Written: Darmstadt, end October 1810.
Published: MMW I, pp. 228–32.
Reprinted: KSS; LKA.

Weber first had the idea of forming a society for the advancement of like-minded colleagues' ideas and music at the beginning of 1810, and plans were discussed with *Gottfried Weber, *Meyerbeer, *Dusch and *Berger. Weber drafted the statutes, sending copies to the others for comment. He also recruited *Gänsbacher, *Danzi and *Berner; and other members they had in mind were *Joseph Fröhlich, *Max Heigel, *Hans Georg Nägeli and *Heinrich Zschokke. After showing his colleagues various drafts, Weber finally drew up the statutes during October 1810. The plans never came to proper fulfilment, through the failure of the members to keep up correspondence after the initial enthusiasm began to wane. It was not intended as a mutual admiration society, and indeed only six of Weber's reviews of members' works survive as compared with dozens about other composers' works. There were also plans for a journal, *Der harmonische Bund*, which Weber hoped to persuade Nägeli to publish, beginning on 1 May 1811; but these were abandoned, partly because Nägeli refused and partly, Weber later told *Rochlitz, out of respect for the *AMZ*.

The judgement of works of art is often one-sided and dictated by party spirit, and publishers even hire writers to praise their publications, so that it is often difficult to obtain a proper hearing and evaluation for works of genuine worth by those who have not yet made a name for themselves. These are the circumstances that have led Carl Maria von Weber, Joh. G. Meyerbeer, Gottfried Weber and Alexander von Dusch to form a Society for mutual support and action in the cause of art. The basis of the Society is a shared enthusiasm for art, shared opinions on its nature and the necessity of paying more attention particularly to aesthetic considerations.

It has not been possible for all the associates to work together in a single locality, and it has therefore been thought necessary to plan and establish a standard practice in order to achieve the Society's objects. An absolutely disinterested conception of the Society is something that must be taken for granted in every member; and since many misconceptions and misinterpretations of the Society are possible, and many obstacles can only be overcome by persistent effort, the motto chosen is 'Perseverance achieves its object'.[1] The title 'Harmonic Society' seems justified by the fact that in it everything is inspired by a single enthusiasm and a single point of view, and in the last resort is a single entity.

1. The nature of the matter demands that the existence of the Society should be kept in the closest secrecy. Its effectiveness would be hopelessly prejudiced by publicity, since it would be difficult to persuade the public that such a Society was impartial and sincere.

---

[1] *Beharrlichkeit führt zum Ziel* – Weber's principal motto, especially in the early years of his life. It appears frequently in his Diary, correspondence and other writing, sometimes abbreviated as B.f.z.Z.

2. Carl Maria von Weber has been entrusted with the General Direction of the society.

3. Mannheim has been decided upon as a regular Central Office, and there Gottfried Weber will act as Secretary of the Society. He will keep the Society's archives and be in charge of the finances, accounting for income and expenditure, and arranging and noting incoming contributions and in general all official documents, so that the progress of the Society's activities can be followed exactly.

4. All correspondence will be addressed to Herr Lizentiat Weber in Mannheim, and he will forward it as soon as possible to the Director, with whom he will be in constant touch.

5. A fixed sum, to be decided later, will be allotted for postal expenses, which will inevitably be considerable.

6. Constituent membership of the Society will be confined to those who are both composers and writers, and care will be taken to choose only those whose character ensures their proper use of the Society.

7. In addition to the aforementioned, literary members will be accepted, that is persons who, without being composers, combine a knowledge of music with a literary gift and can help the cause of music by their poems and other literary works. They will have exactly the same position and rights as other members.

8. The greatest prudence will be exercised in the choice of new members, and therefore no one will be accepted unless his proposer can vouch absolutely for his suitability, and unless,

9. in his form of proposal to the Director, he encloses a full statement of his artistic abilities and general attitudes. This will be communicated to other members for discussion.

10. Those proposed for membership will of course have no previous knowledge of the Society's existence. This will ensure against abuses, though in no way excluding gifted persons from the beneficial activities of the Society.

11. Every member must adopt a pen-name with which his notices will be signed unless he uses his own, thus ensuring against possible unpleasantnesses, since every member will immediately recognize another member's work.[2]

---

[2]   The pseudonyms chosen were as follows: Gottfried Weber – G. Giusto, Julius Billig; Meyerbeer – Philodikaios, also Julius Billig; Gänsbacher – Triole; Dusch – Unknown Man, The Unknown (both in English). Carl Maria himself was to be Melos (or M—s), Simon Knaster, or B.f.z.Z. Knaster was a kind of tobacco, also slang for an old grumbler; for B.f.z.Z. see above, n. 1.

12. Should a member find it necessary to use several different signatures or to choose a new pen-name, he will at once inform the Central Office, which will communicate the information to other members.

13. Two months after election to the Society (or two months after the foundation of the Society) every member is bound to communicate a *curriculum vitae*, with particular attention to his artistic development, to the Secretary; and this must be updated annually. It will be the Central Secretary's duty to contact members who fail to do this.

14. The chief object of the Society, and therefore of each member, is to assist and draw attention to work of high quality, wherever it is to be found, and particular attention should be paid to youthful, budding talents.

15. On the other hand, since the world is flooded by so many productions of poor quality, which are often promoted by officials and by wretched reviewing, it is the Society's duty to draw attention to this and warn the public wherever it occurs. It is to be hoped, however, that in doing so the common style of reviewers will be avoided.

16. On the other hand it will be a pleasant duty to publicize the work of Society members and appreciate its just worth.

17. Members must immediately inform the Director of any public appearance [i.e. performance or publication] of any work of theirs and at the same time draw attention to its individual features. The Director will pass on his own criticisms to another member in a special letter devoted to the subject, and will show this letter to the author of the work.

18. An octavo copy of every review, edition etc. will be sent by members to the Society's archives; and in this way every member will be able to welcome, and if need be to profit by, the effectiveness and progress of the archives.

19. Members must observe the strictest impartiality and adverse criticism must not be glossed over. It should however be expressed discreetly and not in the biting and mocking tone common to newspaper reviewers.

20. In the improbable case of a member submitting work of really poor quality, the Director will be frank with him and urge him to withdraw what he has written. Should the author in question have objections to the Director's judgement, the opinions of two other members will be sought. If one of these agrees with the Director's judgement and

advises the author to withdraw his work, but the author refuses to do this, proceedings will be taken against him under paragraph 15.

21. Although any attempt to exert political influence of whatever kind is against the spirit of the Society, it is to be taken for granted that every member will do his best to help a fellow member in any situation, thereby showing himself superior to that spirit of jealousy which is so deplorable but so common among artists.

Central Archives, 20 November 1810

14. A note on Mannheim

Written: Darmstadt, 26 January 1811.
Published: AMZ xiii (1811), 261–3.   *Signed:* Carl Marie von Weber.
Reprinted: HHS; MMW; KSS.

Weber wrote this report as a first move towards the *Musical Topography* described below (No. 27).

Public utterances and private observations made by the greatest artists, as well as my own experiences, lead me to give public expression to the desire for a modest and reliable guide to the major German cities – something designed to provide touring artists with a correct idea of the position of the arts in each of these towns and the best manner of approach in individual cases. Ideally such a guide would be compiled by artists themselves, whose many contacts with the public give them, after even the shortest acquaintance, a certain ability to divine the artistic quality of an audience. Why should not the artist himself take up his pen, instead of always being the object of comment? We are accustomed to reading the reactions of an audience to the artist; why should we not read his reactions to them? The result would certainly be of interest to many readers, and not only to other artists. If his observations were to carry conviction, he would certainly have to write under his own name, and this would ensure against facile and partisan judgements. It is a common experience that countless unpleasantnesses in life are caused by trivial circumstances which, however, can often have a notable effect on the development of a talent and may even nip it in the bud. There is no means of redressing such things; and it therefore seems to me a matter of necessity to bring to the public notice instances of such deplorable circumstances, which play an unusually large part in the career of an artist. If I may make so bold as to begin with my own humble example, it is in the hope that I shall be followed by others more worthy than myself, whose experiences will be of greater interest to the public.

I should like to begin with Mannheim, a city famous in the past for its artistic glories and still true to this tradition, with a genuine feeling for art and a warm-hearted appeal to the visitor. The orchestra contains some fine artists – the violinist *Frey, the horn players *Dickhut and Ahl, the flautist Apold, the younger Ahl as clarinettist. The conductor, *Kapellmeister Ritter, is known as composer of the operas *Salomon, Der Zitherschläger*[1] etc. and is a man of generally acknowledged talent. It is a matter of regret that his conducting lacks warmth, and that the absence of a strong controlling personality has led to a certain element of chaos in Mannheim's musical life. The playing of the orchestra is capable, and I am glad to have the opportunity to express on paper my gratitude for the precision with which they have performed a number of my works. One experience of mine in Mannheim, however, came as a great surprise. A number of music-lovers invited me to give an additional concert and this was at first agreed upon by the whole committee. Not long afterwards I received a letter explaining that there was a regulation by which the orchestra was forbidden to perform with a guest artist during the winter season. Although this struck me as strange, I accepted it and after explaining the matter to the public, forgot the whole business. A few days later *Kreutzer and Leppich[2] arrived and proceeded – apparently in spite of the existing regulation – to play with the orchestra; and they were followed by a number of other guest artists. I could not conceal my justified astonishment at this, though I do not want to exact an explanation of any kind, particularly as I never had any disagreement with any member of the orchestra. I do however consider it my duty to bring this arbitrary behaviour to the notice of the public and to warn other artists.

[1] See above, No. 5.
[2] Conradin Kreutzer had arrived from Vienna with Franz Leppich, the inventor of the Panmelodicon. This was one of many contemporary attempts at developing a sustaining keyboard instrument. Produced by Leppich in 1810 in imitation of Friedrich Chladni's Clavicylinder, it consisted of a set of tuned rectangular metal bars, controlled by a keyboard, which were sounded by being pressed against a rotating metal cylinder. It was perhaps the interest aroused by the novel instrument that led to the infraction of the rules about guest artists. Weber alleged that the letter forbidding his concert was the result of intrigues by Ritter (letter to *Gänsbacher, 13 January 1811).

15. A note on Darmstadt

Written: Darmstadt (?), February 1811.
Published: Morgenblatt für gebildete Stände, No. 118, 17 May 1811.
Unsigned.
Reprinted: HHS, MMW (both inaccurate); KSS; LKA.

Weber moved from Mannheim to Darmstadt in the spring of 1811, partly because the *Abbé Vogler was established there and partly because he believed that since 1790, under the Grand Duke Ludwig I, the town had developed a flourishing musical tradition. He found it a boring and oppressive town (as he wrote to *Gottfried Weber on 15 April 1810). The opening passage in square brackets was deleted from the MS before publication.

[Like the Hetman in Boieldieu's *Béniowski,*[1] if I speak of the situation of the arts in Darmstadt, I must be understood to mean that the arts actually have no situation in Darmstadt; and this has unfortunately been almost true up to now, and would have remained true if the establishment of the new Hoftheater[2] did not promise to bring about a revolution in their favour.]

There are certainly very few princes who foster the arts as assiduously as His Highness the Grand Duke. Particularly in the field of music, in which His Highness has very sound judgement, a tireless enthusiasm has produced striking results during the last few years. The orchestra contains some very fine players – among them the leader, Mangold,[3] particularly outstanding as an admirable violinist – and is warmly supported by a number of music-lovers from all ranks of society, heartily encouraged by His Highness. A fine large chorus has been formed of amateur singers, stiffened by a few professionals for concert purposes, and the standard of performance will impress the listener

---

[1]   Boieldieu's *Béniowski, ou Les Exilés de Kamchatka* (Paris, 1800) was performed in Brunswick (in French) in 1803, and Vienna (in *G. F. Treitschke's translation) on 20 June 1804. Weber had left Vienna a matter of days previously; but the opera featured in a few German repertories, and Weber records that he saw it in Prague in 1811 (Diary, 17 December 1811). In Alexandre Duval's libretto the Hetman makes only a token appearance; but in the original play by *Kotzebue (who had himself been a Siberian exile) the Hetman is the comic relief, the conventional drunken, cowardly braggart of German comedy. Weber's reference is to his plans to leave the wastes of Kamchatka so as to found a more civilized community in America.

[2]   Darmstadt long lacked a properly organized theatre, and the Hoftheater was not opened until 1810. Based on the Worms company under Xaver Krebs, it began with Mozart's *La clemenza di Tito.*

[3]   Georg Mangold (1767–1835) was one of a large family of musicians who served the Darmstadt court for several generations.

even at a first hearing. With these combined forces, three or four so-called concert-rehearsals have been given every week in the grand-ducal palace, the programmes including such large-scale works as operas, oratorios, cantatas etc. These were performed before a small invited audience and the Grand Duke attended every concert, following a score of each work and taking the liveliest interest in the correctness of the performance. The writer was most impressed by soft playing unique in his experience, but occasionally out of place, particularly after loud passages, where *mezzo forte* and *mezzo piano* were lost and the orchestral *piano* weakened its own effectiveness. The writer also noticed the absence of a strong, resonant *forte*, due to poor tone in the violins and cellos. If attention is paid to this weakness, as His Highness's discernment would lead us to expect, the Darmstadt Orchestra may be counted among the best orchestras in Germany. The unusual condescension and kindness shown by His Highness the Grand Duke in all these matters must assuredly earn him the affection of his subjects.

In spite of such encouragement on the part of the ruler, Darmstadt cannot boast of that genuine musical sense that finds its most lively expression in amateur performances of chamber music prompted by an impulsive need for artistic expression. Music is regarded there rather as a professional duty performed to oblige a master, and once a rehearsal is over a player will not touch his instrument until the next one.

It is the warmest wish of the writer that this cold attitude may eventually disappear and a love of beauty become more general. The influence of the theatre cannot be other than beneficial, as it will mean that a larger number of good artists come to live in Darmstadt. The organization of a new theatre is no small matter and needs before all else an active and experienced director; but the determination of His Highness the Grand Duke, who seems bent on having a really good theatre, will without doubt overcome all difficulties.

Darmstadt has already made an interesting acquisition in *Herr Wohlbrück, and fine individual artists of this kind cannot fail to exercise the most advantageous influence on the development of the artistic situation. *Madame Schönberger[4] has delighted the public in several roles; and the productions of *Die Entführung aus dem Serail* and *Die drei Sultaninnen*,[5] which the writer had the pleasure of attending, were both vigorous and promising for the future. Particularly note-

---

[4]   See above, No. 10, and below, No. 44.

[5]   *Singspiel* in one act by F. A. Hiller, produced Königsberg 1809: unfavourably reviewed, *AMZ* XI (1809), 813.

worthy is the chorus, which consists of some fifty young people who may be regarded as new recruits to the cause of music. The chorus-master is Markwort,[6] an excellent singer who within the incredibly short space of a few months has had such good results that before long Darmstadt will have a chorus such as few theatres in Germany possess. In fact none of the means for achieving a satisfactory end are wanting in Darmstadt, and it is the writer's heartfelt wish that good use may be made of them for the satisfaction of the art-loving ruler and the creation of a sound taste.[7]

[6]   Johann Christian Markwort (1778–1866) abandoned theology for a career as a tenor, becoming chorus-master in Darmstadt in 1810. He also published some theoretical and pedagogical works and wrote some essays for the *AMZ*.

[7]   By 1817 the chorus was said to be well schooled, if not all that large, and the Opera was praised for its organization in the interests of German opera (*AMZ* xix (1817), 736–40).

16. Review of Gänsbacher's *Six Variations on 'Ist denn Liebe ein Verderben?'*

Written: February or March 1811.
Published: AMZ xiii (1811), 280.   *Signed:* Carl Marie von Weber.
Reprinted: HHS (inaccurate); KSS.

*Johann Gänsbacher's piece was published as *Six variations à 4 mains pour le pianoforte sur l'air 'Ist denn Liebe ein Verderben'* as his Op. 9 by Kühnel of Leipzig (later also by Simrock and by Haas). It was dedicated to the Countess Maria Anna Firmian, to whose family Gänsbacher had acted as music teacher and with whom he was then living.

A very attractive trifle, which stands out not a little above the general run of variations that appear in such numbers. The composer combines a good melodic gift with a remarkable knowledge of harmony; and the writer, who is acquainted with a number of larger compositions from the same pen, finds it his pleasant duty to draw the attention of the public to these variations also. They are all well suited to the amiable character of the theme and are brilliant without being too difficult, which means that they should find a place particularly in the repertory of amateur players. The writer was particularly struck by the good part-writing in Variation 1, the sheer charm of Variation 3 and the original gait of Variation 6. The writer finds that the broken figure in bars 5–9 after Variation 8 disturbs the unity of the piece and is ineffective. On the other hand the introduction to the final theme is excellently managed.

17. A new discovery for perfecting the flute

Written: Munich, 30 April 1811.
Published: AMZ xiii (1811), 377–9.   *Signed:* Carl Marie von Weber.
Reprinted: MMW (inaccurate); KSS

Johann Nepomuk Capeller (the *AMZ*'s initial F. is an error) was one of many woodwind players in the early years of the nineteenth century who attempted to improve their instruments, in response to the twin stimuli of more sophisticated mechanical processes and the increased interest in virtuosity and instrumental effect that was to be one of the characteristics of Romanticism. Capeller's most famous pupil was Theobald Boehm, inventor of the modern fingering system, who later described the sliding mouth-hole discussed in this article in a list of the improvements he claimed to have made during the years 1812–17. Weber was naturally much interested in such matters, especially in Capeller's flute. The article appears to be largely Capeller's own work, as is suggested by the similarity of an article in the *Kritischer Anzeiger für Literatur und Kunst* of 11 May 1811, signed 'S—th' (conceivably Gottlob Schuberth; this is not one of Weber's pseudonyms, though he did write for the journal: see below, no. 18). Capeller's ideas were challenged in an answer by the notoriously contentious Leipzig flautist Carl Grenser (*AMZ* xiii (1811), 778), and Capeller returned the attack in the first issue of the *Münchener Gesellschaftblatt* (1812). A somewhat inaccurate translation (probably based on MMW) appears in R. Rockstro, *The Flute* (London, 1890), sections 521–2.

Herr F. Nepomuk Capeller, a member of the Munich Court Orchestra, has made an ingenious discovery thanks to which the mechanism of the flute leaves little further to be desired. The advantages of this invention lie in the increased range, without prejudice to the equal purity of all the notes and intervals, and the ease with which trills may be performed on every note, thus abolishing the chief drawbacks of the instrument. Herr Capeller took the basic conception of his new flute construction from the earlier invention of the so-called English *Metallkopfzug*,[1] whose weakness has already been pointed out by Tromlitz.[2] Herr Capeller's invention must not be confused with this earlier invention, which did indeed enlarge the range of the flute, but at the expense of its pure intonation.

The new flute consists of three sections. The two normal middle sections of the instrument are combined in a single piece; and to avoid

[1]   This was a sliding metal mouth-hole whose position could be varied easily and rapidly so as to smooth out discrepancies in tone between high and low registers.

[2]   Johann Georg Tromlitz (1726–1806) was a Leipzig flautist, composer, flute-maker and teacher, the author of some studies and tutors.

disproportionate length in comparison with the other parts, this middle section has been made shorter and the necessary length added to the mouthpiece. The length of the new flute is in fact the same as that of an instrument with the low C key. It has nine keys, and the B flat key can be opened from two sides: the lower lever can be used in two ways and with the greatest ease, employing the index or middle finger of the right hand without altering the position of the hand (making a trill on F sharp – G sharp easy and perfectly in tune) and constituting the difference between this key and an earlier invention. A newly invented D key, to be played by the index finger of the right hand, is designed to make the trill on D–C sharp more clearly defined and makes both the trill on B–C sharp and the trill on D–C *in altissimo* easier to perform. The lowest C key is so designed that the passage from C sharp to C is easily accomplished, an advantage not shared by the present C key. The other keys are arranged in the usual way and, with the new invention of Herr Capeller's, all notes and all trills, whether the interval concerned be a tone or a semitone, can be produced easily with perfect intonation.

The most interesting advantage possessed by a new flute is the tuning mechanism. In order to ensure consistent purity and clarity of tone, Herr Capeller has provided the instrument with a mouthpiece that retains its exact shape even after long years of use. It consists of an oval gold plate neatly attached to the rounded surface of the flute. Like the stopper of the flute, this mouthpiece can be easily and quickly moved to and fro to obtain the desired tuning, by means of a double screw. This has the great advantage of enabling the player to alter the tuning of his instrument with the minimum of notice and without affecting the intonation over the whole diatonic and chromatic range.

The great advantages of this new improved flute are so obvious that it is unnecessary to insist on them. It should only be added that the instrument was not manufactured by an instrument-maker but by a local turner, Fiegel, whose work does not suffer by comparison with that of the best foreign instrument-makers, even in the matter of finish and elegance of appearance. The price is no higher than that of an ordinary flute of good quality, that is to say about 9–10 carolins, a sum for which Herr Capeller will doubtless have the kindness to present every amateur with his new improved flute.

18. Review of Isouard's *Cendrillon*

Written: Munich, 16 May 1811.
Published: Kritischer Anzeiger für Literatur und Kunst, No. 20, 18 May 1811.
Reprinted: HHS, MMW (both inaccurate); KSS.   *Unsigned.*

The Maltese composer Nicolò Isouard (1775–1818) wrote his *Cendrillon* to a text by Charles Guillaume Étienne, after Perrault's well-known tale; it was produced at the Paris Opéra-Comique on 22 February 1810 (the same text was set by Steibelt in the same year, produced St Petersburg, 26 October). It was very successful in Paris and abroad, especially in Germany as *Aschenbrödel*: a German vocal score was published in 1812. Weber had made friends with the editor of the *Anzeiger*, Professor Spech, who invited him to write this article in the section 'Miscellen'.

The first performance here of the German version of *Cendrillon* (*Aschenbrödel*), a French opera in three acts with music by Niccolo Isouard de Malthe, took place on 7 May. The extraordinary success of this opera in Paris immediately aroused the interest of the German public, always on the look-out for foreign works, and our own theatre was among the number of those anxious to satisfy this interest.

The circumstances of the Paris production make it easy to understand the success of the work there. The whole opera was written for Mlle St Aubin[1] and calculated to display her personality. Every nuance was designed to show her in the most advantageous light, and the circumstances of her life were deliberately caricatured in order to emphasize the difference between her own existence and that of Cinderella, a character whose patience and modesty under oppression cannot be exaggerated and constitute her chief claim on our sympathies. In Paris the production was extremely elaborate and every local resource was exploited in order to increase the excitement of an audience well known for its susceptibility.

The composer in turn has not failed to make use of any and every means of arousing applause. The most notable example of this is the overture, designed as a duet between the well-known harpist Casimir[2]

[1]   Alexandrine Saint-Aubin (b. 1793) was the daughter of Jeanne Saint-Aubin and sister of Cécile Saint-Aubin; all three were successful singers. Alexandrine's brilliant début at the Théâtre Feydeau in 1809 led to Isouard's writing *Cendrillon* for her. However, she retired on her marriage in 1812.

[2]   Casimir Baecker (*c* 1790 to after 1836) played under the name Casimir (some sources give his real Christian name as Friedrich). He went to Paris as a protégé of Mme de Genlis, and had an ephemeral success, 1807–10. Various *AMZ* reports suggest that his style, flashy and somewhat uncertain, was not liked in Germany. He then retired into obscurity, emerging in 1829 with a celebrated *Méthode*.

and the horn player *Duvernoy – something absolutely unworthy of figuring as an operatic overture, consisting as it does of trivial cadenzas and petty details, all of which were no doubt still further ornamented and exaggerated by the players. Generally speaking, the composer has done absolutely nothing to raise the character of the work, and the routine nature of practically every piece in it is only further emphasized by the clumsy instrumentation.

At the climax of the second act, where each sister tries to outdo the other, Cinderella's Romance ought to outshine the talents displayed by her sisters, like a bright, friendly star; and the composer must employ here all the magic of melodic and instrumental invention that he possesses. As it is, however, the melody of the Romance is insignificant and seems to contain nothing to make an effect on an audience. Her sister's earlier Bolero is more substantial and effective, but unquestionably the most successful number is the duet between Cinderella and the King in Act 3. The passionate nature of the situation naturally gave the composer more scope and he has made good use of his opportunity by incorporating the Act 2 Romance mentioned above. This was the song that conquered the Prince's heart, and she here recalls it to his memory. After that the most characteristic number in the work is the duet between the two sisters. Both of them are revelling in their own arrogance and intoxicated by the good fortune that awaits them; and their interweaving scales and ornamental passages express not only self-congratulation but a spirit of rivalry, each challenging the other and vying for her rival's applause. The Romances of Cinderella and the King in Act 1 are quite simply French *romances*, nothing more; and the remaining numbers of the work are so thin and insignificant that it can never be the music of this opera that will bring it success.

Generally speaking, the presentation of the work was fairly successful. *Madame Regina Lang (Cinderella) neglected nothing calculated to suggest her own personal interest in the part. Her simple and sincere acting suggested very well the tender-heartedness and innocence of a young girl who is also clumsy and uneducated. *Madame Harlas as Clorinde and *Frau von Fischer as Thisbe cleverly underlined the fatuousness of a pompous pride of ancestry. Frau von Fischer was particularly successful, but in the Act 1 duet her acting would have been much more telling if, against her sister's singing-test, her dance (to which she hums the tune) had been more rhythmical and more accentuated. *Herr Muck was absolutely in his element as Montefiascone, but the same could not be said of *Herr Mittermayer's Dandini. His industriousness is certainly praiseworthy, but his performance in such roles as this has not yet got the necessary skill. *Herr Weixelbaum (Romiro) brought to the Act 3 duet with Cinderella an admirable expressiveness and agility. The ballet at the beginning of Act 2 was more like a carefully prepared court function than a fairy scene. A few light clouds in the scenery would have given the dances a much more ethereal character and confirmed the impression of gently fleeting dreams.

19. Review of Meyerbeer's *Gott und die Natur*

Written: Munich, 24 June 1811.
Published: AMZ xiii (1811), 570–2.   *Signed:* N.
Reprinted: HHS, MMW (both inaccurate); KSS; LKA.

  *Meyerbeer's oratorio (also known as *Gott und Natur*), to a text by *Aloys Schreiber, was first performed at the Berlin Singakademie on 8 May 1811. Weber was in Munich. He had had the opportunity of studying the score, and Meyerbeer gave him the full account of the performance which he incorporated here. The pseudonymous signature indicates that Weber felt that, in the circumstances, he could not lend his name to the review; it was written in the spirit of the Harmonischer Verein, as a critical exercise to further the cause of music in which they believed. He was proud of this essay, as he wrote to tell *Gottfried Weber: 'God, that was a work of art, the review of *Gott und Natur*! I regard it as one of my most fluent and felicitous articles' (letter of 14–15 September 1811). There is perhaps also to be read into this comment the feeling that a considerable degree of contrivance had been necessary to bring off such an article.

In recent times we have had many new works, some good and some not so good, but one stands out in every respect above the others – I mean the oratorio *Gott und Natur*, with a text by Schreiber, composed by Herr Meyerbeer. This had its first performance in *Kapellmeister [B.A.] Weber's Concert Spirituel on 8 May. Berlin and other papers carried notices of this work, but you may well like to hear something in more detail about a composition by this extremely promising artist, who combines so much learned culture with such an excellent mastery of musical technique. The form of the work is rich and varied without any prejudice to the principle of unity; and there can be no mistaking the full-blooded vitality, the delightful charm and before all else the genuine power of a genius with high ideals. The first chorus (C major) and the fugue which follows are kept prudently *mezzo tinto*, and I only noticed a few unhappy treatments of the text. Nos. 2 and 3 are a bass recitative and aria. The recitative is eloquent and natural; and the aria has such grace and charm that I felt inclined to wish that it had been assigned to some other voice, until Herr Gern's[1] singing convinced me that I was wrong. This aria contains the passage 'da winkt er dem Licht, es schwebt hernieder' – fortunately quite different in conception from Haydn's 'Let there be Light!', and consisting of an E major wind chord in a most unusual position. Nos. 4 and 5 (recitative and aria in B flat) were sung by Herr Eunicke[2] and proved a great success with the audience. It might be objected that two male-voice arias at the very beginning of a work constitute an error of judgement; but the Flower Chorus for women's voices only (No. 6 in G) restored the balance, and had the effect of a welcome ray of light. This was another favourite with the public, and even gave rise to a sonnet in the composer's honour, one of quite a number of poems that appeared in the Berlin paper. Unfortunately the harp accompaniment was almost inaudible. No. 7 was perhaps my favourite piece in the whole work, a soprano aria (C major) of quite unusual power which *Mlle Schmalz's performance succeeded in conveying.

The placing of this soprano aria immediately after the women's chorus is, I think, a real mistake on the composer's part, since both numbers lose by the juxtaposition. No. 8 is a Chorus of the Four Elements – Air (soprano), Fire (alto), Earth (tenor) and Water (bass). Each of the four has its own melody, with illustrative accompaniment, and finally these four melodies and their accompaniments – eight themes in fact – are heard in strict counterpoint together. This was most impressive, especially the *pianissimo* repetition in F of the whole mighty ensemble. Used in this way and handled skilfully and naturally, harmonic *tours de force* of this kind have their place and make their effect, but unfortunately these conditions are not often observed. No. 9 is a bass recitative and No. 10 a chorus – 'Er war, er ist, und er wird sein'. Here the composer's fine rhetorical development of a four-part, chorale-like chorus is interwoven with passages for the solo quartet. No. 11 is a duet between an Agnostic and an Atheist, with

---

[1] Georg Gern (1759–1830) was a successful bass who made his début in Mannheim in 1780 and worked at the Berlin Nationaltheater from 1801. Weber wrote for him the song 'Lebensansicht' (J134) in 1812. He was the first Hermit in *Der Freischütz* in 1821. His most famous roles were Mikéli and Sarastro.

[2] The tenor Friedrich Eunicke (1764–1844) made his début in 1786 and sang in various cities before settling in Berlin in 1797. He published some singing studies. His second wife Therese (born Schwachhofer; 1776–1844) was also a singer in Berlin. Of their daughters, Johanna (b. *c* 1800) was the first Aennchen in *Der Freischütz*; Weber wrote 'Einst träumte' as an extra number for her.

a male-voice chorus preaching trust and faith in God. The different
characters are most aptly drawn and the whole piece is a unified
conception. It was also a good idea to entrust this serious episode to
men's voices only (in G minor). Immediately following comes the C
major chorus 'Hörst du die Posaun' erklingen?', in which I was
delighted to find Herr Meyerbeer avoiding the platitudinous use of the
trombone. From this point onwards the work steadily gathers strength.
The text treats of the Last Judgement, when all the dead return to life.
After a moment of intensity in which the orchestra holds a chord, the
soprano soloist enters *pianissimo* accompanied only by a roll on the
timpani.

This leads to the final fugue, whose theme:

is first given out by the trombones, in augmentation.

This is combined with lively figuration for the violins and moves on
to an extraordinarily powerful conclusion. The use of the orchestra is
always skilful and often new and original. All the themes, even the
most graceful and charming, remain within the limits of the oratorio
style. May Herr Meyerbeer continue his musical career with the
steadfastness, the industry and the modesty which have won him such
a high reputation. Music can expect great things of him.

20. Review of Mayr's *Ginevra*

Written: Munich, 27 June 1811.
Published: Gesellschaftsblatt für gebildete Stände, No. 51, 29 June 1811.
                                                    Signed: Simon Knaster.
Reprinted: HHS, MMW (both inaccurate); KSS.

Johann Simon Mayr's *Ginevra di Scozia*, to a text by Gaetano Rossi after Ariosto's *Orlando furioso*, was produced in Trieste on 21 April 1801, for the inauguration of the Teatro Nuovo. It became popular in Italy, and was given in Vienna (with additions by *Weigl) in 1801, and in Germany from 1802. The first Munich production was in 1805, and it was occasionally revived there.

On 25 June the second performance of *Ginevra, opera seria* in two acts by Simon Mayr, gave all music-lovers a feast such as the present writer cannot remember enjoying in this theatre. Our magnificent *Brizzi seemed to excel himself on this occasion, and although physical circumstances often made his intonation uncertain, this was more than made up for by his excellent acting, the lightness and security of his ornamental passages, the power of his declamation and the perfect mastery of his dramatic presentation. *Madame Harlas, as Ginevra, came next in order of merit and her performance deserves the most honourable notice. Such roles as this seem made for her. In fact the real grandeur of her singing, the security and boldness of her bell-like voice and the altogether exceptional ardour of her performance made her a powerful rival of Herr Brizzi for the honours of the evening.

*Herr Mittermayer's Ariodante showed once again that his laudable industriousness has justified the highest expectations. He has a handsome, resonant voice and all the flexibility needed for its perfecting. *Clearer enunciation* and an increase in ardour and vitality would give his singing more character. The present writer has in mind, for instance, the beautifully sung duet with Polinesso in Act 1 and particularly the scene in Act 2, where the priest discloses Ginevra's imminent death to Ariodante, who flares up in the awareness of his own strength and cries *non morirà* in the conviction that his invincible arm can and will rescue her. The present writer begs Herr Mittermayer to regard these small criticisms as a mark of his admiration for a fine talent.

As far as the music is concerned, the play-bill might just as well have read 'by Weigl, Simon Mayr and Co.', since nearly all the best pieces were Weigl's, for instance Polinesso's aria, the charming Act 1 aria of Ariodante etc. Ginevra's Act 2 aria was also composed by another hand, and the evening opened with Catel's magnificent *Sémiramis* overture.

Totally opposed as the present writer is to the insertion of music by other composers,[1] in this particular opera he found it a blessing. Herr Simon Mayr's compositions show such a complete forgetfulness of his German origin and so exclusive an affection for the weak points of the Italian school that I am only too ready to allow him these insertions and only regret that such good music is performed under his signboard.

The choruses went well and the costumes were very handsome, but the audience was smaller than the writer had expected, and it must be disheartening indeed to have to sing to a half-empty house. The enthusiastic applause and approbation of a discerning audience such as this, however small, must have been all the more welcome to the performers. It may be assumed that it was the better sort of public that was there; and if wild horses are no longer able to drag the other sort to the theatre, what further resources does poor music possess?

[1]   Nevertheless, Weber himself wrote arias for insertion in operas by Méhul, *Cherubini and Spontini.

21. Review of Cherubini's *Les Deux journées*

Written: Munich, 2 July 1811.
Published: Gesellschaftsblatt für gebildete Stände, No. 52, 3 July 1811.
Signed: Dein Freund M—s.
Reprinted: HHS, MMW (both inaccurate); KSS; LKA.

Les Deux journées was first produced in Paris at the Théâtre Feydeau on 16 January 1800, when it had an immediate success; however, this was exceeded in Germany. Performances in French were given in Brunswick (in 1801) and elsewhere; and it was given in German, usually in Heinrich Schneider's translation as *Der Wasserträger*, in Frankfurt in 1801, and then in other German cities. In Vienna it was given as *Graf Armand* at the Theater an der Wien on 13 August 1802, and in *Treitschke's different translation as *Die Tage der Gefahr* at the Kärntnerthortheater on the following night, with *Cherubini himself conducting (and taking the overture's Allegro very slowly, according to the *AMZ*). The work was greatly admired by the Romantics, especially for Bouilly's Rousseau-inspired libretto, in which a Rescue Opera subject included the treatment of peasants as human figures of moral stature. Goethe and Beethoven both ranked its libretto among the best of the day, as the latter told Weber on their meeting. Weber himself was influenced in *Der Freischütz* by its successful handling of everyday life among all classes, and in *Euryanthe* by its use of linked, virtually continuous numbers; he was also, as the present article testifies, impressed by its articulate use of the orchestra.

He included it in his repertories in both Prague and Dresden. The semi-fictional tone adopted in this article is similar to that of No. 11 above, and permits Weber to refer to performances in France which he cannot have heard.

Fragment from a traveller's letter

Imagine my delight when on a passing visit to Munich I saw a playbill with the magic work *Armand*[1] at my table d'hôte. Even if my business affairs had been ten times as pressing as they were, the thought of this divine music played by the Munich Orchestra, and of the delight it would give me, would have decided me. 'No question of leaving today,' I said to the postillion, 'they are giving *Wasserträger!*' He looked at me in amazement and I finally found that he could only be convinced by my pressing a couple of vierundzwanzigers[2] into his hand.

I was the first person to arrive at the theatre and planted myself in the middle of the parterre, full of excitement and in eager expectation of the music which I knew would fill me with a noble enthusiasm. I have absolutely no doubt that *Armand* is a genuinely classical drama. All the effects are well calculated, each musical number is in the right place, so that it is impossible to add or to suppress anything. This opera will always remain green and always popular, thanks to the charming abundance of its melodic inspiration, the powerful declamation and the striking truth of the situations. I have seen it many times, in almost every German and French opera house, and was convinced that here in Munich I should see a really perfect performance.

My hopes were confirmed by the overture, for only the Munich Orchestra could have played it with such a combination of fire, precision and vigour, and I joined in the enthusiastic applause with which the audience responded. (Trumpet parts have been added to the overture and very effective they are, I think, in the Allegro. In the last powerful *crescendo* of the introductory Adagio, however, the single horn-notes are unquestionably more effective without the support of the trumpets, which thus make their first entry at the change of key to E major.) But to my astonishment the first trio had been converted into a duet.[3] In fact I hardly trusted my ears, but confirmed by means of my opera-glasses that the Water-carrier's father was not in fact

[1]   In Cherubini's opera Count Armand is the refugee President of the Parliament of Paris whom the water-carrier Mikéli helps to escape.
[2]   Twenty-four groschen made one reichsthaler.
[3]   This refers to the second part of the opening Romance.

opening his mouth. I must admit that the prospect of the Act 1 finale without a bass did not inspire me with confidence.[4] Was it possible, I asked myself, that the company could not produce a suitable singer for this part? The trio between Armand, his wife and Mikéli was heavily cut, though this was made up for by an excellent performance. There were outstandingly fine moments in the duet between Armand and Constance, but the opening was completely spoilt. You may remember that when the Water-carrier mentions a short separation of husband and wife, there should be an abrupt orchestral entry and Constance should express her feeling of despair at the prospect of her husband's absence in a cry of 'Ich sollte von dir mich trennen?' In the Act 1 finale, Mikéli's father appeared to be absent. Is he supposed to take no part in the scene, and where is the poor old man meanwhile? The spoiling of the composer's conception of the finale came as a most unpleasant surprise. As you may remember, the Water-carrier and Marcelline quarrel, he resents her opposition and she bursts into tears. After this *fortissimo* a single clarinet enters with a phrase [beginning] C C E flat D C. First the bassoon and then the cello enter as a brother starts to comfort his sister. This is a passage that it is extremely effective in every performance that I remember seeing. In Munich the clarinet is replaced by the oboe, producing an entirely different effect from that intended by the composer and, to make things even worse, an accompaniment has been added. In the same way some violin quavers have been added to the Ds sung unaccompanied first by Antonio and then by Mikéli. If no good clarinettist is available, the flute should play this passage, but to add an accompaniment is insufferable; and my knowledge of *Director Fränzl's well-attested perspicacity justifies the hope that he will see to the correcting of this misconception (for which he is in no way responsible) and thereby content not only myself but all admirers of Cherubini's music. The very difficult Act 2 choruses were admirably clean and lively in both singing and action. Altogether Act 2 was better shaped and more vivacious than Act 1. There were further regrettable cuts in Act 3, for instance, the farmer's daughter's [Angéline] 'Antonio n'arrive pas'. The omission of these few words makes an awkward transition from the musical point of view.[5] As the

---

[4]   With the exception of one short ensemble passage, Daniel (Mikéli's father) sings almost entirely in unison with Mikéli in this finale, though his voice provides some necessary bass reinforcement to an ensemble that is otherwise soprano, mezzo, tenor, tenor and baritone. Moreover, as Weber points out below, his presence is dramatically important.

[5]   What it actually does is remove a fascinating chromatic passage, somewhat in Weber's own harmonic manner; the transition effected by its removal is simply from dominant to tonic.

actress who played this part sings elsewhere, she could surely have sung this tiny passage. The best performance of the evening was *Herr Muck's as the Water-carrier. He was wholly successful in suggesting the honest, genial open-hearted character of a man whose awareness of doing a good deed gives him a quiet confidence in the face of every danger; and the loud applause of the audience showed appreciation of his performance.

I fear that I have written at great length about this opera, but I would ask you to bear in mind that it is impossible to say too much about such a masterpiece as this; and I hope that so enthusiastic a music-lover as I may count on your indulgence.

22. Review of Méhul's *Joseph*

Written: Munich, 3 July 1811.
Published: Gesellschaftsblatt für gebildete Stände, No. 54, 10 July 1811.
                                        Signed: Simon Knaster.
Reprinted: HHS, MMW (both inaccurate); KSS.

Méhul's *Joseph* was produced in Paris at the Opéra-Comique on 17 February 1807. It became very popular all over Europe. The first performance in German, in the translation by Matthias Lambrecht, was in Munich on 6 June 1809. It was the first work which Weber gave on his appointment to the Dresden Opera. See below, No. 89.

On 5 July[1] the pleasing sight of a packed house confirmed the writer in his conviction that the Munich public knows how to recognize and appreciate masterpieces. But there can hardly be anyone who is not attracted and irresistibly carried away by such music as that of Méhul's *Joseph*. This work is characterized by a sustained note of antique, I might almost say Biblical, simplicity. The ear is not titillated by any unnecessary ornament, and dramatic effect is achieved by sheer truth to nature, while a skilfully calculated use of the orchestra reveals the experienced composer who can achieve dramatic effectiveness by the simplest means. Whole alphabets would be needed to do justice to all the qualities of this magnificent work; and the writer must therefore content himself with an appeal to the feelings of the audience, which rewarded almost every number of the work with enthusiastic applause. This particular performance was in every way consistent and of sterling quality. No mistake and no unpleasant incident marred the effect of the work, and singers and players seemed to vie with each other in producing a perfect performance.

[1]   Weber presumably added this opening sentence later.

In the absence of *Herr Weixelbaum, the role of Joseph was sung by *Herr Mittermayer. Among all Herr Weixelbaum's roles, that of Joseph is most suited to his powers and personality and therefore one of his most successful; and in addition to this audiences seldom judge a performance objectively. Their usual way is to make comparisons and say 'one performer does one thing better, another another'. It must therefore be counted Herr Mittermayer's greatest triumph that his performance was universally admired. The writer was delighted to note an improvement in the clarity of his enunciation, which gave the delightful Romance 'Ich war Jüngling noch an Jahren' a charm that is absent from Herr Weixelbaum's interpretation. Both his singing and his acting were warm-hearted and mercifully free from all otiose ornamentation, something which however small is intolerable in this purely declamatory music.[2] Perhaps Herr Mittermayer would allow the writer to refer to one or two scenes in which his acting might have been rather warmer, for example, the first time that Joseph sees his brothers, the moment when he sees his father and particularly the narration of his father's dream which reveals his unchanged love for the son he has lost. At such moments Joseph must portray the deepest emotion. In Act 3 scene 2, where Joseph becomes aware of the danger threatening his brothers, we have the single instance in this part of a violent reaction. After finding what he has longed for over so many years, Joseph feels the prospect of losing it again unbearable and even his mild temper is raised to fever heat.

*Herr Tochtermann's performance as Simeon is so widely recognized for its excellence that it is unnecessary for me to say more, except that his truthfulness to nature is deeply moving and that the thoughtfulness of his performance reveals a first-class artist.

The role of Jacob was scrupulously sung and acted by Herr Lanius,[3] and the Act 3 duet with Benjamin was delightfully heartfelt. When in Act 2 Jacob awakes during the solemn Prayer Scene, Herr Lanius forgot to kneel down again and this disturbed the atmosphere of devotion. The writer also found on several occasions that Herr Lanius's movements were too swift and powerful for a man of Jacob's age.

*Madame Regina Lang made a charming and amiable Benjamin,

---

[2] The bass *Eduard Genast was to recall how in Dresden, when he inserted a small flourish into a passage in this role, Weber berated him soundly and sent him home 'to sleep off his Italian frenzy' (E. Genast: *Aus Weimars klassischer und nachklassischer Zeit: Aus dem Tagebuch eines alten Schauspielers* (4 vols., Leipzig, 1862–6; 5th edn, Stuttgart, 1905)).

[3] A bass who was praised as a singer and actor in a letter from the Intendant Joseph Babo (2 September 1810), then sang regularly in Munich 1811–18.

bringing out all the childlike attractions of the part; and we must be grateful to her for singing the role without cuts despite a heavy cold. The brothers' choruses were excellently sung, and grouping and action were most striking. The fine conclusion of Act 3 is the work of *Director Fränzl. It only remains to express our heartfelt thanks to the orchestra, whose admirable performance of this masterpiece added a new leaf to their laurels.

23. Review of Neuner's *Der Dichter Gessner*

Written: Munich, 23 July 1811.
Published: Gesellschaftsblatt für gebildete Stände, No. 58, 24 July 1811.
Signed: Simon Knaster.
Reprinted: HHS, MMW (both printing 'Steuner' for Neuner; other mistakes); KSS.

Carl Neuner (1778–1830) studied with Joseph Grätz, who had once refused Weber as a pupil probably on financial grounds, and with Johann Wallishauser (Valesi), who had accepted Weber after Grätz's refusal. He worked all his life in Munich, where he made a particular reputation as a ballet composer. In 1812–13 he wrote incidental music for F. X. von Caspar's play *Der Freyschütze*: it is possible that Weber saw the score, and was even slightly influenced by the opening of the overture when he came to write his own. *Der Dichter Gessner* was produced in 1809. Salomon Gessner (1730–88) was a Swiss author of Theocritan idylls in poetic prose, depicting a city-dweller's idealized view of country life.

On Sunday 21 July *Max Helfenstein*[1] and *Der Dichter Gessner*, a one-act ballet by Herr Crux[2] with music by Herr Neuner, were given. The present writer has heard several ballets with music by Herr Neuner, but he found none so enjoyable at this. Herr Neuner has been exceptionally happy in catching the delightful idyllic character and the amiable good nature expressed in this pleasing scenario by our Crux. He has preserved absolute consistency of style without becoming monotonous, and the wealth of his melodic invention is further set off by his skilful use of the orchestra.

The present writer cannot help expressing the wish that Herr Neuner would one day apply his admirable talent to something rather more ambitious, as he seems to lack none of the qualities demanded of a good opera composer. There are some really excellent and powerful moments in his ballet *Faust*,[3] and in the entr'acte between the short play and

[1]   *Max Helfenstein*, a *Lustpiel* (1811).
[2]   Anton Crux was court ballet master in Munich.
[3]   Neuner's *Doktor Faust* was produced in 1808.

the ballet the music has a vital buoyancy that seems to justify high hopes of his powers in any genre that he may attempt. The present writer is well aware of the fact that any composer accustomed to working in a single genre finds that all his ideas automatically shape themselves accordingly; but it would surely not be beyond his powers to transcend the limitations imposed on him by the form to which he has grown accustomed, and devote his talents to a more ambitious field with a wider appeal.

The performance of *Max Helfenstein* was that to which we have grown accustomed. *Herr Flerx was his usual comic and capricious self; but Max Helfenstein himself could have been played with a greater liveliness and a sharper edge. The little play itself, it must be admitted, is essentially an ephemeral piece.

24. Review of Dalayrac's *Léhéman*

Written: Munich, 25 July 1811.
Published: Gesellschaftsblatt für gebildete Stände, No. 59, 27 July 1811.
Reprinted: HHS, MMW (both inaccurate); KSS.   *Signed:* Simon Knaster.

Dalayrac's *Léhéman, ou La Tour de Neustadt*, to a text by Benoît Joseph Marsollier, was produced at the Opéra-Comique, Paris, on 12 December 1801. It became one of the most popular Rescue Operas of the day in Germany, first in G. L. P. Sievers's translation and then more widely in the translation by *Max Heigel as *Makdonald*. In this version, the setting is transferred to Scotland, with the Hungarian rebel Ragotzi turned into Bonnie Prince Charlie (or Karl Eduard) and Neustadt into 'Tudor Castle'; Léhéman becomes Makdonald, and his daughter Amélina becomes Adeline (score and other material in D-Mbs). First given in Munich in 1803, it remained very popular in the city (as the *AMZ* reported in 1812 and again in 1819). Dalayrac's operas in general had a good following in Germany. Weber included *Adolphe et Clara* and *Les Deux petits Savoyards* in his Prague repertory, the former also in his Dresden repertory.

On Thursday 25 July Dalayrac's *Makdonald* was given in our theatre. This and *Das Schloss Monténéro*[1] must unquestionably be considered the composer's most accomplished works. The chief characteristics of Dalayrac's music, as shown in his other operas, are naïvety and high spirits, but in these two works there is a new and unfamiliar power of utterance that makes him all but unrecognizable as the composer

---

[1]   *Léon, ou Le Château de Monténéro* was produced at the Opéra-Comique, Paris, in 1798; also successful in Germany, in French and in various German translations, it was produced in Munich, in 1803.

of *Nina*.[2] It is typical, too, that these two operas are not in France considered among his best, and it is chiefly we Germans who appreciate them at their true worth. This has been the case wherever they have been given and in particular with *Makdonald*, produced elsewhere as *Lehmann, oder Der Turm bei Neustadt* and *Der Turm von Gothenburg*.

The overture transports us at once into the atmosphere of the drama by its delightful alternation of charm, excitement and sudden exhibitions of forcefulness. The present writer's only criticism relates to the frequent changes of tempo, which disturb the sense of continuity. The Romance 'Ein Pilger irrt' ['Un voyageur s'est égaré'] holds the attention by its close connexion with the drama, at whose most exciting and critical moments the amiable melody of the Romance appears, like a comforting star, to reassure the anxious listener of his loved ones' rescue. Such passages form the delicate threads in the fabric of an opera, which, spun, as here, by a composer with a genuine dramatic gift, must irresistibly enmesh the hearts of the listeners.[3]

Apart from this, all the choruses in this opera are truly classical. The Drinking Chorus in Act 2, especially, has a popular, martial robustness and its mood of carefree merry-making contrasts splendidly with Makdonald's agitated whispering to his daughter. To achieve this contrast, the chorus must be as powerful as possible; and it is essential that the moment when even the warning to be quiet is disregarded and cheerfulness breaks out again, carrying all before it, is given the greatest dramatic importance. Indeed, this may well be one of the few instances where performers should shout rather than sing. As far as the production is concerned, the present writer cannot deny that he found the whole performance marked by a certain lethargy. The choruses etc. never really achieved complete unanimity or swept the listener off his feet.

*Herr Muck sang Makdonald's music very well as regards isolated numbers, but the present writer feels justified in observing that the character as a whole should have been presented as more noble. Apart from a few passages, Herr Muck's Makdonald was not unlike *Cherubini's Water-carrier,[4] though in fact not even disguise should have concealed his superior character – which, after all, is repeatedly

---

[2] *Nina, ou La Folle par amour* was produced at the Comédie-Italienne, Paris, in 1798; also successful in Germany, in various translations, it was produced in Munich, in 1787.

[3] For a discussion of the remarkable use of Reminiscence Motif in Dalayrac's operas, especially *Léhéman*, see D. Charlton, 'Motif and Recollection in Four Operas of Dalayrac', *Soundings* VII (1978), 38–61.

[4] *Les Deux journées*. See above, No. 21.

emphasized in the dialogue. *Frl. von Fischer as Adeline showed her usual scrupulousness, and the present writer regards this as one of her best roles. Her characterization of the part was absolutely consistent throughout and her singing was marked by a fine ardour and expressiveness. We have become accustomed to hearing our orchestra described somewhat bluntly as 'good'. The duet-quartet (as it might be called) in Act 2, where Eduard and Adeline meet again, might have been taken rather faster and the opening chorus of Act 3 rather slower in order to make the text more easily intelligible. There was a great deal of fire visible on the stage in the final scene, and both the present writer and the rest of the audience took their cue from this and gave the performers a warm reception.

25. Review of B. A. Weber's *Deodata*

Written: Munich, 6 August 1811.
Published: Gesellschaftsblatt für gebildete Stände, No. 62, 7 August 1811.
                                                       Signed: Simon Knaster.
Reprinted: HHS, MMW (both inaccurate); KSS.
    *Bernhard Anselm Weber's *heroisches Schauspiel* to a text from *Kotzebue's *Ritterdrama, Deodata*, was produced in Berlin in 1810. It was one of his most successful works. Carl Maria von Weber (to whom he was no relation) had had some difficulties with him over the production of *Silvana* in Berlin, and was no great admirer of his rather classically orientated music. To *Gottfried Weber he wrote, 'Tell me candidly what you think of W.; I can frankly say that I can find no particular taste in his works – see my review of *Deodata* in the *Gesellschaftsblatt*' (letter of 9 October 1811).

On Sunday 4 August we had the first performance in the theatre here of *Deodata*, a four-act play by Kotzebue with music by B. A. Weber, Royal Prussian Kapellmeister.

    This is a worthy companion-piece to Kotzebue's earlier opera *Des Teufels Lustschloss* and has an even more richly varied plot, if that is possible.[1] *Deodata* provides something for every kind of theatre-lover. There are dangers innumerable, attempted rescues, madness, nobility of mind, bears' caves, prisons, battles, poisons and daggers – and at the end the author finds himself impelled by a sheer sense of reality to

---

[1] First set by Dieter (1802) and Reichardt (*Das Zauberschloss*, 1802), then by Schubert as his first completed opera (1813–14, unproduced). The plot is comparable to that of *Deodata* in that a fantastic, not to say ludicrous, series of events proves to be the fiction of an elderly relation who is putting a pair of lovers on trial. Weber was to satirize this kind of *Ritterdrama* in his mock German opera in *Tonkünstlers Leben* (below, No. 125).

dissolve the whole affair in smoke and flames, and so to give a prophetic vision of his future fate.

But that is more than enough about the text, and we must pass on to the more rewarding subject of the music and the production. The score reveals throughout an experienced and well-tried master of the art, who combines correct prosody with expressiveness and is versed in the subject of orchestration as well as knowledgeable about the theatre. His characters have admirable consistency, and as an example of this the present writer would like to quote all that the Fool sings, and in particular his first little song, 'Wer da will blasen, was ihn nicht brennt, der ohne Not in sein Unglück rennt', where the piccolo accompaniment is original in conception and well written. The present writer particularly admired the little duet between the two girls disguised as gypsies, 'Aus dem fernen Morgenlande'; this is most original in treatment. Of the larger numbers, the present writer would like to single out the Blind Man's Song, which combines with the March, and the Prison Scene in Act 3, where the contrast between Deodata's impassioned prayer and the tranquil, uninterrupted music of the chorus in the chapel is strikingly effective.

The present writer did not find the overture to his taste – old-fashioned in its forms and too plainly indebted (especially in instrumentation) to the masters of the past, notably Gluck. Though excellent in craftsmanship, the music failed to make a general impression despite its high qualities, because it lacks the free play of imagination. Generally speaking there are too many musical numbers, some of which hold up the action to an unbelievable extent, for instance, the scene in Act 3 where Rüdiger falls asleep, and the song which Deodata sings in the prison to her Theobald.

As far as production goes, it must be admitted that no expense was spared to make the work as effective as possible. *Frl. von Fischer was most successful in the title role, particularly in individual scenes such as that in which Rüdiger falls asleep and she gets possession of his keys. The only scene between Rüdiger, Theobald and her, in which she appears to deny her love for Theobald, seemed to the present writer overplayed. About Rüdiger's character there is nothing to say, either good or bad, and nothing therefore remains but to record *Herr Tochtermann's usual scrupulous performance in the part. By the same token Herr Kürzinger made a thoroughly noble Theobald. The Fool is the best character in the piece, and *Herr Mittermayer was excellent – capricious, warm-hearted and never coarse (a common error in playing such parts). The remaining characters play their parts, come and go, and there is really nothing more to say about them except that they were there. The public owes a special debt of gratitude to Herren Crux[2] and Quaglio,[3] the former for an outstanding production (particularly of the fighting scenes) and the latter for his magnificent sets. It was a real feat to make the scenic transformation from the elaborate Prison Scene to the chapel without lowering the curtain. Long life to these two pillars of our theatre, and may they train many pupils worthy to tread in their footsteps.

[2]   Anton Crux was the court ballet master in Munich. See also above, No. 23.
[3]   Domenico Quaglio (1787–1837), son of Giuseppe and brother of Angelo, Lorenzo and Simon, was one of a large number of the famous family of designers who served the Bavarian court. His elegant architectural designs and picturesque scenes, conventionally Romantic but beautifully executed, were very popular. He died at Hohenschwangau while building a mock ruin in the castle grounds for Maximilian I.

26. The Swiss Music Festival, Schaffhausen

Written: Solothurn, 11 September 1811.
Published: Gesellschaftsblatt für gebildete Stände, No. 75, 21 September 1811.
                                Signed: Carl Maria von Weber.
Reprinted: Schweizerische Musikzeitung, No. 10, 7 March 1908; KSS; LKA.
    Weber left Munich at the beginning of August 1811 in order to visit *Nägeli and study *Pestalozzi's educational theories. He was arrested trying to cross part of Württemberg, from which he had been banished eighteen months previously. Released, he went on to stay with his Munich friend Baron Hoggner at Schloss Wolfsberg, above Ermatingen, before going on to Schaffhausen. The Schweizerische Musikgesellschaft was founded in 1808, and its festivals were held until 1867. The original idea came from Samuel Auberleben (see below, n. 2), and the first festival was held in Lucerne on 27 June 1808. Eighty-eight performers took part. The second festival took place in 1809 in Zürich. The Schaffhausen Festival was the third.

After spending several most enjoyable days with Baron Hoggner on the Wolfsberg and enjoying the uniquely beautiful view of Lake Constance and its charming surroundings, which I regarded as a foretaste of the pleasures awaiting me in Switzerland, I arrived in Schaffhausen on 19 August. The number of visitors was so great that although I had taken the precaution of booking a room, I could still only be accommodated in a *dépendance* of the Gasthof zur Krone.[1]

    The reason for this extraordinary activity, however, is in fact so

[1]   Murray's *Hand-Book for Travellers in Switzerland* (London, 1838) gives the inn as 'not recommended'.

unusual that friends may well be attracted from all quarters. The big Swiss Music Society had this year chosen Schaffhausen as its place of meeting, and its combined forces were to perform a number of masterpieces. I must confess that the whole idea stirred my profoundest interest – I mean the unique and daring idea of collecting music-lovers from all parts of the country on a definite date in a place chosen yearly for the purpose, and performing great music which would provide delight and instruction and proof, too, of progress achieved during the last year. Such a plan could only originate among people deeply devoted to the arts, with a real zeal for their furtherance and a unity of purpose sufficient to overcome every obstacle for the sake of the common good. Everyone who attends the festival must travel at his own expense, but in the town itself he will find an accommodation bureau where he will discover in which private house he is to stay, and every visitor receives a warm welcome from his host. I was very curious about the standard of performance; and I must say that the prospect did not seem encouraging when I took into consideration the circumstances – people unknown to each other, a director acquainted with the talents of a mere handful (and therefore obliged to leave to chance the question of whether the most gifted occupied the most important positions etc.) and to crown it all, in order to keep expenses down for members, only one rehearsal!

My surprise was all the more pleasant, and I must confess that I could never have believed it possible to produce such an ensemble in the circumstances. High praise goes to *Herr Tollmann, the present director of music at Basel, for his industry and enthusiasm in steering the whole undertaking. Then mention must be made of Madame Egli, an admirable amateur singer from Winterthur (who has recently profited from studying singing in Munich with *Mme Harlas) and Madame Egloff from Schaffhausen. The choirs contained excellent singers, who had scrupulously prepared their music with Musikdirektor Auberleben[2] in Schaffhausen. There must have been more than a hundred in the chorus and about 150 in the orchestra. A number of performers had been prevented from coming by the distances involved. The main concert took place on 22 August, when the programme

---

[2]   Samuel Gottlob Auberleben (1758–1829) was a Stuttgart composer of songs and choral works who held various posts in South Germany and Switzerland. These included Schaffhausen, where he settled in 1807 as director of music. His autobiography, *Samuel Gottlob Auberlebens Leben, Meinungen und Schicksale* (Ulm, 1824) gives a detailed, and harrowing, account of the hardships and struggles of his life.

consisted of Beethoven's First Symphony and Himmel's *Pater Noster* in the first part and in the second 'Spring' and 'Summer' from Haydn's *Seasons* and the magnificent Gloria from *Abbé Vogler's Mass in C minor. On the following day there was another concert, in which a number of amateurs performed arias etc., an excellent way of encouraging budding talent. There were certainly more than 1500 in the audience of the first concert, but fewer at the second, as a number of visitors had by then left. The church in which the concerts took place (the Kreuzkirche, if I remember aright[3]) is not very good acoustically. At the first concert the troublesome echo was reduced by the numbers of the audience, but this made the second day seem all the worse, the truth being that chamber concerts are not suited to a building in which only large mass effects are possible. I had the honour of being elected by the Music Society as an honorary member, immediately after their first sitting; and this allowed me the interesting experience of attending their meetings. H. G. Nägeli – known to the musical world as a publisher, writer and composer – was unanimously re-elected president for the coming year, when the meeting is to be held in Zürich. I only regret that lack of space prevents me from giving a more detailed account of the society's constitution. What is certain is that such a society must have the most beneficial effects on the development of a feeling for all the arts in general.

You can well imagine that entertainment was not lacking. The town of Schaffhausen did everything to give its visitors an enjoyable time. Particularly delightful were the entertainments at the private club on the Fäsen Staub,[4] where there were balls and firework displays, and everyone must have been struck by the friendly, jovial atmosphere at the Music Society's gatherings. National songs by the former president, Häfliger[5] (actually the founder of the society), and by Hebel,[6] were sung in Swiss dialect; and members said good-bye to each other in the hope of meeting again next year. I left Schaffhausen on the 24th, gave concerts in Winterthur and Zürich to the public's satisfaction, climbed the Rigi and enjoyed the view of thirteen lakes, and am now writing from Solothurn, before continuing my journey either to the Bernese Oberland or to Geneva.

[3]   There is no Kreuzkirche; Weber probably meant the Allerheiligenkirche.
[4]   A promenade in Schaffhausen.
[5]   Jost Bernhard Häfliger (1759–1837) was a pastor and author of folksongs, the most popular of which was 'Was brucht me -n- i der Schwyz' (1796).
[6]   Johann Peter Hebel (1760–1826) was born in Basel and wrote many poems in the dialect he described as *alemannisch*. His collection of *Alemannischen Gedichten* (1803) was highly praised by Goethe.

27. Plan for a *Musical Topography of Germany*

Written: Zürich, 4 September 1811; Jegisdorf, 24 September 1811.
Printed: HHS; MMW; KSS.

Compelled as many eighteenth- and early-nineteenth-century musicians were to earn a living as travelling virtuosos, they had considerable need for some kind of system in the organization of their concert arrangements. In days of poor communications, it was often left to the artist to set about making arrangements for a concert, one upon which his livelihood depended, only on his arrival in a town. On 15 September 1811 Weber wrote to *Gottfried Weber, 'On 2 September I had a marvellous idea which I've immediately put into effect. I intend by means of a little guidebook to help travelling artists to overcome the usual endless trouble with arrangements for a concert when one doesn't know whom to turn to, who can help, what music's popular etc. This will provide a ready account of the contemporary situation of music in Germany. The project is already devised, and will result from circulars in which I'll ask for reports from the brothers' (of the Harmonischer Verein: see above, No. 13). On 22 September 1811 he further wrote to *Gänsbacher, 'The book will cover Germany in the widest sense, and I'll contribute a survey of the artistic situation in every district and every town. I enclose a plan set out as a questionnaire and request you to answer it thoroughly about Prague; and if you know anyone in Vienna who'd take it on, I'd be very grateful...Please be sure to write to me if you come across anything to add to the plan. You needn't hurry with the job; if I have it in 2–3 months, that'll do. I hope it'll be an interesting little work.' He later wrote again to Gänsbacher for information on Vienna (letter of 28 January 1812), acknowledging the information on 16 May. Several other contributions came in, but the book was never finished. Weber tried to complete it, with *Rochlitz's encouragement, in Leipzig in 1812, but the invitation to Gotha by Duke August intervened. The accounts of Mannheim (above, No. 14) and Basel (below, No. 28) would have been included.

An attempted contribution to the history of art and also a companion-book for travelling musicians

Plan according to countries and towns – alphabetical order – list of towns at the end – public transport maps – condition of the arts in each country – frontier points; Lübeck, Stettin, Berlin, Breslau, Prague, Brünn, Vienna, Salzburg, Innsbruck, Geneva, Karlsruhe, Mainz, Kassel, Hanover, Hamburg.

First series: Germany; second: Denmark, Sweden, Russia; third: Italy and France.

Instead of a preface, a dialogue in which the plan and the object of the book is unfolded.

A. Arrangements for concerts. Permit. Hall, church or otherwise. Publicity. Subscription or not. Newspaper advertisements. Tickets.

B. The concert itself. Relations with authorities and singers. Instrumentalists. Orchestra, from what sources drawn and consisting of what. Who is the favourite, what sort of music, what instruments least familiar, most popular. Time of starting, length, how many numbers in the programme and their order etc.

C. Finances. Best time of year. Best day of week. List of days when the theatre or some club is available. Basic expenses. Usual takings, good, mediocre. Free tickets. Note on the currency best used in each place. Concert hall officials. Charges. Time needed to arrange a concert.

D. General remarks. Condition of music in general and importance of amateur interest. Families particularly interested in music. Other important families. Singing schools. Amateur music-making. If possible, a list of the artists who have given concerts there during the last few years. Instrument-makers. Organs. Music shops. Opera house. Short historical account of what has been done for music during the last few years and the present situation. List of newspapers or journals and their specific interest in music or theatre. Any outstanding artists or writers domiciled in the town. Music libraries.

28. Note on Basel, for *Musical Topography*

Written: Schloss Wolfsberg, Lake Constance, 17 October 1811.
Printed: MMW.
Reprinted: KSS.

See above, No. 27, for a note on Weber's plan for a *Musical Topography*. This was the only special contribution he completed himself. Schloss Wolfsberg, above Ermatingen overlooking Lake Constance, was the castle of his Swiss friend Baron Hoggner.

A 1. Permission to give a concert must be obtained from the mayor. It is not likely to be refused.

2. The hall is the public concert hall and this is put free of charge at the disposition of any artist concerned, by the Committee of Direction (see below).

3. If time allows the *Avisblatt* provides publicity. No newspaper is

published in Basel, so that in default of the *Avisblatt* the artist must have a notice printed giving the programme of works to be performed.

4. The basic expenses are not great; arrangements for the musical material must be made with Herr Kachel. As for the orchestra, amateurs have of course to be invited, while the professional members needed will often appear, or at least the majority of them, for no fee. In such a matter all depends of course on the concert-giver's connexions, but during the last years three methods of approach seem to have established themselves:

   a. If the giver of the concert really needs the money and is concerned with every thaler, by sending the subscription from house to house he may obtain, though rather like a beggar, a larger sale of tickets.

   b. An artist whose circumstances do not allow him an unlimited stay in an hotel may choose the subscription method in order to obtain an idea of what interest he may hope to arouse – with the result, in some cases, that he leaves the town without giving a concert at all.

   c. The third method of approach is only for artists who are already established and popular. Their arrival will have been announced in advance, and music-lovers will already have started a subscription list, which merely becomes a kind of public recommendation. It is clear, however, that such a method is only possible in the case of artists who are old friends.

B 1. The concerts, or rather the orchestra, have for six years been entirely under the direction of *Herr Tollmann, whose enthusiasm and disinterested amiability must be appreciated by every artist. At the present moment there are players for all sections, some professional members of the orchestra and some amateurs. There is no oboist. Violins, cellos, horn and flutes seemed satisfactory, at least to us. Mme Hofmann has been the principal singer for the last six years.

   2. There does not seem to be a decided preference for any instrument. Outstanding violinists are of course popular, but so too are players of less well known instruments – violoncello, flute and horn – such as we have recently heard, and very fine artists too. Good singers, whether men or women, are not often found in Germany, but they would certainly be well received. It is a long

time since we heard any outstanding pianist. The hall is not well suited to this instrument and, it should be added, Basel has no really good pianoforte suitable for concert-giving.

3. Concerts generally begin at six, or in winter at half past five.

4. Arrangements with the orchestra can most conveniently be left to Herr Tollmann; Herr Kachel sees to the orchestral parts etc. as part of his official duties.

5. Six items, including a symphony, are enough for a programme. There have been as many as eight quite often and it really depends on each individual artist.

c. 1. The best time of the year is unquestionably the winter, and particularly the second half of October, since at that time –

2. Sunday can still be considered the best day, whereas later in the season it is on Sundays that the ordinary concerts are given. Wednesday is one of the better days, failing Sunday.

3. There is no regular theatre, and if there is no visiting company, the other days of the week are free also. Visiting companies generally give performances on Monday, Tuesday and Friday. There is generally a ball on Thursday, and Saturday is reserved for orchestral rehearsal. Private parties often disturb this normal routine.

4 and 5. Takings are very variable. The top figure would be, I should say, between 200 and 250 gulden, the lowest from 30 to 40; so 100 gulden might be taken as the average. It is worth remembering that an old custom prevents the price of any ticket being more than 1 gulden.

6. The staffing of the concert hall is, as has already been said, in the hands of Herr Kachel, whose charges are very moderate. Herr Stockeisen is the normal cashier and two people are needed to take the tickets.

7. During the winter a concert could be put on in two or three days, particularly if the artist is already well known and has prepared the ground by writing previously. But an artist would have to count on staying a week if he wanted to make personal connexions in the town, obtain maximum publicity for his intended concert and circulate previous notices as a form of recommendation.

d 1. On the state of music in general, the present writer would not like to make any professional judgement, the more so because he has strong feelings of different kinds on the subject; but he is very ready to discuss the matter with anyone who is interested.

Amateurs are indeed genuine lovers of music, but still only amateurs; and it is for that reason that standards are not higher, because in general an understanding and love of music is lacking.

2. For almost a hundred years a public concert has been given every Sunday in winter, and this may really be regarded as a fixture. These concerts are entirely financed by an annual subscription list; and since the sum achieved is often not known until shortly before the concert, it is impossible to make some of the arrangements necessary and to offer good musicians firm engagements. The Concert Committee which controls the whole undertaking consists of twelve music-lovers. The committee is responsible for the financing of the concert, appoints the professional members of the orchestra, corresponds with players who have to be brought in from outside, and is the sole authority capable of making decisions. The orchestra's director of music – at present Herr Tollmann – is paid by the committee and has absolute control of the orchestra, although the hall, instruments, music, furniture etc. are the property of the committee, not the director, since this institution is not a private speculation. Any balance in the accounts is carried forward to the next year and either used for improvements or held over against any possible future deficit, such as has at times occurred. The subscription is for sixteen concerts and amounts to 5 French large thalers; women and occasional guests brought by subscribers to the concerts are admitted free. The subscription is open to everyone without exception.

Recently the committee has found itself in the unhappy position of being obliged, in order to keep up the number of subscriptions, to add a number of balls – eight, in fact, for the higher subscription of 7 thalers, instead of 5. These balls are not given on concert days but quite separately. Though no one can go to the balls who has no concert subscription, the opposite is not true; and it is a melancholy reflection that in order to appeal to men's hearts it is necessary to take their feet into account. The gross annual expenditure must be between 3000 and 4000 gulden.

3. Instrument-makers. Kramer, Immler, W. Kachel.

29. Review of Winter's *Das unterbrochene Opferfest*

Written: Munich, before 6 November 1811.
Published: Gesellschaftsblatt für gebildete Stände, No. 88, 6 November 1811.
Signed: Simon Knaster.
Reprinted: KSS.

Peter von Winter's *heroisch-komische Oper*, *Das unterbrochene Opferfest*, to a text by Franz Xaver Huber, was produced at the Hoftheater, Vienna, on 14 June 1796. It became the most popular German opera between *The Magic Flute* and *Der Freischütz*, and even entered the repertory of Italian Court Opera in Germany (Dresden, 1798–9, as *Il sacrifizio interrotto*). Its most popular number, the quartet 'Kind, willst du ruhig schlafen', was made the subject of variations by a number of composers, including Beethoven (for piano, WoO 75).

Munich, 31 October. *Das unterbrochene Opferfest*, opera in two acts with text by Huber and music by Kapellmeister Winter. It would be quite superfluous for me to try to say something new about the excellence of this music, which is recognized all over Germany, and no proof is more convincing than the fact that the work continues to be given and to reveal new delights to the listener at each hearing. This is one of the few German operas that contains something to show off every type of voice; and today we had a new Murney (Herr Mohrhardt from Frankfurt) and in Mme Willmann[1] a new Elvira.

Herr Mohrhardt confirmed the impression he had already made as Joseph and Palmer,[2] that the theatre can be sure of having found in him a good singing actor. Anyone who saw Herr Mohrhardt a year ago in Frankfurt must have been impressed by the progress that he has made, for his acting then seemed anything but vivacious. In the meantime his singing does not seem to have improved: and even if a listener can accustom his ear to Herr Mohrhardt's not very attractive throaty tone, the lack of variety in his style still leaves much to be desired. The present writer believes in fact that this quality of voice is not natural to the singer but results from faulty vocal training at an early age and could be cured by diligence and application – which would mean that we could congratulate ourselves on a tenor who both

---

[1] Mme Willmann (born Tribolet) was the second wife of the cellist Max Willmann (1768–1813), whom she married in 1792. She sang in Vienna and, from 1805, in Kassel.

[2] Joseph in Méhul's opera (Paris, 1807); Palmer in Carl Cannabich's *Palmer und Amalia* (Munich, 1803).

sang and acted well. However, it is not going to be easy to find anyone who will point out his failings to Herr Mohrhardt with sufficient frankness; and (without any prejudice to his capacity for hard work) the present writer does not in any case credit him with the necessary ability to overcome his own natural failings, particularly when the Munich public repeatedly make it clear that he can already count himself among the best of the small tribe of tenors. All these things taken into consideration, the present writer must reckon this among pious hopes not likely to be fulfilled.

It was a particular pleasure to find the opera treated as an absolutely serious work (and the role of Pedrillo entirely omitted), for although one loses some delightful music, the work profits greatly in unity of style and design. The power and precision of the orchestral playing were, as usual, spellbinding, but the choruses were not so happy. In the Act 1 finale, particularly, they were disadvantageously placed – all on one side of the stage, with the dancers in front of them. The other side of the stage was empty, and as the soloists' ensemble became increasingly animated the chorus found themselves pushed to the back of the stage from where it was difficult to hear their voices.

The great delight of the evening was *Mme Regina Lang's Myrrha. The present writer has heard innumerable singers, and among them many fine artists, in this role, but he has never felt so moved as he was by Mme Lang's singing and acting. Indeed it was not Mme Lang, but Myrrha herself! The Mad Scene, which often fails to come off and is given too exaggerated a character, especially delighted the present writer, and no applause was ever better deserved than that which greeted Mme Lang's performance.

*Director Fränzl earns our warmest thanks for abolishing what might appear to be a trifling annoyance – I mean the prompter's double knock at the beginning of each musical number. This, like other small nuisances, could often mar – even if it did not completely destroy – the effect of the music. An improvement of this kind obviously cannot meet with actual applause: it is its own reward. The public is impressed without knowing the reason, and the few who do know why the music is so much more effective make a silent acknowledgement of their gratitude on behalf of the audience.[3]

[3]   Weber naturally took greater exception to this practice than to the long-enduring triple knock to signal the start of the whole performance, since it undermined any sense of musico-dramatic continuity even in number opera.

30. Review of Gottfried Weber's E minor Mass

Written: End of 1811 or early 1812.
Published: Gesellschaftsblatt für gebildete Stände, No. 16, 19 February 1812.

Signed: Ph—s.

Reprinted: KSS.

*Gottfried Weber's Mass No. 3 in E minor (Op. 33) for soloists, chorus and orchestra was probably written a year or so before the performance here reviewed. On 27 June 1811 Carl Maria von Weber wrote to *Gänsbacher, 'For some time I've been agitating over a Mass of Weber's, and I hope it will come off.' To Gottfried Weber he wrote on 29 November urging him to follow up an approach he himself had already made to Winter about a performance with some flattery to oil the wheels: Winter was an odd and touchy character. The pseudonym Ph—s is not one that Weber otherwise used, and might suggest Philodikaios, that belonging to *Meyerbeer in the Harmonischer Verein. Weber's usual pseudonym in the *Gesellschaftsblatt* was Simon Knaster (see above, Nos. 20, 22–5, 29). But he did, in exceptional circumstances for the paper, use another pseudonym, M—s (see above, No. 21); and it was known for members to share pseudonyms, e.g. Gottfried Weber and Meyerbeer both signed themselves Julius Billig. Moreover, an article in the *Gesellschaftsblatt* (No. 19, 4 March 1812) on the singer *Marianne Schönberger, suspiciously similar to No. 44 below, is signed Philokalos. The supposition must be that Weber is the author of them both, and so could have signed himself Ph—s. It was part of the spirit of the Harmonischer Verein that its members should regard themselves as a unit, with more or less interchangeable identities. Georg Kaiser, summarizing some of the above evidence in KSS, is convinced of Weber's authorship; and though there are no other instances of such a devout tone in Weber's writing about his undoubted religious beliefs, there are certainly stylistic resemblances to his other writings which make the attribution possible. It is perhaps more likely that some passages stemmed from Gottfried Weber himself, for instance the defence of the intentions of the Agnus Dei, which is not very characteristic of Carl Maria; the whole may then have been put together with critical comments by Carl Maria.

The composer of this Mass has been known for several years to the present writer, from musical papers and other journals, as an acute and thoroughly polished critic; and it was for this reason all the greater pleasure to hear a composition of his in the court chapel here. Gottfried Weber's theoretical works and, more recently, his reviews in the *Heidelberger Jahrbuch der Literatur* have shown a wide range of knowledge, which raised our expectations of his music to an unusual degree.

The present writer can testify that this work does indeed show a profound study of harmony and, more especially, a fine liberality in aesthetic matters; and it is from this last, and from no other root, that the flower of every art springs, just as the absence of this fine liberality explains the fact that the music of many accomplished composers lacks the breath of life and only flatters the ears without appealing to the heart.

At the very opening the devout listener is struck by the profound sense of other-worldliness in the Kyrie and prepared by the solemn gait of the chorus and the steadily growing movement of the violins for the great idea of God's presence, an idea which returns again (only in the major key) by a skilful design in the Sanctus. Unfortunately the Gloria is not sung at this season of the Church's year, and the present writer regrets not having heard it, chiefly for the loss of the contrast which it would have furnished. The Credo is admirably designed, with the rich harmonies and fresh radiance of the *Et incarnatus est* standing out against the plain recitation of the articles of faith and forming the highlight of the whole work. On the other hand the present writer would have preferred the *Osanna* fugue to be fully worked out instead of merely sketched in, however promisingly. The composer's handling of the Agnus Dei is novel and will therefore doubtless give offence to many. First the soprano and alto, and then the tenor and bass, conduct a most charming duet in 6/8 time, all four voices eventually combining and interweaving with each other in the most affecting harmony. The intermezzo, designed as a foil to the rest, casts in the present writer's opinion too strong a shadow over the movement as a whole by its plainness, being too drastically different from the main body of the movement, beautiful as the return is. Many critics will consider that the very charm of the Agnus Dei makes it unsuited to church, as an offence against the strict ecclesiastical style in music. But they will be wrong. Why should not the Lamb of God appear to men in a childlike, friendly guise? Why should we be for ever on our knees before the Godhead, dazzled by its radiance? Why should we not also on occasion look with confidence on its splendour dimmed to human form, and make this part of our daily existence, as the Bible teaches us on every page to do? We adore God's greatness and recognize the immeasurable gulf which separates us from Him, making us no more than worms in the dust; but His love we can touch with our own love, which makes us godlike and fit for heaven. This is the spirit in which Gottfried Weber has conceived his Agnus Dei – with the Lamb of God descending in loving benevolence and consolation and sending the worshipper home more closely united to the Godhead. It will be a real enrichment of good music if this thoughtful composer shares his creations with the public.

31. Review of Gottfried Weber's Sonata in C

Written: Dresden, 11 February 1812.
Published: AMZ xiv (1812), 179.   *Unsigned.*
Reprinted: MMW (error in music example); KSS.

Early in 1810, in Mannheim, *Gottfried Weber sent Carl Maria a copy of his new sonata with the request that he should play it one evening. They had a convention that letters between them should be couched as canons; and Carl Maria acknowledged the work with his canon 'Die Sonate soll ich spielen, welche namenlose Pein' (J89). Its dolorous chromatic lines mock the seriousness of Gottfried's music. The sonata was published by Simrock as 'Sonata per il cembalo, Op. 15, dedicata al suo amico Carlo Maria Barone di Weber, da Goffredo Weber'. On 23 September 1810 Carl Maria wrote to Gottfried to say that he had written a review of the sonata; however, this seems not to have been printed, for a year later (15 September 1811) he wrote again to say that he was having trouble in arousing interest in the sonata, and suggesting, 'I'll tell you what, I'll send it to the *AMZ* and express surprise that it hasn't been reviewed, and add that I'd like to do it and include some sort of review in my letter, and you'll see, they'll snap it up, print it, and you'll be in everyone's mind again.' Not until 14 February 1812, though, did he send the following review to *Rochlitz, asking him to print it as soon as possible as it had been lying about for too long.

Herr Gottfried Weber of Mannheim is known to the readers of this journal as a percipient and firmly based theorist, as is proved by a number of substantial essays; and the present sonata provides delightful proof of his practical musical ability. It is remarkable for its firm, robust style, which despite their very different character, welds the two movements into a unity – the Adagio is to be thought of as an introduction to the final Allegro.

The first Allegro (C major, 3/4) opens with a complete musical statement, whose decisive gait immediately announces the sustained note of resolution and the sharp distinction of sections and individual phrases. This seems to have been the composer's overriding concern, and may also well account for a number of harsh passages which struck the present writer at the beginning of the second part and remain brush-strokes of too glaring a character, despite their probably deliberate placing. But the manner in which this Allegro flows, with increasing strength, from E major back to the original C major and the theme, which makes a welcome and unexpected reappearance – this is admirable.

The last Allegro, in C minor, is, however, by far the better movement. It is full of ardour, vitality and tenderness, maintaining a

vigorous impulse and motion from beginning to end. The most
delightful figures are developed from an opening theme as swift as
lightning:

There is nothing alien here to disturb the impression, and forceful
statement and peaceful development are all part of a single idea.

The chief essential in performance is a firm style that clearly
delineates the character of each section. It is rather the style of a
quartet that the player must try to reproduce on the keyboard. Every
note is organic, every middle part demands its right to be heard. There
is none of the usual piano passage-work to be found here; and it is
only by the wit which the player can extract from the music that he
can hope to shine. If he achieves that, however, he will give his hearers
the pleasure of appreciating a contemporary sonata written with an
industriousness rare in our times, with clarity and wit.

32. Review of B. A. Weber's *Der Gang nach dem Eisenhammer*

Written: Berlin, 10 April 1812.
Published: ?
Printed: HHS; MMW; KSS.

*Bernhard Anselm Weber's melodrama, for speaker with chorus and
orchestra, was written in about 1810 and published by Peters. Together with
the opera *Deodata* (see above, No. 25) it was his most successful work.
Schiller's ballad *Der Gang nach dem Eisenhammer* appeared in the 1798 volume
of his annual, the *Musenalmanach* (pp. 306–18). In thirty 8-line verses, it tells
how Fridolin, servant of the Countess of Savern, arouses the envy of the
huntsman Robert, who accuses him of being her lover. Enraged, the Count
orders his blacksmiths to hurl into their furnace the first man he sends to
enquire if his orders have been carried out. Fridolin is delayed on this errand
by the Countess, who asks him first to hear a Mass for her sick son. He returns
from the forge safely, to the Count's astonishment: Robert has meanwhile
gone to enquire if the deed has been done, and been seized and killed. The
penitent Count acknowledges that holy intervention has brought about grim
justice. The poem had many admirers, including Wagner.

Concert in aid of the Pension Fund for widows of members of the Royal Orchestra, Berlin, 5 April 1812

In the vast spate of concerts which flooded Berlin this winter, the above-mentioned proved in many ways one of the most interesting; and the present writer was particularly interested because it included a composition which had aroused many divergent opinions in the press and in private conversation.

Der Gang nach dem Eisenhammer, ballad by Schiller, with musical accompaniment by B. A. Weber, Royal Prussian Kapellmeister, is the work in question. Much ink has been spilt on the question of whether such a poem can properly be set to music and, if so, how. The present writer, in an attempt to analyse and describe the music, starts from the same premises as the composer, namely, he regards the music as the background of a picture constructed on this foundation and as a heightened, emotionally more intense expression of what the text conveys.

There can be do doubt that from this point of view Kapellmeister Weber's treatment of the subject is highly successful. He shows the wise economy characteristic of an experienced master of effect in this music, where the chief emotions are those of powerfulness and strength, by always retaining something in reserve for a dramatic *crescendo* and by avoiding certain keys. His powers of selection, his use of powerful rhythms and his excellent calculation of where to introduce music as an accompaniment to declamation all show the quality of Kapellmeister Weber's talent and experience.

The introduction (C minor) is restless, full of passion and seething emotions; it suggests both the huntsman's malicious insinuations and the violent reaction of the Count. After a half-close in G the composer conjures up an image of the forge itself (E flat major) by means of a powerful rhythmic figure introduced by horns and bassoon. This is followed after thirteen bars by a return to the first, swift-moving C minor figure, which gathers strength until it is interrupted by the oboe solo in C major leading, like a beneficent light over the orchestral storm, to the words 'Ein frommer Knapp[1] war Fridolin.' From here to the words 'Ihr klares Auge mit Vergnügen hing an den wohlgestalten Zügen' the composer leaves the speaking voice unaccompanied. At this point the oboe takes up its melody again, but is interrupted after twelve bars by the first C minor figure – 'Darob entflammt[2] in Roberts Brust,

---

[1]   In Schiller, *Knecht.*   [2]   In Schiller, *entbrennt.*

des Jägers, gift'ger Groll.' The unison D flat of the violins coming after the half-close in G, at the Count's words 'Was red'st du mir, Gesell?' is most effective. From here onwards the spoken text is interrupted at ever shorter intervals by the music. The return of the opening movement (this time in D minor) forms an admirable accompaniment to the malicious muttering of the furious huntsman – 'Nun ja, ich spreche von dem Blonden' until after the lines

> Die gute[3] Gräfin sanft und weich
> Aus Mitleid wohl verbarg sie's Euch,
> Mich reuet jetzt, dass mir's entfahren,
> Denn, Herr, was habt Ihr zu befahren!

These words are accompanied by the clarinet's hypocritical lament – and suddenly the hideous thought of the forge flashes through the Count's mind, and the E flat major phrase associated with it in the introduction is heard in the orchestra. The present writer considers this to be one of the finest and psychologically most penetrating passages. The music continues to illustrate the text whose sense is given by the words 'Der Funke sprüht, die Bälge blasen als gält es, Berge[4] zu verglasen.' Only when Fridolin says 'Es soll geschehen' does the orchestra fall silent and only a clarinet solo (A flat) punctuates the speech until it comes to a halt at 'Und froh der viel willkommnen Pflicht.' The composer shows great skill in preparing the following scene in church by giving the violins a chorale-like accompaniment to answer the voices. The listener feels drawn with the rest to the holy place and takes a deep delight in the unaccompanied Sanctus, for four solo voices, in the solemn key of E major which has not hitherto appeared in the work. It is all part of the picture which poet and composer wish to conjure up, and nobody will take offence at the scene – except perhaps those rationalists who think that they can only enjoy an effect when they have analysed it and reviewed, as it were, the skeleton, with their cold intelligence. At the words 'Drauf, als der Priester fromm sich neigt' the tentative accompaniment figure appears again in the violin until the 'Amen', where the singers break off. There is no more music until the words 'Zwölf Paternoster noch im stillen.' Then the orchestra once again reminds us of the terrors of the forge. Fridolin receives the mysterious answer and brings it to his master, apologizing for his tardy arrival:

> Die Messe, Herr, befahl sie mir
> Zu hören, gern gehorcht' ich ihr.

---

[3]   In Schiller, *gnäd'ge*.   [4]   In Schiller, *Felsen*.

At this point the violins recall the earlier scene in church (F major). They then continue in D flat *rinforzando* and express the amazement and horror aroused by the Count's deed, until the words

> Nun ruft der Graf und steht vernichtet,
> Gott selbst im Himmel hat gerichtet

(dominant seventh on B flat and the timpani enter *fortissimo* for the first time).

This entry is immensely effective. Hosts of composers would have been unable to restrain their love for the timpani so long, especially in the case of a poem which might be thought to offer so many opportunities for their use. The forge itself, for instance, would surely seem to demand timpani, as would the many other horror effects. But this heroic act of self-denial in order to achieve a great effect in the end is the hallmark of a really exceptional composer.

The public was certainly gripped, shattered by this divine thunder, so effective because it had not been used previously for any lesser, profane purpose. As the thunder gradually dies away (E flat major) a solo flute (C major) enters in the highest register and spreads sweetness and light, expressing the divine sense of a crime prevented and innocence rescued. The Count brings Fridolin to the Countess, and after the words

> Dies Kind, kein Engel ist so rein,
> Lasst's Eurer Hold empfohlen sein;
> Wenn schlimm wir auch beraten waren,
> Mit dem ist Gott und seine Scharen.

the full chorus and orchestra break out in C major jubilation with drums and trumpets, and the work ends with an inspiring tutti. No member of the audience will have left the hall without being deeply moved and filled with gratitude for the magnificent experience provided by the ingenious composer.

The unusual effectiveness of this finale can be explained firstly by the fact that, after many passionate and restless melodies, the listener here encounters cloudless serenity for the first time, and in that key (C major) which the composer has hitherto avoided; and secondly by the characteristic sonority of trumpets and drums employed here for the first time. Earlier in the work the trumpets were always associated with the four horns, and their effect was therefore so overclouded that the listener did not associate it with the pure trumpet sound which only appears in the final rejoicings.

This work will be an enduring monument of Kapellmeister Weber's genius. Vigorous and well thought out, it will be found effective everywhere and conquer all small-minded objections.

I should like to say one word more, about the wholly admirable declamation of Generaldirektor Iffland.[5] It really is a pleasure to hear declamation that is so thoroughly alive and that observes so nicely the distinction between this vitality and mere theatricality. This performance could well serve as a model and made a deep effect on the audience by its combination of power and sobriety.

Also in the programme were Righini's *Tigrane*[6] overture and *Cherubini's cantata on Haydn's death.[7] Madame Müller[8] and Madame Schmidt sang a duet from *Sargino*[9] with their accustomed skill. Herr Schwarz[10] brought a fine full tone to Winter's Adagio and Rondo for bassoon;[11] and Herr Möser,[12] the great favourite of the Berlin public, delighted the audience, as usual, by his playing of a violin concerto by *[Rodolphe] Kreutzer to which he brought his characteristically free and generous style.

5   August Wilhelm Iffland (1759–1814) was one of the leading men of the theatre of his day, equally successful as actor, director and author of sentimental dramas. In Mannheim, in 1782, he was the first (and for many years the dominating) Franz Moor in Schiller's *Die Räuber*. Their relations were not unclouded, but Schiller was later, in a letter to Goethe, to praise Iffland's originality in character roles and skill in handling noble roles that did not truly suit him. *Der Gang nach dem Eisenhammer* doubtless appealed to his own taste for somewhat sentimental tales of vice punished and virtue rewarded.

6   Vincenzo Righini (1756–1812) was director of the Italian Opera in Berlin from 1793 until it was discontinued in 1806. *Tigrane* was produced in Berlin in 1800.

7   Cherubini's *Chant sur la mort de Joseph Haydn*, for three voices and orchestra, was originally written to words in honour of Haydn in 1805, but revised on Haydn's death in 1809 and performed in 1810.

8   Marianne Müller (born Hellmuth; 1772–1851) was a principal singer in Berlin from 1789. According to both LTB and FétisB, her voice was small but she sang with taste and expressiveness.

9   *Paer's *Sargino, ossia L'allievo dell'amore* was produced in Dresden, 26 May 1803. It became popular in Germany, in various translations: the first Berlin performance was on 3 February 1808.

10   Christoph Gottlob Schwarz (1768–1829) was the son of the bassoonist Andre Gottlob Schwarz. He toured with his father, and settled for a time in England in the orchestra of the Prince of Wales. On its disbandment in 1787 he returned to Germany and joined the Berlin Royal Orchestra.

11   The Winter MSS of bassoon works in D-Mbs include a rondo, a rondo and variations, a concerto and a concertino. The Adagio and Rondo were perhaps the last two movements of the concerto.

12   Carl Möser (1774–1851) was the leader of the Berlin Court Opera Orchestra and a popular and respected musical figure in the city. He conducted the Berlin première of Beethoven's Ninth Symphony in 1826.

The Royal Orchestra's playing was marked by power and precision; and the present writer welcomes the opportunity of expressing his best thanks to all the members of the orchestra for the readiness and kindness with which they supported Herr Heinrich Bärmann and himself in two concerts.

33. Review of Six Songs by G. W. Fink

Written: Berlin, 13 April 1812.
Published: AMZ xiv (1812), 427–32.   *Signed:* Carl Marie von Weber.
Reprinted: MMW (without music and verses); KSS.
Gottfried Wilhelm Fink (1783–1846) first studied theology and was then active as a composer and critic. He contributed to the *AMZ* from 1808, and was editor from 1828 to 1841. Under him, the *AMZ* took up a position against the younger Romantics and particularly Schumann, whose own *Neue Zeitschrift für Musik* was in part intended to counter the influence of the *AMZ*. Schumann disguised Fink as Knif in some of his writings (e.g. 'Florestan's Shrove-Tide Oration', 1838). Fink's compositions, chiefly songs, included settings of his own verses, like those reviewed here. They were published by Breitkopf and Härtel. The original *AMZ* review included the complete music and all the verses of No. 5.

This is indeed a pleasant surprise in times not exactly rich in song-writers, either poets or composers! Herr Fink has already made a name for himself by his excellent folksongs and his *Häusliche Andachten*, which show an exceptional talent in both fields. In fact they justify expectations of an achievement to which the present writer devoutly hopes to pay tribute, as in the present case.

All six songs bear witness to a profoundly sensitive and imaginative personality; but it is warm-heartedness and good nature that predominate. Only No. 4 ('Gottes Engel') introduces a new note of grandeur. Text and music are admirably suited to each other. The demands of song form are satisfied to an outstanding degree. By placing the same accent on the same syllable in each line, the composer is able to preserve a single melody for four or five verses without prejudice to either prosody or expressiveness. Let us look briefly at each song.

1. 'Glück der Sehnsucht'. C major. The longing of a pure, innocent soul can, in the present writer's opinion, hardly be better expressed than by quoting the last two lines:

> Noch scheut' ich die Lüfte und weiss doch was,
> Bin glücklich – doch werden die Augen mir nass!

The lengthening of the rhythm in bars 7–8 makes a delightful effect. The composer in fact often abandons the confines of the usual 4–8 bar structure, but only in order to achieve some particular effect and thus to make a more deliberate impression by this decisive and personal procedure.

2. 'Die Täubchen der Liebe'. This is a pretty song, but seems the least significant of the six.

3. 'Die Treue'. This can be performed either by four unaccompanied voices or by a solo voice with pianoforte accompaniment. The music expresses all the tranquil happiness of a sensitive and loyal heart, and the choice of A major is particularly appropriate.

4. 'Gottes Engel'. This is the song of a paternal but still vigorous greybeard, and will only be effective if sung by a man. The text expresses a pure and lofty sense of the Eternal, and the language is firm and full of religious feeling, the music apt and dignified, though to the present writer less remarkable than the text. The end of the song lies rather high for a bass, since it is also marked *piano*.

5. 'Die Liebenden'. Duettino in G major. In the present writer's view this is the most successful of the set. It is hard to imagine anything more naïvely touching than both words and music. The novel use of musical declamation and rhythmical patterning already mentioned is particularly impressive here. It goes without saying that this unpretentious little duet must be performed in exactly the same simple, innocent manner as that in which it is written.

6. 'Abschied vom Liebchen'. B flat major. This song most closely resembles the traditional Lied in style and expression and is less personal in character, though still a delightful piece.

To end this notice the present writer feels obliged to draw the composer's attention to a few small points, if only to show how scrupulously he has examined each of these pieces. There are, for instance, certain phrases and harmonies which seem anomalous and might catch the severe critic's eye, e.g. bar 17 in No. 1:

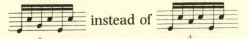

The present writer would have taken these to be misprints had he not found other instances, e.g. bar 24 of the same song, bar 5 in No. 6 (last two crotchets) etc., where the same progression is correct. Can it be that Herr F., who certainly has a good reason for everything he writes, has his own views on these passages?

The type is clean and clear, the price moderate, and there is therefore no external circumstance to prevent these songs becoming popular and finding a regular place on all pianofortes.

34. Review of Friedrich von Drieberg's *Don Tacagno*

Written: Berlin, 24 April 1812.
Published: AMZ xiv (1812), 347–9.   *Signed:* Melos.
Reprinted: HHS, MMW (both inaccurate); KSS.

Friedrich von Drieberg (1780–1856) gave up a military career to study composition with Spontini and, briefly, *Cherubini. He won a reputation in his day for his researches into ancient Greek music, though his work has long been superseded. Drieberg's friendly but candid criticism of *Silvana* – in particular, of the vocal writing, the grasping after effect, and a certain monotony – impelled Weber to revise the work (Diary, 13 May 1812). *Don Tacagno* had some success in Berlin and elsewhere, and the overture and some of the numbers were published by Schott.

Don Tacagno, a comic opera in two acts by Dr Koreff,[1] the music by Herr von Drieberg, had its first performance at the Königliche Bühne, Berlin, on 15 April 1812 and was given again yesterday.

Any composer may consider himself worthy of congratulation whose first work for the theatre makes such an impression as this and enjoys so sympathetic and enthusiastic a reception from the public. Both librettist and composer (but especially the latter) have taken as their models the better sort of Italian comic opera. The style and versification of the libretto are greatly superior to those of the general run of operas, the dialogue is often witty and the plot attractive, with the exception of the Madhouse Scene at the end of Act 1. Since, however, such scenes are unfortunately frequent in the theatre, this should not prejudice listeners against the opera as a whole. The present writer will concern himself with the music, which he will attempt to judge with the frankness and open-mindedness that an intelligent man like Herr von Drieberg is justified in claiming as his right and must certainly be more welcome than misplaced praise.

It is only in the last five or six years that Herr von Drieberg has devoted himself exclusively to composition, and during that period he

---

[1]   David Ferdinand Koreff (1783–1851) was a doctor who had spent some time in Paris, where he numbered among his patients Mme de Staël, Benjamin Constant and the Schlegels. He then settled in Berlin. His colourful personality attracted many friends, among them *E. T. A. Hoffmann, in whose *Serapions-brüder* he features. His opera texts are described as 'worthless' in W. Kosch, *Deutsches Literatur-Lexicon* (Bern, 1953).

has accomplished an extraordinary amount. His music is individual in colour and style; his melodies are fluent and convey a real sense of character. Modulations are simple except on occasions when richer harmonic resources are demanded by the stage action, for instance, the Act 1 finale. The overture is an attractive unity in itself and its vivacious character is effectively concentrated in the coda. The style of the music is light but does not provide a satisfactory transition to what follows. This is the function of the introductory trio, which gives the listener an immediate taste of the composer's wit. The duet between Blanka and Salpeter (No. 4) is very theatrically effective and had by general demand to be repeated.

The Act 1 finale is unquestionably the most successful number in the work. The composer has here proved that comic opera may count him as a valuable acquisition. Well laid out, with good climaxes and an admirably economical use of the orchestra, the work contains a number of well-drawn characters. In addition to this there is a quartet and a quintet, and the duet between Salpeter and Fültrin in Act 2 shows a fund of comic invention. In fact the present writer is only prevented from going into greater detail by the hope that this opera will be given in a number of German theatres, and that he will have achieved his object of drawing attention to what should prove a useful and rewarding work to any company.

The present writer would nevertheless like to make a few additional comments. The strength of the opera lies in its ensembles, and the arias are almost without exception rather duller, lacking the necessary variety of colour. In particular the composer seems to have a certain preference for uneven metres and to exercise too little discretion in his choice of melodies. This applies chiefly to the *semi-seria* arias, for instance, Bannau's and Blanka's first arias. These are not always sufficiently distinct in style from *parlando*, a criticism that also applies to the orchestration. Particular attention should also be paid to the prosody in these pieces. Herr von Drieberg will certainly present us with other operas, and it is to be hoped that he will accept these words of criticism in the spirit in which they are written.

Much devotion and hard work had plainly gone into the production. The general effect was greatly heightened by the acting of Madame Eunicke,[2] *Herr Wurm and Herr Rebenstein[3] (altogether outstanding

---

2   Therese Eunicke (born Schwachhofer: 1776–1844) was the second wife of the tenor Friedrich Eunicke and mother of the soprano *Johanna Eunicke, Weber's first Aennchen (see above, No. 19, n. 2).

3   Ludwig Rebenstein (1795–1834) was a tenor and actor, a protégé of Iffland, whose entire career was spent in Berlin. He was the first Ottokar in *Der Freischütz*.

both as actor and singer, and about to undertake a tour including Mannheim, Darmstadt, Frankfurt etc.). The orchestra, which was under Kapellmeister Weber's[4] perspicacious direction, played with wonted precision.

    4   *B. A. Weber.

35. Review of Gottfried Weber's Twelve Four-Part Songs (1)

Written: July 1812.
Published: AMZ xiv (1812), 515–17.   *Unsigned.*
Reprinted: KSS.
    *Gottfried Weber's Twelve Four-Part Songs with Piano (Op. 16) were dedicated to *Vogler and published by Gombart of Augsburg in three volumes. This review was first attributed to Carl Maria von Weber by Kaiser. See also below, No. 37.

So much music is being composed that it becomes increasingly impossible to discuss even the most outstanding works at any length. The case is further complicated by the consideration that this publication must see to it that no branch of musical composition and no class of music-lover is neglected for too long a period. The present work stands out in a genre which has recently become very popular; but even so, discussion of its merits must be short. This is made easier by the fact that the composer is already known to readers of these pages as a true connoisseur of music and to knowledgeable music-lovers as a sound composer of high ideals.

    These pieces are not true Lieder, nor are they – as is often the case with works entitled 'four-part songs' – basically a single line harmonized by the three other voices. They are indeed genuine four-part pieces resembling, in both conception and execution, those which Haydn published not long before his death to the delight of innumerable music-lovers. (These are to be found in the collection of his work issued by Breitkopf and Härtel, Leipzig.)

    The texts are almost without exception well chosen and suitable for this cheerful form of private music-making. In every case the composer has been successful in catching the poem's character, and has been particularly clever in giving each piece individuality and vitality by expanding and emphasizing isolated phrases. The pieces are very varied in character and contain something for all tastes, from deep melancholy to whimsical humour and strong manly feeling, In the first volume No. 1 is good, but even when sung by four voices not really effective until the return of the *tempo primo*. On the other hand, no one can fail to agree with us in finding No. 2 excellent, whether considered (as it should be) as a whole or, as is also permissible, in detail, for instance, the closeness to the text and its illustration, the skilful part-writing and so forth. No. 3 is, like its subject, less remarkable, but attractive and true to character. One of its chief charms lies in the unusual and effective harmonic progressions in the middle of the piece; and in fact there is if anything too much rather than too little ingenious harmony throughout. Dignity and expressiveness mark No. 4, which provides a commendable support to the poem. The passage starting from bar 2 on page 15 will certainly attract the notice of attentive listeners, not so much for the admittedly choice harmonic progressions (which are not unique and are to be found in C. P. E. Bach) as for the part-writing, which is conceived and laid out with maximum clarity and effectiveness without making too severe demands on the performers. Particularly impressive is the turn to F sharp major precisely on these words. In Vol. ii and iii we can only mention those which particularly delighted us – in Vol. ii, p. 10, p. 15 (despite the roughness of the drone), and in Vol. iii, p. 4 (admirable!) and p. 6.

These pieces demand intelligent and warm-hearted singers with an accurate intonation and a serious musical education, but also give them scope to indulge in what may be called fancifulness. Some of the pieces are in fact quite easy. The accompaniments are admirably written, providing support where this is necessary either to assist the singers or to add to the effect, and also contributing to the general impression of the piece.

36. Introduction to the score of J. G. W. Schneider's trio

Written: Berlin, 27 August 1812.
Published: ?
Reprinted: MMW; KSS.

Johann Georg Wilhelm Schneider (1781–1811) first studied theology before turning to music. He was a pupil of Türk. He wrote a number of larger works for piano, some songs, a melodrama, *Ilse* (Op. 4, 1806), and an opera, *Der Reise nach der Quelle* (*c* 1809). Weber probably wrote this introduction for a projected edition that did not materialise.

Like all artists who have had a higher conception of their art than mere pleasant entertainment, J. G. W. Schneider has often been misunderstood and particularly by those who were closest to him. Those few who were able to appreciate the spark of genius in his works championed him with enthusiasm; but those who judged his music coolly and by conventional standards saw only the frequent difficult, perhaps even unnecessarily complex, passages in his music; and took for mere novelty-seeking and lack of true design what is really evidence of a still unexpressed attempt to find new modes of expression. Only long experience will give a composer that clarity which enables him to give new points of view and new ideas a form that the listener can immediately grasp; and in no art is it more difficult than in music to create a satisfactory whole in which diversity is combined with a sense of unity.

Schneider was in every way unfortunate. In the first place, neither his surroundings nor his circumstances gave him the stimulus and the leisure needed for a composer to reach full maturity. More important still, his health was so poor that only very seldom was his imagination free from the handicap of physical suffering. He died after a slow decline, and his trio was his last work, completed a few days before his death. Indeed the music bears signs of having been conceived when he was literally struggling to live and artistic inspiration could only appear in occasional flashes. The present writer happens to have had the opportunity of making a closer acquaintance with Schneider's music, and has also heard opinions of his talent as a performer from many expert judges. He has therefore thought it right to acquaint both the performers and the critics of this work with the circumstances of its composition, to enable them to judge it in the right perspective and to prevent an unjust attitude. It is true that neither critics nor public need information about the circumstances in which a work of art is created: the work must speak for itself. But in a case where a mere hint can ensure that justice is done to an artist of talent and where, as in this case, it is possible to trace the last gleams of this talent in detail, critics will take these facts into consideration and psychologists will find matters to interest them. This is not the place to undertake an evaluation of Schneider's trio; and the present writer must content himself with observing that the composer himself thought the minuet the most successful movement, and after that the opening Allegro, in which the inspiration is maintained right up to the last bar. The final Allegro was composed by fits and starts and was often largely rewritten, costing the composer great efforts at a time when he was really too ill for any sustained intellectual activity. The movement therefore resembles a mosaic with only occasional gleams of inspiration.

It would be only just if every reader of these words would regard the trio as the final effort of a man of genius who died, alas, before that genius had found the clear and well-defined expression which is the hallmark of a master's productions and can only be achieved by uninterrupted thought and consideration.

37. Review of Gottfried Weber's Twelve Four-Part Songs (2)

Written: Berlin, 29 August 1812.
Published: Berlinische Nachrichten von Staats- und gelehrten Sachen (Haude- und Spenersche Zeitung), No. 107, 5 September 1812.

Signed: M—s.

Reprinted: KSS.
   See also above, No. 35. This review of *Gottfried Weber's songs also appeared in the *Badische Magazin*, No. 239, 1812.

Herr Gottfried Weber of Mannheim is best known to the musical world by his many well-informed articles in the musical press. In these pieces he presents amateurs of part-singing with something very much above the ordinary. Their chief characteristics are suitable texts, mostly cheerful or inclining to the tender, first-class word-setting, fluent part-writing and by no means commonplace harmony. They are chiefly distinguished from the majority of pieces in this genre by the fact that they are not simply a single melodic line with three accompanying parts, but genuine four-part music, in which each part is independent and has a separate life of its own. Each of the three volumes contains four pieces. The present writer regrets that lack of space prevents him from discussing individual pieces in greater detail and must content himself with drawing attention to the following –

Vol. i. The polymetric 'Tränen gabst du, O Gott', a fascinating and immensely effective piece.
Vol. ii. 'Geselligkeit', a vivacious and quick-moving piece.
Vol. iii. 'Minneglück'.

The not inconsiderable difficulties presented by these songs will be found richly rewarding to performers, and the present writer would like to see these songs in the hands of all music-lovers. *Alexander von Dusch appears from these texts to be a talented and witty poet and we can only hope that he will often collaborate with this admirable composer in works to delight the public.

38. Friedrich Kaufmann's Trumpeter

Written: Gotha, 12 September 1812.
Published: AMZ xiv (1812), 663–6.   *Signed:* Carl Maria von Weber.
Reprinted: MMW (inaccurate); KSS.

Friedrich Kaufmann (1785–1866) was the son of Johann Gottfried Kaufmann (1752–1818) and father of Theodor Kaufmann (1823–72). All became famous as constructors of mechanical instruments. Among the instruments which Friedrich and Johann Gottfried built together was the Belloneon (1805), a free-reed automatophone worked by a pinned drum (described below by Weber). This was the forerunner of the Trumpeter (1808). The harmonichord, built by Friedrich and Johann Gottfried in about 1810, was one of many contemporary attempts at constructing an effective sustaining keyboard instrument. In the form of a giraffe piano, it used a resin-coated cylinder, controlled by the feet, to sound strings pressed against it by means of wooden bars controlled by the keyboard. Weber wrote his Adagio and Rondo (J115) for it in 1811.

Herr Kaufmann of Dresden caused a great sensation with the tour that he made through part of Germany last year with his invention, the harmonichord. Acousticians in particular will now find his latest inventions so remarkable that they deserve to be presented to as wide a public as possible. The inventor Maelzel[1] in Vienna is well known as the designer of the first device by which the natural embouchure of the human mouth on the trumpet has been copied. With this he has made a notable improvement to the organ and other instruments, which have hitherto had to make do with pipe stops and reeds that imitated the tone of the trumpet. He later brought his invention to such a pitch of perfection that by means of this artificial embouchure several notes could be produced on a single trumpet instead of needing a trumpet for each note, as was earlier the case. Continuing along these lines, Herr Kaufmann has now produced an artificial trumpeter in every way superior to Maelzel's. During his time in Dresden the present writer had an opportunity of seeing and hearing this machine before it was completed, while it was still on the work-bench and had no ornamental superstructure, so that there could be no question of deception by any means not visible to the observer. The machine is simple and neat, and capable of producing, by means of attaching a

---

[1]   Johann Nepomuk Maelzel (1772–1838), celebrated as the inventor of the metronome which bears his name, was a maker of mechanical instruments and automata. His mechanical Trumpeter played Austrian and French cavalry marches and calls, and military music by *Weigl, Dussek and Pleyel.

trumpet to it (which the present writer changed several times, in order to make the experiment), a perfectly round, even tone and quick tonguing on the following notes:

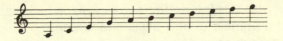

in different fanfares, calls etc. The notes A and B, together with the clarino notes, are of particular interest and unobtainable by Maelzel's method. Still more interesting, and indeed verging on the incomprehensible, is the production of two simultaneous notes absolutely equal in power and clarity. Your reviewer was quite taken aback when, after a number of monophonic passages, he suddenly found himself listening to a number of scales in octaves, thirds, fifths etc., and a very handsome double trill on F–D. Acoustic experiments have of course shown the possibility of accessory notes belonging to a chord sounding with that chord; and some performers, generally flautists or horn players, have experimented with the same phenomenon.[2] Their results, however, have been unreliable in quality and regarded more as tricks; and it is therefore all the more remarkable for the theory of tone-production to find an instrument capable of achieving as satisfactory a sound as two trumpets. If such a result can be produced by a machine, it ought not to be beyond the bounds of possibility to produce it by the natural human mouthpiece, which served as the model for that machine. Hitherto the notes A–B could only be produced by the familiar hand-stop and were therefore ruled out as being impracticable, difficult to produce, uneven and different in quality from the so-called natural notes. By the new system, however, we have them perfectly in tune and dynamically even, and what is more, with no other assistance than that provided by the mouthpiece. Even if double notes were to prove normally impracticable, their feasibility represents an enormous enrichment of the instrument and will enable composers in future to write with much greater effect and to more purpose for the trumpet.

It is an odd fact that Herr Kaufmann has not yet, for all his industry, contrived to produce sixths, although he has managed seconds, major and minor thirds, fourths, fifths and octaves. As far as the outward

[2]   Weber is referring to a phenomenon to be exploited by him in his Horn Concertino (J188) in 1815. The player hums a note at a fixed interval above the one he is playing; this has the property of strengthening some normally inaudible partials so that one or two other notes are also heard.

appearance of the machine is concerned he has all but achieved perfection (a trumpeter in old Spanish costume and with a clock inserted in his headpiece, by means of which the time at which he will automatically play can be regulated), and it is to be hoped that he will make a tour with this interesting work of art, which will at the very least prompt a number of new ideas and attempts.

Beside the Trumpeter Herr Kaufmann has also on display the following:

1. A mechanism[3] consisting of twenty-four trumpets and two drums (as well as a clock) which plays several pieces. In this case each trumpet plays only a single note, but their number ensures variety, and the present writer was particularly interested to find that alternations of *forte* and *piano* can be achieved. A *crescendo* drum-roll is produced by an ingenious bobbin-like device which also ensures against the automatic double strike which is a disadvantage in Maelzel's invention. The bronze and mahogany case, in which the trumpets themselves form a natural trophy, is in excellent taste as well as practical. This whole machine is in general modelled on Maelzel's, but represents an improvement in the matter of *forte* and *piano* etc.

2. A machine of his own invention, with a clock. It plays the fortepiano (and not the harp, as in the usual musical clock), the flute and the flageolet, and the repertory contains several overtures, concertos etc. Another novelty in musical clocks is the fact that the fortepiano is played in the natural way, by hammers which are controlled in the normal way by dampers or stops, which are raised from the cylinder according to the demands of the music. By controlling the violence with which the hammers strike it is possible to produce *piano*, *crescendo*, *decrescendo*, *sforzando* etc.; and a *crescendo* and *decrescendo* are also obtainable from the flute, the quality of whose held notes is particularly good. All these circumstances make it possible to produce a far more lively and characterful performance than has hitherto been possible with machines of this kind. The whole contrivance is enclosed in a mahogany writing-table, with an ornamental marble-columned temple enclosing a clock in the dome.

Herr Kaufmann has moreover constructed a new harmonichord since his last tour, and this is more powerful and rounder in tone, less

3   The Belloneon. According to A. Buchner, *Mechanical Musical Instruments* (London, n.d.), one was installed at Charlottenburg Castle which played Prussian military marches and bugle calls. On the night after the Battle of Jena, one of Napoleon's aides accidentally set it off, causing the Emperor to start in alarm from his bed.

shrill in the treble and with a quicker action, which ensures greater clarity than was the case in the earlier model.

The two musical clocks were invented by Herr Kaufmann's father, J. G. Kaufmann, and the harmonichord is the joint work of father and son. The Trumpeter, on the other hand, is entirely the work of the son, Friedrich Kaufmann.

We can only hope that this industrious and talented young man's admirable efforts will meet with the support and encouragement that they deserve!

39. Anton Dreyssig's Singakademie

Written: Gotha, 27 September 1812.
Published: Zeitung für die elegante Welt, No. 198, 4 October 1812.

Signed: Melos.

Reprinted: MMW (very inaccurately); KSS; LKA.

Anton Dreyssig (1775–1815) was an organist and composer who worked at the royal court in Dresden. His Singakademie was founded in 1807 in conscious imitation of Zelter's famous Berlin Singakademie, out of a group of enthusiasts who met in the house of the Court of Appeal Councillor Christian Gottfried Körner (father of *Theodor Körner). In 1814 Dreyssig gave Haydn's *Creation* as the first of what was to be a long series of distinguished oratorio performances. The Singakademie was directed by Johann Gottlob Schneider from 1832 to 1857, when it achieved great renown for its performance of then neglected classics including the St Matthew Passion (only five years after Mendelssohn's famous 1829 revival), many works by Handel, and music by Lassus and Palestrina; it also gave works by Spohr, Mendelssohn and Schumann, among many other new composers. It sang in Wagner's last Dresden concert, the performance of the Ninth Symphony on Palm Sunday 1846. Schumann took over as conductor in 1847. The society retained its high reputation in Dresden musical life into modern times. A square in the city is named after Dreyssig. The passages in square brackets appear in MMW but not the original.

Musical novelty is something in which we are not in fact very rich. Foreign artists seem not always to obtain the reception they might [so that their visits become less frequent and may well cease entirely]. All true art-lovers must on the other hand be delighted to observe the increasing success of an institution that promises excellently for the future and has hitherto been virtually unique to Berlin – I mean Court Organist Dreyssig's Singakademie. The increasing deterioration of vocal, and especially choral, music and the example of Berlin's admirable institution determined Dreyssig to found a choral society devoted exclusively to church music. [The classical masterpieces of Handel, Mozart, Haydn etc. were new to us and had never been heard.] As a general rule the Catholic Hofkirche performs only music written by composers who have held official posts in Dresden. The remaining Protestant churches have little or no music, and the performance of classical masterpieces by Handel, Mozart, Haydn etc. has meant a rich feast for us. It was this circumstance, taken in necessary conjunction with a number of other conditions, that determined Dreyssig to restrict himself to church music.

He began rehearsals in March 1807 with six or seven singers, and slowly the numbers of those taking part grew. A large number of prejudices had to be overcome. [The chief obstacles lay in the very marked class distinctions prevailing here, and still more in the preference for foreign, especially Italian, music. Regardless of the fact that two of its greatest singers, Mara[1] and *Häser, are German, the great majority of the Dresden public certainly believes it to be impossible for a German to sing, let alone to teach singing.] Meanwhile, by 1809 the society was already able to take a small hall; and eventually, thanks to the founder's iron determination, the large Post Hall was hired last year and the chorus now consists of 16 sopranos, 12 altos, 11 tenors and 12 basses.

Meetings are held at 6 every Thursday and generally last until 8. In addition to this there is a meeting at 5 on Mondays in Herr Dreyssig's own house, where beginners and those particularly keen are coached by him in whatever is to be sung on the coming Thursday. Solo parts are shared out in turn by the director among those whom he considers most proficient.

A subscription of 8 thalers a year is paid by every member towards such expenses as music, lighting, heating etc. Of course this hardly covers the actual costs, and the founder of the society makes not the smallest profit and has no prospect of doing so. This admirable and indefatigable zeal on Herr Dreyssig's part is not supported by any petty considerations and does him the very greatest credit. In fact every music-lover must be deeply touched to see that there are still men who are ready to sacrifice their own interests in order to foster and to further the cause of art.

Happily the director's efforts have met with a corresponding success. Anyone acquainted with the difficulties of training an amateur chorus (with no more than a piano accompaniment) to achieve a standard

---

[1] Gertrud Mara (1749–1833), one of the most famous German singers of her day, was in fact trained by Italian singers.

enabling them to sing clearly and with precision the often very difficult choruses and fugues of the best-known masterpieces will leave the Singakademie with feelings of warmth, gratefully acknowledging Herr Dreyssig's efforts and wishing him prosperity, support and recognition.

40. Review of Ludwig Hellwig's piano score of Gluck's *Iphigénie en Tauride*

Written: Gotha, 27 September 1812.
Published: Zeitung für die elegante Welt. No. 199, 5 October 1812.
Signed: Melos.

Reprinted: MMW (inaccurate); KSS.
  *Carl Friedrich Ludwig Hellwig made a number of piano scores of major works, including Bach's St John Passion and Handel's *Judas Maccabaeus*. He was one of the first arrangers to include indications of the original instrumentation in his piano scores. The word 'great' in square brackets does not appear in the original, but was added in MMW.

The need for a complete and judiciously prepared piano score of this evergreen masterpiece has long been felt, and the present work represents an extremely satisfactory answer. Herr Ludwig Hellwig is himself the author of a number of attractive songs, and in the work under discussion he displays the necessary familiarity with the spirit of the [great] composer, and also the knowledge and care necessary in preparing a piano score which is as faithful as possible to the original in the preserving of details of voices and part-writing, without presenting excessive difficulties to the performer. The print is clear and almost faultless, with French and German text, and the whole undertaking does much credit to Herr Hellwig and his publishers.

41. Review of the score of Lauska's Grande Sonate (Op. 30)

Written: Gotha, 27 September 1812.
Published: Zeitung für die elegante Welt, No. 201, 8 October 1812.
Signed: Melos.

Reprinted: MMW (inaccurate); KSS.
  Franz Lauska (František Louska) (1764–1825) was a successful pianist, organist and composer of Bohemian origin who travelled widely before settling in Berlin in 1798 as a virtuoso and teacher. His B flat Sonata (Op. 41) was dedicated to Weber. The F minor Sonata (Op. 30) of 1812 was

dedicated to Countess Gurowska. He was one of the circle of Weber's Berlin friends, and Hinrich Lichtenstein has left a comparison of them: 'Even Lauska, whose charmingly meticulous and delicate playing remains so unforgettable to so many of us, had to yield to the younger master, in that his extemporization, although exceptionally fluent and natural, always had the mark of prepared and considered work rather than of immediate inspiration and lacked the manifold invention that Weber possessed to such a high degree' (memoir in E. Rudorff, ed., *Briefe von Carl Maria von Weber an Hinrich Lichtenstein* (Brunswick, 1900)).

No paper could be more appropriate for a notice of Herr Lauska's sonata than *Die Zeitung für die elegante Welt*. Herr Lauska's compositions fill a notable gap in the musical literature of the present day, which is devoted either to the highest and technically most demanding works or to what is routine stuff, trivial and easy. The composer of the sonata under discussion treads an attractive middle path, thus assuring himself of the gratitude of amateurs and the respect of professionals. The chief characteristics of his music are an almost unexceptionable quality of style and development, delightful melodies and grateful passage-work. The present work is no exception. Although in the key of F minor, it is not marked by any great degree of passion, but is thoughtful and eloquent, especially the middle section of the first Allegro. The Adagio and Rondo are well matched to the Allegro, making the work a well-rounded whole such as we can recommend with a clear conscience to all amateurs, the latest production of a composer who is also an outstandingly fine performer. Print and paper are both good.

42. Review of concerts in St Margaret's Church, Gotha

Written: Gotha, 3 October 1812.
Published: Journal des Luxus und der Moden XXVII (November 1812), 724–9.
Signed: Melos.
Reprinted: MMW; KSS; LKA.

Weber was asked for this double concert notice and for the article on *Mme Schönberger (below, No. 44) by Bertuch, editor of the Weimar *Journal*, and was paid 3 thalers, 3 groschen for the pair.

Considering how rarely we have the pleasure of public performances of music, the public owes a real debt of gratitude to Cantor Schade[1]

---

[1]   Johann Gottfried Schade (1756–1828) lived in Gotha from 1776, and was town cantor from 1804. He conducted a famous performance of Haydn's *Creation* in 1801, only two years after the first performance, with an orchestra of 60–70.

for putting on two concerts in St Margaret's Church[2] on 29 and 30 September. The artistic resources of the town itself were in fact supplemented by the collaboration of a number of artists living in the neighbourhood, so that there was never any doubt of variety in the programme or of an unusually high standard of performance. In addition to this, Cantor Schade had seen to it that we should be given works belonging to highly contrasting styles.

On the 29th the concert, which was at 5 p.m., began with the overture to Mozart's *Don Giovanni*. This was followed by a horn concerto of *Duvernoy's, played by Herr Sommer[3] of Rudolstadt, who has a good tone and a secure technique. It is a pity that in Duvernoy's generally very mediocre works the horn is treated as such a wretched hybrid instrument, and that no real use is made of either the magnificent power and roundness of tone in the lower register or the cantabile qualities of the upper. Duvernoy uses at most an octave and a half, within which all melodies and passages are constricted, thus emphasizing the slightly monotonous nature of the instrument.

Our esteemed *Spohr and his wife gave us a sonata for violin and harp, of his own composition.[4] Most unfortunately we were able to hear only the first part of the Allegro and the potpourri of Mozart themes. In fact, your correspondent has seldom felt more uncomfortable than on this occasion when, towards the end of the first part, a pedal came loose and then, after this had been mended, a string broke. Such things, disturbing enough for the listener, are enough to put the player off completely; and the two artists are to be all the more complimented for their admirable performance. The sonata itself, which is Spohr's latest, is excellently written and rewarding for the players.

The second part of the concert opened with the greatest of all symphonies, that by Mozart in C major with the fugal finale.[5] This music inspired the orchestra to new life, and it is a rare experience to hear this difficult work so well played. Tempos were spirited and well

2   The twelfth-century Margarethenkirche, one of the principal churches of Gotha, was rebuilt in the state in which Weber knew it in 1652.

3   Sommer was court musician and first horn in the Rudolstadt Orchestra. Several *AMZ* reviews support Weber's opinion, and he was described as 'certainly one of the leading horn players of our time' (*AMZ* XIII (1811), 311).

4   Spohr's E flat Sonata for violin and harp of 1811 (Op. 114) includes a potpourri of themes from *The Magic Flute*, 'done with spirit and taste' (*AMZ* XLIV (1842), 800). Spohr's wife Dorette Scheidler (1787–1834) was one of the leading harp virtuosos of the day, and a fine pianist. See also below, n. 11.

5   K551.

chosen, and light and shade assured by careful observation of *piano* and *forte* markings. Wind and strings vied with each other to produce complete unity of feeling.

The present writer's pleasure was only modified by his awareness of the fact that perfection such as this is not likely to come his way again for some time, since Spohr is leaving on 5 October for a tour which includes Leipzig, Dresden, Prague, Vienna and elsewhere, and is taking with him his pupils, who provide an important support to our concert life. The symphony was followed by a setting of Psalm 84[6] by the worthy *Schicht, director of music in Leipzig. Here the fugues and choruses show an unusual clarity and power. The arias and solos may not have been found quite satisfactory by the connoisseurs of today's melodies, and perhaps the whole work might with reason be called heavy-handed. The choruses were sung well, if with somewhat weak tone.

On the 30th the concert began at 10 a.m. The present writer must admit that daytime concerts – let alone those that take place in the morning – always put him in rather a bad mood, and this was certainly not made better by the fact that it was market day, with all the attendant traffic noise, cracking of whips and so on, right next to the church. Cantor Schade no doubt had very good reasons of his own for making this arrangement.

The programme opened with a lively and well-disciplined performance of *Bernhard Romberg's D major Overture, a fine, powerful work built on a large scale.[7] This was followed by a performance of Spohr's superb C minor Clarinet Concerto[8] played by the justly admired *Hermstedt, to whose reputation no words of mine can add anything. It must be said that perhaps on this occasion he seemed to outshine himself particularly in the Adagio; and when he has travelled a little and heard outstanding singers, he may well give a little additional roundness to his own tone, after which perfection will be within his grasp. As far as the composition was concerned, it was the Rondo that the present writer most admired.

Carl Maria von Weber, the composer and pianist who has recently

---

[6] *Herr Zebaoth* ('Wie lieblich sind deine Wohnungen, Herr Zebaoth' in Luther's Bible; 'How amiable are Thy tabernacles, O Lord of Hosts' in the Authorized Version).   [7] Concert overture in D (Op. 34).

[8] Op. 26, composed *c.* 1808. The first of a series of works which Spohr wrote for Hermstedt, first performed in Sondershausen, 16 June 1809. In his preface to the first edition, Spohr writes that Hermstedt made special mechanical modifications to his instrument so as to master the technical difficulties more effectively.

come here from Berlin, played only a short Fantasy and Variations on the delightful theme from Méhul's *Joseph*[9] (by common report completed only since he arrived) on the fortepiano. He seemed momentarily taken aback by some out-of-tune notes in the treble of what was otherwise a fine, full-toned instrument; but his playing was then in the manner which we have come to expect from him. Herr Methfessel,[10] from Rudolstadt, sang with Madame Scheidler[11] – a delightful performance of one of his own duets written in the best Italian style.

Schiller's *Glocke*, set by *Andreas Romberg,[12] completed the programme. So much has already been written for and against this work that the present writer will do no more than comment on the performance, which was excellent. The soloists were Mlle Karoline Schlick[13] and Herren Methfessel and Schiffner.[14] This was Mlle Schlick's first public appearance here for some considerable time; and although her voice is not of the strongest, her performance was distinguished by admirable clarity of enunciation and good vocal technique. Mlle Schlick has spent a long time in Italy and it is to be hoped that we shall have many opportunities of hearing her. This would enable her to conquer a certain natural timidity and develop her potentialities unimpeded. It is well known that we have in her in any case an efficient and tasteful pianist. As Konzertmeister Spohr had had the opportunity of hearing this work in Hamburg conducted by the composer, we can be sure that the tempos – which have often been mistaken – were correct on this occasion.

Finally the present writer would like to observe that it was a pity that this performance had to be given in a church. For one thing, many small details of interpretation are simply not heard in so large a building, and for another the performers are deprived of their only real

9   Variations on 'A peine au sortir de l'enfance' (J141). Composed in Gotha, 22 September 1812. 'Damned out-of-tune piano; put me out of tune, too, though I played the new *Joseph* variations well, and for the first time in public' (Diary, 30 September 1812).

10   Albert Gottlieb Methfessel (1785–1869) was court singer at Rudolstadt from 1810, later court Kapellmeister at Brunswick, 1832–42. He wrote a large number of very popular songs. Weber recommended him as his successor in Prague, unsuccessfully.

11   Sophie Scheidler (born Preysing) was the wife of the Gotha cellist Johann David Scheidler (1748–1802), and the mother of Spohr's wife Dorette Scheidler. She made her début in 1776.

12   *Das Lied von der Glocke* (Op. 25).

13   Karoline Schlick was the daughter of the cellist and composer Johann Konrad Schlick (?1748–1818) and the violin virtuoso Regina Strina-Sacchi (1759–1839).

14   Schiffner was a baritone of the Prague Opera.

reward, namely the immediate enthusiastic response of public applause. Instead the whole proceedings take place in a deadeningly chilly atmosphere. Without a doubt both the music-loving inhabitants of the town and the many strangers who came here for the concert would have liked to express their gratitude audibly. Her Serene Highness the Duchess graced both concerts with her presence, but we were deprived of that of the Duke[15] by a serious indisposition.

43. Schlesinger's Music Shop in Berlin

Written: Gotha, 3 October 1812.
Published: Morgenblatt für gebildete Stände, No. 258, 27 October 1812.
                                    Signed: S. K . . . r [Simon Knaster].
Reprinted: MMW (inaccurate); KSS.
   Adolf Martin (born Abraham Moses) Schlesinger was working as a bookseller in Berlin before 1795, and operating a lending library in collaboration with Breitkopf and Härtel, *Nägeli and Simrock. In April 1810 he opened A. M. Schlesinger's Musikhandlung at 8 Breitenstrasse, and in the following year began publishing music. He became Weber's principal publisher through an agreement contracted on 5 August 1814. Adolf's son Moritz secured some of Beethoven's later works; he then (as Maurice) became an important figure in Paris musical life, especially through his publication of the *Revue et Gazette musicale.* The new Berlin premises at 34 Unter den Linden, occupied in February 1823, became a meeting-place for musical Berlin. Schlesinger also issued journals, including some numbers of *Der Freimüthige* (founded by *Kotzebue in 1803), out of which developed the Berlin *Allgemeine musikalische Zeitung,* 1824–30, edited by A. B. Marx. The firm was sold to Robert Lienau in 1864. The words in square brackets appear in MMW, not in the original.

It is hard to believe that in such a town as Berlin there has hitherto been no proper music shop, considering that the work of German artists is in general encouraged there and that one can be sure of finding the latest and best musical productions from the rest of Europe. It is devoutly to be hoped that this lack, which is becoming increasingly felt, will be supplied by the [new music] shop established some eighteen months ago by Herr Adolf Martin Schlesinger. Apart from a publishing house and a bookshop, he has opened an admirable lending library, with French, English and Italian books [and maps]; and he has all the energy and resources needed to establish his undertaking on the highest footing, if he is well advised by unprejudiced connoisseurs and is willing to make good use of their advice. If he continues as he has

[15]   Duke August of Saxe-Coburg-Gotha (1772–1822).

begun, the omens are excellent. In the case of new works that he has published, composers have been properly paid and the greater part of the music has been of exceptionally high quality.

The present writer would like to draw particular attention to a number of excellent piano arrangements – Gluck's *Iphigénie en Tauride* *[C.F.L.] (Hellwig), Méhul's *Joseph* (Hennig), Kapellmeister Reichardt's *Der Taucher*,[1] *Kapellmeister B. A. Weber's *Deodata*[2] and C. M. von Weber's *Sylvana* etc. Some of these, with other pieces, are issued as a theatrical journal under the title 'Selection of overtures, marches, songs and dances from the latest operas performed at the Königliche Theater, Berlin, in piano arrangements' etc. Until a new business such as this has won the confidence of the leading artists and enjoys their support, it can hardly be expected to publish many important new works, and must rather cater for immediate demands. Nevertheless, Schlesinger has in fact published several sonatas by the excellent Lauska,[3] an admirable concertante for flute and oboe by *Westenholz and a splendid trio for pianoforte, violin and viola by Wollank,[4] while several works by the well-known composer and pianist C. M. von Weber are in the press.

Both paper and type-face are good, and the present writer would like to repeat that in view of the above-mentioned considerations we can expect great things of Herr Schlesinger.

[1] A *Liederspiel* (1810).	[2] See above, No. 25.

[3]   See above, No. 41.

[4]   Friedrich Wollank (1781–1831) was a lawyer and amateur composer, a prominent figure in the Berlin Singakademie (see above, No. 39) and Liedertafel and a close friend of Weber. His works include a three-act opera, *Die Alpenhirten*, which had some success in Berlin in 1811. This was not repeated when Weber gave it in Prague in May 1815 (with *Caroline Brandt as Betty); he noted that it was 'too long, after one performance shortened to two acts and five numbers cut' (Notizen-Buch).

44. Marianne Schönberger (2)

Written: Gotha, 16 November 1812.
Published: *Journal des Luxus und der Moden* XXVII (December 1812), 799–801.
                                    Signed: T.f.z.Z.[1]

Reprinted: MMW (inaccurate); KSS.

*Marianne Schönberger impressed not only Weber on this Weimar visit, but also Goethe: 'The presence of Mme Schönberger stimulated the most

[1]   *Tätigkeit führt zum Ziel*, 'Action achieves its object', a variant of *Beharrlichkeit führt zum Ziel*; see above, No. 13, n. 1.

satisfying performances' (Diary for 1812), ed. E. Bentler, *J. W. von Goethe. Gedenkausgabe der Werke, Briefe und Tagebücher*, XI, *Tag- und Jahreshefte* (Zürich, 1950). Georg Kaiser, in KSS, draws attention to another essay on her in the *Gesellschaftsblatt für gebildete Stände*, No. 19, 4 March 1812, signed Philokalos, with such stylistic and other similarities as to suggest Weber's authorship. See also above, No. 10, and the introduction to No. 30.

We too [in Weimar] had the pleasure of admiring Mme Schönberger (born Marconi) in three guest performances as Murney, Joseph and Titus.[2] The present writer of course knew her reputation well and was most intrigued by the many, often puzzlingly contradictory, opinions of her voice and the new conception of what constitutes a woman's role. For that reason he was careful to form no previous judgement before going to the opera.[3] He went with that open mind, ready for any and every impression, which is the prerequisite of any balanced judgement. Madame Schönberger's first notes cannot fail to surprise by their novel quality; but in fact the ear soon grows accustomed to this, and the listener is then in a position not only to do full justice to her fine, vibrant delivery and well-considered acting but to admire and applaud her generally excellent vocal production, the flexibility of her voice and her mostly admirable taste in ornamentation of the vocal line.

It is inconceivable to the present writer that anyone should entertain doubts because Mme Schönberger's voice is not a tenor. Nature, in her case, must have made an unique exception in the formation of her vocal organs. Her voice is in fact an exceptionally beautiful, rich and sonorous contralto; and it was the scarcity of major roles conceived for such a voice that caused her (as she has modestly confessed) to attempt high-lying tenor roles. Her undertaking has been highly successful and much applauded, though no one will maintain that she can replace a real tenor. Her vocal range may be the same, but the balance of the voice is not. In acoustic terms, the quantity of the notes is identical, their quality different. It is in fact the same phenomenon as when a violin or viola plays a melody ranging between the low G and the G two octaves above it, and this seems far lower than exactly the same notes played by a violoncello. What lies easily and naturally for a man's voice, well within his upper and lower limits, represents an extreme – the lowest range possible – for a contralto.

Mme Schönberger's regular development of the lowest range of her

---

[2]   Murney in Winter's *Das unterbrochene Opferfest*, Joseph in Méhul's opera, Titus in Mozart's *La clemenza di Tito*.

[3]   See, however, above, No. 10.

voice has indeed given this lowest register a power which is quite exceptional even in contraltos. But in the higher range (the tenor's F G A etc.) her voice develops its own beautiful characteristics; and as these notes generally demand some degree of effort for a tenor and are not often reached and held without using the head voice, falsetto etc., it is naturally here that Mme Schönberger's listeners find most to admire, and most to puzzle them.

To go into the matter more deeply would take the present writer too far, and he may well already have broached matters too abstract for his readers, in which case he can only plead the attraction and interest of the subject, which have led him on. Mme Schönberger's Murney was little short of perfect both vocally and dramatically, and she fully deserved the comparable success which she obtained in the part of Joseph. She is an artist as modest as she is excellent, and she showed the full extent of her art in the role of Titus, to the admiration of all present. Here no small part in her success was played by her admirably well-considered and dignified acting.

45. Invitation to librettists

Written: Prague, 12 March 1813.
Published: AMZ xv (1813), Intelligenz-Blatt iv.
                              Signed: Carl Maria von Weber...[see below]
Reprinted: KSS.

Weber had not written an opera since *Abu Hassan* of 1811, and had just taken up his post as director of the Opera in Prague. The reasons for the silence that was to last until *Der Freischütz* of 1821 are complex. They include difficulty in absorbing the influences relevant to his intentions for German opera, and the necessity of gaining more theatrical experience; but the lack of good librettists was among them. Though a few composers, notable *Poissl, attempted their own librettos, these were generally in the conventional Italianate mould: Weber was after something new, from writers with proven theatrical experience. Accordingly he sent this advertisement to *Rochlitz, with a covering letter saying, 'I'm properly thirsting for a good opera text: if you find it acceptable, would you put the enclosed Invitation in the AMZ and if need be a couple of times in the *Literaturzeitung*. No matter if it doesn't help' (letter of 12 March 1813). The Invitation was not in fact printed in the Leipzig *Literaturzeitung*; and it does not seem to have brought Weber any libretto, at any rate none that he found acceptable.

The undersigned wishes to acquire as soon as possible a good opera libretto for setting to music, and is prepared to pay a good price. He hereby invites any German poet prepared to undertake this work to submit a manuscript, stating his terms; and he undertakes to return this manuscript to the author, should it prove unsuitable to his purpose, without in any way misusing the copy.

Prague, 12 March 1813

Carl Maria von Weber

Kapellmeister, Director of the Opera of the Königliches Böhmisches Ständisches Theater in Prague

46. Gottfried Weber's *Te Deum*

Written: Prague, summer 1814.
Published: AMZ xvi (1814), 677–80.   *Unsigned.*
Reprinted: KSS.

*Gottfried Weber's *Te Deum*, *Deutschlands siegreichen Heeren gewidmet* in D minor, for chorus and orchestra, was his Op. 18. It was written to celebrate the defeat of Napoleon, and published by André. As Carl Maria told *Gänsbacher, he conducted a performance in the Wallenstein Gardens in the first summer of his arrival in Prague (letter of 5 March 1814); but that did not prevent Gottfried, who felt his original compositions underrated beside his theoretical work, from taxing his old Harmonischer Verein comrade with neglect. 'A little while ago I had a letter from Gottfried that upset me so much that I can't decide how to answer it. He feels bitter that I don't do anything for him and hadn't once announced the performance of his *Te Deum* etc. I've owed the *Musikzeitung* [*AMZ*] a review for a year and a day, so now I'll do it. You don't know how much this sort of thing upsets me' (letter to Gänsbacher, 15 July 1814).

In recording his judgement of the above-mentioned work, the present writer recalls having read a notice of it in these pages. This is to be found in No. 22 of the present year, from Mannheim, by von Weiler.[1] Not wishing to write anything that is useless or superfluous, he does not intend now to add a great deal about the work, since the notice that has already appeared goes into considerable detail and is clearly written by someone who has studied and heard the music, quotes from the score and in general agrees in his judgement with the present writer. Bearing in mind this earlier notice, he will touch only lightly on points where he is in agreement and will merely treat rather more fully any matters which seem to have been neglected, or those on which his opinion diverges from that of the earlier reviewer.

If full justice is to be done to this work and possible objections to

---

[1] *AMZ* xvi (1814), 373–7. This was a review of the performance in the Mannheim Stadtkirche on 17 April 1814.

details of structure, style, instrumentation etc. for the moment laid on one side, attention must be paid to the dedication of the piece 'to Germany's victorious army'. In fact the composer has written a *Te Deum* to celebrate the victory not of one army over another, but of a people's alliance to liberate themselves from the yoke of a foreign tyranny. We are well aware from the pages of this journal that Weber is a man who undertakes nothing without first considering the justification of his action; so much we may take for granted. In view of the circumstances of this composition, he chose to write with a maximum of concision and effectiveness, brilliance, strength, volume of sound and mass effect. To achieve this he has used all valid means, especially loud and resonant instruments, and emphasized effects of contrast, particularly stressing passages of the text which might be closely related to the occasion, more especially those expressing praise and jubilation. Quieter and more clearly intercessory passages are given heartfelt expression but kept as short as possible; and the work shows that he has consistently borne these and similar considerations in mind while composing. The severe critic may well remark that priorities such as these will produce a work remarkable more for its suitability to the occasion than for absolute artistic value. This must be allowed, provided that it is also granted that to produce a work perfectly suited to such an occasion is also in itself a great achievement. Moreover, the critic who is acquainted with this *Te Deum* will be obliged to add that the composer has made extensive and well-planned use of truly artistic principles as the occasion permitted and as is demanded by the fact that this is church music, which itself imposes certain conditions if it is to be true to its essential nature. Certain passages may remain, in spite of everything, questionable. Is the volume of sound produced by four trumpets (three in E flat and one in B flat) perhaps excessive? Is the treatment of the Sanctus too hasty and too little varied? Is the *Te ergo quaesumus* too short, and was it necessary to omit an important section of the text? No general answer can be given to these questions, as all depends on the circumstances of individual performances. Having himself directed a performance of the *Te Deum*, the present writer can only make the following points. With a large chorus and a large body of strings, and using a good organ to support the basses with the pedals in appropriate passages, he did not find the four trumpets excessive. On the other hand he, and connoisseurs in the audience, felt that up to the fugue the whole work seemed rather hurried, and that it was only the short but sturdy fugue that first gave the music real stability and formed the real introduction. As for textual omissions, he felt strongly that of *salvum fac populum tuum* etc., an important passage and one particularly relevant to the occasion. Finally he, too, like the earlier reviewer of the *Te Deum*, found that the repeated rolling of the timpani defeated its own object and before the work ended became almost objectionable.[2]

The musical content of the work and the purpose and construction of the individual numbers have already been sufficiently described by the first reviewer, but it may not be superfluous to repeat a few points. After a short *maestoso* introduction there is a more extended Allegro, in which the words *Te Deum laudamus* are reiterated. There follow the short Adagio of *Te ergo quaesumus*[3] and then the final fugue (*Laudamus nomen tuum in saeculum saeculi*) mentioned above and carefully analysed by the first reviewer of the work. The present writer finds the preparation and introduction to this fugue original, excellently designed and most effective. This too was mentioned by the earlier reviewer, who illustrated his points by quoting from the score.[4]

The *Te Deum* is written for four trumpets, bass trombone, timpani, clarinets in B flat, bassoons, strings and four-part chorus. The omission of horns, flutes and oboes is not to be explained by the desire to lighten an orchestra which is not in any case very large (though such a consideration would be welcome, particularly in such a work as this), but rather by the fact that the instruments omitted, especially flutes and oboes, would have been ineffective. The printing of the score and the parts is clear and good. The vocal parts are printed both with the familiar Latin text and also with a very successful German translation, facilitating the performance of the work by conductors who are not allowed to give works with Latin texts.

It is worth adding that the composer has marked his tempos chronometrically, an easy and readily intelligible method recommended by him in No. 27 of this journal.[5] As far as the present writer knows, this *Te Deum* is the first work in which this admirable method has been employed, and it is very much to be hoped that other composers will follow Herr Weber's lead in this matter. The present writer's personal experience has confirmed the simplicity and certainty of the chronometrical method.

[2]   A similar opinion was expressed by *Spohr (*Selbstbiographie*, diary entry for 19 October 1815).

[3]   This consists of only sixteen bars.

[4]   Weber does not mention that Weiler disliked the introduction, in which first bassoon and then clarinet enter unaccompanied, with chorus and orchestra coming in at the eighth bar.

[5]   'Über die jetzt hervorstehende wirkliche Einführung des Taktmessers', *AMZ* xvi (1814), 445–9, 461–5.

47. Prague

Written: Munich, end July 1815.
Published: AMZ xvii (1815), 617–22.   *Signed:* M—e [Marie].
Reprinted: HHS (inaccurate); KSS; LKA.

Weber had been director of the German Opera in Prague since the beginning of 1813, and the work needed to reorganize the company – which he undertook, in every department, with characteristic thoroughness – gave him little time or occasion for journalism. In the summer of 1815, beset by a number of personal problems of which the worst was a break with his future wife *Caroline Brandt, he left for Munich. Here he found old friends, a cheerful social life, and the exhilaration of a city *en fête* in the wake of Waterloo. He was able to resume composition, and to write the present article on his adopted city.

It really is high time that the reading public of the musical world was given some hint of the artistic life of our city. A number of different circumstances have prevented me for the last two years from making full reports, and I was also anxious to wait until I could point to the success of certain new elements, new undertakings and new activities. Having been silent for so long, I should like first, before going into details, to give you a general idea of the prevailing artistic temper of the city, from which conclusions may easily be drawn.

There was a time when the capital city of Bohemia could claim almost the same status as a capital of music. Certainly a public that was the first to recognize Mozart's genius had good reasons for such a claim.[1] If this has since become merely titular, it is owing to a number of historical circumstances which have changed the nature of society and the atmosphere of the town, often for the worse. It is a well-known fact that those whose claims to any right are empty insist on their privileges more loudly than those to whom such claims are in fact due. The great noble and princely families, who once had their own orchestras, and the respected bourgeois families who used to foregather to make or listen to music – all these have yielded to the pressure of circumstances and drawn in their horns. The forces that brought about their downfall have raised up other layers of society, who have replaced the former leaders of the musical world and now form the music-loving public. The numerous musicians among the population of Prague have been reduced by the demands of many, mostly newly

---

[1] Mozart had been especially treasured in Prague since writing *Don Giovanni* for the city in 1787 and *La clemenza di Tito* for the coronation of Leopold II as King of Bohemia in 1791; he had previously had a great sucess with the performance there of *Figaro* in 1785.

recruited, regimental bands. Death, too, has naturally played its part. Neither support nor instruction could make up this loss, and the standard of musical culture gradually sank, and with it musical taste declined, leaving nothing but the memory of past glories and the old connoisseurs, whose inherited laurels were claimed as their own and boasted of by the young generation of music-lovers. They have often been assured that the musical taste of the Prague public is excellent, and so they believe it.

The chief source of all genuine culture is social intercourse and the exchange of ideas, and this is absolutely lacking in Prague. There is no centre where people meet, no large, wealthy or scholarly house with a circle of members who create public opinion and influence those who themselves set the tone of society. Each of the 'estates' or classes – noble, merchant and bourgeois – lives in a watertight compartment, yet they still fail to form entities. It would be true to say that each family leads a separate existence, only concerned with its immediate neighbours and relations. Many of the nobility spend their money in Vienna and visit Prague for a few weeks of the year at the most on the way to and from their estates. A large number of foreign visitors might act as a unifying force among these centrifugal elements in society, as is the case in Vienna, Berlin and so on. But owing to Prague's position and its lack of sufficient attractions, this element is absent. The few artists and scholars who live here often complain of these circumstances, which make it difficult for them to achieve the mentality and the spirit which mark the artist who is a real cosmopolitan and therefore free. Every artist in Prague owes his existence to some noble family and bears the title 'Composer to His Excellency Count So-and-so'. His opinions are those of his patron, who in his turn champions his own composer against the rest. The result is an absence of the spirit that refuses to be content with merely earning a livelihood and longs to embark on the high seas of art in search of new discoveries.

After this description, I shall hardly be believed when I say that in spite of these circumstances (which I have painted if anything in mild colours), the indefatigable efforts of a few have enabled Prague to take its place among Germany's most famous towns. In my notes on the existing institutions concerned with the arts in Prague, I shall give proper pride of place to the theatre, as exercising the widest influence.

The proprietor and director of the theatre, *Herr Karl Liebich, is one of those rare directors for whom art is more important than financial gain, as is clearly shown by his strenuous effort to influence public taste. (He is assisted in these efforts by the provincial authorities and a number of excellent men on the committee of the Ständisches Theater, and this should be mentioned in their honour.) This unremitting labour is all the more admirable in view of the fact that the Prague public is pretty cold-blooded and – as one wit[2] put it – volatile and apt to take off into the blue. They judge everything by foreign standards and never really support the director with the genuine fire of enthusiasm which he deserves as his reward.

Until 1813 *Herr Wenzel Müller was the music director of our opera house. Much as I appreciate his amusing popular pieces, he was not really the right man for the post, and Herr Liebich saw no way of effecting an operatic renaissance except by dissolving the company and suspending it for a time. He then engaged Herr Carl Maria von Weber, who was visiting Prague on one of his tours, and handed over the direction and reorganization of the whole opera to him. [I do not need to introduce Herr von Weber to you or any of your readers, as he is known to you as an imaginative, knowledgeable and experienced artist and a bold, industrious man of wide culture; and no one who knows him will deny him any of those qualities.][3] Herr von Weber tackled the situation with all the enthusiasm to be expected of a man whose devotion to art is total and wholehearted. The directors did their best to carry out his suggestions, and so after a period of only four months' closure the opera house once again opened its doors with a performance of Spontini's *Cortez* on 9 September 1813.[4]

There was an entirely new spirit in the house. Proper choruses were once again to be heard. The orchestra was led by *Herr Clement of Vienna, whose playing had tenderness, fire and precision and has never lost its original high quality, so that it would be difficult to find a better leader. On the 19th we had Catel's *Les Aubergistes de qualité*,[5] and on the 26th Méhul's *Joseph*.[6] And so things went on with uninterrupted activity, so that despite the marked deterioration of circumstances – the closing of the frontier, the war and the consequent loss of many potential members, not to mention much trouble with illness – our repertory includes all the outstandingly interesting works of the past and the present day.

This strenuous activity speaks volumes for the readiness and

[2] *Rochlitz, in a letter to Weber.
[3] This sentence was added in print by Rochlitz.
[4] With Wenzel Müller's daughter Therese Grünbaum as Amazily and her husband Johann Grünbaum in the title role.
[5] Catel's *Les Aubergistes de qualité* was first produced at the Paris Opéra-Comique on 17 June 1812. Though not then a great success, it did have, as *Die vornehmen Gastwirte*, a certain following in Germany.
[6] See below, No. 89.

enthusiasm of the members, who are united among themselves and well aware of the Kapellmeister's aims, and therefore work with pleasure and devotion. I shall later have an opportunity of proving this, though for the moment it would engage too much of my space. But I must mention our wonderful Mme Grünbaum (born Müller), whose superb gifts and capacity for work have not been properly appreciated, or even known, in Germany.

The second interesting institution that promises well for the future of music in Prague is the conservatory founded by the aristocracy.[7] As in the Paris Conservatoire, all instrumentalists receive their training here. It is directed by *Herr Dionys Weber, a remarkable theoretician and an enthusiastic and hard-working director. The other professors are for the most part chosen from among members of the theatre orchestra. The only one I have space to mention is the outstanding violinist *Pixis, whose playing has a strength and a spirit which he succeeds in communicating to his pupils. Although this institution is still young, the concerts given there last winter justified the highest expectations.[8]

Church musicians in Prague are in a bad way. The best are to be found in the Templars' Church and the cathedral. The latter has lately acquired *Herr Vitásek, well known as a pianist and composer and a man whose appointment promises well. There is no regular series of concerts in Prague, I am sorry to say, and we have to content ourselves with the summer concerts in the Wallenstein Gardens or the afternoon concerts at which *Herr Wenzel's pupils play. The only quartets are given weekly at the house of the banker Herr Kleinwächter,[9] who is himself a respectable violinist and a true friend of the arts, known as such by his fellow citizens and foreigners alike.

One quite outstanding branch of the art in its practical side is dance music, and it would be difficult to find any other town except Vienna where this is better cultivated. In fact local musicians are so enthusiastic that during Carnival there are often as many as three or four hundred balls – I repeat, three or four hundred – every evening. *Horribile dictu*! But police records prove it. Yes, it looks as though for years the love

---

[7] See below, No. 104.

[8] See below, Nos. 64 and 65.

[9] Ignaz Kleinwächter was director of the Prague bank Balabene and Co., and an amateur violinist and pianist. Weber first met him in 1811. His house became something of a second home to Weber, who often played there on his beautiful Streicher piano. Weber dedicated the Nine Variations on a Norwegian Air (J61) to him. His son Alois (1808–40) became a composer before turning to the law.

of music has been sinking – into the feet, and only a few remains of it are to be found higher up.

Concerts by foreign artists are on the whole rare. On the other hand, charity concerts are common. Every winter we can rely on anything from eight to ten such concerts, very pleasant occasions mostly organized by the staff of the opera house under their director Weber. The two concerts given annually by local musicians in aid of former colleagues' widows and orphans could be excellent, as those taking part form a large enough body to perform something quite exceptional. But since these gentlemen are more interested in notes – banknotes – than in rehearsals, it is luck if the performance is merely adequate. I should like to ask them if in future they could not be more discriminating with their programmes, and look for quality rather than quantity.

I close with the promise to give you more detailed information, with chapter and verse, in the future about the delights of our artistic life. I hope that I shall have plenty to discuss and that I shall have the pleasure of reporting an advance in taste. Hitherto so many splendid efforts in achieving this noble end have been ineffective, and ignored by the public.

48. The Frankenhausen Music Festival

Written: Prague, 10 September 1815.
Published: AMZ xvii (1815), 653–5.   *Signed:* Carl Maria von Weber.
Reprinted: HHS, MMW (both inaccurate); KSS; LKA.

The Frankenhausen Music Festival was founded in 1810 by Georg Bischoff (1780–1841), a local cantor and schoolmaster; and the first meeting took place on 20–21 June under the directorship of *Spohr. Its success, which gave encouragement to other festivals, was described by Spohr (*Selbstbiographie*), quoting *in extenso* E. L. Gerber's enthusiastic review (*AMZ* xii (1810), 745–58). The second followed in 1811; then war and other difficulties intervened to impose an interval until 1815. In the aftermath of Waterloo, there was now great enthusiasm for a festival that would reflect the upsurge of patriotism caused by Napoleon's defeat. The date selected was the second anniversary of the 'Battle of the Nations' before Leipzig two years previously, on 19–20 October 1813, and the works were chosen to express national pride and thanksgiving. Possibly Bischoff was worried about the success of the festival in difficult times, and hence encouraged Weber to write the present article drawing attention to it. Afterwards he was faced with a deficit, perhaps partly due to the quartering of Russian troops in the area and the consequent restraint upon movement by potential visitors. At Spohr's suggestion, the visiting musicians agreed to defray their own expenses, covering their costs

by concerts on their return home. It is a measure of the respect the festival
had won that they seem all to have agreed. The passages in square brackets
do not appear in the original *AMZ* review, but are in HHS and MMW.

It is encouraging to see the hope of international peace blossoming in
new initiative, and both art and science promising new life and
progress as the fairest fruits of peace! I congratulate myself on being
able to furnish further proof of this. The director of music at
Frankenhausen, Herr Bischoff, arranged a number of major concerts
in 1810 and 1811, and these were duly noticed in this journal as
something of interest to all art-lovers. It was a bold undertaking for
a little town far removed from major resources – the musical legions
of Vienna, the republican solidarity of Switzerland – and one entirely
due to the unremitting energy of a man who has thereby earned the
gratitude of his neighbours and the respect of the musical world.

According to the programmes announced by the organization in
Frankenhausen, this year's performances will be marked by a patriotic
tendency, which will make them of even greater interest and value to
every German. The general title runs 'German Musical Victory
Celebrations at the conclusion of the commemoration of the Battle of
the Nations' [19–20 October 1813]. We may confidently predict that
the festival, to be worthy of this title, will be even more brilliant and
distinguished than those of the last two years. An orchestra of three
hundred (including a chorus of 150) and the collaboration of
Germany's most highly honoured artists, *Andreas and *Bernhard
Romberg, Kapellmeister Spohr, the outstanding clarinettist *Hermstedt,
the excellent Matthäi[1] from Leipzig etc. make this prediction a certainty.
The festival will consist of two concerts in Frankenhausen's large and
handsome Hauptkirche. On October 19, from 2 to 5 in the afternoon,
Kapellmeister Spohr (who is postponing his departure from Germany
on a visit to Italy solely for this reason) will conduct in person a large
symphonic work written for the occasion, *Das befreite Deutschland*, with
a text by Caroline Pichler.[2] The respected name of Spohr is quite
enough to justify the highest expectations [and this performance will

---

[1]   Heinrich August Matthäi (1781–1835) was a celebrated leader of the
     Gewandhaus Orchestra.
[2]   Caroline Pichler (1769–1843) was a Viennese novelist and minor poet who
     ran the most celebrated Romantic salon of the Congress period. Schubert set
     three of her poems. Her complete works, which include historical novels,
     stories, plays and opera librettos, and translations (especially from Scott),
     run to sixty volumes. She found Weber's piano playing 'like that of Mozart
     and Beethoven – whom I often heard – rather than Liszt or Thalberg'
     (C. Pichler, *Denkwürdigkeiten aus meinem Leben* (Vienna, 1844)).

be followed by a ceremony of farewell as he undertakes yet another journey to prove German artistic prowess abroad]. It is a pleasure to know that we shall then hear a new work by the spirited and powerful composer *Gottfried Weber (Mainz), to whose pen readers of these pages are indebted for much excellent work [and indeed this will show him similarly able to speak with as much fire and vigour to the heart as to the intelligence]. His Te Deum[3] (published by André of Offenbach, score and parts) will form the conclusion of the festival and has in fact already proved its worth in many excellent ways. (In this connexion I cannot help expressing the wish that Gottfried Weber's superb four-part songs[4] [published by Gombart, Augsburg] and the twelve songs with guitar accompaniment [Simrock, Bonn] were better known to music-lovers.) [His Majesty the King of Prussia has expressed his appreciation by sending Herr Weber a gold medal. The Austrian Verein der Musikfreunde has also asked for the Te Deum, in addition to other works by the same composer; and its inclusion on this occasion is particularly happy, as an expression of his admiration for Germany's victorious armies.] On 20 October, from 10 till 1, there will be a concert consisting of performances by the artists associated with the festival, the programme to be announced a few days previously. Lists of subscribers for each concert (price 1 thaler) will be kept open until 18 October. The Town Clerk is making every arrangement possible to make the stay of visitors easy and agreeable; and I can only wish good luck to those whom time and circumstances allow to attend this festival at which the power of music will give them new courage, new ardour and new strength.

[3]   See above, No. 46.   [4]   See above, Nos. 35 and 37.

49. Introduction to Musico-Dramatic Articles

Written: Prague, 13 October 1815.
Published: KPZ, No. 293, 20 October 1815; revised version, DAZ, No. 25, 29 January 1817.   Signed (DAZ): C. M. von Weber.
Reprinted: MMW (Dresden version); KSS; LKA.

On 26 January 1816, Weber wrote to *Gänsbacher to say, 'On the 13th [October 1815] I started a new scheme for working on the public and wrote the enclosed articles which I've since published before each new opera.' He wrote in similar terms to *Gottfried Weber on 2 February, adding, 'This enterprise has aroused much carping and cavilling, but its usefulness is acknowledged, and I'm employing it with each new opera. One more thing to do, of course, but my aim really and truly is to work for quality.' These introductory articles were to be one of the most important areas of his criticism, and a vital instrument in his work on behalf of Romantic opera. So necessary and effective did Weber feel this policy to be that he repeated it when he moved to Dresden, prefacing his articles with a revised, and stylistically improved, version of his introduction (with a few minor local references slightly amended). It is this revised version which is here translated, with the passage printed in square brackets added from the Prague version.

Musico-Dramatic Articles
as attempts by means of art-historical observations and suggestions to facilitate the appreciation of new operas given in the Landständisches Theater.

Preface

Primitive man is content to watch anything that is happening; civilized man wishes to have his feelings touched, and reflection is agreeable only to the fully educated.   Goethe[1]

The course of history has given the genius of today a direction, which increasingly threatens our relationship to the art of the ideal. Such an art must abandon practicality and show itself superior to necessity, with the proper boldness; for art is a daughter of liberty and it is from spiritual, not material, necessity that she must receive her mandate. But today necessity holds sovereign sway and holds wretched humanity beneath a tyrant's yoke. Utility is today's idol and to utility all powers must submit, all talents bow the knee. On such crude scales as this the spiritual profit of art weighs nothing, and, deprived of all encouragement, disappears in the noisy market-place of this century.   Schiller[2]

I should like these magnificent words of Goethe and Schiller to serve here as an introduction; and the reader – on whose forbearance I rely in my efforts – will not hold it against me if, in my novel and rather bold undertaking, I take refuge behind the writings of great men as a kind of rampart. I feel that my present position is a challenge, involving as it does the welcome duty of influencing public taste and feeling by the beneficial agency of art. Long vanished are those happy days when the blessings of a universal and lasting peace encouraged everyone to dedicate his free time to the fine arts and sciences, when the appearance of a new work of art formed the topic of the day in all social gatherings, and when everyone – free of all external pressure –

[1]   From *Wilhelm Meisters Lehrjahre*, Bk 2, ch. 3 (1795–6).
[2]   From *Über die aesthetische Erziehung des Menschen, in einer Reihe von Briefen* (1795), No. 2.

spontaneously concerned himself with the higher things of life, as necessary to all men of feeling and nourishment for the spirit. Those happy days are vanished, and with them, inevitably, that essential concern of the public with artistic productions. Of course a really good work eventually establishes itself and becomes popular by its repeated appeals to human feeling. The effect, however, is quite different if such feeling is, as it were, prepared for the enjoyment to come.

It is the same in all departments of life. Does not everyone seek to be introduced into a social circle by someone who is already a member of it, and does not the introducer seek in a few words to communicate to that circle his friend's nature? From the cradle to the grave we rely on friends who take on themselves the duties of godparents. May I, then, also be allowed to recommend the works committed to my care, on their appearance, to those to whose service, entertainment and improvement these works are dedicated?

Of course, there is one danger against which I must be especially on my guard. I mean that in informing the public of the chief characteristics of my protégé, his artistic career and that of his creator, I must not present what is only a point of view – and one meant to facilitate the proper evaluation of a work – as though it were anticipating a judgement. That would be to affront the most precious right of public opinion. To have recognized this danger is already half-way towards avoiding it, as my efforts will show. Nevertheless, I feel that here too I must count on your indulgence towards what may well amount to excessive zeal in the good cause. The artist's enthusiasm, which he is so anxious to share with the rest of the world, may indeed on occasion lead me to overstep the bounds of plain reporting.

My overriding consideration will be that love of truth which is imperiously demanded of those who plead a cause before the public. I shall not allow the previous histories of the works concerned to go unnoticed, without being thereby concerned about their future fates. Not every plant flourishes in every situation: what will blossom in one climate may wither in another. Careful tending will at least prevent malformation, and in my efforts to cultivate what is good I shall not be led astray by the opinions of partisans who have no individual opinions and are only comparatively well qualified to judge. Experience teaches us that public opinion, taken in the round, is almost always right[, and that many fine works were appreciated here that only later won recognition in the capital, whose opinion we have so often had to follow. Finally, I should like to express the hope that my efforts in promoting the good cause will not be misinterpreted but appreciated].

50. Introduction to Meyerbeer's *Wirth und Gast*

Written: Prague, 13 October 1815.
Published: KPZ, No. 294, 21 October 1815.   *Signed:* C. M. von Weber.
Reprinted: HHS, MMW (both inaccurate); KSS; LKA.

*Meyerbeer's *Wirth und Gast* was a *Lustspiel* in two acts to a text by
*J. G. Wohlbrück. The plot was taken from 'The Story of the Sleeper
Awakened' in the *Thousand and One Nights*; it may be found in supplementary
vol. I of Sir Richard Burton's translation (London, 1885–8). Wohlbrück uses
the first part of the tale; the second had been already used by *Hiemer for
Weber's own *Abu Hassan*, which is no doubt why the characters' names are
altered. Meyerbeer had abandoned an *Abu Hassan* setting in 1810. The opera
was produced in Stuttgart on 6 January 1813, and, in spite of what Weber
says, was not a success. The performance cannot have been helped by the
theatre's standards, which, as Weber recorded in 1809, were low (see above,
No. 3) and which were not improved by the troubles of war. Little time was
given to rehearsal, and in winter the poor lighting and heating meant that
the house was often empty (*AMZ* xvi (1814), 334–9) – unfavourable
conditions even for so modest a novelty as Meyerbeer's little comedy. But the
new version, given as *Die beiden Kalifen* at the Kärntnerthortheater in Vienna
on 20 October 1814, fared no better, as Weber describes below. On 20
January 1816, he wrote to *Gänsbacher about the present revival, 'You can
imagine how delighted I am to have rescued the good fellow's reputation in
defiance of the Viennese.' The Prague performance was on 22 October 1815,
with the following principals: *Franz Siebert (Caliph), *Josef Kainz (Giaffar),
*Wilhelm Ehlers (Alimelek), *Therese Grünbaum (Irena). Weber gave the
work under the title *Alimelek, Wirth und Gast*, later repeating it (as *Alimelek*)
in Dresden on 22 February 1820.

Alimelek, Wirt und Gast, oder Aus Scherz Ernst.
Comic opera in two acts, text by Wohlbrück, set to
music by Meyerbeer.

It is a great pleasure to me to introduce right at the outset a guest who
will certainly himself play host to his listeners and one whom we are
doubly pleased to recognize – because this is a genuinely German
original work. The present writer regrets the fact that the repertory
of German theatres is flooded with foreign works. What is more, these
works generally appear not in their original form, but poorly translated
and subjected to cuts that are thought essential for local reasons. These
mutilations are often carried out according to the caprice of a single

powerful personality; and if the work is successful, it is for the most part thanks to the reputation that it has won elsewhere.

The librettist of the present work, Herr Wohlbrück, is himself an actor, who worked first in Hamburg and is now a member of the Hoftheater in Munich. He is a man of varied culture, loved and valued everywhere as an excellent and discerning artist. He is noted for his knowledge of the theatre, his eloquent delineation of character and his masterly elocution. The German stage is indebted to him for several other works beside the present libretto, and I hope to have occasion to return to these later.

In answer to the criticism relating to the appearance of slave-girls in the first finale (a gross libel on Turkish society), I must make clear that no blame attached to the composer in this matter. The slave-girls were first introduced in the Vienna production, probably with a view to filling the theatre, and at the same time obtaining women's voices for the chorus.

The composer, Herr Meyerbeer, is one of the finest, if not actually the finest, pianist of today. He is the son of a much-respected house in Berlin and has dedicated himself to music out of pure devotion to the art. He is an exceptionally well-read man and a good linguist, as well as one of the few composers of recent years to have made a really serious study of the art and its most recondite mysteries. In addition to being himself a thinker and a scholar he owes much of his culture to the two years he spent with *Abbé Vogler. His music is particularly remarkable for its lively imagination; attractive, often voluptuous melodies; correct prosody; good musical characterization; rich and novel harmony; and careful instrumentation, often marked by unusual combinations. As a tribute to his outstanding talents he was three years ago appointed chamber composer to His Royal Highness the Grand Duke of Hesse-Darmstadt, a personal choice.

The present opera was written for the Königliches Hoftheater in Stuttgart, where it was much applauded. The composer later rewrote the work with a special view to the Vienna production. It was given at the Kärntnerthortheater, where is was a failure – or rather, a number of unfortunate circumstances limited the performances to a single one, so that the public had no opportunity to acquaint themselves with it.

Without saying too much about that particular performance of a difficult work, which is full of the finest and most varied nuances, and demands little less than the ensemble expected of a quartet, I should like to make a few general remarks. The part of Alimelek was written for the singer Herr Ehlers, who was however prevented from appearing by unavoidable circumstances and was replaced by *Herr Forti. The melodic lines were altered, and thereby deprived of their original charm; whole numbers were transposed; and – without any reflection on Herr Forti's artistry – the whole conception of the title role, carefully designed to fit Herr Ehlers's personality (so popular with the Viennese public), was very largely lost. *Mlle Buchwieser was not well that evening and proved unable to perform her role with the power which has made her such a favourite with the public, who went so far as to give audible expression to their disappointment.

Accidents of this kind are quite enough to cause the temporary failure of a work of art, whose life and success hangs on such fragile threads. This is to leave aside a host of other minor circumstances which may prove unfavourable, among which I would myself count the presence of the composer. Personalities give rise to too many prejudices, both favourable and unfavourable, and partisan feeling is already high even before the performance. Time, however, ripens judgement, and time is the natural ally of all good causes. There was hissing at the first performance of *Don Giovanni* in Frankfurt, and *Joseph in Egypt* was given much the same reception a few years ago in Vienna, where it is now a great favourite.[1]

---

[1]   Méhul's *Joseph* was first given in Vienna in 1809; a new production was given at the Kärntnerthortheater a few months before Weber wrote this article, on 14 June 1815.

51. Review of Meyerbeer's *Wirth und Gast*

Written: Prague, 3 November 1815.
Published: AMZ xvii (1815), 785–8.   *Signed:* Carl Maria von Weber.
Reprinted: HHS, MMW (both inaccurate and abbreviated); KSS.

Wirth und Gast was given in Prague on 22 October 1815 (see above, No. 50, for further details). On 7 November Weber wrote to *Rochlitz, submitting this review to the *AMZ*: 'The only good and rewarding thing about my present job is the chance of winning recognition for some misunderstood work of quality, and of showing that something good must have a good performance if it is to be properly appreciated. The success of *Meyerbeer's opera has given me untold pleasure, and I ask you to find this little essay a corner in the *Musikzeitung*.' Weber's version was in three acts. It was repeated a number of times, with *Kainz replacing *Siebert, *Johann Grünbaum replacing Kainz, and *J. A. Stöger replacing *Ehlers.

During my holiday abroad this year it was repeatedly brought to my notice that this town and the works produced here are seldom if ever mentioned in the press. In the literary wilderness in which we live here I find myself ill-informed and also uncertain as to whether this regrettable situation may not have been changed during the recent months. I nevertheless take up my pen in order to acquaint the readers of your much-respected and influential paper with an excellent new German work and the reception that it has received from both critics and public. I feel doubly impelled to do this because, despite our repeated references to 'Germanness', and our desire to be free of all prejudice, foreign works are all too easily idolized here. Works by our own composers, on the other hand, are frequently subjected to so much carping criticism, so run down and so dissected, that they can give the public no pleasure, or only win acknowledgement after a long interval.

Herr Meyerbeer has made his name hitherto chiefly as a great pianist. This is a title which can be proved before the public, whose applause can be won, as it were, in the open field where it cannot be disputed. There can be no question of the listener asking the pretentious amateur or the cognoscente (who is often moved by envy) what opinion he is allowed to express about a pianist. Herr Meyerbeer's merits as a composer have not been so easily accepted. In the majority of places where his major works have been given, no allusion whatever has been made to them. In fact the only judgements passed on his gifts have been at best ambiguous and belittling, and this is true of his grand opera *Jephtha* in Munich, his *Wirth und Gast* in Stuttgart, his oratorio *Gott und die Natur*[1] in Berlin and even of his piano recitals in Munich, Vienna and elsewhere which were a great popular success.[†]

It is deplorable enough that the results of a public success, which the artist has had to purchase with his life-blood, often depend on individual caprice and are in the hands of those whom chance, garrulity, the itch to appear in print, or even plain hunger, have made the heralds and mouthpieces of public opinion. It would be something if their judgements and pronouncements were at least the expression of honest conviction. In fact, however, they are more often dictated,

[†] Neither is true of this journal, though Herr von Weber may well be right in asserting that too little notice has been taken of this young artist. We personally only knew Herr Meyerbeer in earlier days, as a charming and talented boy. At that time we heard a fine small choral work of his, which was printed as a supplement to this journal.[2] The Editor [of the *AMZ*].

[1] See above, No. 19.
[2] 'Preis Ihm!', for SATB, No. 2 of *Geistliche Gesänge* (Klopstock); published *AMZ* xv (1813), no. 4, suppl. 2.

for good or evil, by petty irrelevancies. There are plenty of sad instances in which failure to leave a visiting-card or a concert ticket has had disastrous results. But enough of such matters, and let us return to the subject which prompted this digression, the opera *Alimelek*.

The plot is taken from the story of the sleeper awakened, in the *Thousand and One Nights*. It is treated with unusual wit and whimsicality, and we must therefore congratulate the composer on the choice of *Herr Wohlbrück as a librettist. When a plot is handled with so much knowledge of the stage and feeling for character, both expressed in verses that seem to demand music, a composer cannot fail to be stimulated and inspired: such is strikingly the case here. Few musicians have the advantage of a text of such consistency and quality. What evidence, too, of serious artistic studies, what skilled transitions between independent melodic shapes, and logical consistency in characterization! No digression, everything dramatically true and full of vital imagination and charming, often voluptuous melodies, correct prosody, much rich and novel harmony and instrumentation revealing the greatest care and frequently marked by surprising combinations – I could easily produce examples of all these things, if experience has not taught me that the quotation of such features away from their context is never convincing, because their character depends on the contribution that they make to the whole work.

Exactly a year ago, on 20 October 1814, *Alimelek* was given at the Kärntnertortheater in Vienna, and failed – owing to a host of reasons of which I will only give a few, in order to explain this failure of such an excellent work. Herr Meyerbeer originally wrote this work for the Stuttgart Hoftheater. He rewrote it for Vienna, having special regard to local circumstances and in particular to the singer Herr Ehlers, who in such roles as that of Alimelek was a long-standing favourite with the public. This casting was frustrated by a number of unavoidable circumstances, and much of the music was changed, transposed etc. *Mlle Buchwieser, who was not well, had not the volume of tone needed for her difficult role and did not live up to her great reputation. Indeed, the public, with whom she is a great favourite, gave audible expression to their discontent. Thus a series of misadventures cast a gloom over the whole production and destroyed the uninterrupted concentration demanded by music in which so much depends on fine shades of expression. *Alimelek* received only one performance and therefore never had a chance of becoming known to the general public.

Here, there were two handicaps to be surmounted – first the knowledge of the Viennese fiasco, and then the Sunday audience, which is never so attentive or so judicious as the audiences on weekdays. On the other hand, we had Herr Ehlers, a singer of *Mme Grünbaum's calibre, and a universal devotion to the work. The reception was doubtful at the first performance, and this made the triumph of the second performance all the more decisive. This was on 24 October, when every number was applauded and many numbers aroused real enthusiasm. Even at the first performance the overture, a duet, trio, finale etc. were successful; and at the third performance, on the 30th, a full house and repeated applause made it clear that the Prague music-lovers still recognize quality and that the general public is always right in the last resort.

I cannot say more about the performance itself, since its direction was entrusted to me. Even so, I must be allowed to say a word not only about Herr Ehlers's gifts and enthusiasm, but also about our own admirable Mme Grünbaum. Her work always enchants the public; and her powerful, agile voice and pure intonation, coupled with the vivacity of her acting, made no small contribution to the revelation of the work's many beauties. At the same time, I should like to take this opportunity to thank publicly my orchestra and chorus for their indefatigable enthusiasm and diligence.

No doubt the vocal score of *Alimelek*, which should appear in the near future, will be welcomed on many pianos; and I shall have achieved my object if these few words draw music-lovers' attention to a new source of pleasure.

Herr Meyerbeer is at present in Paris and will soon continue his journey to Italy. He is writing a theoretical work, which should fill a notable gap in musical literature.

52. Report to Karl Liebich, director of the Prague Theatre

Written: Prague, November 1815.
Printed: HHS; MMW; KSS; LKA.

Weber had been appointed director of the Prague Opera in succession to *Wenzel Müller in 1813, largely under the pressure of *Karl Liebich's famous powers of persuasion. At the time he was hailed by the Board of Directors as the saviour of the Opera, and he set about reversing the decline into which it had fallen with the greatest energy and attention to detail. His repertory, which included a strong emphasis on French *opéra comique*, was planned to act as the creative springboard for German Romantic opera; his company was

formed with the intention of building up a true ensemble of singing actors;
his administration took account of every detail of operatic presentation in
pursuit of his ideal of opera as an art unifying all the theatrical means.
Inevitably, his reforms aroused some hostility from the same Directors who
had once welcomed him, but were accustomed to a simpler view of opera;
and Liebich's slackening grip – he suffered from disabling attacks of kidney
stone – meant that the theatre's policy came under fire when a new President
took over in 1815. By the summer of 1815, Weber himself had begun to fret,
finding Prague a backwater in which his career had become bogged down;
but he was nonetheless upset to receive the formal complaint from the
Directors which Liebich had to pass on to him, as he indignantly wrote to
*Gänsbacher on 20 January 1816: 'On the 13th [November 1815] I got a
letter from Liebich in which he told me that he'd had a complaint from the
Governors to the effect that *for the last three years he'd done nothing for the Opera.*
I wrote an immediate reply, which I wished you could have read. There
followed nothing but verbal excuses, it wasn't meant, etc. Isn't it unbelievably
wounding to find everything so misunderstood, even to be reprimanded, in
a place where one's done *everything*, and has sacrificed one's time, body and
mind? This has set the seal on my resolve to leave Prague at all costs.' Though
Weber's reply was in the form of a letter, not intended for publication, it is
included here as a statement of his artistic aims.

I must admit, my dear friend, that the communication which you have
sent me on behalf of the authorities, with reference to the position of
the Opera and claiming that nothing has been done on its behalf since
1812, has given me the bitterest moment of my whole career. In view
of my zeal in the cause of the Opera, I felt doubly surprised both by
the complaint and by the quarter from which it comes, one in which
my indefatigable activity has meant staking both my health and the
time which I could otherwise have devoted to my work as a composer,
writing for the world and for my own reputation – simply in order to
have the pleasant awareness of maintaining Prague's long-standing
reputation for musical excellence and at the same time showing that
there is at least one musical institution whose policies and actions are
dictated not by the usual myriads of petty considerations of the
profession and its jealousies, but by a spirit that is untouched by such
things and free from all irrelevancies.

On my arrival here in January 1813, nothing was further from my
mind than tying myself down by accepting any post. This was
incompatible with my views on an artist's influence on the public. The
only things that persuaded me to accept the direction of the Opera were
the above considerations and hopes – and the confidence that was
placed in me on all hands (though quite unsolicited) and chiefly the
personal respect and friendly feeling inspired in me by your attitude

and behaviour. There I imagined that I should have never-failing support in furthering my plans for improvement. I am thankful to say that I am shielded from the suspicion of any other motives by my circumstances and by the confidence inspired throughout the rest of Germany by my actions and my work.

I took up my post with the unshakable confidence needed by anyone who is at the head of an artistic institution and is therefore the target of any individual who differs from him in taste, mood or characteristics or who simply enjoys fault-finding. The musical taste that I encountered had been given a peculiar character by the Italian opera in former days and then in Mozart's time. It was unstable and undependable, not really sure of itself in any way. Italian opera demands, by its very nature, a few outstanding artists – brilliant individual gems, in what setting is irrelevant. Everything else is of secondary importance. The German goes deeper: he demands a work of art in which all the component parts are united in a satisfying whole. He is not indifferent to the French taste for lively action, which demands a series of events on the stage. His serious temperament seizes on and comprehends all that is excellent and tries to adopt it for himself. The first necessity seemed to me to be the building up of a good ensemble; nothing seemed to me irrelevant, for in artistic matters every smallest detail is significant. This point of view was approved by our monarch, who is a true and perspicacious friend of the arts. I later had a number of opportunities to learn from his own lips that he was pleased with the way that chorus and orchestra and theatre staff were collaborating.

Correspondence was opened on a large scale with artists whom I had met on my travels or such as had made a great reputation. At the same time we were concerned to make good use of the material at hand. The orchestra and the chorus were so organized as to ensure the quality of our performances by a careful adaptation of all our forces. After considerable efforts the services of *Herr Clement, the oboist *Sellner and a number of other players were obtained.

The war and other circumstances that I need not detail but are matters of public knowledge unfortunately prevented us from completing the staff according to our original intentions. We still retained, or more often newly engaged (since they were won to us by means of new agreements), a number of performers of whom any theatre would be proud. Among the singers I need only mention *Mme Grünbaum, Mlles Bach,[1] *Brandt and *Böhler and *Mme Allram;

---

[1]   Her few roles included Countess Almaviva and Elvira (*Das unterbrochene Opferfest*).

among tenors Herren *Grünbaum, Morhardt,[2] Neumeyer[3] and among basses Herren *Siebert, *Kainz, Manetinsky,[4] *Allram etc. Among those already engaged who could not come because of the war were the tenor Herr Tolle[5] and his wife, and Herr Rode[5] (*buffo*), and in the cases of a number of artists, whose names I list below, negotiations that had been begun eventually came to nothing owing to unavoidable difficulties, all of which can be explained in detail.

*Mme Harlas	Herr Pestaker[7] (tenor)
*Mme Fischer	Herr Tarti[5] (bass)
*Mlle Buchwieser	Herr Rosenfeld[7] (tenor)
Mme Gervais[6]	Herr Wild[10] (tenor)
*Mme Reg. Lang	Herr Schikaneder[11] (bass)
Mlle Herz[7]	*Herr Flerx (bass)
Mlle Seidler[8]	Herr Scharbök[7] (bass)
*Mme Flerx	Herr Kramer[7] (bass)
Mme Eberwein[9]	*Herr Stöger (tenor)
*Mme Weixelbaum	Herr Schiele[7]
*Herr Häser	*Herr Weixelbaum
*Herr Stümer (tenor)	Herr Hanabacker[7]

[2]   This name has been variously transcribed by editors from Weber's MS scribble as 'Mankard' and 'Markward', but what was intended must have been Morhard[t]. He was a tenor who sang various roles, including Alvaro (*Fernand Cortez*), Méhul's Joseph, and Armand (*Les Deux journées*) in 1813 and February 1814. He died early in 1814. Weber's manner of reference to him after the tabulated list suggests that he had already been mentioned. He is likely to be the 'Mohrhardt' Weber would have remembered as singing the first Rudolf in *Silvana* in Frankfurt in 1810; he also sang in Munich in 1811 (see above, No. 29).

[3]   His roles included Alvaro (*Fernand Cortez*), Mozart's Masetto and Annius, Jacquino (*Fidelio*) etc., but his name does not appear in the cast lists after February 1815.

[4]   Manetinsky (not Maletinsky, as transcribed in HHS and copied by others) sang Morales (*Fernand Cortez*), Antonio (*Les Deux journées*), Pedrigo (*Jean de Paris*), Masetto and many other roles in 1813–14.

[5]   These singers have not been identified.

[6]   This name was mistranscribed by all editors, following HHS, as 'Pewais', but Mme Gervais is certainly meant. Weber praised her to *Franz Danzi (letters of 16 March and 24 May 1816), and mentions her appearances in May 1816 as being well received. See also above, No. 5, n. 1.

[7]   No singer of this name has been identified. Weber's scrawl may conceal some other name or variant spelling.

[8]   Caroline Seidler (1790–1812) was the daughter of the composer Anton Wranitzky. In 1816 she moved from her native Vienna to Berlin, where in 1821 she was Weber's first Agathe.

[9]   Henriette Eberwein (1797–1849), daughter of the composer Johann Wilhelm

Morhardt died and Mlle Bach and Herr Neumeyer failed to satisfy the expectations that we had formed from the reports of those qualified to give an opinion. It may be said in passing that the public suffered less from these circumstances than did those whose business it was to ensure the supply of performers. It was difficult to build up a satisfactory repertory with a reduced staff and great efforts were often required to keep the existing repertory going. What we managed to achieve with the means at our disposal is vouched for by the complimentary notice that we received from all foreigners and those who had the opportunity of comparing our repertory and standards of performance with those of almost any noteworthy foreign theatre, not by any means excepting Vienna. Can you point to any of the recognized masterpieces that were not in our repertory, and are there any new works that we did not perform soon after they appeared? The recent engagements of *Herr Ehlers and *Mme Czegka are proof of our seizing every opportunity to complete the company. Let anyone who complains of the company point out artists who can do better and are not elsewhere engaged. Every theatre and every court keeps a hold on the good singers it already has and the troubled times have made talent hard to find. They are not a commodity which has only to be paid for and secured in writing in order to own them. What after all have we to offer a foreigner as a bait or an attraction? I have more than once been unpleasantly impressed by the criticisms of some pen-happy and uninformed critics in the public prints, as for instance a recent paragraph in the *Sammler*,[12] where the writer 'had hoped in

Hässler, married the Weimar opera composer Carl Eberwein in 1812, and made her career in Weimar as a light soprano.

[10]   Franz Wild (1792–1860) was one of the most successful Viennese tenors of his day. After singing in various theatres, he joined the court opera in 1814; here he became enormously popular, especially during the Congress. He worked in Darmstadt 1817–25, and toured widely, returning to Vienna 1830–55. He sang Max seventeen times in London in 1840. He was much admired by Beethoven, who arranged the song 'An die Hoffnung' for Wild and accompanied him in it.

[11]   Karl Schickaneder (d. 1845) was the son of Emanuel Schikaneder's brother Urban, and studied with his uncle. After working as a mining engineer, he joined the Josephstädtertheater as a director, then moved to Brünn and back to Vienna as a *buffo* bass. Though he evidently refused Weber's invitation, he did work in the Prague theatre 1820–34; and his name appears in Weber's cast lists, as Mikéli (*Les Deux journées*) and Dr Bartolo among others. A mother and daughter named Schickaneder, presumably his wife and daughter, also sang in Prague, the elder singing minor roles such as Lorezza (*Jean de Paris*), the younger Barbarina and Luisa (*Les Deux journées*).

[12]   A Viennese newspaper.

vain' that I should do something to improve the Opera. Of course for him and his like it means nothing to hear the precise yet impassioned orchestral ensemble in a finale. He seems to imagine that, like a musical second Prometheus, I can conjure up singers from clay. These masters of public opinion dogmatize with a confidence which the public may take for the truth; but the conclusion that I draw is that in Prague it is possible to diminish a well-earned reputation but not to increase it. In spite of that I don't allow myself to be misled in my actions, and never have, but rather place my confidence in the perspicacity of those who are knowledgeable and fair. If on the other hand those whose respect and satisfaction are my only reward, if they too are discontented with my work, then I have failed in the purpose for which I came here and have shown that I was unable to fulfil what was expected of me. For myself I only have the consolation of knowing that I have always done my best and must ask you to appoint – the sooner the better – an opera director better able to carry out the wishes of the public.

Please do not imagine that there is any bitterness – let alone any culpable defiance – in what I write. It is a matter of *pure conviction* that I can no longer be of service here. But so long as I am in command I can promise that the same enthusiasm and the same tireless effort will mark my actions until the very last moment, and you can be assured that my relations with you, both as artist and as man, will always be marked by the same respect and affection as hitherto.

53. Review of a concert by Franz Siebert

Written: Prague, after 30 November 1815.
Published: KPZ, No. 363, 29 December 1815.   *Unsigned.*
Reprinted: HHS, MMW (both inaccurate and incomplete); KSS.
    *Franz Siebert was a principal bass in Weber's Prague company, and one of the most versatile and active of his artists.

On 30 November a concert was given by the opera singer Herr Siebert. *Cherubini's brilliant *Anacreon* overture was followed by a duet from Niccolini's *Traiano in Dacia*,[1] sung by Mesdames *Grünbaum and *Czegka. It was a real delight to hear these two voices in duet; and performed by such artists as these, even such music as this, designed

---

[1]   Giuseppe Niccolini (1763–1842) wrote numerous operas, of which one of the most successful was *Traiano in Dacia* (1807). It was given in German, in *F. K. Hiemer's translation, in Stuttgart in 1812 and in Darmstadt later the same year.

simply to flatter the listeners' ears and to give the singer the widest possible scope for virtuoso display, made a great effect.

A Mozart pianoforte concerto was played by Herr Gläser,[2] a pupil of *Herr Wenzel, but proved a not very happy choice on this occasion. Herr Wenzel has the great merit of producing excellent pupils, but such a work as this demands considerably greater artistry. Herr Siebert sang 'Das Grab' with guitar and glass armonica accompaniment, and then a Polonaise with a highly coloured orchestral accompaniment. The public thoroughly enjoyed Herr Siebert's unusually fine voice, which combines strength and softness. It is greatly to his honour that he continues to work for further vocal development; and it is to be hoped that he will not be misled by public applause and attempt to achieve, by florid ornamentation and passage-work quite unsuited to the bass voice, that agility which is only natural and pleasing in sopranos and tenors. The text of his first song was particularly unsuited to this kind of singing, and a simple heartfelt style would certainly have been more effective. This criticism is inspired solely by admiration for his great talent and by the wish to prevent him from following by-ways which can only lead him astray in his search for perfection. The hymn from *Cortez* was very well sung and it was a pleasure to hear it again. Kapellmeister von Weber's *Lützows wilde Jagd* [J168], sung by a male-voice chorus of forty, did not fail to make its effect, though it cannot be denied that this effectiveness was not increased by the size of the chorus, which prejudiced the accuracy of the ensemble.

Two amateur players were good enough to make contributions to Herr Siebert's programme. Herr Dr Mertlik[3] played an Adagio on the glass armonica, and a pupil of Herr Wenzel's, the son of the late Madame Gläser, the actress, a pianoforte concerto. The public in each case expressed their gratitude.

[2]   Probably Franz Joseph Gläser (1798–1861), later famous as the composer of the very successful opera *Des Adlers Horst* (1832). At the Prague Conservatory (1813–17) he studied the violin with *F. W. Pixis and composition with *Dionys Weber; Wenzel taught the piano during these years. BKP mentions him as an Absolvent of the conservatory.

[3]   Vincenz Mertlik was a doctor and amateur musician who also translated a number of German comedies into Czech. Among these was Paul Weidmann's *Der Bettelstudent, oder Das Donnerwetter,* as *Neslýchaná nahóda strašlivehó hromobytí, aneb Zebraný student.* This popular comedy had been set by various contemporary composers, including Schenk, Winter and *Wenzel Müller. It is possible, however, that Weber was referring to Mertlik's brother Franz. Both registered at the faculty of medicine in 1782 as coming from 'Boemus Crumloviensis', i.e. Český Krumlov (*Schematismus für das Königreich Böhmen auf das gemeine Jahr 1813,* Abt. VII, p. 26).

54. Review of a concert by Anna Czegka

Written: Prague, after 8 December 1815.
Published: KPZ, No. 363, 29 December 1815.   *Unsigned.*
Reprinted: HHS, MMW (both inaccurate and incomplete); KSS.

*Anna Czegka was one of the senior singers in Weber's company, and a distinguished teacher (her pupils including Henriette Sontag) as well as performer. As the present review reveals, she was not only a striking singer but a fine pianist.

On 8 December a concert was given by Mme Anna Czegka, born Auernhammer. The programme opened with the magnificent, serene but impassioned overture to *Cherubini's *Medea*,[1] after which Mme Czegka sang a Cavatina from Niccolini's *Coriolano*.[2] Once again it was a pleasure to observe how much this excellent artist has profited from hearing the best singers of the day. The voice is full and powerful and her execution shows admirable taste. She must beware of accenting certain letters, for instance the letter 'i', which gives a slight sharpness to her tone. Apart from that her singing leaves nothing to be desired, and we may congratulate ourselves on having her in the company.

'Des Kriegers Abschied von seinem Liebchen' is a poem by *Theodor Körner to the melody 'La Sentinelle', with a final verse by Karl Schall[3] on the poet's death, set with full orchestral accompaniment. *Herr Ehlers sang this in a style of melodic declamation. Since mention has been made of Herr Ehlers's style, we can only add that the singer quite fulfilled the promise of his advertisements, and the deep feeling of his interpretation was rewarded by well-earned applause. The instrumentation of the accompaniment proved most successful.

Next Mme Czegka played a pianoforte concerto (No. 4) by Eberl,[4] and displayed a facility and brilliance which showed her to be a worthy daughter of her mother, who was recognized as an exceptionally fine pianist. We then had the pleasure of admiring the remarkable budding talent of *C. M. von Bocklet, whose performance of some violin variations by *Rode revealed the strides that he has made since we

[1]   *Médée* (1797) was first performed in German (translated by C. A. Herklots) in Berlin in 1800, and had a long and successful career on German stages.

[2]   *Coriolano* (1808) was one of Niccolini's most sucessful operas: it reached Vienna in 1810.

[3]   Karl Schall (1780–1833) was a Breslau playwright who also interested himself in politics and aesthetics.

[4]   Anton Eberl (1766–1807) was a friend of Mozart; his many works were popular in their own day, and included six piano concertos.

last heard him. May the Genius of Art continue to protect and guide him on the path on which he has made such a brilliant beginning, to the delight of all friends and admirers of beauty. The orchestra accompanied him excellently, and we cannot remember ever having heard such a perfect choice of tempo in the last variation but one (Adagio). The duet between *Mme Grünbaum and Mme Czegka, from Niccolini's *Coriolano*, confirmed the opinion which we expressed in our review of the previous concert [*Siebert's].

55. Review of a concert by Joseph Sellner and Michal Januš

Written: Prague, 15 December 1815.
Published: KPZ, No. 363, 29 December 1815.   *Unsigned.*
Reprinted: HHS, MMW (both inaccurate and incomplete); KSS.

*Joseph Sellner, one of the most celebrated oboists of his day and the founder of a dynasty of German players, joined the Prague Opera Orchestra as principal at Weber's invitation. He also played several other instruments, besides the guitar, and while in Prague (until 1817) studied composition with Tomášek. *Michal Januš was the first flute in the orchestra, and also a composer for his instrument. He taught at the conservatory until 1823.

On 15 December a concert was given by two members of our orchestra, Joseph Sellner (oboe) and Michael Janusch (flute).

The programme opened with a solid, well-written overture by J. W. Tomaschek.[1] This was doubly rewarding as it is seldom that we hear works by our native composers, who have nevertheless many fine works to their credit, as was shown by the warm applause which greeted Herr Tomaschek's music.

The flute concerto by Wilms[2] is for the most part dull and routine music, and it was only included to show our Janusch's full, handsome

---

[1]   Václav Tomášek (Johann Wenzel Tomaschek) (1774–1850) was by 1815 one of the most important musicians in Prague, as pianist and composer but especially as teacher and musical sage. However, though introduced to him on arrival in Prague by *Gänsbacher, Weber seems not to have had close contacts with him. Tomášek's most famous opera was *Serafina* (Op. 36: Prague, 1811); but as Weber does not mention this by name in his review, the work played was probably the Concert Overture, Op. 23.

[2]   Jan Willem Wilms (1772–1847) was a Dutch flautist and composer who played an important part in Amsterdam concert life. He wrote the Dutch national anthem which remained in use during much of the nineteenth century. Of his concertos for various instruments, there are two for flute, in D (Op. 24) and in G minor.

tone and expressive interpretation. In the event his uncertain health prevented him from playing his best on this occasion. A duet by Simone Mayr was then sung by *Mme [Katharina] and *Mlle [Marianne] Kainz. Mme Kainz's powerful contralto reminded us of her excellent training and vocal method, and all that we need recommend her daughter to add to her natural gifts is a diligent continuation of her studies, with particular attention to achieving a pure intonation. Herr Bayer[3] gave a virile and deeply felt recitation of a poem by Buri,[4] *Skizzen aus meinem Leben*. The guitar variations played by Herr Sellner revealed his mastery of the instrument but at the same time its insufficiency as a concert instrument. In spite of a noticeable hoarseness of voice *Mme Czegka was good enough to sing an aria by *Zingarelli, though for this reason she did not please the public as much as usual. Herr Sellner displayed his excellence as an oboist in *Westenholz's Concertante. Precision, judgement and purity of tone, coupled with technical mastery, marked all his playing and, combined with his fine tone and style of playing, reminded us once again of our good fortune in having him in the orchestra here.

[3] Franz Rudolf Bayer (1780–1860) was engaged as an actor by *Liebich in 1802, and remained in Prague as a mainstay of the company until 1842. At first outstanding in classical heroic parts, he later made a name as a character actor: he was especially famous as Schiller's Wallenstein and Goethe's Götz, and in Shakespeare. In 1817 the *Wiener Theaterzeitung* called him one of the few remaining tragedians of whom Germany could be proud. Weber's Diary for 9 December 1813 records, 'Chorus for *Romeo and Juliet* written for Bayer. In the theatre, Bayer's Benefit. *Romeo and Juliet*. The chorus was sung.' No trace of this work survives.

[4] Ludwig Ysenburg von Buri (1747–1806) was a soldier and the author and composer of various *Singspiele*. Stationed at Neuwied in 1785, he staged several of his works there, and became (at Goethe's suggestion) director of the local group of literary dilettantes and writers, the Arcadian Society of Phylandria. He was also a talented violinist. He married the singer Ludmilla Schetky (d. 1771).

56. Introduction to Weigl's *Die Jugend Peters des Grossen*

Written: Prague, before 24 December 1815.
Published: KPZ, No. 358, 24 December 1815.

Signed: Carl Maria von Weber.

Reprinted: KSS; LKA.

*Joseph Weigl's *Die Jugend Peters des Grossen* (1814) was one of the earliest of the many operas based on the episode in Peter the Great's youth when he worked incognito in the Saardam shipyards: it was preceded only by Grétry's *Pierre le Grand* and Shield's *The Czar* (both 1790), and Lichtenstein's *Der Kaiser und der Zimmermann* (also 1814). It was in three acts, to a text by *G. F. Treitschke adapted from Bouilly's libretto for Grétry, and was first performed in Vienna on 10 December 1814. Weber's final comments are clearly a reference to the Congress of Vienna, which began assembling in September 1814. Alexander I of Russia made a considerable impression on the city, with his intriguing mixture of moral idealism and political ruthlessness, and with his personal charm. It is possible – and, perhaps Weber is shrewdly implying, probable – that Alexander was the real model for a work that was hastily put together from Bouilly's original libretto that autumn and performed while the Congress was still in full session.

The first performance in Prague was on 26 December 1815, with *Wilhelm Ehlers (Peter), *Josef Kainz (Lefort), *Therese Grünbaum (Chatinka), *Franz Siebert (Gregori), *Marie Allram (Feodora) and *Caroline Brandt (Marina). On 10 January 1816 Weber wrote to *Gänsbacher, 'On the 26th there was the première of Weigl's opera *Peter the Great*; it failed, as it deserved, because of its dullness.'

On Tuesday 26 December there will be given, for the first time on this stage, *Die Jugend Peters des Grossen*, an opera in three acts, libretto by Bouilly freely arranged by F. Treitschke, music by Weigl.

I really need only mention the composer's name to be relieved of any further comment or explanation. Kapellmeister Weigl has conquered the public by his charming imagination and his understanding of the theatre; and they will be well disposed towards one of the latest productions of his muse. This represents a kind of relaxation on the part of the composer of *Die Schweizerfamilie*;[1] but it also indicates a new direction and a new gait, as any comparison between his present and his earlier productions will show. It is always attractive to observe how an artist and his public mutually shape, educate and guide each other. A single successful, widely appreciated work will not only spawn imitators and mere copiers; it also inclines the author himself to continue in the vein which has brought him success, and to prefer the means which have once proved effective to the risk involved in new attempts to win the elusive applause of his contemporaries.

The works of Weigl's first, Italian period are quite different in style and manner from his later works. Both have found a public; and in Prague, too, *Der Korsar aus Liebe*[2] and *Die Schweizerfamilie* are favourites

---

[1]   Weigl's most famous work, first performed in Vienna on 14 March 1809 and enormously popular on virtually every German stage. It reached Prague in the autumn of 1809.

[2]   *L'amor marinaro*, a *dramma giocoso* in three acts (1797) that also became popular in its German translation as *Der Korsar, oder Die Liebe unter den*

with theatre-goers. The atmosphere and colouring characteristic of the latter work are still to be found in this new piece, which will be sure of finding friends if only for its simple, catchy melodies and the instrumentation to which Weigl has given a very personal note in these later works. I should like to draw special attention to the overture, which is an unusually clearly constructed, passionately eloquent piece, most effective instrumentally and perhaps one of the finest things the composer has written.

As regards the treatment of the story, this is set in the interesting period of the Tsar who turned himself into a ship's carpenter and did not disdain any means of furthering his great plan; and we can trace at once the hand of the original French author, who has not hesitated to attribute to the rough and lusty monarch the gallantry for which his own countrymen are famous. On the other hand Herr Treitschke has tried to adapt the story to more modern ideas. At the time of composition European royalty (including the Tsar) were much in Vienna, and this must have had an effect. Human beings are inclined to view everything in their immediate surroundings in a sympathetic light and to allow their imaginations to attribute present characteristics to figures belonging to an earlier age.

> *Seeleuten*. Weber gave it, as *Der Korsar aus Liebe*, in Prague on 16 October 1814, with a cast that included the Grünbaums, Siebert, Kainz, Allram and Caroline Brandt (as Lucilla).

57. Review of a concert by F. W. Pixis

Written: Prague, after 6 January 1816.
Published: KPZ, No. 36, 5 February 1816.   *Unsigned.*
Reprinted: KSS.

Like some of the others which follow, this review was not included in HHS or MMW. It was first attributed to Weber by Kaiser, with good reason: from the end of 1815, Weber was the sole concert critic of the *KPZ*, and the reviews (which according to the paper's normal practice were anonymous) have the marks of his style and approach. *Friedrich Wilhelm Pixis taught at the Prague Conservatory from 1810, where he founded a distinguished line of pupils that included *Jan Kalivoda.

On 6 January Herr F. W. Pixis, violin teacher at the conservatory, gave a concert.

1. Overture by P. Pixis.[1] This extremely gifted young composer has

---

[1]   J. P. Pixis's four operas date from later: this must be some earlier concert overture.

already given much evidence of his talent and this substantial work makes it clear that he lacks neither ideas nor the ability to handle them effectively nor knowledge of instrumentation.

2. Violin concerto, composed and played by F. W. Pixis.[2] This shows that the artist has satisfactorily avoided the fault common among composers who write works for their own performance, namely the piling up of commonplace difficulties without considering the overall effect. The work as a whole shows taste and brilliance, and is so naturally put together that even the rich decoration gives the impression of being organic rather than merely ornamental. Herr Pixis's style is too well known to need describing in detail. He was as impressive in the Allegro, with his agility and virile strength, as he was with his ability to move the emotions in the Adagio and to frolic in the most delicate and gentle manner in the Rondo.

3. Scene from *Zingarelli's *Giulietta & Romeo*[3] sung by *Mme Grünbaum. Almost every day we have occasion to admire the talent of this artist, but on this occasion in particular we were impressed by the sincerity of her performance and the expression that she gave to every phrase.

4. Variations in the form of a march, composed and performed by Herr Pixis.[4] These contained exceptionally difficult double stops and gave the artist an opportunity to demonstrate the wealth and variety of his energetic bowing, for which he is famous. He was rewarded by the loud and repeated applause of a large audience.

5. Duet from *Paer's *Sargino*,[5] sung by Mme Grünbaum and *Mme Czegka. We have on several occasions in the past alluded to what these two singers can achieve together, and fear to repeat ourselves should we try to say something more on the subject of their joint artistic endeavours.

6. Double concerto for two violins by Schall,[6] played by Herr Pixis

---

[2]   Probably his Violin Concertino (Op. 1).
[3]   Produced in Milan in 1796. An adaptation of Shakespeare, with a happy ending, it remained popular throughout Europe largely through its championship by Malibran.
[4]   Variations on 'War's vielleicht um eins', for violin and orchestra.
[5]   *Sargino, ossia L'allievo dell'amore* was produced in Dresden in 1803. One of Paer's most successful works, it was given in Prague in the following year in Italian, and in German there in 1808.
[6]   Claus Nielsen Schall (1757–1835) was a Danish dancer, violinist and composer whose name had been known in Prague since a visit on which he had coincided with Mozart. On 8 October 1820 in Copenhagen he conducted a triumphant first performance of the *Freischütz* overture, eight months before the Berlin première of the opera.

and his admirable pupil *Herr C. M. von Bocklet. It is difficult to imagine a more rewarding contest than that of a master exercising his art to the full and his promising pupil doing his utmost to reach and support him. If indeed there is a more delightful feeling than admiration of this scene, it must be the thought of what both master and pupil feel on such an occasion.

Herr Pixis had prepared a further surprise for his audience by substituting, for the orchestra, students from the conservatory. Under the direction of their excellent conductor, *Herr F. D. Weber, these young players exerted themselves most laudably in accompanying the solo artists of the evening and were rewarded for their efforts by the generous applause of the artists themselves and the connoisseurs in the audience.

58. Introduction to Isouard's *Joconde*

Written: Prague, before 10 January 1816.
Published: KPZ, No. 10, 10 January 1816.   *Signed:* Carl Maria von Weber.
Reprinted: HHS; MMW; KKS.

Nicolò Isouard's *Joconde, ou Les Coureurs d'aventures*, in three acts to a text by Charles Guillaume Étienne, was produced in Paris at the Opéra-Comique on 28 February 1814. It was one of Isouard's most successful works, and became popular in Germany in various translations: the first was by Joseph von Seyfried, given in two Vienna theatres on 12 March 1815 and 1 April 1815. It was this version which Weber produced on 11 January 1816 as a Benefit for *Therese Grünbaum. The cast included *Josef Kainz (Robert), *Johann Grünbaum (Joconde), *Franz Siebert (Lysander), *Joseph Allram (Official), *Marie Allram (Lukas), *Anna Czegka (Matilda), Therese Grünbaum (Edita) and *Caroline Brandt (Hanka). See also above, No. 18 and below No. 95.

On Thursday 11 January there will be given the first performance here of *Joconde, oder Die Abenteurer*, a comic opera in three acts adapted from the French of Étienne by J. R. von Seyfried; the music is by Niccolo Isouard.

It is some years since productions of the French muse began to dominate the repertories of German theatres, and there is a growing taste for these pieces, light, easily staged here, whose delightful superficiality provides a pleasant form of entertainment. Among the more recent of such works, the opera *Joconde* is in many ways outstanding. The composer of *Cendrillon*[1] and many other works has

---

[1]   Produced at the Opéra-Comique, Paris in 1810. See Weber's review of the German première, above, No. 18.

here added to his familiar qualities – genuine high spirits, knowledge of theatrical effect, and so on – some Italianate vocal sweetness which will certainly not lose him any admirers.

I feel bound to observe that everyone who knows the opera must be puzzled by its title. It is not only the fact that the German *Abenteurer* is not at all the same as the French *coureurs d'aventures*, but also the choice of Joconde for the title role, considering that this character plays only a comparatively unimportant part in the story and is one of the least interesting participants. We have had the opportunity of comparing the translation with the original text and of suggesting a number of changes to obtain a closer approximation to the French. But it was not, as might be imagined, the Vienna adaptation that was to blame. Only one of the Count's arias was not translated; and for the rest the adaptation was as faithful to the original as could be expected in the short time available for such undertakings and so far as is permitted by the stiffness of our serious language compared with the playful, equivocal use of French. It can only be the fact of this opera's outstanding success in Paris and Vienna under its present title that accounts for an unwillingness to give it here under another. The fact remains that this title is quite misleading, since it suggests that the chief interest resides, as in *Jean de Paris*,[2] in a single character, whereas in fact the chief reason for the opera's success is the lively intrigue with its piquant situations.

   [2] Boieldieu's *Jean de Paris*: see Weber's introduction, below, No. 94.

59. Review of a concert by Ferdinand Fränzl

Written: Prague, after 12 January 1816, probably after 15 January.
Published: KPZ, No. 37, 6 February 1816.   *Unsigned.*
Reprinted: KSS.

*Ferdinand Fränzl became director of the Munich Opera in 1806, but continued to tour as a virtuoso, albeit one living to some extent on his early fame. Weber had known him since 1811, and was naturally called upon to help with the arrangements for this visit to Prague: he wrote to *Gänsbacher on 20 January 1816, 'Now I must solemnly tell you that Fränzl arrived on 1 January, stayed with me, I had to look after everything for him, take him everywhere, arrange his concert, which he gave on the 12th, leaving on the 15th.' Fränzl's old-fashioned manner, delicately alluded to by Weber, was more bluntly described by *Spohr the year previously: 'His playing is just as antiquated [as his music], and retains of its former excellence nothing but its vigour, which now frequently betrays him into indistinctness and poor intonation' (*Selbstbiographie*).

On 12 January a concert was given by Herr Ferdinand Fränzl, music director of the Bavarian court.

1. Overture *Prometheus* by L. van Beethoven. This magnificent, clear and solidly composed work was this evening played with exceptional ardour and precision by the orchestra.

2. Violin concerto, composed and played by Herr Fränzl.[1] He is a good, honest composer of the Mannheim School, which has produced many excellent violinists. His father held a high place among these and was largely the founder of that neat, clean and amiable style which makes no pretentious claims but has long proved a sound ideal for violinists.[2] Herr Fränzl's playing proved to possess all these merits, though he has not adopted the practice of the more recent school in such matters as variety of bowing, intensity of expression and often extreme technical virtuosity. His compositions are like his playing and their prolixity would relegate them in many people's opinion to an earlier age, as would the repeated cadenzas.

3. Aria by Wolfram[3] sung by *Herr Siebert. This seemed already rather overloaded with flourishes, to which the singer added some of his own. It is to be hoped that Herr Siebert will not be misled by the general applause which greeted his performance into this habit of adding ornaments – often quite unsuitable – to the works that he sings. It really constitutes an abuse of his fine voice.

4. Clarinet concertino by C. M. von Weber played by *Herr Farnik. It was a great pleasure to hear once again the talented playing of this honoured member of our orchestra in a concerto which revealed his agility and purity of tone. The same is true of his playing in:

5. Aria by *Paer, with obbligato clarinet. Here *Mlle Grünbaum sang with an accomplishment that seemed to excel even her own high standard of performance.

6. Concertino for violin[4] composed and played by Herr Fränzl. This proved a more attractive work than the concerto and was performed in the same style.

[1]   Fränzl published a set of nine violin concertos (André).
[2]   Ignaz Fränzl's playing was admired by Mozart, who described him as 'no great wizard [*Hexenmeister*], but a very sound fiddler' (letter to Leopold Mozart, 22 November 1777).
[3]   Joseph Maria Wolfram (1789–1839) studied law at the University of Prague, and later counterpoint with Koželuh. He held various civic posts while writing much music, including some ten operas. He became Mayor of Teplitz in 1824. The success of his opera *Alfred* in Dresden in 1826 led to his being offered the post of Kapellmeister after Weber's death, but he declined it.
[4]   Fränzl's Concertino (Op. 13e) was published by Simrock.

60. On composing the cantata
Kampf und Sieg

Written: Prague, 26 January 1816.
Printed: HHS; MMW; KSS; LKA.

Taking a much-needed break from professional and personal difficulties in Prague, Weber travelled to Munich, arriving on 18 June 1815 – the day of Waterloo. When the news came through, the victory rejoicings included a thanksgiving *Te Deum* in the Michaeliskirche, and on leaving afterwards with the idea of a victory cantata in his mind, Weber met *Johann Gottfried Wohlbrück. They discussed a plan, and by 2 August the text of *Kampf und Sieg* (J190) was ready. The music went more slowly, though it was all but finished by 11 December. The first performance was on the 22nd, a stormy day which served to keep the audience thin, Weber noted: 'The weather was foul, and the hall not very full. E flat Symphony went very well. *Grünbaum's aria, too. I played my C major Concerto [No. 1, J98] *well*. The applause was leaden. Finally the cantata. Went very well, and made a great effect' (Diary, 22 December 1815). The singers included *Anna Czegka, Therese Grünbaum, *Christine Böhler, *Caroline Brandt, *Josef Kainz, *Franz Siebert and *Johann Grünbaum. Despite the immediate enthusiasm, the work was severely criticized; and Weber was stung into sending the text to *Rochlitz, who printed it with an introductory 'Report from Prague' that is clearly modelled on Weber's reports and includes phrases from his comments on *Kampf und Sieg* (*AMZ* XVIII (1816), 154–8). Kaiser further identified other articles which include Weber's own phraseology. The assumption is that the present article was circulated to various sympathetic journals and friends as a defence and explanation of so unusual a work. Weber had particularly tried to avoid some of the excesses of other contemporary victory cantatas, as he told Rochlitz: 'I don't want to involve myself with an occasional poem shrieking praise and glory, with "Vivat Blücher", "Vivat Wellington" etc. every minute' (letter of 27 August 1815). There was no shortage of such examples to avoid, hastily turned out to catch the mood of the moment (see, for instance, below, No. 72). Weber was clearly affronted by the nature of the attacks, which he refused to take lying down: hence the writing and circulation of the present article. KSS, and LKA following, add music examples in relevant places; but there is a danger that these, in isolation, may emphasize the moments of literal illustration at the expense of the structure and other originalities which Weber was anxious to defend. The article is best read in conjunction with the score.

It was during the last days of July 1815, in Munich, that Wohlbrück and I decided to write the above cantata. We were both in a state of enthusiasm, excited by the recent great events, and believed that we could recreate for future listeners that strange, shifting series of emotions which must surely dominate any future perspective of our times, and give as it were a bird's-eye view of this period.

The form of such a cantata must inevitably differ in many ways from the conventional; and our real difficulty lay in making the picture that we had before us at the time equally clear to any unprejudiced listener who might in the future enter the concert hall with no more knowledge of the work than that provided by the title. Our first concern was to ensure a more dramatic handling of the material than is common in cantatas; and this of course meant problems for the composer. Nevertheless, the close relationship between the feelings aroused by the course of events and their immediate expression made this insistence on the dramatic element essential if the work were to be really alive. To the composer, what seemed most difficult of all was to unite, without any theatrical appeal to the eye, the two elements – music and drama – which were often contrasted and even emotionally contradictory. Only the reception of the work by the public and the judgement of connoisseurs can decide how successful I have been in this attempt.

In order to preserve the rapid sequence of events, I dispensed with the individual 'closed numbers', such as arias etc., which are normal in cantatas but could only be distracting in this case. Before turning my attention to details I sketched in my mind a complete plan of the tonal canvas and determined the basic colour of each section. That is to say, I wrote out clearly the sequence of keys, and hence of emotional moods, which I hoped would be effective. Then I considered the orchestration. I had determined on confining myself to a normal large orchestra, partly in order to make performance easier but also for another reason. The use of extraneous means and strange additions to the percussion section seemed to me unworthy of the noble art of music, and indeed proof of an underrating of music's particular powers. Nor was I interested in suggesting cannon or grapeshot fire, or the groans of the dying. My chief aim was to express human feelings on such an occasion by means of the different melodies of each nation, such as are in all mouths and ears and serve as the surest and most easily intelligible guide to the different national characters.

I will now pass on to matters of detail and shall hope by analysis to throw the right light on what I have already said.

To you, my friends, who know me, I need hardly say that when I call one of my melodies 'great', 'noble', etc. I am only referring to the intention, not the achievement. Thank God, I hope that I can say that I am still progressing, as I found that according to the 'temperament chart' recently published in *Musikalische Zeitung* (the essay on the artist's discontent, No. 35, 1815)[1] I am still, very properly, absolutely discontented with myself.

The mood of the musical introduction (D minor, strings with four horns, bassoon and timpani) is abrupt – stormy – lamenting – vehemently accented. Towards the end it becomes more powerful and finally dies away with a kind of ill-suppressed throbbing. It contains anticipations and hints of things to come (for instance, the passage which begins 'nun enger und enger umdrängt der Dränger') followed by the full chorus (also in D minor) beginning 'reisst wieder sich die Zwietracht los' in the same mood. Faith (bass) then has a recitative in B flat, with clarinet and bassoon – 'Völker, verzaget nicht'. The trio which follows ('Brüderlich, Hand in Hand') is sung by soprano, tenor and bass and is in G major, with a cello obbligato. The agitated opening ritornello has a *ritardando* which gradually gathers strength and introduces the chorus of warriors (C major). At the words 'Horch! das war Freundes Jubelklang' a passing reference to the Austrian Grenadiers' March is heard in the orchestra. The chorus ends powerfully and impressively with the words 'Die Hyder in den Staub gedrückt'. N.B.: no trumpet or timpani. Two muffled drum-rolls on E are followed by an arrogant 'March of the Enemy' in A major with shrieking piccolos, oboes, horns and bassoons, the 6/8 rhythm set by the side-drum (eight bars). I wanted to introduce the warriors' prayer into this march, and believe I found a satisfactory way of doing so. The prayer is heard in long notes, in a measure different from that of the march, so that the two are independent of each other and are self-contained. As the march gradually fades, sinister forebodings of disaster gradually approach in isolated trumpet calls, and finally the battle itself explodes, in D minor. It rages up to a certain moment, when it seems to die down; whereupon we hear the arrogant 'Ah! ça ira' (D major) in the wind instruments, interrupted by the warriors' exclamations ('Der Feinde Spott?'). After this the whole orchestra takes up the 'Ça ira' and the movement ends in an infernal exaltation with a blaze of trumpets. A pause follows. Then come isolated horn calls (E flat and high B flat) for which I used the correct Prussian Jäger regimental bugle calls – 'Avantgarde vor!' 'Masse formiert!' 'Angriff!' etc., against which are heard the warriors' exclamations – 'Ha, welch ein Klang!' etc. (voices alone); and the melody taken from my own setting of *Körner's *Lützows wilde Jagd* [J168] at the passage

[1] 'Die Unzufriedenheit des Künstlers mit sich selbst', *AMZ* xvii (1815), 581–9. This was an essay on the artistic temperament, especially on its self-questioning aspect.

'O Himmelslust in Todesdrang, das ist Freundes mutiger Schlachten-gesang'. The battle blazes up again (E flat; and, for the first time, trombones). The warriors have hardly sung the first four lines ('den Kampf erneut') when the enemy's 'Ça ira' is heard. They believe themselves to be the victors, but they are immediately interrupted by chords on full orchestra, in ever briefer segments, which finally drown them. The music now modulates in unexpected ways, making it impossible for the listener to be sure of its direction, until at last it reaches E major as the 'Turkish music' is heard for the first time and we hear the terrifying cry of 'Hurrah!'. After the words 'Setzt an den zersprengten flüchtigen Tross den letzten Hauch von Mann und Ross' the 'Hurrah!' is repeated and finally all the wind, with trumpets and trombones, break into the noble 'God save the King!',[2] while the strings, side-drum etc. continue the battle to its final moment. Rhythms and instrumental figures pursue here such an unusual sequence that the immediate transition from quick 4/4 to 3/4 is hardly noticeable, as each crotchet of the 3/4 has the same value as a whole bar of the earlier tempo and the demisemiquavers have the same value as the earlier quavers.

In this way I believe that I have suggested the true greatness of the German and English peoples as in the first flush of victory they raise their hearts to heaven in thanksgiving, in contrast to the devilish glee of the enemy. Faith now embarks, after three solemn and simple chords in C major (cello and trombones), on a recitative 'Söhne des Ruhms' ending with the words 'preisen Euch als des Jahrhunderts Glanz'. The soprano then enters with the words 'wo ewiger Friede ist', the tenor 'wo keine Träne fliesst', the bass 'sich jeder Wunde schliesst', and all three together 'dort in Unsterblichkeit', with all three concluding the recitative at 'lohnt Euch der Kranz'. Then the full chorus sings (F major) in unision 'Das Wort des Herrn ist Felsengrund'. There follows a simple, noble melody for clarinet and bassoon, which is taken up by three solo voices at 'wo auch nur zwei im festen Bund'. A lively D minor ritornello introduces the soprano recitative from 'die Ihr des Unterdrückers Macht' to 'preis't, Völker, Gottes Namen'. Then the whole chorus, unaccompanied, sings a chorale-like melody, to the words 'Herr Gott, Dich loben wir', which later becomes the theme of the fugue and is always associated with a full close. We now hear the full splendour of the orchestra (D major), exultant but filled with awe. The remaining words are treated as a prayer, accompanied by a winning violin melody – 'gib und erhalte den Frieden der Welt' – sung

---

[2]   Weber later used this orchestration in his *Jubel-Ouvertüre* (J245).

by four voices and leading up to the fugue, whose theme, after taking many different forms, is combined with that of the four solo voices and closes in jubilant thanksgiving.

And so, my dear friends, you have my account of all that I thought and felt and of what I sought to depict in moods of different colour. *How* the whole work has come about is a question of a gift from above, and I leave it to the judgement of the world.

61. Introduction to Gaveaux's *L'Echelle de soie*

Written: Prague, before 11 February 1816.
Published: KPZ, No. 42, 11 February 1816. *Signed:* Carl Maria von Weber.
Reprinted: HHS; MMW; KSS.

Pierre Gaveaux's *L'Echelle de soie*, in one act, to a text by F.-A.-E. Planard, was produced in Paris at the Opéra-Comique on 22 August 1808. It was translated for Vienna by *Treitschke as *Die Strickleiter* (1814), and though it did not match the popularity of *Le Petit matelot*, Gaveaux's most successful work in Germany, it did have a following. Exceptionally, Weber does not give a cast list for the Prague performance in his Notizen-Buch; and despite his remarks about authenticity, he describes the work as being by 'Isouard and others'. Planard's play is also the source of Rossini's *La scala di seta* (1812).

Today, Sunday 11 Feburary, will witness the first performance in our theatre of a one-act opera entitled *Die Strickleiter*, with a libretto by Treitschke based on the French of Planard, music by Gaveaux. This is the composer of *Le Petit matelot* and several little operas very popular in France and Germany. Only a few of Gaveaux's musical numbers remain in this version, as four other numbers were substituted for the originals in Vienna. But these extraneous additions are so well chosen, belonging (with the exception of the first duet) to the same musical world and forming together such a charming bouquet, that on this occasion we can only applaud what is, in principle, deplorable and unhappily becoming increasingly common – I mean the prejudicing of the uninstructed against a composer by inserting what are often the most alien pieces into his works. Since such things are precisely the concern of these notices, I append a list of the pieces inserted into Gaveaux's work: No. 1, duet by *Weigl; No. 2, Cavatina by Spontini; No. 3, Polacca by Gaveaux; No. 4, duet by Isouard; No. 5, ariette by Gyrowetz; Nos. 6, 7, 8, 9, by Gaveaux.

The story and characterization of the work reveal French skill and

French manners in the handling of the material. The whole is amusing and carefree, continues to be a success in Vienna and certainly deserves to be.

62. Review of a concert by Franz Král

Written: Prague, 6 March 1816.
Published: KPZ, No. 113, 22 April 1816.   *Unsigned.*
Reprinted: HHS, MMW (both very inaccurate); KSS.

František (Franz) Král was the son of the veteran violinist Václav Král (1756–1824), who had played in the opera orchestra in the première of *Don Giovanni* under Mozart. In Weber's day, Václav played second to *Franz Clement on the first desk of the first violins; his son played on the second of the two desks, and was marked by Weber in the Notizen-Buch as 'soloist'. DKB describes him as 'one of the best violinists', and records that he gave his first concert in 1807, with great success.

On 2 March a concert was given in the Redoutensaal by Herr Franz Kral, member of the orchestra of the Landständisches Theater. If in fact only great virtuosity justified the giving of a public concert, many of last winter's concerts would not have taken place; public interest would have been less, but better concerts might have had larger audiences. Certainly we should applaud Herr Kral's striving for perfection, and this indigenous talent deserved the encouragement of his fellow citizens. His performance of a violin concerto by [*Rodolphe] Kreutzer and some variations by *Rode showed that he has made great progress during the last few years; and we hope that his diligence and devotion will soon enable him to leave nothing more to be desired in the way of pure intonation and more especially clarity of execution.

The programme opened with the Grand Overture to the opera *Der Beherrscher der Geister* by C. M. von Weber, which was well played throughout. *Mme Grünbaum charmed us all, as usual, in an aria by Liverati.[1] Beethoven's *Egmont* also went well, and held the audience spellbound; and it was only in a duet from *Paer's *Die Wegelagerer*,[2]

---

[1] Giovanni Liverati (1772–after 1835) was a tenor and composer who travelled widely in Europe (including to London) and had considerable success in his day with his many operas.

[2] *I fuorusciti di Firenze* (1802), in two acts to a text by Angelo Anelli, was the first opera Paer wrote for Dresden, when it was praised as one of the best works written by an Italian for the German stage (*AMZ* v (1802), 206). It was given in Prague in Italian in the same year, and in C. W. Franke's translation as *Die Wegelagerer* again in 1808; in this version it was popular throughout Germany.

sung by *Mme Czegka and *Herr Siebert, that we could have wished for a more precise ensemble.

63. Review of Therese Grünbaum's concert

Written: Prague, after 6 March 1816.
Published: KPZ, No. 113, 22 April 1816.   *Unsigned.*
Reprinted: HHS, MMW (both inaccurate); KSS.

*Therese Grünbaum was one of the singers Weber admired most in his company; and she had been a favourite with Prague audiences since her arrival with her father, *Wenzel Müller, in 1807. This seems to have been her last public concert before she left to take up a new engagement in Vienna later in the year. The final, bracketed sentence does not appear in the original published version but was first added in HHS.

On 6 March Mme Therese Grünbaum (born Müller) gave a concert in the Redoutensaal.

The overture and introduction from Spontini's *Cortez*[1] proved once again that music written for the stage and dramatic effect loses much of its effectiveness in the concert hall. This would account for the cool reception which these excellent pieces met, despite the excellent performance, both orchestral and choral. Mme Grünbaum sang *Zingarelli's Cavatina with all the magic that an agile and well-trained voice can give to the well-chosen decorations proper to this kind of music, and she was as usual warmly applauded by the public.

*Herr F. W. Pixis, professor at the conservatory, adorned the programme by performing a violin concerto of his own.[2] His powerful and spirited playing was admirably suited to the attractive music, excellently written for the solo instrument, and shone in the most difficult passages. It is to be hoped that he will not go too far in piling up such demanding passages.

The scene with chorus from *Paer's *Sofonisba*[3] is one of the best examples of its kind, and here Mme Grünbaum displayed true grandeur

---

[1]   *Fernand Cortez* was the opera with which Weber had chosen to open his Prague repertory on 9 September 1813, when Therese Grünbaum sang Amazily.   [2]   Cf. above, No. 57.

[3]   *Sofonisba,* in two acts to a text by Domenico Rossetti after Girolamo Francesco Zanetti's text for Jommelli (1746), was produced in Bologna for the inauguration of the Teatro del Corso in 1805. It was given in Dresden in 1806, when the *AMZ* made it the text of a sermon against the Italian refusal to treat opera as 'a large, lyric-dramatic entity' (*AMZ* VIII (1806), 490).

and power, both of interpretation and vocal range, at the opposite pole to the charm which she had earlier demonstrated. The duet from *Vogler's *Castore e Polluce*[4] (actually written for two sopranos) was sung by Mme Grünbaum and her husband but proved unimpressive; and Beethoven's *Coriolan* overture was not so effective as our excellent orchestra usually makes it. [It should be said, by the way, that the duration of these concerts is dictated by the fact that the orchestra has to play in the theatre on the same day and this causes a sense of haste which spoils the enjoyment of the performance.]

> [4] *Castore e Polluce* was produced in Munich in 1787. It long remained a tradition in the city for the Chorus of Furies to be introduced into the finale of *Don Giovanni*, as Weber mentions without comment in the letter to *Gottfried Weber (11 March 1811) and as the *AMZ* reported (*AMZ* xxvi (1824), 585).

64. Review of the first concert by pupils of the Prague Conservatory

Written: Prague, after 19 March 1816.
Published: KPZ, No. 113, 22 April 1816.   *Unsigned.*
Reprinted: HHS, MMW (both very inaccurate); KSS; LKA.
    The Prague Conservatory was founded in 1811, and quickly made a good impression on the musical life of the city. For Weber's account of the new institution, see below, No. 104.

On 19 and 26 March the pupils of the conservatory gave their annual concerts. The present writer has sincere pleasure in dwelling on the high musical standards achieved by the co-operation of private individuals and the efforts of an excellent staff, who devote themselves to the musical future of Bohemia. In the few years of its existence, this splendid enterprise has already promised to bear handsome fruit, and the individual performances heard for the first time on this occasion suggest that this fruit will not be long in maturing. This is an admirably public-spirited institution, and its foundation and organization are not as widely known throughout the country as they should be. In answer to the requests of a number of true music-lovers, we shall be giving our readers a short sketch of its work in our forthcoming pages.[1]
    The programme of the first concert was:
    1. Symphony by Mozart (the large one in C major).[2] A highly

> [1] Below, No. 104.
> [2] K551. The work was not known as the 'Jupiter' until after Mozart's death, and the nickname was not used by Weber.

exacting task, which was exceptionally well and gratefully fulfilled. The playing throughout was precise and spirited. The ability to relax without losing intensity will come with time.

2. Clarinet concerto by *Cartellieri, played by Franz Blatt.[3] After some initial nervousness, this performance was fairly secure. Any lack of tonal beauty may well be put down to his instrument, but this young artist is urged to pay particular attention to pure intonation.

3. The aria from Così fan tutte[4] by Mozart, sung by *Mme Grünbaum, received an excellent accompaniment. As this is notoriously the most difficult task for any orchestra, success was particularly gratifying in this instance.

4. Double concerto for two violins by [*Rodolphe] Kreutzer, played by Vinzent Bartak[5] and Johann Taborsky.[6] This is a well-designed study in simultaneous bowing and in that mutual adaptability of each player to his partner, which is in fact the secret of good performance. This was a most laudable performance.

5. Horn concertino by *Duvernoy, played by Joseph Zwrczek.[7] Everyone in the audience must have been surprised and delighted to hear such control, such beauty of tone and interpretation from so young a player. If he continues in the way that he has begun, we can promise ourselves a first-rate horn player.

6. The powerful overture to Winter's Tamerlan[8] closed the programme. The performance was admirably accurate and powerful. The present writer would only like to emphasize that, in his opinion, a

[3]   Franz Blatt (b. 1793) first studied painting before taking up music; at the conservatory he was a pupil of *Dionys Weber and of the clarinettist *Farník (principal in Weber's orchestra). In 1820 he himself became professor at the conservatory, then (1832?) co-director. FétisB calls him 'the most famous contemporary clarinettist in Germany', and praises his brilliant and expressive playing and the beauty of his tone.

[4]   Così fan tutte had been popular in Prague ever since 1791 (one of the earliest productions), and was revived in various German adaptations based on *G. F. Treitschke's translation.

[5]   Vincenc Barták (1797–1861) studied with *Pixis at the conservatory 1811–17, subsequently joining the opera orchestra and also becoming a respected teacher. He wrote an early Czech Singspiel, Pražští sládci (1821–4).

[6]   Jan Taborský came from Kraštice, and was a student at the conservatory 1812–17.

[7]   Joseph Cvrček (Zwrczek, Zavertschek) was a student at the conservatory 1811–17, and one of four scholars (the others being Gellert and Maršíček (see below, No. 65) and *Kalivoda).

[8]   Winter's Tamerlan was produced in Paris, at the Opéra, in 1802. It was his only French opera, and subsequently became known in Germany in Joseph Sonnleithner's translation.

slightly slower tempo would have made the performance even more effective.

65. Review of the second concert by pupils of the Prague Conservatory

Written: Prague, after 26 March 1816.
Published: KPZ, No. 113, 22 April 1816.   *Unsigned.*
Reprinted: HHS, MMW (both inaccurate); KSS; LKA.
    See above, No. 64; also below, No. 104, for Weber's account of the Prague Conservatory.

The programme of the second concert, on 26 March, opened with Beethoven's magnificent, lucid and fiery Symphony in C major, which was given a lively and carefully nuanced performance. A number of people observed after the first concert that the basses were rather weak, and today therefore their numbers were increased. The authorities concerned must pay the greatest attention to ensemble, especially in the wind. The present writer is very well aware of the difficulties that all orchestras experience in this matter and of the cause, which lies in a number of technical, physical and mechanical circumstances. Even so, young players cannot be too forcibly impressed with the importance of the matter.
    2. Oboe concerto by Bahrdt[1] played by J. Marschitschek[2] – a secure performance characterized by excellent, but perhaps too frequent, staccato.
    3. An aria from *Cherubini's *Faniska*[3] was beautifully sung by *Mme Grünbaum and were accompanied by the orchestra. But it proved not very effective in the concert hall and needed a stage setting.
    4. Adagio and Polonaise by *Rode played by *Johannes Kalliwoda

----

[1] Friedrich Philipp Barth (1773–1804) was the son of a famous oboist, Christian Samuel Barth, and brother of another oboist, Christian Friedrich Barth (1787–1861). Both brothers wrote oboe concertos, among other music for their instrument.
[2] František Maršíček came from Michle, and was at the conservatory 1812–1817 as a scholar.
[3] *Faniska* was produced in Vienna, at the Kärntnerthortheater, in 1806. It was Cherubini's only *Singspiel*. The first performance in Prague, on 3 May 1807, was to inaugurate the German opera house. Weber revived it, as his seventh new production, on 7 November 1813, with Therese Grünbaum in the title role.

who, considering his extreme youth, gave an efficient and expressive performance.

5. There was apparently not time for more than a single movement from Stumpf's bassoon concerto.[4] Anton Gellert[5] gave every sign of becoming a very respectable performer – a well-controlled performance and a good, secure tone.

Mozart's overture to *Die Zauberflöte*,[6] taken at a very fast tempo and very well played, was the last work in the programme. Every member of the audience must have left the hall delighted by the standard of performance and by the flourishing state of the country's music students.

[4]   Johan Christian Stumpf (d. 1801) was a celebrated bassoonist who worked in Paris around 1785, then moved to Germany and became répétiteur in Frankfurt. He wrote four bassoon concertos.

[5]   Possibly a relation of the Czech composer Josef Gellert (1787–1842). He was at the conservatory 1813–17, and then took up a post in Russia.

[6]   *The Magic Flute* received its first production after the Vienna première in Prague on 25 October 1792, and was subsequently performed there in Italian and in Czech (1794).

66. Review of the first concert for the Workhouse inmates

Written: Prague, after 22 March 1816.
Published: KPZ, No. 119, 28 April 1816.   *Unsigned.*
Reprinted: HHS, MMW (both incomplete and inaccurate); KSS.

This review was accepted by HHS and, following him, MMW, as being by Weber, though they omitted the sentence in square brackets. Possibly it was an editorial addition: though happy to draw attention to his own enterprises and intentions (as in the first paragraph), Weber did not use the cloak of anonymity to praise himself.

On 22 and 29 March two concerts in aid of the fund for the inmates of the Workhouse were given in the Redoutensaal. They were organized and conducted by the director of the Opera, C. M. von Weber, who is plainly concerned on every occasion with accustoming the public to a diet of the more serious kind of music, and through whom we often hear a number of great works that ordinary concert-givers omit from their programmes, in their concern to attract the public by variety. In the first of these concerts we had a whole symphony by Haydn, well performed except for a few small blemishes in the Adagio. This was

followed by Beethoven's oratorio *Christus am Ölberge*[1] with Herr and
*Mme Grünbaum, *Herr Siebert and the chorus of the Landständisches
Theater.

Beethoven's genius often shines out here in individual numbers; but
the present writer finds that the work as a whole lacks unity of
conception and style, and also that noble simplicity which should be
the distinguishing mark of the oratorio. The dramatic choruses often
recall the theatre and prompt a wish to hear them in such
surroundings – a wish that speaks well for the dramatic character of
the music but not for the actual character of the genre. The present
writer also missed what is the crowning glory of the more serious style,
namely the fugue. An attractive fugal theme appeared but was almost
immediately abandoned. If great composers allow themselves these
breaks with tradition and casual treatment of important ideas, their
example has a bad effect on the deepest forms of musical study, which
is already in decline.

The orchestral playing was precise and the choral singing really
outstanding. A few years ago we could not boast of any good choir,
so that the present success was all the more rewarding[; and we must
express here our thanks for the power and precision of our present
chorus, acknowledging at the same time that we owe this to our worthy
Opera director, Herr Carl Maria von Weber]. The rather thin audience
was tepid, and showed that it did not greatly care for this kind of
serious music.

[1] *Christus am Ölberge* (Op. 85) was first performed in 1803, but not published
until 1811 (in revised form). It became quite popular in Germany, and
reached England in 1814 (in a performance under Sir George Smart).

67. Review of the second concert for the Workhouse inmates

Written: Prague, after 29 March 1816.
Published: KPZ, No. 119, 28 April 1816.   *Unsigned.*
Reprinted: HHS, MMW (both inaccurate); KSS.

As with the previous review, there are signs of an editorial hand at work.
The comment on 'empty Italian tinkling' (*leere italienische Kling-Klang*) is in
Weber's authentic voice, but he would not have allowed himself to praise his
own work. His Diary contains a laconic account of the event: 'Concert at
5 o'clock. Everything went excellently. Chinese overture. *Grünbaum sang her
aria very well, Freytag good, also *Erste Ton*' (Diary, 29 March 1816).

The second concert, which took place on the 29th, had a more varied programme without being any better attended.

1. Overture to Schiller's *Turandot*, on a genuine Chinese folk-tune, arranged by C. M. von Weber. Pipes and drum introduce the strange, bizarre melody, which is then taken up by the whole orchestra and presented in a number of different shapes, figurations and keys. The impression on the listener is not exactly pleasing, for this would mean going against the nature of the melody, but it must be acknowledged to be a respectably conceived character piece.[1]

2. Mme Grünbaum gave pleasure in an aria by Weber[2] with her expressive singing, which solved all the difficulties of this considerable undertaking and did so with such amazing facility that the composer added his own applause to the public ovation.

3. Phantasie for the pianoforte, with orchestra and chorus by Beethoven,[3] played by Herr Freytag[4] from Berlin. This was the first time that we had heard this ingenious composition, and we were very pleased to discover that the title 'Phantasie' was not used as an excuse for a possibly excessive looseness of construction, but for a well-planned work, whose structure is made clearly intelligible only by the words of the chorus at the end. For this same reason, the work will no doubt make a stronger impression at a second hearing. Herr Freytag has come here from Berlin to study composition with our Opera director, Weber, and to perfect his piano playing. He showed both good sense and good taste in his performance and overcame the often considerable difficulties of the solo part by the power and sureness of his playing. Even so, we should like to ask him to pay especial attention in his studies to his trills, and we shall without doubt find in him an exceptional pianist. The unusually difficult orchestral accompaniment went with great accuracy; and those citizens of Prague who know that even under the composer's own direction in Vienna a disaster occurred on one occasion will justly congratulate themselves on this success.

4. Duet by Farinelli.[5] Charming perhaps, this empty Italian tinkling seemed very jejune amongst the luxuriant wealth of German harmony.

---

[1]   For a discussion of this work, J75, and the theme's origins, see J. Warrack, *Carl Maria von Weber*, 2nd edn (Cambridge, 1976), pp. 74–5.

[2]   Possibly the scena and aria, 'Ah, se Edmondo fosse l'uccisor!' (J178), since it was one of Weber's most recent arias, written on 1 January 1815, for insertion in Méhul's *Héléna*, especially for Therese Grünbaum.

[3]   Op. 80.

[4]   Freytag was one of Weber's comparatively few pupils. He died young.

[5]   Giuseppe Farinelli (1769–1836) was one of the most popular Italian opera composers of the early nineteenth century before the rise of Rossini.

*Herr Siebert appeared to be afflicted with hoarseness and it was hardly possible for Mme Grünbaum to earn applause entirely by herself.

5. *Der Erste Ton* [J58], poem by *Rochlitz with orchestral and choral accompaniment by C. M. von Weber, nobly declaimed by *Herr Wilhelmi. This work was enthusiastically greeted on Herr von Weber's first appearance here. He seems to have put the poem in the shade by using it merely as a pretext for the creation of extended musical composition. The present writer finds particularly felicitous the idea of first making the speaker rehearse the creation of music and its beneficial effects and then making the chorus, acting as representative of humanity, burst into praise of music, completing the work with a powerful fugue. The performance was immaculate.

68. Review of a soirée by Therese Brunetti

Written: Prague, after 30 March 1816.
Published: KPZ, No. 135, 14 May 1816.   *Unsigned.*
Reprinted: HHS, MMW (both inaccurate and incomplete); KSS.

Therese Brunetti (born Frei; 1782–1864) began her career while still a child in Vienna, joining Domenico Guardasoni's Company as an actress and dancer and moving with him to Prague in 1798. She married the ballet master, Joachim Brunetti (b. 1771), in 1799 or 1800, and after his death married the guitarist and song composer František Kníže (1784–1840). She became very popular, and continued to appear as an actress, occasionally singing soubrette roles; she retired in 1834. She was lively, capricious, wayward and very pretty, with red-gold hair and blue eyes: within a few weeks of his arrival in Prague, Weber was involved in a tumultuous affair with her. He actually lived with her in a *ménage à trois*, during which time he gave piano lessons to her daughter Therese (Resi) Brunetti (1803–92), who later married *Jan Kalivoda. The affair came to a stormy end early in 1814, but Weber was clearly still willing to review her soirée despite his involvement with another artist appearing in it, his future wife *Caroline Brandt. His Diary records many painful scenes with Caroline during these months, and it is difficult to suppose that she can have been in ignorance of the Brunetti affair.

On 30th March Mme Therese Brunetti, actress at the Ständisches Theater, gave an evening of music and recitation in the Redoutensaal. Mme Brunetti knew exactly how to attract the public by the charms of variety and by the many different offerings and artists. We have not space here to mention by name the eleven different numbers in the programme, and must content ourselves with saying that the standard of performance throughout was high. Outstanding, however, among the recitations were the following:

*Castelli: *Gespräch eines Bauernmädchens*, performed by Mlle Brandt.
*Schreiber: *Trifolium*, performed by Mme Sontag.[1]
Langbein:[2] *Das Not- und Hilfsbüchlein*, performed by Mme Brunetti.
Schütze: *Mädchengedanken*, performed by almost all the ladies in our theatrical company, in order to make this witty poem as delightful as possible. And indeed the pleasure would have been still greater, had not each piece recited reminded us painfully of the loss of our unforgettable Schröder,[3] who will remain in a class by herself for many a long year.

The musical part of the evening was rather lost in the quick succession of events. The first Allegro of Beethoven's septet was the opening piece, followed by a Cimarosa aria sung with her usual charm by *Mme Czegka. She was then loudly and rightly applauded for a performance of Steibelt's somewhat lengthy sonata for two pianos, which she played with Frau Professor Wawruch,[4] an amateur who played with great taste and feeling. *Herr Ehlers, too, gave spirited and expressive performances of a notturno by Reinhardt and of Goethe's *Hochzeitslied* with guitar accompaniment.

[1]   Franziska Sontag (1798–1865) was a famous actress who joined the Prague company in 1814, succeeding Sophie Schröder.
[2]   August Friedrich Langbein (1757–1835) was a writer of light tales and anecdotes, also of plays, poems and novels.
[3]   Sophie Schröder (1781–1868), the mother of Wilhelmine Schröder-Devrient, was one of the greatest German actresses of her day. She joined the Prague company in 1813, but remained for only two years.
[4]   She was the wife of Jan Ondřej Wawruch (1773–1842), professor of pathology and amateur musician. He was the physician in attendance during Beethoven's last illness.

69. Review of a concert by Franz Clement

Written: Prague, after 6 April 1816.
Published: KPZ, No. 135, 4 May 1816.   *Unsigned.*
Reprinted: HHS, MMW (both inaccurate); KSS.
*Franz Clement was one of the most important artists whom Weber was able to secure for the Opera. He led the orchestra, and also deputized as conductor when Weber was absent – though with a good deal less effect. His compositions include chamber and orchestral music, as well as a number of concertos such as the one introduced in this concert.

On 6 April Herr Franz Clement, Kapellmeister of the Ständisches Theater Orchestra, gave a concert in the Redoutensaal.

1. The storm from *Cherubini's *Medea*.[1] Although there is no doubt that this great man can only do excellent work, the piece did not make much effect because it is not an independent work, like Haydn's storm,[2] but calculated entirely in connexion with the scenic effect which Cherubini has made so gripping in the opera.

2. A new violin concerto, composed and played by the concert-giver. Herr Clement here showed himself once again a real master in all points of violin playing. His tone is pure and full in even the most technically demanding passages and his control, his security and his stamina command the warmest acknowledgement. The present writer will say no more about his style and his attitude to the works he plays. These are universally familiar and have much to recommend them; and it is moreover unjust to ask an artist to go against his own artistic personality and transfer his allegiance to another school or style of playing, when he is a perfect master in his own way. All species are good, as Voltaire says, except the boring. The work itself provides evidence of great care and is marred only by the ceaseless chains of modulation and harmonic progressions, which have the effect of over-seasoning the music.

3. Quartet from Mozart's *Idomeneo*[3] sung by Mesdames *Czegka and *[Katharina] Kainz, *Mlle [Marianne] Kainz and *Herr Ehlers.

4. Pianoforte trio by Eybler;[4] and in conclusion, Beethoven's *Wellingtons Sieg, oder Die Schlacht bei Vittoria*.[5] The present writer is unable to give his opinion of this work, since the appalling din of cannon, rattles etc. made it impossible for him to hear the actual music properly. As far as the public went, they did not seem to find the expectations with which they went to the concert realized. There is always something dubious about such works as this, which lie outside the proper boundaries of music, since each individual forms his own idea of what he expects; and when he is disappointed in his expectation he finds the work mean in comparison with its title. The Victory Symphony obviously contains strokes of genius such as we can hardly fail to find in works by this great composer. Here and there he catches to perfection the jubilation of victory; and the introduction of 'God save the King' at one point is most skilful and individual, as is the accompaniment.

[1] *Médée* (1797) was first performed in German (translated by C. A. Herklots) in Berlin in 1800, and had a long and successful career on German stages.
[2] Presumably the chorus 'Hark! the deep tremendous voice', from *The Seasons*.
[3] 'Andrò ramingo e solo', from Act 4.
[4] Josef von Eybler (1765–1846) wrote a large amount of chamber music as well as operas and oratorios.
[5] Op. 91 (1813).

These are the present writer's first impressions, and he hopes in a future number to discuss the whole work in more detail.[6]

[6] See below, No. 72.

70. Review of a concert by Leopold Czapek

Written: Prague, after 8 April 1816.
Published: KPZ, No. 139, 18 May 1816.   *Unsigned.*
Reprinted: HHS, MMW (both very incomplete and inaccurate); KSS.

Leopold Eustach Czapek (Čapek) (dates unknown) was an amateur at the time of this concert, but later became a composer and teacher of the piano in Vienna. FétisB says that he wrote some sixty works for the piano. He is perhaps the father of Joseph Čapek (1825–1915), who studied at the Prague Conservatory and then worked in Copenhagen.

On 8 April Herr Leopold Eustach Czapek, student of law, gave a grand concert in aid of the Workhouse, at the Redoutensaal. It is always a pleasure to see cultured amateurs devoting their artistic skill to the assistance of suffering humanity. And although it would be unsuitable for a critic to give a formal account of such a concert, it is nevertheless a pleasant duty to chronicle both the object of the undertaking – which was supported by the acknowledged talents of *Mme Czegka and *Herr Clement – and its successful accomplishment.

71. Review of a concert organized by Johann Christian Mikan

Written: Prague, after 9 April 1816.
Published: KPZ, No. 139, 18 May 1816.   *Unsigned.*
Reprinted: HHS, MMW (both incomplete and inaccurate); KSS.

Johann Christian Mikan (1769–1844) was a distinguished botanist and entomologist, professor at the University of Prague from 1800. He was also 'an enthusiastic occasional poet, whose products reveal his good intentions rather than their artistic worth. He...also organized concerts to raise money for the poor' (C. von Wurzbach, *Biographisches Lexicon der Kaiserthum Oesterreich*, xvii (Vienna, 1867). St Elisabeth of Hungary (1207–31) was born at Pressburg (Bratislava, Poszony), the daughter of Andrew II of Hungary, and while still a child married Count Louis IV of Thuringia. She became famous for her charitable works. The conversion of her much-loved husband through the Miracle of the Roses (see below) has been the subject of many German poems, pictures and pieces of music: it was the series of paintings by Moritz von Schwind in the Castle of the Wartburg that inspired Liszt's *St Elisabeth*. The Elisabetherinnen were an order of nuns – Franciscan tertiaries, as Elisabeth herself became after the death of her husband on the Sixth Crusade. They were founded in the fifteenth century, and were a nursing order with special charge of the aged and the sick. They had houses in Prague, Brünn and Pressburg, among many others. The staging of tableaux, representing pictures or famous scenes, was a contemporary fashion, as Goethe describes in *Die Wahlverwandschaften*.

On 9 April, in the Ständisches Theater, Prof. Dr J. Chr. Mikan gave an evening of music and recitation, with a tableau, in aid of the Order of St Elisabeth.

The indefatigable care which Prof. Mikan devotes every year to such an institution reveals also in truly remarkable fashion his inventiveness in amusing and delighting the public in a novel and attractive way, while also arousing their charitable instincts. With tireless enthusiasm he lays under contribution every artistic medium, by which means he certainly hopes to please the public and to win the support of those who are well disposed to each branch of the arts; his only reward is the consciousness of having done everything in his power to assist a noble cause – the relief of the needy – and of having succeeded.

The evening began with an excellent performance of a powerful overture by *Bernhard Romberg, richly endowed with instrumental effects.

2. Aria with chorus for *Titus*,[1] by *Weigl. Though excellently sung by *Herr Ehlers, it did not prove very effective; and this was inevitable with a public which admires Mozart's genius to such extremes that it is disinclined to accept anything attached to his work. Though recalling ideas from the march and ending with the chorus, this number strives in vain to win equal civic rights with the others.

3. Double concerto for two violins by Eck,[2] played by *Kalliwoda and Taborsky,[3] students at the conservatory. As always, this was a pleasure to hear; and on this occasion the pleasure was increased by the former player's presence of mind, for when one of his strings snapped he remained perfectly calm and completed the piece in fine style on a borrowed instrument.

4. *Die Kuh* by Bürger[4] is rather a sentimental little poem. The subject

---

[1]   A number for insertion in Mozart's *La clemenza di Tito*.

[2]   Johann Friedrich Eck (1766–1810) was a violin virtuoso and composer who had worked in Munich and was admired by Reichardt, *Spohr and Mozart. The work performed was the Concertante, Op. 8.

[3]   See above, No. 64, n. 6.

[4]   Gottfried Bürger (1747–94) was best known for his popular ballad *Lenore* (1774) and his versions of the Baron von Münchhausen stories. His poems were savagely attacked by Schiller in a notorious review of 1791. *Die Kuh*

matter was very suitable to the occasion, and *Mlle Brandt recited with the greatest charm and spirit.

5. A duet for *Titus*, sung by *Mme Czegka and *Herr Schnepf. This was not much more successful than its predecessor. Mme Czegka sang excellently; but we could not help wishing that Herr Schnepf, with all his talent and culture, would pay more respect to the character of his fine baritone voice and not insist on performing music lying in the highest tenor register, thereby depriving his voice of its greatest asset and its purity. Your correspondent also noted the absence of that careful ensemble essential in duet singing.

6. Psalm by *Nägeli. A fine, serious piece in a style that is rather strange here but well loved in Protestant countries, where it originated and still plays an important part in church music.

7. *Des Königs Ladislaus Wahl* by *Castelli (one of his best poems)[5] was admirably recited by *Herr Ehlers, who on the eve of his departure appeared in this new and interesting role.

8. Chorus for the tragedy *König Thamos* by Mozart.[6] This is a magnificently powerful and noble conception which must be most effective in its context and even here held and delighted the audience.

9. Allegro for wind instruments, played by students from the conservatory. Unhappily this failed almost entirely in its effect owing to the fact that preparations for the tableau necessitated the lowering of several curtains, while the public's impatience showed in a certain restlessness.

10. *Die Wunderrosen*, a legend by J. Ch. Mikan, recited by Mme Sonntag.[7] The poet has taken the beautiful story of the Countess

(1784) concerns the return of a stolen cow to a pious widow as a result of her prayers, and was presumably included for its mention of God as the protector of widows and orphans.

[5]   Ignaz Castelli published in his *Gedichte* (Berlin, 1835), I, 140–50, the poem *Die pohlnische Königswahl*. It describes how Ladislaus is elected by acclaim, with one dissenting voice – that of an old peasant. When Ladislaus then declines the throne as there is a single honest and humble voice against him, the old man, impressed, withdraws his opposition and the election proceeds. Prince Władysław of Poland (1456–1516) was chosen as King Ladislas II by the Bohemians in 1471 in the hope of obtaining help from the Poles against the Hungarians. He proved, in the event, something of a failure as a king.

[6]   Tobias von Gebler's tragedy *Thamos, König in Ägypten* was printed in 1773 in Prague, where he was a Councillor of State and Vice-Chancellor. The chorus sung was probably the opening number of Act 1, 'Schon weichet dir, Sonne', which Gebler himself found *sehr schön* (letter of 13 December 1773 to Nicolai, quoted in R. Werner, *Aus dem Josephinischen Wien* (Berlin, 1888)).

[7]   Franziska Sontag (1798–1865); see also above, No. 68, n. 1.

Elisabeth disobeying her husband the Count and giving food to the poor in a basket. When stopped on her errand by him, she said that it contained roses; and when he removed the cloth, the contents had been miraculously transformed into roses. The narrative poem chosen by the poet expounded the two moments shown in the tableau; and Mme Sonntag's recitation was marked by a charm, warmth and sincerity that reminded us once again of our good fortune in having acquired this thoughtful artist for our theatre. She had penetrated the spirit and meaning of the poem and her heartfelt delivery conveyed both to her listeners' hearts, earning their enthusiastic applause.

In the tableau, *Mlle Bohler took the part of Elisabeth; and the beauty and nobility of her figure and the tender devotion in her face perfectly expressed the idea of this glorious German woman from our German past. Herr Polawsky[8] gave a strong and dignified impersonation of the forbidding Count; and the Countess's ladies (Mme Clement and Mme Junghans) and the Count's courtiers (Herren Löwe, Gerstel, *Wilhelmi and Dorsch) formed excellently posed and poised groups on either side of the stage. An Adagio for wind instruments accompanied the tableau.

> [8] Ferdinand Polawsky (1779–1844) was an actor who had been a protégé of Iffland and had worked in the Döbbelin Company and elsewhere before accepting a Prague engagement in 1803. Here he made himself one of the most important actors in the company, and on *Liebich's death he became one of the Directors. A catalogue of 1821 lists his parts as lovers, bon vivants, knights and schemers; he was also a famous Shakespearean, his roles including Hamlet, Shylock, Capulet and many others.

72. Review of a concert in aid of the Institute of Musicians' Widows and Orphans

Written: Prague, after 14 April 1816.
Published: KPZ, No. 145, 24 May 1816.   *Unsigned.*
Reprinted: HHS, MMW (both inaccurate); KSS; LKA.

All his life Weber was very charitably disposed, and his accounts in his Diary record many gifts to the poor even when his own funds were very low. This was a charity that would obviously have meant much to him, especially at a time when, already a sick man, he was contemplating marriage.

On 14 April a grand concert was given in the Ständisches Theater in aid of the Institute for Musicians' Widows and Orphans.

1. Grand Symphony in D major (the so-called *englische*) by Mozart.[1] A grandly designed, lucid and powerfully paced work, excellently performed under Kapellmeister Witasek [*Vitásek].

2. Oratorio, *Der grosse Tag des Vaterlandes*, written for voices and wind alone, by I. Sauer.[2]

It is most reprehensible, and irresponsible to the public, to select from the works available for performance such a feeble concoction as this. It is hard to imagine more commonplace melodies, insipid harmonies or a more unintelligent handling of a text; and the audience displayed remarkable patience in refraining from a more explicit expression of their dissatisfaction.

After this the successful performance of Beethoven's martial tone picture *Die Schlacht von Vittoria*[3] was all the more rewarding. The advantages of the venue were cleverly exploited to give as much realism as possible to the approach of troops, as the composer has imagined it. The cannon, rattles and side-drums proved effective later in the work, but they were kept so much in the background that it was quite possible to follow the course of the music without having one's ears deafened by an overwhelming din.

The presence of *Kapellmeister Hummel, of Vienna, who has heard this work under the composer's own direction, enabled the conductor, Kapellmeister Carl Maria von Weber, to be sure of the effects to be emphasized; and this he did with all the devotion and zeal that he always shows in good causes. The whole piece went really excellently, yet even so it did not make a great impression on the audience – for reasons related to those mentioned above. The effectiveness of the actual battle scenes appears to be prejudiced by their beginning too early in the work. This means that no reserves are left, and without them the music falls flat, despite the magnificently vigorous figure of the assault with its chromatic movement. The present writer thinks it an open question whether the same effect could not have been achieved by other and more conventional means. There was a full house, and for this reason the battle was in fact effective.

[1]   No symphony of Mozart's was generally known as the 'English'. It is possible that Weber's adjective *englische* really means 'heavenly', especially as elsewhere he gives *Englisch* a capital letter when meaning 'English'. He may be referring to K504, the D major Symphony written for Prague.

[2]   Ignaz Sauer (1780–1863), not 'T. Sauer' as transcribed by KSS and LKA.

[3]   *Wellingtons Sieg, oder Die Schlacht bei Vittoria* (Op. 91, 1813). W. M. Thackeray had heard the work under Hummel in Weimar, and has left a description in ch. 62 of *Vanity Fair* of the performance, in 'Pumpernickel', at which Tapeworm, the British Chargé d'Affaires, 'rose up in his box and bowed and simpered, as if he would represent the whole empire'.

73. Review of a concert by Jan Wenzel

Written: Prague, after 14 April 1816.
Published: KPZ, No. 145, 24 May 1816.   *Unsigned.*
Reprinted: KSS.
  *Jan Wenzel (1762–1831) was a famous Prague piano and singing teacher, and was organist of St Vitus's Cathedral for forty years from 1791.

This Lent, Herr Wenzel's Amateurs' Concert gave the same satisfaction as in former years to those taking part. Since *Director F. D. Weber's concerts ceased, this is the only one of its kind. There is no other occasion on which music-lovers can enjoy an exhibition of youthful, budding talent in all departments of music, with all it promises for the future. The choice of a pleasanter and more spacious hall has recently facilitated attendance at the productions of this musical seminary. There are some excellent pianists among Herr Wenzel's pupils for whom these concerts are largely designed as a form of practice, encouragement and perfecting. The most impressive artist, however, was a young singer of extraordinary promise. Although hardly more than a child, she already has a handsome, well-rounded voice and shows an excellent sense of style. A number of mature performers also adorned these concerts by their contributions. *Herr Schnepf, for instance, sang a Cavatina by Rossini and took part in a number of concerted pieces. Herr Zavora[1] sang in a trio by *Paer, and gave an unusually fine performance of a Rondo for violoncello. *Herr Hause, who is a professor at the conservatory, gave the assembled public the unusual pleasure of a double bass concerto by Herr Maschek;[2] and several unusually gifted amateurs added their talents to those of Herr Wenzel's pupils. As far as the programme is concerned, most of the pieces selected were 'brilliant' examples drawn from recent operatic or chamber music. We heard symphonies and overtures by Beethoven, *Cherubini, Himmel, Kunzen, Vogel, Wilms and Winter; concertos by Beethoven, Mozart, Polledro, *Rode, *[?Andreas] Romberg and Wölfl; and vocal music by *Cartellieri, Häser, Maurer, Paer (the most popular of all), Rossini, C. M. von Weber and Witasek [*Vitásek].

[1]   Dionys Weber had invited Závora to be his assistant in 1811, without success. DKB refers to Benedikt Záwora, 'a good tenor and cellist'; he was also a member of the Prague Tonkünstler-Gesellschaft.
[2]   Vincenc Mašek (1755–1831), composer of much music in different forms.

74. Review of the first concert by Jan Nepomuk Hummel

Written: Prague, after 19 April 1816.
Published: KPZ, No. 154, 2 June 1816.   *Unsigned.*
Reprinted: HHS, MMW (both incomplete and inaccurate); KSS; LKA.

*Hummel's first tour of Bohemia was made in 1788, and he retained an affection for a city to which he had been commended by his teacher Mozart. In 1816 he was still at the height of his powers; his last visit was made in 1836, the year before his death, when he was long past his prime and had only a *succès d'estime*, though he still 'created a very favourable impression as an improviser' (W. Kuhe, *My Musical Recollections* (London, 1896)). To the present review, Weber added a letter to *Rochlitz (22 April 1816), which was made the basis of an article on Hummel's visit (*AMZ* XVIII (1816), 318–19). Another review (*AMZ* XXII (1820), 358–69) makes use of material in Weber's article without acknowledgement.

Kapellmeister Hummel delighted us with two concerts in the Redouten-saal on 19 and 26 April. The programme of this first concert was as follows.

1. Overture to Hummel's opera *Die Rückfahrt des Kaisers*.[1] This is a very lively, *galant* and effectively written piece and it was very well played under the composer's own direction.

2. Piano concerto,[2] composed and played by Hummel, who completely justified the reputation which had preceded him. A very large audience gave him an ovation for the precision, accuracy and polish of his playing, his stamina in the longest and most fatiguing passages and the smoothness and elegance of his interpretation. The concerto itself is not one of the composer's finest works and the present writer was disappointed particularly by the extended Adagio.

3. An aria by *Paer, sung by *Mme Grünbaum. This rather long and ample scene was excellently sung, as usual, and we were only nervous of the effect on the singer of the excessive heat, which often makes the voice husky.

4. Grand Septet for the pianoforte, composed and played by Hummel.[3] This is without doubt one of the composer's most successful

[1]   *Singspiel* in one act (Op. 69), text by E. Veith, produced in Vienna in 1814 and published in piano reduction in the same year.
[2]   Probably the Second Concerto in C (Op. 34), for piano solo or with orchestra.
[3]   Grand Septuor in D minor (Op. 74), for piano, flute, oboe, horn, violin, cello and bass (1816). Apart from Hummel himself, the players were *Michal Januš (flute), *Joseph Sellner (oboe), Václav Zalužan (horn), *Franz Clement (violin), Joseph von Kučera (cello) and *Wenzel Hause (bass), all members of Weber's orchestra.

works, upon which he seems to have lavished great care and feeling. There were five movements[4] and of these the present writer particularly admired the Variations and Minuet, partly for the fine development and execution of the ideas and partly for the clever ensemble writing. The Trio section of the Minuet is unusually delightful and attractive, with its simple horn melody. This fine septet did not quite receive its due from the audience, who can hardly be blamed for this after a single hearing, particularly as the work is rather long by today's standards, being designed to stand alone and not in a programme.

The performance by our own excellent players (Clement, Kutschera, Sellner, Janusch, Zaluzan and Hause) was very fine, while the composer's playing was of course excellent.

5. *Die Orakelglocke* by Tiedge and *Der Stein der Treue* by Bürger,[5] recited by *Mlle Brandt. These proved two charming trifles and they were spoken with all the sincerity and charm that we have often had occasion to remark in the performances of this versatile young artist.

6. Herr Hummel then improvised at the pianoforte, and here he displayed for the first time his mastery of every kind of figuration and an unhesitating resourcefulness in all the different phases and moods prompted by the caprice of the moment. It is impossible to play with a greater purity and precision than Herr Hummel brought to his improvisations. His audience were fascinated by the robustness of his playing and certain individual, delicate little turns of melody.

What he values most highly in piano playing are elaborate passage-work and perfect clarity. Perhaps in order to achieve these he rather neglects other potential qualities of the instrument. It may be remarked in passing that, along with many others, those pianists who insist on raising the pedal in scales etc. can make him their example. This admirable artist received an ovation such as the present writer has never before witnessed.

4   Actually four.
5   Christoph August Tiedge (1752–1841) was most famous in his day for his philosophical poem *Urania* (1801). For Bürger, see above, No. 71, n. 4.

75. Review of the second concert by Jan Nepomuk Hummel

Written: Prague, after 16 April 1816.
Published: KPZ, No. 155, 3 June 1816.   *Unsigned.*
Reprinted: HHS, MMW (both inaccurate); KSS; LKA.
    For a note on *Hummel's Prague concerts, see above, No. 74.

The second concert, on the 26th, began with Hummel's overture to the tragedy *Marpha*.[1] A serious work, solid and powerful in character.

2. 'An die Entfernte',[2] a Romance with piano by Hummel, sung by *Mme Grünbaum. A charming trifle, which was given an unpretentious, but by no means unornamented, performance.

3. Piano concerto[3] composed and played by Hummel, in which his already proven qualities appeared again in the fairest light.

4. 'La Sentinelle',[4] sung by Herr Pohl, with variations for violin, guitar and pianoforte, played by Messrs *Clement, *Sellner and Hummel. This showed a pleasant vein of invention worked out in the modern style, and gave much pleasure.

5. Messrs Hummel and Clement gave a free improvisation for pianoforte and violin with no preliminary preparation. Without some form of prearranged plan which still places no narrow limits to the players' imagination, this communal improvisation is a precarious undertaking. The players are bound to have recourse to familiar melodies, and the result is more like a potpourri than a free fantasia. It is almost impossible to follow Herr Hummel's flow of ideas and wealth of harmony as they deserve without giving the appearance of interrupting or making unwanted comments on the music. This is especially true if the players do not exercise a certain amount of mutual forbearance. This item excited much interest, but the present writer will not decide whether this interest was maintained throughout the performance itself.

This much is certainly true – that Herr Hummel enjoyed a reception and an appreciation such as few artists have met with before. This second concert was, if anything, even better attended than the first, and we hope that the artist too was satisfied with his reception in Bohemia's capital.

[1]   Hummel wrote the music for this long-forgotten tragedy in about 1800–10.
[2]   Op. 84, No. 1, composed in Berlin probably in 1816.
[3]   Possibly the Concerto in A minor, Op. 85 (*c* 1816).
[4]   Op. 71, originally for voice, violin, guitar or cello, cello and optional double bass (*c* 1815). It was sung by the tenor Pohl, with *Franz Clement (violin), *Joseph Sellner (guitar) and the composer.

76. Introduction to Poissl's *Athalia*

Written: Prague, 17 May 1816.
Published: KPZ, No. 142, 21 May 1816.   *Signed:* Carl Maria von Weber.
Reprinted: KSS.

*Poissl's *Athalia* was a grand opera in three acts with a text by *J. G.
Wohlbrück after Racine's *Athalie* (1691). It was produced in Munich on 3 June
1814, when the *AMZ* praised the composer for writing not out of professional
need but from conviction. It added, 'If Italian grand opera gives priority to
song, less to accurate declamation and still less to dramatic truth; if French
opera gives priority to declamation and correct staging and allots singing a
secondary place; then there is in this work a striving to find a middle course
between the two extremes' (*AMZ* xvi (1814), 441–5). The work was also
given in Stuttgart (1815), Frankfurt (1815) and Berlin (1816, when it
received another long review in *AMZ* xix (1817), 258–63). It was revived in
Munich in 1828. *Spohr, who greatly disliked the work, records that it was
given on thirty consecutive nights by the Grand Duke of Hesse, who
conducted it himself (*Selbstbiographie*). The Prague performance 'went well
and was favourably received' (letter to *Franz Danzi, 24 May 1816).

Today, 21 May, a grand opera in three acts, *Athalia*, with a libretto
by J. G. Wohlbrück and music by Baron von Poissl of Munich, is being
given its first performance here. Baron von Poissl's outstanding talent
includes a strongly appealing attraction to German artistic resources,
and it is a great pleasure to me to bring to the notice of the public one
of his most successful works. Many German stages have already given
his works a friendly, in some cases an enthusiastic, reception. Baron
von Poissl, who is a chamberlain of the Bavarian court and a Knight
of the Order of St George, has devoted himself wholly to music, for some
ten years giving it all his time and energies; and indeed no less is
demanded of those who wish to attain some rank as artists. His most
important assets have been his own private studies and the friendly
advice of the excellent *Kapellmeister Danzi. After the Baron had
written a number of stage and chamber works, an Italian opera which
was received with almost unparalleled enthusiasm in Munich, the
two-act *Ottaviano in Sicilia*,[1] decided him to write exclusively for the

---

[1]   *Dramma eroico*, libretto by the composer after Metastasio, in other versions
three or four acts; produced in Munich on 30 June 1812. Its success cheered
a wet summer, wrote a critic in *AMZ* xiv (1812), 652–3, finding everything in it lucid and well proportioned. It played to three full houses, with
*Antonio Brizzi as Octavius Caesar, *Josephine Weixelbaum as Scribonia and
*Helene Harlas as Cilona.

stage. He has scholarly inclinations, and is in fact himself a talented poet, as is shown by his last opera, *Der Wettkampf zu Olympia*.[2] This is a metrical adaptation of Metastasio, and marks a notable advance in the Baron's career as an artist. An indefatigable diligence has enabled him to produce within a short space of time not only these works but a three-act opera, *Aucassin und Nicolette*,[3] an adaptation of Sedaine by Hiemer, and more than half another opera, *Merope*,[4] as well as a number of concert arias and other pieces. His music is characterized by a scrupulous attention to prosody, a youthful richness of harmony and apt, well-varied orchestration. His melodies lean strongly towards an Italian cantabile – tender, and well written for the voice – with that true regard for the vocal chords which German composers are often accused of neglecting. This valuable trait is explained by his acquaintance with such outstanding singers as Bertinotti,[5] Harlas, Brizzi and others, whom he has often heard and above all for whom he has chosen to write a number of operatic roles.

The opera under discussion, *Athalia*, also possesses this vocal quality to a high degree, though belonging in character rather to the declamatory genre. Certainly many of the recitatives are models of their kind. The emotional crises in the action are judiciously characterized and contained by highly charged melodies which recur at crucial points. What were at first no more than hints are sure to appear later in undisguised form and with satisfying conviction. The dramatic action is well sustained throughout. Athalia herself emerges as a terrifying personality, well contrasted with the noble dignity of the High Priest, Jehosheba's tender solicitude, the childlike purity of Jehoash and the chorus of boy victims, and the combined strength and noble bearing of the Chosen People. Finally I must content myself with observing that the librettist has done excellent work and given devoted care to the verse dialogue as well as the sung numbers. In

---

[2]   Grand opera, text by the composer after Metastasio's *Olimpiade*; produced in Munich on 21 April 1815. It was also given in Stuttgart (1815), Darmstadt (1816) and Weimar (1819), when Poissl was favourably compared to Rossini (*AMZ* xxi (1819), 655–7).

[3]   *Singspiel* in three acts, text by *F. K. Hiemer after Michel-Jean Sedaine's text for Grétry (1779), in turn after a thirteenth-century story. See below, Biographical Glossary *s.v.* Poissl, for *AMZ* comments.

[4]   Poissl wrote an overture and nine numbers for Sebastiano Nasolini's *Merope* (1796), given in this version in Munich, 1 September 1812. A revival led the *AMZ* to praise the general style at the expense of individual items, finding the invention too simple and second-hand (*AMZ* xxii (1820), 441).

[5]   Teresa Bertinotti (1776–1854) sang while still very young in Italy before making a European career; she first appeared in Munich in 1807.

Germany it is rare for a librettist to obtain proper recognition, and he must content himself with the modest assurance of having expended all his powers and diligence on this libretto. *Athalia*, together with other operas by the same composer, has already been given in Munich, Stuttgart, Frankfurt and Darmstadt, and the work is eagerly awaited in Berlin.

The following information about the state of the Kingdom of Judah, particularly from the religious point of view, will perhaps not come amiss.

The Scriptures tell us that this kingdom consisted of the two tribes of Judah and Benjamin, and that the other ten tribes seceded under King Rehoboam and founded the Kingdom of Israel. The reigning house in Judah was that of David, and both Jerusalem and the Temple formed part of this inheritance. All the priests and levites were united in loyalty to the throne, since after the building of Solomon's Temple it was forbidden to offer sacrifice in any other place and lawful worship could only take place in Judah. These priests and levites formed a numerous tribe. They were divided into different classes, which took turns in performing the Temple liturgy from sabbath to sabbath. The priests belonged to the tribe of Aaron, and only they might officiate in the Holy Place. The levites were concerned with the Temple chant, the preparation of the sacrifices and the care of the Temple buildings. Those who were on duty lived, like the High Priest, in the buildings surrounding the Temple and forming part of it. The whole building was called the Holy Place, and this name was applied particularly to the inner part, where the golden candlesticks, the altar of incense and the shewbread were kept. The ark stood in the Holy of Holies, which the High Priest was allowed to enter only once in the year, on the Day of Atonement.

So much for the general picture; now to the details of the story. Jehoram, the son of Jehoshaphat, was the seventh member of David's house to occupy the throne of Judah. He married Athalia, daughter of Ahab and Jezebel, who were notorious – especially Jezebel – for their savage persecution of the prophets. Athalia was as impious as her mother and soon persuaded her husband to introduce idolatrous practices and to build in Jerusalem a temple of Baal, a god of the people of Tyre and Sidon. All Jehoram's children had been killed by the Arabs and Philistines, except one, Ahaziah. After Jehoram's miserable death of an internal malady, Ahaziah continued his parents' impious practices, and after reigning only a year he too was involved in the destruction of the house of Ahab and was killed on the occasion of a visit to Jehu, King of Israel and the instrument of divine wrath. Jehu destroyed the whole house of Ahab and threw Jezebel out of the palace windows. Elijah's prophecy was then fulfilled, and she was devoured by dogs in the vineyard of that same Naboth whom she had had killed earlier, in order to take possession of his inheritance.

When news of these executions reached Athalia in Jerusalem, she in her turn determined to destroy all the house of David, and she had all Ahaziah's children, her own grandchildren, put to death. Fortunately Ahaziah's sister, Jehosheba, found a way of saving one of her nephews from strangling. This was the infant Jehoash, whom she entrusted to his nurse, the wife of the High Priest, and hid both of them in the Temple, where the young Jehoash was brought up until the day that he was proclaimed King of Judah.

History gives no exact dates for this.[6] Racine chose the feast of Pentecost. This commemorated the giving of the Law on Mount Sinai, and it was also known as the Feast of the First Fruits, because the first loaves from the new harvest were then offered to God.

6   Modern scholarship suggests the ninth century BC, with Athalia's death c 835.

77. An incident in Abt Vogler's youth

Written: Prague, before 22 July 1816.
Published: KPZ, No. 204, 22 July 1816.   Unsigned.
Reprinted: KSS.

Weber had long had the intention of writing a full-scale biography of *Vogler (see above, No. 7), and he appears to have made various notes towards it at various times. The publication of this anecdote was clearly connected with the circumstances of his private life at the time. In the wake of his disastrous affair with Therese Brunetti, he had fallen in love with *Caroline Brandt and was anxious to marry and settle down. Previously, he had taken a Romantic view that family life was not for the artist's untrammelled spirit. To *Gänsbacher he once wrote, 'You've already married me off fifty thousand times, but it's no good: you know my views and my position on the matter. It's indeed hard that human happiness must be sacrificed by artists, but that's how it is, one can only be one thing completely, and I hate half measures' (letter of 15 July 1814). He reiterated these sentiments to his friends in several other letters, and was disconcerted by Caroline's down-to-earth nature: 'To my great distress I've noticed that her attitude to noble art doesn't rise above the usual shoddiness, namely that art is simply a means of getting soup, meat and clothes' (letter to Gänsbacher, 18 March 1816). After a far from easy courtship, they were married on 4 November 1817.

Abt Vogler is equally well known as virtuoso organist, masterly composer and theorist. He was born at Würzburg in 1749 and even as a child showed an unmistakable artistic and scholarly bent which easily persuaded his father, an instrument-maker, to have him educated. At the Prince Bishop's Gymnasium in Würzburg the boy was remarkable not only for his outstanding gifts but also for an indefatigable diligence. The normal course of studies could not satisfy his desire for knowledge, and his lively intelligence sought new fields to conquer. He therefore devoted all his leisure time to music. With almost no instruction he learnt to play first the violin and then the piano, and without any teacher, he started to compose, confidently following his own natural promptings. By the time that he reached man's estate his compositions had already won him a considerable reputation in his own country, and many music-lovers from the neighbouring towns were anxious to make his acquaintance. Among other visitors were a rich wine merchant and his pretty daughter. Both were devoted to music and wished to make Vogler's acquaintance, partly out of natural interest and partly in order to develop and perfect the girl's musical gifts. At their first visit Vogler was not only pleased and flattered but deeply impressed by the daughter's charming looks, which aroused a love whose ardour was such as might be expected in a young man of his lively temperament. The girl soon came to reciprocate his feelings, and the father appeared to approve of the young people's mutual understanding. Vogler would indubitably have married and eventually taken over his father-in-law's large business, thus robbing music of his genius, had this first love not been destroyed by a ridiculous incident. On the feast of St Kilian, the patron saint of the diocese of Würzburg,[1] Vogler took his betrothed to the cathedral. It was raining hard and he had an umbrella. At the church door he let her go ahead and then followed her up the nave. The magnificence of the high altar with its many hundreds of candles, the rich festival vestments of the Prince Bishop and the other clergy taking part in the High Mass, the solemn music played by the full court orchestra – all this captivated the girl's eyes and ears, so that she paid little attention to the young man at her side. He, too, may well have been aware of a certain novelty in experiencing all these things with his betrothed by his side, and may therefore have been in his turn distracted. Both stood there in total unawareness until they were rudely awoken by the laughter of various of Vogler's neighbours. He looked round and saw nothing but laughing

---

[1]   8 July. Kilian was an Irishman who converted the local ruler in Würzburg and on his martyrdom, c 684, became the city's patron.

faces. His embarrassment grew with every moment and he did not dare to seek the cause of this strange phenomenon which, as he feared, was in some way connected with himself. Finally he noticed that some of his neighbours kept looking upwards, and he then realized with horror that he was still holding his open umbrella above his head. Quick as a flash he lowered it and then hurried out of the church, leaving the girl standing there. After this his embarrassment was so great that he never dared to look her in the face again. Was this chance or the work of his guardian angel?

78. Review of a concert by Johann Peter Pixis

Written: Prague, after 22 July 1816.
Published: KPZ, No. 212, 30 July 1816.   *Unsigned.*
Reprinted: KSS.

Johann Peter Pixis was at this stage of his career still living in Vienna, where he contributed much to the city's musical life. As a young man he had toured Europe with his father and his brother *Friedrich Wilhelm Pixis, who was by now established in Prague as a teacher and conductor. He was widely admired for his virtuosity, though some found it rather showy. His compositions, numbering some 150, were praised by Schumann, who made him one of the Davidsbund; he was also a friend of Liszt.

A pleasure rare at this season of the year was provided for us on the 22nd by the grand concert given Herr J. P. Pixis, a composer from Vienna. The following works were in the programme.

1. Overture by J. P. Pixis, which opens with a powerful Adagio and moves in the most astonishing manner into an Allegro which consists for the most part of a thematic working of the material, with a richly varied use of the orchestra. This was loudly applauded.

2. Pianoforte Concerto in E flat major, also by J. P. Pixis. A number of admirable features contribute to make this one of today's most interesting works – invention and novelty in the most technically demanding passages in the first Allegro; felicitous choice of accompanying instruments in the Adagio (three cellos, three horns, and double bass and timpani) which proved most effective; finally a fiery and vivacious Rondo, in which hair-raising difficulties are combined with lyrical passages in a way that grip the attention.

3. Variations for the violin, composed and played by the brother of the concert-giver, Herr F. W. Pixis, violin teacher at the conservatory.

This work was new to Prague. A pleasant cantabile melody is followed by six variations, each in a different form, always showing different musical resources and great charm, as well as really colossal virtuoso passages. The player overcame these with astonishing ease and sureness and earned unanimous and enthusiastic applause.

4. Polonaise concertante for pianoforte and violin, composed by J. P. Pixis and played by both brothers. There are not many works in which these two instruments can both assert their own rights in such a happy union as here. The composer has been particularly successful in pitting the virtuoso display of one player against another, and in the most original manner bringing each back to the opening theme. The whole piece is most effective and the performance by the two brothers was marked by an ideal combination of strength and precision.

5. Cavatina by Nasolini,[1] sung by *Mme Grünbaum (born Müller). The magical quality of her voice, the powerfulness of her expression and the elegant new ornamentation with which she clothed this simple and harmonically unadventurous music won her an ovation.

6. Caprice for the pianoforte by J. P. Pixis. In this the artist revealed, within the narrowest limits, all his mastery of the instrument. After a serious opening passage he piles one difficulty on another, ending in a Prestissimo, which he performed with extraordinary strength and precision. Unusual harmonies, bold leaps over two or three octaves taken at top speed, the most elaborate chordal passages in both hands and long stretches of polyphonic writing, facilitated no doubt by the wide span of the player's hands – all these things give this pianist a unique character calculated to arouse the greatest excitement.

He was accompanied by a students' orchestra from the conservatory, under the director, *Herr F. D. Weber, by special permission of the governing body of the Association for the Promotion of Music in Bohemia. Once again it was a pleasure to note the progress made by this youthful orchestra in the art of accompaniment; and indeed they performed these works, which bristle with difficulties of every kind, with admirable accuracy and feeling.

---

[1]   Sebastiano Nasolini (c 1768–c 1806) wrote some thirty operas.

79. Review of a concert by Ignaz Moscheles

Written: Prague, August 1816.
Published: KPZ, No. 242, 29 August 1816.   *Unsigned.*
Reprinted: KSS; LKA.

*Moscheles's concert took place in Carlsbad, whither Weber's friend Dr Jungh had gone for the cure. There is no record of Weber's having gone too. The supposition must be that Jungh sent this account to Weber, who rewrote it and used it as his August contribution to the *KPZ*. *Giuliani often shared concerts with Moscheles in Vienna.

Among the many enjoyable evenings of music during the past summer special mention should be made of that given in the Sächsicher Saal by Herr Moscheles, the popular pianist from Vienna.

This young artist already has an exceptionally high reputation here, and his performance certainly bore this out. Strength, agility and accuracy are the hallmarks of his playing, and these enabled him to confront successfully even the greatest technical difficulties. He was given an ovation for his performance. If such dexterity and taste justify his claim to be called an exceptional pianist, he also won applause for his compositions. His success as a teacher was proved by the delightful playing of an eight-year-old girl, who played a Polonaise with orchestral accompaniment to general satisfaction.

The universally acknowledged master of the guitar, *Herr Giuliani, also contributed to the enjoyment of the evening by performing a brilliant potpourri of his own. This both confirmed his reputation and delighted his audience.

80. Introduction to Spohr's *Faust*

Written: Prague, 27 August 1816.
Published: KPZ, No. 245, 1 September 1816.
                              Signed: Carl Maria von Weber.
Reprinted: HHS, MMW (both with minor inaccuracies); KSS; LKA.

As Weber notes, *Faust* was intended for the Theater an der Wien, where *Spohr was conductor. The libretto (which is not derived from Goethe) was offered to him by Joseph Carl Bernard, and the opera was composed, so Spohr writes in his *Selbstbiographie*, in less than four months. He acknowledges much encouragement from *Meyerbeer, who later conducted it in Berlin. The cast he had in mind included *Anton Forti (Faust), Carl Weinmüller (Mephistopheles), Franz Wild (Hugo) and Antonia Campi (Kunigunde), but he admits that his inexperience in writing for voices led him into miscalculations for these particular singers, and it was this which was given as an excuse for the work's rejection by Count Palffy. At the première in Prague on 1 September 1816, the cast included *Josef Kainz (Faust), Gned (Mephistopheles), *Johann Stöger (Hugo), *Therese Grünbaum (Kunigunde), Johann Grünbaum (Franz), *Caroline Brandt (Röschen) and *Marie Allram (Sycorax). The performance was, Weber thought, a success. He told *Rochlitz that he was sorry not to be able to write about it for the *AMZ*, and especially that, as far as Spohr himself was concerned, 'I can't tell him about his favourable reception as I don't know where he is' (letter of 22 November 1816). Spohr later rewrote the work, replacing the spoken dialogue with recitatives for the London production at the Prince's Theatre in 1840.

On Sunday 1 September there will take place the first performance of *Faust*, a Romantic opera in two acts, with a libretto by J. C. Bernard and music by Louis Spohr. It was an honour for our Prague theatre to be the first to stage this fine example of German art. It was commissioned in 1814 and, according to the libretto, written for the Theater an der Wien; but it was never performed there, sharing this fate with a large number of works which have been delivered to Vienna theatres and – for reasons I prefer not to mention here – simply left, unperformed, to gather dust on the shelves.

Herr Bernard's treatment of the well-known story, so rich in many kinds of interest, differs in a number of ways from that to be found in earlier versions; and indeed it seems as though this very richness of interest explains the wide divergence of treatment, despite the similarity of each writer's intention, namely to achieve the maximum dramatic effect. The same reason may well explain the fact that each writer's imagination has made demands in the matter of spectacle that have never hitherto been satisfactorily met by any stage representation of the story. As far as music is concerned, Herr Bernard has opened up a wide field of possibilities, and the present writer is of the opinion that this libretto could have fallen into no better hands than those of this composer.

Herr Spohr's admirable instrumental compositions of every kind have won him such a high place among contemporary composers that his name is mentioned with affection and respect by all artists. The general public does not know him so well as an operatic composer; but he has a number of operas to his name which have aroused expectations among connoisseurs such as only the completely dispassionate can observe without forming judgements. The work which the present writer remembers best is *Das Duell mit der Geliebten*[1], written

---

[1] *Der Zweikampf mit der Geliebten.* Singspiel in three acts (Hamburg, 1811).

for Hamburg and performed there and elsewhere. The subject of *Faust* clearly corresponds very closely to the spirit to be found in the majority of Spohr's works: and this dark, Romantic spirit-world is ideally matched with the composer's inmost musical character. Owing to this fact the work as a whole is marked by great aptness of colour – big musical and dramatic effects of charm and tenderness alternating with shatteringly powerful effects in the ensembles and choruses.

Individual features of the score, such as instrumentation and harmony, bear witness to that intensely scrupulous attention to detail and strictness of taste that we have come to expect from this master. A few melodies, felicitously and aptly devised, weave like delicate threads through the whole, and hold it together artistically. In this connexion I might add that the overture, though highly effective, is only fully intelligible after one has heard the whole work. The composer himself alludes to this in his preface to the printed libretto.

The composer has tried to present in the overture a musical impression of the circumstances of Faust's life. In the Allegro vivace it is Faust's sensual life and the riot of debauchery that is suggested. With satiety comes an awakening of his better self, and pricks of conscience, though these are overwhelmed by the return of sensual impulses. In the Largo grave he at last pulls himself together and seriously attempts to renounce the evil of his ways; and in the fugato there is a suggestion of good resolutions being formed. It is not long, however, before he is again the prey of new and stronger sensual temptations (tempo primo) and, blinded by the deceptive power of the Evil One, he abandons himself more completely than ever to the most uncontrolled desires.

Like all Spohr's works, this opera bristles with difficulties of a technical musical kind, and these will no doubt tell against its being performed in many theatres. The present writer, however, is happy to be able to inform the music-loving public that, owing to the good-will and industry of the whole company, chorus and orchestra, no effort has been spared in bringing such novel – and often for that reason more difficult – works to the attention of the public.

81. Review of a Carlsbad concert by Amalie Schmalz

Written: Prague, before 17 September 1816.
Published: KPZ, No. 261, 17 September 1816.   *Unsigned.*
Reprinted: KSS.

    See above, No. 79, for the possible source of Weber's Carlsbad reviews.

Among the more recent and, in both senses, attractive artistic delights a high place must be accorded to the grand vocal and instrumental concert given in the Sächsischer Saal by the well-known Prussian court singer *Mlle Auguste Amalie Schmalz, in aid of the Fund for Impoverished Mountain Villagers. It is always refreshing to see art displaying its charms in aid of our needy fellow men, and particularly when the undertaking is pioneered by such a remarkable talent, who has collected colleagues of similar calibre to support suffering humanity and at the same time to provide benefactors with such a delightful evening.

Among a number of virtuosos taking part special mention should be made of the young Ritter von Eskeles, who shows remarkable gifts as an amateur violoncellist. He played for Mlle Schmalz and, with the addition of *Herr Giuliani and *Herr Moscheles, formed a fascinating ensemble. The programme opened with an overture, after which Mlle Schmalz sang a Cavatina by Portogallo[1] and fully justified the great expectations formed in the present writer's mind by the accounts of those who had heard this remarkable artist. Next came a potpourri for violoncello and pianoforte composed by Herr Moscheles, who played it with Herr von Eskeles. Much was naturally expected of the talents and artistic understanding of an amateur confident enough to appear in public with an artist of such calibre; but there is no denying that Herr von Eskeles was equal to every demand made on him and more than fulfilled our expectations. Particularly praiseworthy is the taste with which he handles his instrument – not exactly an easy one for the average music-lover to appreciate – and this prompts us to form the highest hopes for his future career.

Mlle Schmalz then sang an aria by Portogallo and finally a Romance, 'La Sentinelle', with variations, by Herr von Eskeles, Herr Giuliani, Herr Moscheles and a number of amateurs. Both works gave the singer even more opportunity than her first song to display the mastery of her art, the power and agility of her voice and the fine taste and production that she commands. She was rewarded not only by the silent gratitude of music-lovers, but also by the enthusiastic applause of the general public.

[1]   Marcos Antonio Portugal (1762–1830), known as Portogallo in Italy and elsewhere, wrote some twenty-one Portuguese comic operas and thirty-five Italian operas.

82. Review of a Prague concert
by Mauro Giuliani

Written: Prague, after 6 September 1816.
Published: KPZ, No. 282, 8 October 1816.   *Unsigned.*
Reprinted: KSS; LKA.

From Carlsbad, *Mauro Giuliani came on to Prague. Weber wrote to *Rochlitz to say, 'A number of performers, Giuliani, *Mlle Schmalz and others helped to keep my head warm and inflame the rest of me for a bit.' Weber was of course himself a skilled guitarist. See also above, No. 81.

On 6 September the great and universally acknowledged guitarist Herr Mauro Giuliani gave a concert in the Redoutensaal. Our expectations beforehand were high, thanks to the artist's reputation which had preceded him; but it is impossible to deny that Herr Giuliani's performance not only fulfilled, but even exceeded them.

The guitar is the most meagre and unrewarding of all concert instruments, but his playing was marked by such an agility, a control and a delicacy that he often achieved a real cantabile, much to our delight and admiration. The present writer enjoyed most of all the concerto, which may well be the most idiomatic and well written of all concertos for this instrument. The musical ideas themselves are attractive and well arranged, and the instrumentation, in particular, is cleverly designed to ensure that the solo instrument is as prominent and effective as possible. The potpourri for two guitars, in which *Herr Sellner did noble service as the second guitarist, was less satisfactory and appeared less substantial without the light and shade provided by an orchestral accompaniment. *Mme Grünbaum's singing added distinction to the programme, and both she and Herr Giuliani were given an enthusiastic reception by the audience. *Herr Stöger also gave an outstanding performance of an aria by *Kapellmeister Hummel and shared the unanimous applause of the public.

83. Review of a Prague concert
by Amalie Schmalz

Written: Prague, 19 September 1816.
Published: KPZ, No. 282, 8 October 1816.   *Unsigned.*
Reprinted: KSS.

*Amalie Schmalz had, like *Mauro Giuliani, travelled on to Prague from Carlsbad. See also above, No. 81.

On 19 September Mlle Schmalz from Berlin delighted music-lovers with a grand concert in the Redoutensaal. This excellent artist laid the foundations of her high reputation during her time in Italy, Vienna, Berlin and elsewhere, and we were charmed to find in her an outstanding bravura singer, possessed of an unusual range which she exploits with great confidence. Both her taste and her excellent production display the benefits of having studied in Italy, the classical home of singing. Her second aria, composed by *Kapellmeister Gürrlich, was especially remarkable: here, where the German conception of art combined with Italian brilliance, Mlle Schmalz displayed all the qualities of her voice to such advantage that she received an ovation from the public.

That excellent young artist *Herr Carl Maria von Bocklet played a violin concerto by *Rode which displayed the great advance that he has made in the development of his fine talents. On every new appearance he gives further justification of our great expectations for his future career. It was most regrettable that Mlle Schmalz's tour schedule made it impossible for us to hear her in dramatic music.

84. Farewell to Prague

Written: Prague, 3 October 1816.
Printed: KSS.

Weber concluded his duties as director of the Prague Opera on 30 September, and took his leave of the company on 7 October. This notice was written for the *KPZ*, but for some reason was never published.

Since September 1813 I have been responsible for the direction of the Opera at the Landständisches Theater, and I am now resigning that office. I feel that I cannot deny myself the duty and the pleasure of expressing my warmest thanks to all members of the Opera, the chorus and the orchestra, for their untiring efforts and the boundless confidence which they have reposed in my policies. Wherever I may be, these will always constitute some of the happiest memories of my life. I am further prompted to express my gratitude by the fact that a number of difficult circumstances, musical and non-musical, obliged me to make a number of exceptional demands. These passed unnoticed by the outside world – as was inevitable from their nature – and were for that very reason doubly appreciated by the only person fully acquainted with the good-will displayed and its effect on the organization for which he was responsible.

I should like to think that you too will have happy memories of our collaboration; and nothing could give me more welcome assurance of this than the knowledge that the institution, to which I devoted such unfailing enthusiasm, will continue to prosper and to flourish, endued with this same admirable spirit.

Prague, 3 October 1816

Carl Maria von Weber

Former Director of the Opera at the Landständisches Theater.

85. Warning to the public

Written: Berlin, 22 November 1816.
Published: AMZ XVIII (1816), Intelligenz-Blatt x; *Zeitung für die elegante Welt,* 1816, Intelligenz-Blatt xx.   *Signed:* Carl Maria von Weber.
Reprinted: MMW; KSS.

Weber sent this notice to *Rochlitz on 22 November 1816 with a covering letter: 'I respectfully hope to be favoured with a corner for the enclosed note as soon as possible in the *Allgemeine musikalische Zeitung.* The nuisance caused by this sort of thing is maddening, and if it had afflicted someone else I would have spoken up still more vigorously; but as it affects me, I think the simplest and most moderate course is the best, and the disgraceful behaviour of the publisher and of Herr Ebers will be adequately exposed.' Carl Friedrich Ebers (1770–1836) was a composer and arranger who led an itinerant life that included a period in Seconda's Theatre Company. Sir George Grove, who reprinted the controversy in the first edition (1890) of his *Dictionary of Music and Musicians,* declared him to be 'a man evidently of great ability, and as evidently of little moral stability'. German opinions do not substantially differ. Weber's gesture, a pioneering one, is a characteristic Romantic blow for the sovereignty of the artist.

The music publisher Herr Friedrich Hofmeister of Leipzig has issued an arrangement of my Quintet Op. 34 (for clarinet, two violins, viola and violoncello) as a solo piano sonata, with the following misleading title.

Sonata for pianoforte
arranged from a clarinet quintet
by
C. F. Ebers
of
Charles Marie de Weber
Op. 34

I urgently requested Herr Hofmeister to withdraw this publication, which defaces, and in many places destroys, the sense of the original.

His only reply was that 'if the arranger has been guilty of mistakes, he must expect the sharpest criticism; but this hardly concerns me'. I have therefore had no choice but to warn the public most solemnly and confine myself to the following observation – that apart from a number of possible misprints, the melodic line has been unnecessarily altered in forty-one places, and that a number of bars have been altogether omitted – 1 in one passage, 11 in another, 1 in a third, 8 in a fourth, 1 in a fifth and 4 in a sixth.

Ebers replied in the next number of the *AMZ* and in Intelligenz-Blatt xxii of the *Zeitung für die elegante Welt* as follows:

Herr Schlesinger of Berlin has published as Carl Maria von Weber's Op. 34 a quintet for clarinet and strings – when five people play together I believe it is called a quintet – which is so completely inaccurately engraved that no clarinettist unfamiliar with the work could possibly detect and avoid mistakes in certain places, for instance bar 60 of the second part of the first Allegro. I took the trouble to score the thing and found that the charming melodies would not sound at all bad on the piano; and as such pieces are available for arranging, I made out of it all a solo piano sonata which I can conscientiously recommend to music-lovers. As clarinet figuration does not always suit the piano, the arranger is at liberty to alter and omit whatever is repetitious and ineffective. It has been done with insight, and there can be no question of misrepresentation. Mozart and Haydn – great men who did not seek to make a musical effect with din and showiness, with bombast and bizarrerie – were happy with arrangements of their compositions, and it happens daily to the great Beethoven. If it still distresses Herr Weber to see his child in a new dress, and should he therefore withdraw his paternity from it, I shall be obliged to ask the public to acknowledge me as its foster father. But the public has a right to insist that Herr Schlesinger corrects the mistakes in his publications, for as long as a single work remains uncorrected he is open to the reproach, *ne sutor ultra crepidam*.[1]

---

[1]   Ebers appears to be misquoting the origin of the proverb *ne supra crepidam sutor judicaret* ('let the cobbler stick to his last') in the Elder Pliny (*Nat. Hist.* 35, x). However, Schlesinger did bring out a new edition of the quintet, 'corrigé par l'Auteur'.

86. A correction

Written: Berlin, 20 December 1816.
Published: MMW (erroneously superscribed 'Prague').
Reprinted: KSS.

Weber had been annoyed by a report in the Berlin *Dramaturgische Wochen-blatt* that referred to *Liebich's funeral, and by a dismissive review describing *Caroline Brandt as a *Dreissigerin.* Liebich actually died on 21 December, the day after Weber wrote. The *Wochenblatt* did not print his letter in their No. 28 of 11 January 1817, carrying instead a notice to the effect that public announcements of Liebich's death corrected their previously published information. Nothing was said about Caroline Brandt.

In No. 24 (14 December last) of your versatile journal there appeared, under the date of 25 November in Prague, the description of the much-respected theatre director Liebich's funeral as a sad event. I am sorry to have to contradict this, but feel obliged to point out that such a funeral cannot possibly have taken place, since Director Liebich was still alive on 14 December and well on the way to that recovery which has in the event proved such a delight to all good musicians and music-lovers.

In addition to this I should like to draw attention once more to the conscientiousness which marks all your reporting; but your Dresden correspondent's report of 26 November is evidence of your willingness to publish the unjustified views of your correspondents even when these conflict with your own correct convictions. In the interests of veracity, then, I must point out that Mlle Brandt is indebted to your reporter, or his source of information, for ten years of her age, since she has just celebrated her twenty-first birthday.

I feel convinced that you will welcome this information since you have often emphasized your love of accuracy. I too consider it a pleasure to be able to make an occasional contribution to the perfecting of a journal which has so justifiably high a reputation in Berlin, where there is daily opportunity to convince oneself of its true worth. Finally I should like to ask, as a favour of the editor, for an assurance that this information will appear in the next (28th) number and I have the honour to remain, yours respectfully...

87. Review of E. T. A. Hoffmann's *Undine*

Written: Berlin, early January 1817.
Published: AMZ xix (1817), 201–8.   *Signed:* Carl Maria von Weber.
Reprinted: HHS, MMW (both incomplete and inaccurate); KSS; LKA.

*Hoffmann's *Undine* was produced at the Berlin Schauspielhaus on 3 August 1816 with, in the title role, the sixteen-year-old Johanna Eunicke (later to be Weber's first Aennchen). The text was by Baron Friedrich de la Motte Fouqué, after his own story (1811), which had given wider Romantic currency to the popular legend. The twenty-third performance was on 27 July 1817, when the theatre burnt down and the scenery and costumes were destroyed. Apart from an unsuccessful revival in Prague in 1821, the work was not seen again until 1922, when it was championed by Pfitzner.

When I formed the intention of saying something about this fine work in the public prints, I had an involuntary vision of all the other announcements, notices or whatever you like to call them devoted to the same subject; and it was only then that I fully realized the extreme difficulty of forming any clear picture of the work under discussion or anything approaching the impression that it is capable of making. It seemed to me that there are almost always two alternatives. On the one hand one can content oneself with the usual opinions of society, some favourable and some hostile, without more ado, or with more moderate opinion inclined neither wholly to accept nor wholly to reject, and all depending on the importance and credibility of the individual judge and the confidence that he inspires, which is a purely subjective factor. On the other hand, in the case of large works on which not everyone is going to be able to lay their hands, any detailed technical examination of structure and so forth entails a minute dissection in which the work as a whole simply dissolves. The greatest effects and beauties of a work depend on their presentation and arrangement; removed from their context they mostly lose their whole individuality and even seem, as it were, to testify against themselves by virtually losing their significance when viewed in isolation. Even the most vivid description can only very rarely communicate the sense of their organic relationship to the rest of the work.

Of course there are plenty of exceptions to this rule, especially in the case of works that are generally familiar, where structural analysis can be most instructive to the student. In the present case, however, all that is needed is to draw the attention of the public to a work by indicating the imaginative world to which it belongs and briefly sketching the form chosen by the composer. First, then, we must become clear in our own minds how in fact the judge of a work of art – *this* work of art – himself sees, believes and thinks; and there should then be no difficulty in each person deciding to what extent he can consent to the resulting judgements. In this connexion, I think I cannot do better than preface my actual discussion of the opera by quoting the following passage from a larger work of mine, since it applies for the most part to the formation of the opera *Undine*.[1]

In order to judge properly any work of art that depends on a performance within the temporal dimension, it is essential for the critic to have a tranquil and unprejudiced mind, open to every kind of impression but scrupulously free of any definite opinion or emotional inclination, except of course a conscious preparedness to accept the subject matter in question. It is only in this way that we can give the artist complete sway over our state of mind and enable his emotions and characters to transport us into the world of his creation, where he is the master of all emotional stimulation and impels us to share his sorrow, his delight, his agony of mind, his joy, hope and love. It will very soon be shown beyond any doubt whether he has been able to create a work of the imagination that makes a lasting impression, or whether his work is no more than a succession of brilliant but irregular and uncertain flashes of brilliance, individually attractive but leaving no lasting impression as a whole.

In no art form is this latter so hard to avoid, and therefore so frequently encountered as in opera. Of course when I speak of opera I am speaking of the German ideal, namely a self-sufficient work of art in which every feature and every contribution by the related arts are moulded together in a certain way and dissolve, to form a new world. In most cases individual numbers decide the fate of an opera. It is only rarely that such attractive individual features, which strike the listener immediately, disappear in the final impression of the work as a whole, as should ideally occur. For ideally the listener should fall in love with the whole work and only later pick out the details of which it is composed.

The very nature and inner constitution of opera – as a whole containing other wholes – has this essential drawback, which only a few heroes of the art have managed to surmount. Every musical

---

[1]   The following four paragraphs are repeated in *Tonkünstlers Leben*, ch. 5 (below, No. 125), initially in general sentiment but soon literally, word for word. The only significant alteration is that in his famous definition of the unified work of art, Weber in *Tonkünstlers Leben* speaks of 'the German and French ideal'; here he mentions only the German.

number has its own proper architecture, which makes it an independent and organic unity; yet this should be absorbed in any study of the work as a whole. Ensembles, in particular, can and should show a number of different aspects simultaneously, a Janus-like image, whose different faces are visible at a single glance.

Herein lies the great and profound secret of music, something that can be felt but cannot be expressed in words. The ebb, the flow and all the conflicting tides of anger, love and 'the pleasure that's all but pain' are here united, where Salamander and Undine[2] mingle and embrace one another. In a word, what love is to human beings, music is both to the other arts and to human beings, for it is indeed love itself, the purest and most ethereal language, myriad-faced and containing all the colours of the rainbow in every mode of feeling, uniquely true, to be understood simultaneously by human beings of a thousand different emotional complexions. This veracity of music's language, in whatever unexpected form it may appear, is finally victorious in asserting its rights. The fates of all eras of musical and representational art prove this completely and on many occasions. For example, nothing could seem more improbable than Gluck's works at a time when all sensibilities were overwhelmed and unmanned by the flood of Italian music, with its powerful sensuous charm. At the present time the artistic errors that threaten us are of quite a different kind, though perhaps even more dangerous. The circumstances of life today have made it inevitable that the two extremes of death and pleasure rule our lives. The horrors of war have depressed our spirits, and misery has been all too common, so that relief has been sought in the coarsest and most primitive forms in the arts. The theatre has become little more than a peepshow in which the noble and satisfying excitement associated with true artistic pleasure has been carefully avoided, and in its stead we have been content with the titillations of trivial jokes and melodies and dazzled by pointless stage spectacle. Accustomed in everyday life to being astonished, nothing but astonishment will serve us in the theatre. Following the gradual development of a passion or a witty building-up of all the interests involved is considered exhausting, boring and – to the unobservant – unintelligible.

I have been obliged to listen to absolutely contradictory opinions of *Undine*, and for precisely these reasons. I have tried to be as far as possible unprejudiced in my own judgement, although my knowledge

---

2   The four elemental creatures, as conceived by Paracelsus, were Salamander (fire), Undine (water), Sylph (air) and Gnome (earth). Pope refers to them in the Prelude to *The Rape of the Lock*, and they passed into Romantic lore.

of Herr Hoffmann's writings impelled me to expect something out of the ordinary from his opera. Anyone capable of appreciating the spirit of Mozart with the warmth of imagination and the penetration to be found in Hoffmann's *Phantasiestücke in Callots Manier* Part 1, the story *Don Juan*,[3] is simply incapable of producing anything mediocre. He might at the outside verge on the mediocre, but could never lose himself beyond the dividing line.

La Motte Fouqué's arrangement of the original seems to the present writer to be as a dramatic fairy tale in which a number of interior connexions might indeed well have been interpreted with greater emphasis and clarity. The author in fact knew his own story only too well, so that he has often been betrayed into a kind of self-deception – the belief that others would know it as well as he did himself. On the other hand, to maintain that the work is unintelligible, as many have done, is simply not true.

To compensate for this weakness, the composer has made the colours and outlines of the music all the more explicit and unambiguous. The music is in a single mould, and after repeated hearings the present writer cannot remember a single passage that even for a moment broke the magic spell cast by the composer. Indeed, the fascination of the musical development is so powerful from beginning to end that one can grasp the whole work after a single hearing and individual details simply disappear, with the innocence and reticence proper to all great art.

Only those who know what it means to sacrifice the glory of the spontaneous burst of public applause can fully appreciate the magnitude of Herr Hoffmann's refusal to enrich one musical number at the expense of the others by drawing greater attention to it – easily achieved by a broader and more protracted handling – than its place in the whole really warrants. He goes steadily forward, visibly guided by the determination to achieve dramatic truth and intensity instead of holding up the swift progress of the drama or shackling it in any way. However differently and tellingly depicted the various characters in the story may be, they are still surrounded by that spectral story-book atmosphere and the delightful thrills of fairyland.

The most powerful impression is that made by Kühleborn (the present writer, like the composer, takes an acquaintance with the story for granted) and the characteristic melodies and instruments which always accompany him and announce his uncanny presence. Since he appears, if not as an actual personification of Fate then as Fate's

[3]   Published in *AMZ* xv (1813), 213ff.

immediate agent, this is also absolutely right. Next in order of interest comes the lovely water-nymph Undine, whose music is alternately playfully rippling and striking enough to suggest her magic powers. To the present writer it is the aria in Act 2 that most successfully suggests both sides of her character; and indeed the handling is so charming and spirited that it may well serve as a sample of the whole work and is therefore appearing as a supplement. Next come the ardent, vacillating, love-lorn Huldebrand and the simple, devout priest with his austere chorale. More in the background are the figures of Berthalda, the fisherman and his wife, and the Duke and Duchess. The choruses of the retainers breathe a gay vitality, amounting in some cases to a quite exceptional sense of euphoria and in strong contrast to the gloomy choruses of the spirits of earth and water with their strange, harmonically dense progressions.

The finale of the opera seems to the present writer the most successful thing in the work, truly grand in conception, with the composer crowning and topping the harmonic wealth of his music with an eight-part chorus to the words 'Gute Nacht aller Erdensorg und Pracht'. Here the melody is touchingly devout in character and marked by a sense of deep significance, grand and melancholy at the same time, so that the actual tragic ending leaves a strong sense of consolation. Here, too, the overture is taken up in the final chorus, rounding off the whole work. The overture conjures up and evokes the world of magic. It starts quietly, gathers strength and fire and passes straight into the first act. The final chorus brings universal consolation and satisfaction. The work as a whole is one of the most imaginative of recent years. It is the happy outcome of complete knowledge and understanding in its own field, achieved by deep thought and consideration and a careful calculation of all material means; and its fine, deeply felt melodies give it the hallmark of a true work of art. To say this is tantamount to saying that it contains handsome, and often in fact novel, instrumental effects, correct prosody, etc., for these are the means of which every true master must freely dispose, since without this the musical imagination is severely hampered.

With an eye to Herr Hoffmann's future development, and since neither praise nor blame can be unmixed, the present writer would like to express a few hopes. First, however, it should be said that in *Undine* itself he would not wish anything altered, since everything is just as it should – and indeed must – be, and one may well wonder whether the same will be true of a later work. Even so, one can get a very good idea from a single work of a composer's favourite turns of phrase, and good friends should always warn him of the possibility of these becoming mannerisms. What particularly struck the present writer as something to be guarded against was a certain preference for small, short figures which can both easily lack variety and disturb or cloud the melodic line, and to which only a conductor of unusual intelligence and scrupulousness will be able to give proper prominence. Then mention should also be made of Herr Hoffmann's marked preference for violoncello and viola and for chords of the diminished seventh, and also of a certain brusqueness in cadences which, at least at a first hearing, makes a disturbing impression and if not actually incorrect is nevertheless unsatisfactory. Finally, there are certain middle parts of a kind often to be found in *Cherubini, and therefore liable to make the general public look out for other resemblances.

As far as the sets and costumes are concerned, the production was magnificent;[4] and both singing and acting could be called successful. Public interest in the opera is demonstrated by the continuing full houses. The malicious attribute too much of the work's success to the stage sets. But the present writer has observed that in other pieces of which this is true the public wait for these spectacular moments and then leave, whereas in *Undine* their attention is engaged uninterruptedly from beginning to end, which provides sufficient proof of their interest in the work itself. Almost every number would be applauded to the echo were it not for the small number of full closes, since the work moves forward steadily at a swift pace.

Let us hope that Herr Hoffmann will soon give the world another opera of such worth as this; and that his versatile spirit, which quickly won him a literary reputation and a respected position among his colleagues as a civil servant (member of the Prussian Supreme Court in Berlin), will continue its creative activity in this branch of the arts also.

4   These famous designs were by Carl Friedrich Schinkel.

88. To the art-loving citizens of Dresden

Written: Dresden, 26 January 1817.
Published: DAZ, No. 25, 29 January 1817.   *Signed:* Carl Maria von Weber.
Reprinted: HHS; MMW; KSS; LKA.

To preface his work in Dresden as director of the German Opera, Weber felt it useful to publish an article setting out his aims and beliefs. The main part was reused from a similar article he had written on arrival in Prague, slightly revised and stylistically improved (see above, No. 49), and this he added to the new introduction here translated. It generated considerable controversy, as Weber told his wife: 'The enclosed essay has caused a good deal of sensation, delight, attention and alarm: all of them necessary in this world!... Good men have already begun to like me, and the others are thoroughly alarmed, as they well know that I'm not to be trifled with!' (letter from Dresden, n.d.).

Musical-Dramatic Articles,

an attempt to assist music-lovers in forming their opinions of new operas given at the Königliches Theater, Dresden, by means of notes and suggestions relating to the history of the art.

To the Art-Loving Citizens of Dresden

The amiable foresight and proven love of the arts of their gracious monarch have provided the inhabitants of Dresden with a handsome enrichment of their lives in the form of a new German Opera now being founded; and it seems as though a valuable and perhaps necessary contribution to the success of this undertaking might be made by the individual in charge of the institution, if he were to try to explain the nature, method and circumstances of the whole operation.

Man naturally takes a warmer interest in anything whose origin, growth and progress he can see with his own eyes. He loves and values more than anything something whose constitution and construction he has come to understand; and nothing can touch him more nearly than matters relating to the arts – the creation of human vitality raised to its highest power and something to which every member of the community makes an invisible, but by no means an unconscious, contribution.

Those entrusted with the management and organization of this public treasure-house have therefore a duty to tell the public what it can expect and hope for, and to what extent the success of such an undertaking depends on their benevolent and indulgent attitude. Great expectations are easily and swiftly aroused; but from the nature of the case it is difficult to satisfy even the most legitimate demands.

No people has been so slow and so uncertain as the German in determining its own specific art forms. Both the Italians and the French have evolved a form of opera in which they move freely and naturally. This is not true of the Germans, whose peculiarity it has been to adopt what seems best in other schools, after much study and steady development; but the matter goes deeper with them. Whereas other nations concern themselves chiefly with the sensuous satisfaction of isolated moments, the German demands a self-sufficient work of art, in which all the parts make up a beautiful and unified whole.

This being the case, the present writer believes that the formation of a good ensemble is of the first importance. If an artistic production is not marred by any alien elements, it has already achieved something very valuable, namely the impression of unity. This can only be brought about by enthusiasm, devotion and the correct use of all the elements concerned.

Ornament, brilliance and enthusiasm are only bestowed on any artistic institution by men and women of exceptional gifts, and these are everywhere rare. They are in an assured and established position wherever they may be; and it is only time and the blessing which alone makes any human undertaking prosper, that can eventually secure them. And so if we speak now of initiating German operatic perform- ances, we can only be referring either to attempts to form an artistic corps or to opportunities to become acquainted with foreign talents and to judge their qualities in performances here – or finally to providing opportunities for artists to further their musical development.

What we achieve with our present forces I can only commend to the indulgence and benevolence of the critical public. Later, when the company is stronger, we shall be able to make more effective use of the talent we already possess and place it in the most advantageous light; and not until then shall we be able to initiate a planned policy in the choice of operas to be performed, varying them according to their musical and dramatic character and thus giving the public the best of every period and country with the same eye to quality of performance in every case. In order to demonstrate this wish to music-lovers, the first performance of any new work will be preceded by articles such as the following. Thereby I shall at least demonstrate my desire to further the good cause so far as in me lies; and I hope that I may express the hope that the public will understand this.[1]

---

[1]   The article first published in Prague (above, No. 49) then followed.

89. Introduction to Méhul's *Joseph*

Written: Dresden, January 1817.
Published: DAZ, No. 25, 29 January 1817.

Signed: Carl Maria von Weber.

Reprinted: HHS; MMW; KSS; LKA.

Joseph was produced at the Opéra-Comique, Paris, on 17 February 1807. It became very popular all over Europe. The first performance in German, in the translation by Matthias Lambrecht as *Jakob und seine Söhne in Ägypten*, was in Munich on 6 June 1809. Weber greatly admired the work (see above, No. 22), and it suited the limited resources he found awaiting him in Dresden. It requires only one female singer, for the travesty role of Benjamin, and does not make very severe demands on any singer: the German company had not been well recruited, and the most serious lack was of a good female lead. The chief roles were taken by a newly engaged tenor, *Johann Gottfried Bergmann (Joseph), the house producer *Friedrich Hellwig (Jacob), and the actress Schubert (Benjamin). *Friedrich Burmeister, then forty-five and engaged for 'noble father' roles, played another of Jacob's sons, and *Georg Wilhelmi played Simeon. Later there were several cast changes: the most successful performance was by *Heinrich Stümer, from Berlin, as Joseph. As there were no women in the theatre chorus, Weber had to dress up the boys of the Kreuzschule for the Virgins of Memphis, which caused a good deal of hilarity even though he took the precaution of posting some female soloists and actresses in the front row. Rehearsals began on 18 January, and there were eleven in all, the last on the morning of the performance, 30 January. 'Went very well. At the end was twice applauded with shouts of "Bravo Weber"' (Diary, 30 January). *Theodor Hell's *Abend-Zeitung* review (No. 34, 8 February 1817) was favourable, making special mention of the décor, Hellwig's production and the orchestral playing under Weber. The playing was also singled out for praise in a poem, 'An Maria von Weber', by 'a musical layman' (*DAZ*, No. 41, 17 February 1817). The *AMZ*, referring to the new company as 'Institut für deutsche Oper', praised the orchestra but was more reserved about the singing (*AMZ* xix (1817), 182).

On Thursday 30 January the first performance in our theatre will take place of the opera *Jakob und seine Söhne in Ägypten*, after the original French of Alexandre Duval, the music by Méhul.

After *Cherubini, Méhul is unquestionably the finest of the composers who have formed and developed their art chiefly in France and eventually, by their unfailing truth to nature, become the property of the whole world. Cherubini may perhaps have more genius, but Méhul is more thoughtful, and his music shows the best-judged calculation and employment of the means at his disposal and a certain solidity and purity evidently achieved by a thorough study of the oldest Italian masters and more particularly of Gluck's dramatic works. The chief hallmarks of his music are great dramatic truth and a vivid forward movement with no irrelevant repetitions, the achievement of great effects often with the simplest means and an economy in his use of the orchestra which leads him to confine himself to what is strictly necessary.

Many of his hymns and songs became something like the folk music of the Revolution after 1789, and he has been credited with the authorship of the music of the *Marseillaise*.[1] Of some twenty operas, those on which his reputation chiefly rests are *Euphrosine* (first given in Paris in 1791),[2] *Adrien, Ariodant, Une Folie, Héléna, Joseph* and *Les Deux aveugles de Tolède*, which have confirmed his mastery in the most diverse genres. Particular enthusiasm was aroused by his overture to *Le Jeune Henri*, although the opera itself was a failure.[3] The overture was repeated day after day with perpetual calls of 'encore!' Almost all the works mentioned above have been given throughout Germany. The least well known are *Adrien* and *Ariodant*, and the most popular *Une Folie*, which has everywhere enjoyed a great success under the title *Je toller, je besser* or *Die beiden Füchse*; after that come *Héléna* and *Les Deux aveugles*, and most recently *Joseph*, or *Jakob und seine Söhne in Ägypten*.[4]

Those who know and admire the light-hearted charm, the popular high spirits, the humour and *bonhomie* of *Une Folie* will rightly be amazed by Méhul's versatility of mind and mood when they hear *Joseph*. A truly patriarchal atmosphere and way of life are here combined with a childlike purity of religious devotion. Strong characterization and a passionate sincerity of expression are unmistakable in the overall mastery, the theatrical experience and the clear grasp of what such a work demands. The composer here disdains all tinsel and tawdry; truth of expression is his endeavour, and beautiful, moving melody guides his genius.

The present writer would like to make it clear that the end of the opera – Joseph's short solo and the chorus which follows it – was

[1] Rouget de Lisle's authorship of both words and music was not so famous in Germany as in France.
[2] *Euphrosine*, Méhul's first opera, was actually given at the Comédie-Italienne on 4 September 1790.
[3] The presence of a king on the stage led to boos by Republicans.
[4] Of Méhul's operas listed by Weber, those which press notices show to have been especially popular in Germany include *Héléna, Ariodant, Joseph* and *Une Folie* (also staged as *Wagen gewinnt*). He does not mention *Irato*, which had successful performances in Berlin and Leipzig (as *Der Tollkopf*) in 1804.

composed by *Musikdirektor Fränzl of Munich, who has modelled his style closely on Méhul's. The present writer is the declared enemy of all such additions, cuts and other mutilations of an original work, and he will later find a number of occasions to speak his mind on this subject. If he shows himself tolerant in the present instance, it is owing to a feature common to all French operas, namely the almost complete triviality of the final chorus. This can be explained by the fact that after the final dénouement of the drama the lively French intelligence tends to lose interest in a work and to let it play itself out without paying any attention. The German listener enjoys savouring the dramatic situation, and his sympathies are still engaged by the emotions of the stage characters who have won his affection. The fact that the opera is definitely improved by this addition and, incidentally, that this is the form in which it is always given in Germany, decided the present writer to leave it thus.

Since the dissolution of the Institut National and the Conservatoire, of which he was in one case a member and in the other a professor, Méhul has retired from public life. He lives in Paris and is reputed to be working on a large opera.[5]

[5]　Méhul died on 17 October 1817, with *Valentine de Milan* incomplete.

90.　Introduction to Anton Fischer's
Das Hausgesinde

Written: Dresden, 13 February 1817.
Published: DAZ, No. 42, 18 February 1817. *Signed:* Carl Maria von Weber.
Reprinted: HHS; MMW; KSS.

Anton Fischer (1778–1808) was a Swabian by birth. Moving to Vienna, he was obliged to find employment in the chorus of the Josephstädtertheater, and then sang secondary roles in Schikaneder's company at the Theater auf der Wieden, later Theater an der Wien. His early attempts at composition, according to FétisB, were so closely modelled on Mozart, *Cherubini, Méhul and Elsner that he was reproached with plagiarism. However, a certain success led to his appointment as second Kapellmeister at the theatre. *Das Hausgesinde* (1808) was the most popular of some dozen operas given in Vienna. It was adapted from *Le Désespoir de Jocrisse* (1791) by Dorvigny (pseudonym of Louis-François Archambault, 1742–1812). The comic servant Jocrisse gave his name to a type of amiable, credulous simpleton, deriving from the *commedia dell'arte*, who reappeared in much French farce. He owed much of his popularity to the actor Brunet (pseudonym of Jean Joseph Mara, 1766–1853), whose performance of the piece at the Théâtre des Variétés in 1796 made his own name as well as that of Jocrisse. As Weber suggests, the character 'travelled' better than some national comic types: it reached not only Germany, where Schlegel's praise aroused the interest of the Romantics, but even Poland, where 'Zokrys' became popular through the actor Józef Zdanowicz. The Dresden performance of Fischer's opera was not a great success, Weber recorded in his Diary, in part because the hoarseness of *Emilie Zucker meant that Fräulein Schubert (the Benjamin of *Joseph*: see above, No. 89) was obliged to sing her part from the wings. The review in the *Abend-Zeitung* dismissed it in a few lines (*DAZ*, No. 49, 26 February 1817).

On Tuesday 18 February there will take place the first performance of a one-act opera *Das Hausgesinde*, based on a French original, with music by Fischer. This is an entertaining play designed for all who enjoy a good-humoured joke and the few moments of amusement that it entails. Popular humour is for the most part restricted by local considerations and expresses itself in figures and characters familiar to the inhabitants of a single region, associated if not identified with their own form of humour or burlesque – hence each country's possessing a comic character who represents the humorous or whimsical elements in the national character. Nevertheless, some of these comic characters do occasionally migrate from the stages of one country to those of another, where they undergo a process of adaptation and become more or less nationalized. This is seldom a complete success; and the appreciation of such figures generally depends on critical consideration and a knowledge of the distinguishing characteristics of each country. Such appreciation is therefore confined to the comparatively few capable of fully understanding their significance. A full enjoyment of the English Falstaff and John Bull, or the Italian Arlecchino (not, by the way, to be confused with the German Hanswurst) and Policinello, depends in each case on a familiarity with the national character.

For the last twenty years or so a brilliant comedian (Brunet, in Paris) has succeeded in making a character called Jocrisse a favourite in France with all those who enjoy a good laugh. He was, and is, the mainstay of the Théâtre des Variétés, where everything revolves round him, and plays innumerable roles, in each of which he delights the public. There are similar recurrent comic figures in some parts of Germany, and the place once occupied all over Germany by Hanswurst (the famous Prehauser, in fact) is now taken in Vienna by Kasperl and in Bavaria by Lipperl.[1] A combination of stupidity and doltishness with

---

[1]   Gottfried Prehauser (1699–1769) was an Austrian comic actor, most famous for his impersonation of Stranitzky's classic version of Hanswurst. Though connected to Arlecchino in the *commedia dell'arte*, perhaps also with something in him of the company of English strolling players who were an influence on *Singspiel*, Hanswurst is as crafty as his Italian ancestor but more buffoonish, with a grosser sense of humour and a gluttony denoted by his

a certain degree of mother-wit, which stands out by contrast and emphasizes the comic side of every situation, often in the least expected manner, seems to be the fundamental nature of such comic characters everywhere. Of all Jocrisse's innumerable adventures – which have eventually (1809)[2] landed him in hell – the present work, adapted from *Le Désespoir de Jocrisse*, is to the best of my knowledge the only one to have reached the German stage. It was first given in Vienna by the well-known comedian Hasensuth,[3] who under the name of Taddädl has created an extremely amusing comic character of his own (making particular play with the pitch of his voice, using falsetto) and then, slightly differently adapted, by the comedian *Wurm who used to be in the Berlin company. In Vienna the music of the French vaudeville was of course pointless and was therefore replaced by music supplied by a talented young man named Fischer, who was composer-in-chief at the Theater auf der Wieden. He has recently died at a tragically early age, leaving behind him as earnest of what he might have achieved a mass of delightful songs, whimsical in character but thoroughly sound musically. Apart from a heap of isolated pieces inserted, in accordance with the lamentable Viennese practice, into other men's operas, Fischer left two operas of his own which were notably successful and plainly show his gifts – *Die Festung an der Elbe*[4] in three acts and *Die Verwandlungen*[5] in one act. The present work, too, is by no means without merit, and one can only hope that it will make its effect as a whole. Such works as these depend chiefly on the whim of the moment and the mood of both performer and listener. Those given to analysing their own enjoyment always fall short of the mark; and in fact it is impossible to sum up this genre better than in the words used by Millin in his *Magazin encyclopédique*[6] ('Jocrisse corrigé'): 'Ils font rire, c'est tout ce qu'il y a de mieux à en dire.'

protruding belly. The stupid but sly Kasperl is a subtler and more specifically Austrian manifestation – owing his fullest characterization to the actor Johann Laroche (1745–1806) – as Lipperl is specifically Bavarian.

[2]   Weber seems to have mistaken the date of *Das Hausgesinde*, actually 1808.

[3]   Anton Hasenhut [*sic*] (1766–1841) was an Austrian comic actor whose stage name, Taddädl, was taken from Taddeo in the *commedia dell'arte*. His characteristic squeaking voice was made use of by *Wenzel Müller in *Der lebendige Sack* (1787), and this ensured his fame: he was the original Lorenzo in *Das Hausgesinde*. He was much admired by both Tieck and Grillparzer.

[4]   1806.

[5]   1805.

[6]   Aubin Louis Millin de Grandmaison founded his *Magazin encyclopédique, ou Journal des sciences, des lettres et des arts* in Paris in An III (1795). It eventually ran to 122 volumes.

91. Introduction to Himmel's *Fanchon*

Written: Dresden, before 24 February 1817.
Published: DAZ, No. 47, 24 February 1817. *Signed:* Carl Maria von Weber.
Reprinted: HHS; MMW; KSS.

Friedrich Himmel (1765–1814) showed such precocious talent that he came under the patronage of Frederick William II, who had him trained under *J. G. Naumann at Dresden, and then in Italy. Here his first operas were produced; but his greatest successes were with *Liederspiel* and *Singspiel*. His most famous work was the three-act *Fanchon*, to a text by *Kotzebue after a French vaudeville by Joseph Marie Pain and Jean Nicolas Bouilly. It was first produced in Berlin on 16 May 1804, and won immediate and widespread popularity: it was translated into several languages, and staged all over northern and eastern Europe. The *AMZ* gave it a dubious reception, praising the melodious songs but deploring the lack of general control (*AMZ* vi (1804), 488). Another critic, writing from Stettin on Himmel's visit there, reached similar conclusions, also finding fault with the libretto and calling the music 'a dainty potpourri scented with a few pretty blossoms' (*AMZ* vii (1805), 219). Weber noted that the Dresden performance went 'so-so, on the whole' (Diary, 24 February 1817). The cast included Mme Lindner (Fanchon). She was said to have 'neither voice nor technique, like most of the rest of the company' (*AMZ* xix (1817), 225), and to have 'overdone her part' (*DAZ*, No. 54, 4 March 1817). The remainder of the cast included *Georg Wilhelmi (Francarville), *Emilie Zucker (Florine), Herr Zwich (Abbé); Mlle Schubert learnt her part in two days when another singer fell ill.

On Monday 24 February there will take place the first performance here of *Fanchon, das Leiermädchen*, adapted from the French by Kotzebue, music by Himmel. The revival of this opera, so popular in Germany and at one time the centre of attention in Paris as a vaudeville and much parodied, is explained by the presence of Mlle Lindner from Kassel, who will be singing the title role as guest artist. Kotzebue originally arranged the work for the Berlin theatre, and Himmel wrote new music for the same production.

Friedrich Heinrich Himmel was born in 1765 at Treuenbrietzen, and he has a sort of claim on the interest of Dresden music-lovers owing to the fact that he studied with our admirable Naumann. It is to Naumann, in fact, that he was indebted for the knowledge of harmony, the smooth part-writing and skilled use of the orchestra which give his attractive compositions the charm of a certain solidity and skilfulness. A naturally pleasure-loving disposition and youthful high spirits prevented him from devoting the time needed to penetrate to music's deepest secrets, which no amount of natural genius will discover without long and arduous study; for really great things are only achievable by a personality capable of absolute concentration and cut off from the distractions of society.

For this reason, Himmel made his name chiefly by his touching, well-written songs, his setting of Tiedge's *Urania*[1] and the opera *Fanchon*. These individual examples of his admirable talent are marked by a happy blend of Italian charm and German sense of form; each seems to form a highpoint of pleasure, a glass of musical champagne. Himmel's music shows a natural, even a conscious inclination to the sentimental, and his works contain things that fall well below the ideal in this manner. *Fanchon* is a bouquet from just such a garden, a play of the most various moods and emotions, a butterfly quivering in the garden of the arts. The scene is laid in the most elegant and luxury-loving circles of Parisian life and every number is a witticism caught on the wing, a joke or some other point of heightened feeling.

There is no question of elaborate or protracted musical numbers in an opera, or really *Liederspiel*, such as this, modelled as it is on the French vaudeville. The piece originally owed its extraordinary success chiefly to the fact that each of the characters was ideally suited to one of the most outstanding artists in the Berlin theatre of the day (1803).[2] The excellent, well-rounded performance which resulted from this and the ease with which every member of the audience absorbed the music could not fail to make *Fanchon* a favourite work with the public of the day; and judged by these standards it will always remain an outstandingly enjoyable theatrical experience.

Among Himmel's larger works, the most successful were his *Vasco da Gama* and his Funeral Cantata on the death of Frederick William II. A later opera, *Die Sylphen* (1807), was less successful, and his last opera, *Der Kobold*, written for the Theater auf der Wieden, was a complete failure.[3] As a pianist, Himmel had a charming touch and an ingratiating manner which was found universally delightful, though he had no pretensions to virtuosity. At his death two years ago he was Royal Prussian Kapellmeister, and he can with justice be mourned by all those with a taste for amiable, expressive melody.

[1]   Christian August Tiedge (1752–1841), who settled in Dresden in 1819, was most famous for his philosophical poem *Urania* (1801). Himmel set songs from it as his Op. 18, published *c* 1800.

[2]   Actually 1804.

[3]   *Vasco da Gama* was a three-act *opera seria* (Berlin, 1801). *Die Sylphen* was a three-act *Zauberoper* after Gozzi's *La donna serpente* (thus anticipating Wagner's *Die Feen*), produced in Berlin, 1806 (*sic*). *Der Kobold* was a four-act comic opera (Vienna, 1813). The Funeral Cantata, to a text by Herklots, was given in Berlin in 1797.

92. Morlacchi's oratorio *Isacco*

Written: Dresden, 20 March 1817.
Published: DAZ, No. 78, 1 April 1817.   *Signed:* Carl Maria von Weber.
Reprinted: HHS; MMW; KSS; LKA.

Francesco Morlacchi (1784–1841) was a native of Perugia, but by 1810 was established as director of the Italian Opera in Dresden. As the favoured protégé of the court, where Italian taste in music had reigned since the days of Hasse, he found himself in opposition to Weber when the latter arrived with a commission to form and develop the German Opera. Their rivalry was not so bitter as their partisans like to suggest, nor was Morlacchi's behaviour so discreditable as some German biographers of Weber indicate; but he did take advantage of his rival's energy and good nature to absent himself for unnecessarily long periods and make other exhausting demands. Initially, they both felt that they could work together in the same city, and the present article (which Weber had translated for the benefit of the Italians in the city) is witness to the good-will on Weber's part and his hopes for a friendly co-operation. *Isacco* had a long, favourable review in *AMZ* xix (1817), 343–8.

When the deepest and holiest feelings are aroused and the soul is penetrated by the sublime images and memories of religion, the elevating power of music must also play its part, for it is the purest expression of human feeling. A daughter rather than a mimic of Nature, music in her solemn and mysterious language arouses and creates the sense of devotion; she works directly on man's emotional system and is the mistress of his deepest stirrings. With what wisdom the Church's usages run the gamut of human feelings – a solemn and awful silence to match the deepest affliction and a free burst of music to express thanks to the Creator for grace restored. It is a wonderful and solemn privilege to use one's powers for such an end, and an artist might well be content with the simple knowledge that his work has served its purpose. Yet no one could well hold it against him if he should wish to bring his labour of love nearer to the understanding of his listeners. The result of long periods of effort only rarely makes itself known, and is gone in a moment. And so the artist must be allowed to seize it as it passes, particularly if he believes that in his treatment of his material he has employed procedures unknown to his predecessors and of such a nature that a closer description would spare the listener doubt and puzzlement.

Kapellmeister Morlacchi has made a new setting of Metastasio's oratorio *Isacco, Figura del Redentore*. He has done me the honour of wishing to entrust me with translating the text into my native language and with explaining to the public his attitude and his intention in composing this oratorio. It is with joy and with the enthusiasm of an artistic colleague that I will attempt to fulfil his request.

The general public often condemns a work as dry or hard because it has not grasped the scale of values inherent in the work's conception, or else does not see it from the point of view determined by the composer's talents, cultivation and convictions. Generally speaking, Italians and Germans find each other's music alien and unsatisfying. A closer familiarity and wider musical education will bring greater understanding and the ability to distinguish what is outstanding in either field. But in every sphere perfect truth asserts her rights victoriously over all critical opinions, which after all must all be finally reconciled in the one truth. The criticism that is desirable and genuinely positive is that which is based on a friendly understanding of the composer's point of view but at the same time reveals him to himself by unravelling his secrets – for after all every human being is, very naturally and pardonably, the prisoner of his own individual field of vision and ability.

It is a most creditable achievement, and one which should be fully acknowledged, for a man who has been formed by the artistic beliefs and demands of a foreign country to come to understand that these do not necessarily apply elsewhere. This is already a great step forward, and the only danger that still remains is the possibility of mistaking the form of a work for the work itself. Kapellmeister Morlacchi has manifested such an achievement in his most recent works, and this oratorio suggests that he is even more aware of this situation than formerly. Earlier settings of Metastasio's text were, in his opinion, suited only to the demands of an older generation. The secco recitatives, the many arias and the paucity of choral pieces created a sense of void and would be hardly tolerable to modern music-lovers, whose ears have become accustomed to such musical opulence. He has therefore arranged the whole work into more clearly defined musical forms. Such portions of the text as do not fall naturally into the forms of aria, duet etc. are not set simply as accompanied recitative (in which truth of expression depends to a great extent on the quality of the singer) but are wedded to a definite musical and rhythmical declamation. In this way the whole work becomes more of a unity, a single movement in different metres and tempos. Then he has been greatly concerned with the clear characterization of the actors in the drama, and has found material for duets, trios and choruses in passages of the text designed for solo. This was a praiseworthy solution to the problem, particularly as it would have been a crime to deface the poem of a

Metastasio by alien additions, which proved less of a danger than the threat of cutting.

I think that I have now made the composer's intentions and his attitude to the work sufficiently clear; and I should indeed be delighted to think that in so doing I may have made some contribution to the greater effectiveness of his intentions. The path to the goal is broad and diverse; we can all find room on it. It is also steep, and we all need each other's help. May the outcome be joy, peace and a thriving art! That is my proclamation in the name of all honest and truly devoted artists.

93. Introduction to Méhul's *Hélèna*

Written: Dresden, 19 April 1817.
Published: DAZ, No. 96, 22 April 1817.　　*Signed:* Carl Maria von Weber.
Reprinted: HHS; MMW; KSS; LKA.

Hélèna was produced at the Opéra-Comique, Paris, on 1 March 1803. The text was by Jean Nicolas Bouilly and Jacques Antoine Révéroni de Saint-Cyr. *Georg Friedrich Treitschke's German version was first given in Vienna on 22 August of the same year, and it quickly became popular throughout Germany: a vocal score was announced as published in 1804. The first Prague performance was on 4 January 1815, as a Benefit for *Therese Grünbaum, who sang the title role; Weber wrote an extra aria for her, 'Ah, se Edmondo fosse l'uccisor!' (J178). The Dresden performance does not seem to have included this, but to have had inserted numbers by *Paer and Nasolini. However, the revival in January 1818 did use Weber's number. The singers included *Josephine Weixelbaum (Hélèna), *Georg Weixelbaum (Constantin), *Friedrich Hellwig (Moritz) and *Georg Wilhelmi (Bastian).

Concerning the announcement of the first performance here on 22 April 1817 of the opera *Hélèna*, after the French of Bouilly by Treitschke, with music by Méhul: in last January's number of this paper I tried to sum up the characteristics of this excellent composer's music in connexion with his opera *Joseph*.[1] All that I have to add to what I then wrote is that *Hélèna* was written five years before *Joseph* and presents a strong contrast between a serene rural existence and passionate personalities and action. Although *Hélèna* differs in character and atmosphere from *Joseph*, the shrewd observer will have no difficulty in recognizing Méhul's independent and consistent musical individuality.

In accordance with the practices of musical hospitality, which assure

[1]　Above, No. 89.

visiting artists every opportunity to employ and demonstrate their powers on the largest scale, the roles of Constantin and Héléna (sung by Herr and Madame Weixelbaum) were enlarged by the addition of a Cavatina, a duet and an aria, all by Italian masters. The respect due to a composer demands that this fact should be pointed out if the work is to be fairly assessed.

It is perhaps not out of place in this connexion to recall once again that we must still refuse the honour of calling ourselves a German operatic company; and that as far as that goal is concerned, none of our performances is more than an attempt to bring into being an artistic body which does not yet exist. In this way we can hope to form judgements of outside talents that we shall later be able to engage, and at the same time give our present artists an opportunity to extend their range. Only time brings roses.

94. Introduction to Boieldieu's *Jean de Paris*

Written: Dresden, before 2 May 1817.
Published: DAZ, No. 105, 2 May 1817.   *Signed:* Carl Maria von Weber.
Reprinted: HHS; MMW; KSS; LKA.

Jean de Paris was produced at the Opéra-Comique, Paris, on 4 April 1812. The text was by Claude Godard d'Aucour de Saint-Just, one of Boieldieu's favourite librettists for his early operas, and was later used by Romani as the basis for his libretto for Morlacchi (1818); Romani's text was in turn used by Donizetti (1839). The first German version, *Johann von Paris*, was by *Ignaz Castelli, performed in Vienna on 28 August 1812; other German versions within a year of the première were by Joseph von Seyfried, *F. K. Hiemer and Carl Herklots, and the work remained long popular in Germany. The Dresden cast included *Therese Grünbaum (Princess), *Georg Wilhelmi (Jean), *Eduard Genast (Seneschal), *Julie Zucker (Olivier) and Christiane Unzelmann (Lorezza). The opera is set in the seventeenth century, and describes how the French Crown Prince arrives at a Pyrenean inn incognito, as 'Jeañ de Paris', so as to observe secretly, and entertain splendidly, the bride selected for him whom he knows to be travelling there too. The production was Weber's first great success in Dresden, as he told his wife Caroline: 'My *Jean de Paris* went excellently yesterday, and Unzelmann delighted the public: she was nervous in Act 1, and I've heard better from her, but in Act 2 she was quite heavenly. It all went splendidly, and the production is very good. We even managed to put together some dances with castanets. On the table we had the King's silver dinner service. Grünbaum had a curtain call, which she took very modestly. Wilhelmi as Jean was fine. So was Genast as the Seneschal, also the Innkeeper; only the Page could have been better, but poor Julchen was as you know her to be. Chorus and orchestra!!! Now! – the King was overcome and absolutely delighted' (letter of 4 May 1817). Weber had previously produced *Jean de Paris* in Prague in 1814, as well as *Le Calife de Bagdad* and, in 1815, *Le Nouveau Seigneur de village*. In Paris in 1826 he was delighted with *La Dame blanche*, and wrote home recommending it for Dresden.

On Saturday 3 May the first performance will be given of *Johann von Paris*, an opera in two acts after the French of Saint-Just, with music by Boieldieu.

The genre to which this opera belongs has developed during the last decade in France and spread from there to Germany. An attempt has been made to designate it as 'conversation opera', since the majority of these works concern themselves very little with historical facts (something that indeed often alienates us not a little) and present a picture of present-day society, more particularly of French society. They are in fact the musical sisters of French comedies and, like them, give us a picture of the most agreeable features of that nation. High spirits and a lively wit, displayed in a series of cleverly arranged situations, are common to all these operas and, in accordance with French taste, play the most important part. In fact we could name (as with their comedies) a large number of these French operas that resemble each other so closely in invention, cut, treatment and character-drawing that they are only distinguished by their more or less successful treatment of familiar material. The Italian and German character touch greater depths of feeling and passion, whereas these French pieces represent the claims of humour and intelligence, particularly, and most noticeably, as far as the music is concerned. A single idea is enough to stimulate the German imagination to create a musical picture of magnificent proportions; and the warmer Italian imagination often needs hardly more than a single word – love, hope, or whatever it may be – to work the same wonder (and when stripped of words, this same eloquent image of the soul may lead its own independent life, as in the highest forms of instrumental music); while the essence of French music is to achieve its quality more often than not through words alone, so that it is intelligent after the fashion of its nationality and its nature.

It is reserved for masters of the art to effect a rapprochement between these national styles, to amalgamate them and thus to create music of truly universal significance. Among these few, Boieldieu might well claim the first rank in France today. True, the public applaud Isouard with equal enthusiasm, and indeed both composers have admirable gifts. But Boieldieu stands head and shoulders above his rivals by the freedom and elegance of his vocal line, the skilful construction of both individual numbers and the work as a whole, by his careful and excellent use of the orchestra and that masterly correctness which alone confirms a composer's claim to durability as a classic. He may be as worthy of respect as Méhul, but he is more attracted by light-hearted Italian forms than Méhul and pays more attention to melody as such, though without prejudicing the truth of his verbal expressiveness.

This characteristic trait of his works provides a double proof of his independence, since he is a great admirer of *Cherubini and is said to have studied chiefly with him. Boieldieu learnt the first rudiments of music from Broche,[1] cathedral organist in his native town of Rouen, where he was born in 1770. He came to Paris in the nineties and occupied a post as piano teacher at the Conservatoire, very soon attracting public attention by a number of successful works for the theatre and popular Romances. Of some dozen of his operas from this period, two that became particularly popular in Germany were *Ma Tante Aurore*[2] and *Le Calife de Bagdad*.[3] In 1813 Boieldieu was given a court appointment in St Petersburg, but since then he has returned to Paris.[4] His *Jean de Paris* has made the greatest impression and has been everywhere admired. We are obliged for its performance here to that excellent artist Mme Grünbaum (born Müller), leading singer of the Ständisches Theater in Prague, who is to sing the Princesse de Navarre as guest artist. Boieldieu's recent successes include *Le Nouveau Seigneur de village*[5] and most recently of all *La Fête du village voisin*.[6] The Paris stage is expecting two new works from his pen, a grand opera, *Charles de France*, and a comedy, *Le Petit Chaperon rouge*.[7] As an instrumental composer Boieldieu is known for a number of sonatas, concertos etc. for pianoforte and harp, but these add nothing to his reputation, which has developed all the more successfully in the dramatic field.

[1]   Charles Broche (1752–1803) had been a pupil of Padre Martini, and was the Rouen organist for most of his career. Boieldieu only later took lessons from Cherubini.

[2]   Paris, 1803; popular in Germany in French, and then in translations by Matthias Lambrecht and Carl Herklots.

[3]   Paris, 1800; popular in Germany in various translations, and given by Weber in Prague in 1814.

[4]   Boieldieu was in Russia 1803–11.

[5]   Paris, 1813; popular in Germany in Ignaz Castelli's translation.

[6]   Paris, 1816; popular in Germany in various translations.

[7]   Boieldieu had already written *Charles de France*, with Hérold (1816), and this was followed by *Le Petit Chaperon rouge* ('Little Red Riding Hood') (1818).

95. Introduction to Isouard's
Le Billet de loterie

Written: Dresden, 7 May 1817.
Published: DAZ, No. 111, 9 May 1817.   *Signed:* Carl Maria von Weber.
Reprinted: HHS; MMW; KSS.

The Maltese composer Nicolò Isouard's *Le Billet de loterie* was produced at the Opéra-Comique, Paris, on 14 September 1811. The text was by Augustin Creuzé de Lesser and Jean François Roger. It was popular in Germany in translations, as *Das Loterieloos*, by *Ignaz Castelli, Carl Herklots, and G. Freund. See also above, Nos. 18 and 58. Weber gave it in a double bill with *Das Mädchen aus der Fremde*, a *Lustspiel* by E. Willig. The cast was headed by *Therese Grünbaum (Adele), who was much praised by *Theodor Hell in his review (*DAZ*, No. 125, 26 May 1817); the others included *Julie Zucker (Betty), *Johann Grünbaum (Blinville) and Herr Metzner (Jackson).

On Sunday 11 May the first performance will be given here of *Le Billet de loterie*, a one-act opera adapted from the French, with music by Nicolo Isouard.

Isouard, favourite composer of the French musical world today, was generally known for family reasons as 'Nicolo de Malta'. I do not have the pleasure of being the first to introduce him to the public here, as his first opera, *L'avviso ai maritati*,[1] written in Florence, was given here as early as 1795. He was born in Malta in 1775. He began his musical studies there, before going on to Palermo, Naples, Florence and later Paris. As a result, his lively and active temperament seems to have been attracted primarily to theatrical effectiveness rather than to obtaining complete mastery of all the secrets of harmonic architecture in its classical perfection. A rich faculty of invention and a certain novelty in the delineation of character have won almost all his works a very decided success with the public. To the more discerning critic, however, the absence of internal finish and attention to detail will make them appear no more than spirited sketches, with genuine vitality in the melodic lines but without that solidity of style that is the hallmark of the real master.

Isouard wrote ten or twelve operas in Malta and Italy, none of them well known elsewhere.[2] Of a score of operas written in France, the majority have been most successful. The most remarkable is *Cendrillon*[3]

---

[1] Florence, 1794; Dresden, Carnival 1795.
[2] Nine of Isouard's operas were given in Malta and Italy before he went to Paris, two of them later receiving Paris productions.
[3] See above, No. 18.

(1810), which had ninety successive performances in Paris and has enjoyed an almost uninterrupted success in Germany. It is perhaps characteristic that despite the popularity of these operas their author-ship is often known only to very few; and that, in Germany especially, Isouard's operas are popular but his name is not par-ticularly honoured. His operas most popular with German audiences are *Un Jour à Paris*,[4] *Michel-Ange*[5] and, most recently, *Joconde*.[6] *Le Billet de loterie* is another of his most charming works, and in it his exclusively 'conversational'[7] gift is sustained most clearly by flowing melodies and by colours which communicate the purest high spirits.

Isouard has retired and lives in Paris, where he is also admired as an outstanding pianist. He is at present engaged on a libretto by Étienne, *Aladin, ou la lampe merveilleuse*, for the Opéra.[8]

[4]   Paris, 1808; popular in Germany in French, also in translation by Carl Herklots.
[5]   Paris, 1802; popular in Germany in French, also in translation by Carl Herklots.
[6]   See above, No. 58.
[7]   See above, No. 94, for Weber's comment on 'conversation opera'.
[8]   *Aladin*, Isouard's last work, completed by Angelo Beninconi, was not produced until 1822, when it was the first work to make use of the newly installed gaslight at the Opéra.

96. Introduction to Grétry's
Raoul Barbe-bleue

Written: Dresden, 13 May 1817.
Published: DAZ, No. 118, 17 May 1817.   *Signed:* Carl Maria von Weber.
Reprinted: HHS; MMW; KSS; LKA.

Raoul Barbe-bleue was produced at the Comédie-Italienne, Paris, in 1789. The text was by Michel-Jean Sedaine, whose vivid librettos for Philidor, Monsigny and especially Grétry were a substantial contribution to the evolution of Romantic opera, and also to Beethoven's *Fidelio* by way of such successful Rescue Operas as the present work (which includes an off-stage trumpet to warn of new arrivals at the castle); nevertheless, its description was the old-fashioned one of *comédie mêlée d'ariettes*. The first of many Bluebeard operas, it became popular in France, and in Germany in various translations. Weber used the one by Heinrich Gottlob Schmieder, revised by Joseph Sonnleithner, first given at the Theater an der Wien in 1804, with the music revised by Anton Fischer (see above, No. 90). The Dresden performance, which had *Therese Grünbaum as Maria and *Friedrich Hellwig as Bluebeard, was remarkable for the splendour of its sets and its production. It included the use of two horses on the stage, and the sensational appearance of

Bluebeard through a trapdoor with drawn sword, as *Theodor Hell reported enthusiastically in his review in the *DAZ* (No. 133, 4 June 1817). Afterwards Weber himself wrote to his wife Caroline to say, 'Must just tell you, our *Bluebeard* production this evening was splendid, and went so well and was so sumptuously staged that it was also a great success. The costumes were magnificent, quite fabulous, and very expensive, taken from the main wardrobe. We also used the Royal Armoury and two lovely horses with velvet saddle-cloths picked out in gold to bear Bluebeard and Marie away' (letter of 17 May 1817). The *AMZ* praised the performance, including Weber's conducting and the manage of the horses (*AMZ* xix (1817), 425–6). The *DAZ* wrote that 'Weber's conducting could not be too highly praised' (No. 134, 5 July 1817).

On Sunday 18 May the first performance here will be given of *Raoul Blaubart*, an opera in three acts, arranged by Dr Schmieder from the original French of Sedaine, music by André Erneste Modeste Grétry. The guest performances by that admirable mistress of the art of song, Mme Grünbaum, have included this interesting work as the cornerstone of the present series, which may well be said to have achieved the singer's intention of displaying her art in the most widely differing genres.

Grétry's works have an especial interest in their pure and natural musical language, which is that of an original genius. The received conventions of the art proved in his case a maze in which he easily lost the way, whereas his transgressions of the rules often have a quite particular charm. Indeed Grétry has inaugurated a new musical era in France, and his melodic forms and the treatment of the musical numbers in his works have provided a kind of accepted model for all other composers who have wished to catch the public ear.

He was born in 1741 in Liège, and went in 1759 to Rome where, according to his *Mémoires*, or *Essais sur la musique* (Paris, 1797), his real teacher was the composer Casali.[1] His observation that Casali was exclusively concerned with theatrical effect explains a great deal in Grétry's own later views and manner of working. The most salient and characteristic feature of Grétry's music during the sixties was in fact his concern to give the maximum of dramatic truth to his prosody and to his delineation of character by melodic means. For this reason his contemporaries coupled Grétry's name with that of Pergolese who, however, was a far more correct and resourceful writer. Grétry balked at no obstacle in his search for dramatic truth and often had difficulty in bringing his melodic ideas into alignment with the principles of

[1] Giovanni Battista Casali (*c* 1715–92) liked Grétry, but regarded him as a musical ignoramus.

harmonic structure. In fact he frequently had recourse to the most out-of-the-way solutions, including really childishly unsophisticated false relations, which nonetheless clearly showed his search for dramatic truth.

Grétry may well be the only French composer to have displayed in his music an unmistakable lyrical, and indeed often even a romantic, sense. His rhythms are always determined by the dramatic needs of the moment rather than by conventional formulae, and the ingenuousness of his melodies has proved inimitable. His works have outshone those of his contemporaries Monsigny, Dalayrac, Martini etc., who followed the line which he inaugurated and which, with a few modern adjustments, was still followed by Berton, Le Sueur, Boieldieu and others in their lyrical and comic operas. In fact there has been no marked change in this field comparable to that brought about in the opera, where the giant figure of Gluck opened up new horizons.

Grétry is the author of some seventy dramatic works, the majority of which have had countless performances all over Germany. Of these I will only mention *Le Tableau parlant*, *Les Deux avares*, *Zémire et Azor*, *La Rosière de Salency*, *Le Jugement de Midas* and *Richard Coeur de Lion*. The least well known pieces include *Pierre le Grand*, *Guillaume Tell* and *Amphitryon*.[2]

The *Bluebeard* story comes from an old fairy tale and, together with *Richard Coeur de Lion* and *Zémire et Azor*, the opera has remained Grétry's most popular work, endlessly in demand and repeatedly performed. The demands of today's taste have been thought here, as in Vienna, to justify a richer and more piquant orchestration in order to make the music more effective. This task was carried out with great single-mindedness and perspicacity by the late Kapellmeister Fischer; and although the real connoisseur would unquestionably prefer to hear the opera in its original form, it cannot be denied that Fischer's arrangement brings the work more into line with the musical ideals of the present day, yet without prejudice to the character of Grétry's music. The cases of Shakespeare, Calderón and other great playwrights of the past are very similar.[3] Our decision to use Fischer's version rests on a number of grounds, but chiefly on the conviction that we are doing no injustice to the composer's memory but rather making his

[2]   All the operas in Weber's first list were repeatedly performed in Germany both in the original and usually also in several different translations. *Pierre le Grand* (1790) also had several productions in Germany in both languages.

[3]   Though both Shakespeare and Calderón were enormously popular and influential in Germany with the Romantics, their works were performed in distorted versions.

work more familiar and attractive to the intelligence and critical faculty of today's public.

Grétry also distinguished himself by his political writings (*De la vérité* (3 vols., 1801)).[4] On the other hand, his musical essays betray the most complete ignorance to be found in the literature of music, and reveal his total dependence on his own feelings. Things that every choirboy in Germany has known for decades are hailed by Grétry as entirely new discoveries. But that belongs in the grand record of French scholarship.

[4]   Actually 1803.

97. An attempt to express in tabular form the organization of a German opera company in Dresden

Written: Dresden, 22 May 1817.
Printed: HHS, MMW (both incomplete); KSS; LKA.

After over four months in Dresden, having staged several new productions, conducted many performances and familiarized himself with conditions in the theatre and city, Weber submitted this set of recommendations to his patron and supporter at court, Count Vitzthum, together with the tabulated list of what voices were needed and which artists might be used. Some were really actors willing to sing, and these usually received a measure of public tolerance; some were highly trained singers with little dramatic ability, and in general were less well liked; Weber's intention was to form an ensemble of actor-singers. The purpose of his appointment by Vitzthum had been for him to establish a German Opera, side by side with the Italian Opera under Morlacchi, on the lines he had pursued in Prague. Though a private memorandum, not intended for publication, the document is important as a statement of his artistic aims. The complete text was first established from the MS by Georg Kaiser in KSS.

A number of the artists tabulated by Weber had made or were to make wider careers, among them *Eugenie von Schüler-Biedenfeld, *Therese Grünbaum, *Julie and Emilie Zucker, *Johann Gottfried Bergmann, *Friedrich Burmeister, *Christian Geiling, *Eduard Genast, *Ludwig Geyer, *Friedrich Gerstäcker, *Friedrich Hellwig, *Johann Stümer and *Georg Wilhelmi. However, some of the others remained obscure; and there was a considerable turnover of artists from this initial situation. Mlle Lembert was possibly the daughter of the Prague-born actor Wenzel Lembert (or Trembel), Mlle Amberg of the actor Johann Amberg. Mlle Schubert was cast in sentimental and sometimes travesty roles, as well as those mentioned. Camille Mieksch, wife of the chorus-master and singing teacher Johann Aloys Mieksch, was a member of the Italian company who occasionally appeared with the German company, though her stage presence and her voice were equally disliked by the public. Metzner was an actor and *buffo* bass engaged in 1816 whose wife sang coloratura roles; he also helped to train the chorus and instruct them in dance, mime and movement.

An attempt to express in tabular form the organization of a German opera company in Dresden, with short explanatory notes.

Introductory remarks

Both Italian and French opera have their recognized vocal types and dramatic figures, in *opera seria* and *opera buffa*. When it comes to a German opera company, however, these different types have to be combined, seeing that Italian and French opera are given in translation; and the singers for the characters proper to German opera have also to be found. Hence the need for a larger and more versatile company, and one for that reason more difficult to bring to a really high standard of accomplishment. In choosing performers it is particularly important to see that they should be capable of singing a wide variety of roles. A man may be very gifted, yet difficult to make use of, as is shown by a number of otherwise admirable artists. This observation implies no adverse criticism of such artists' talent or usefulness; it merely underlines the necessity of forming a company able to satisfy the just demands of the musical public.

The members of the company marked with a cross(†) are either beginners or else used more for the spoken drama than for the opera; and they therefore lack the opportunity to develop their talents as singers. The following table makes it plain that although large numbers of singers are available as stopgaps and stand-ins, the chief types of singer needed to give colour and substance to an opera are in fact lacking. Except in a few cases this confusion is damaging. In the first place, the use of the organs of speech is directly harmful to those required for singing – and for this reason it is a great relief to the singer to be able, as in the case of Italian works, to sing throughout – and in the second place the system of doubling is wasteful of both time and energy. This last reason brings me to the clear distinction between German and Italian opera companies, in fundamental principles and provisions, always of course bearing in mind the exceptions formed by individual cases of perfecting an artist in one style or the other. The accompanying list by no means exhausts the highest demands that can be made in forming a German opera company. It represents only the minimum needed to form such a company, since the choice of repertory as determined by the existent forces remains the responsibility of whoever is in command.

It is absolutely necessary to engage singers in classes 1, 2, 3, 6 and 10. In the case of class 1 (and indeed most of the others) there is the difficulty that it is not until Michaelmas that one knows who can be engaged in a year's time. This problem can only be solved by engaging a second leading singer who is free at an earlier date and can also stay on with the company. In this connexion (as also with classes 3, 6 and 10) it will be necessary to keep in touch with all singers who might be considered as possible future members of the company; and their gifts and qualities must be carefully investigated by inviting them to give guest performances. Many talents develop, and some fall off in quality, with time and chance circumstances. In order to obtain outstanding artists one must have luck and also the ability to seize them whenever they appear. Artists of rank are such rare birds, and so much in demand everywhere, that to capture them generally needs a quick and determined action.

The generally recognized necessity of an independent opera chorus also means a trainer or coach for the chorus, as well as for the less musical members of the company. Even the smallest theatres find this essential. A regular opera chorus is a great advantage since, properly trained and well rehearsed, it can produce an ensemble capable of the most striking effects. Even more important is the fact that such a chorus serves as a regular nursery from which outstanding talents can be picked for further training.

Ideally there should be a dancing master as well as a singing master. He would be responsible for training every member of the company, without exception, in the rudiments of dance and mime, for individual scenes in particular and more generally for effective grouping on the stage. Children could attend his dancing classes for periods of three years, during the first of which the parents would pay no fees, and their children could be used on the stage. During the second three-year period they would receive a small fee for appearing. In this way the opera house would have a regular supply of child performers, half of whom would cost the company nothing.

If the suggested salaries of the singers seem too high, I should like to point out that I have based my figures on the salaries paid to Italian singers, knowing that every newly appointed singer will certainly do the same. If he feels that he deserves more either because of his superior artistry or because his youth promises a longer period of service in the theatre, he will certainly believe that he has not been excessive in his demands.

	Artist needed	Specification	Proposed ensemble	Salary (approx.)
1	A principal woman singer	Roles in which the chief accent is on the singing	Mme Grünbaum. But as no eventual agreement can come into force in less than 18 months, the choice of operas will have to take this into account, and the next best singer be employed	3400 th.
2	A principal woman singer	Character parts, male roles, Athalia, Iphigenia, Sextus, Sargino and the more declamatory roles, such as Medea	Mmes Waldmüller, Lembert etc.	2000 th.
3	A principal woman singer	Ingénues, light-hearted roles – Savoyarde, Cendrillon, Zerlina, Aline, etc.	Mlle Amberg, and in some cases Julie Zucker†	1500 th.
4	A woman singer	Dignified roles, mothers and comic parts	Frau von Biedenfeld, Mlle Schubert†	
5	A woman singer	Less important parts, confidantes, etc.	Mme Mieksch†, Mlle Emilie Zucker†	
6	A principal tenor	Chief lovers, youthful heroes	Herr Stümer, Herr Gerstäcker	2000 th.
7	A second tenor	As above, but less important roles	Herr Bergmann†	
8	A tenor	So-called character roles, especially in French opera. Jean de Paris, occasional servant's parts	Herr Wilhelmi†	
9	A *buffo* tenor		Herren Geyer, Burmeister	

Artist needed	Specification	Proposed ensemble	Salary (approx.)
10 A principal bass	Serious cantabile parts, Duke in *Camilla*, Mafferu, Sarastro etc.	In these two categories fall Herren Hellwig† and Genast, but a really powerful bass is needed	
11 A principal bass	Character roles. Seneschal, Bluebeard, Moritz in *Héléna* etc. where dramatic ability is the most important		1600 th.
12 A bass	For subordinate roles, comic or minor characters	Herr Metzner, also Herr Huber	
13 A singer	Low comic roles	Herr Geiling	400 th.

98. Therese Grünbaum

Written: Dresden, 25 May 1817.
Published: DAZ, No. 134, 5 June 1817.   *Unsigned.*
Reprinted: Berlin *Dramaturgische Wochenblatt*, No. 50, 14 June 1817; *Leipziger Kunstblatt*, No. 91, 1818 (incomplete); HHS; MMW (misdated 2 June).

Weber's appreciation of *Therese Grünbaum was included in a review of *Raoul Barbe-bleue* by *Theodor Hell, in which he declared the need for a more thorough professional evaluation of her than he felt able to give: 'it is with pleasure,' he added, 'that we append here, given in his own words, Herr Kapellmeister von Weber's opinion, which we sought for a more detailed appreciation of this matter'.

You want to know my opinion of Mme Grünbaum, and here is what I have to say about her most individual qualities. The voice itself is a natural asset which I discount, since everyone can hear whether it is remarkable or mediocre: and however fine it may be, a voice by itself no more constitutes a good singer than a good figure makes a good dancer. What constitutes the true artist is complete control of the physical organ – whether that be cold, flexible or weak – so that it appears to adapt itself easily and naturally to every form of musical exercise. Many people speak of this as 'perfect schooling' of the voice.

Just think for a moment of the demands made on a German singer! In the first place she must have all the fascination of Italian charm and flexibility and the full range of French naturalness and expressiveness in declamation. Add to these the simple, deeply felt German style, with its emphasis on truth to nature. How easy in comparison is the life of the Italian singer, who spends her whole existence perfecting her performance in a single field! It is the composer's business to see that what he writes suits her voice and her powers; her natural weak points are skilfully concealed, natural beauties and advantages emphasized. If she finds any passage awkward, no matter how fine it may be musically, she has only to say 'not for me' and it is rejected for some conventional *fioritura* or other.

Mme Grünbaum is the complete mistress of her voice. She can hold every note, *crescendo* and *diminuendo*, with absolute purity, either in isolation or in any context required. Her passage-work is clear and perfectly articulated, not a torrent of clumsy descending notes or an awkward upward scrabbling. Every interval is given its precise value and in her runs, for instance, one could stop her short at any moment, whether in an ascending or a descending passage, and the last note would be as pure and fully nourished as one generally finds only with instrumental players. Then – to her everlasting honour be it said! – she has a real respect for the work of art in whose performance she is taking part, and does not regard it as a construction of notes humbly put together to provide her with an opportunity to shine. For this reason she gives every work its true character – how simply, for instance, she recently sang the Romance from *Le Billet de loterie*, refusing the easy applause that she could have won by a bold flourish or two. In ensembles her precision resembles that of an instrumental player, and she never destroys or neglects either the musical beat or the ritornellos, where all too often one hears singers ending half a bar after the orchestra, so as to make sure of an affecting final phrase. That Mme Grünbaum is never guilty of such things shows that she is a real musician, which is also confirmed by her ornaments and cadenzas. These are never arbitrary firework displays, but always fall into clear rhythmic and harmonic divisions, despite their improvisatory character, so that every listener is able to follow and to understand. The ease with which she achieves such things and her mastery of every nuance of volume at the top and bottom of her range mark her out as a real mistress of her art. This also explains the listener's delight in the appreciation of an artistic skill which seems absolutely secure. It is hardly necessary to add that her intonation is pure, that her trills are good, that her breathing is correct and unnoticed by the listener and that her *portamento* in grand cantilenas is as well judged as her *leggiero* singing; for these are accomplishments without which no singer can lay claim to greatness.

If I were to say that there are things in Mme Grünbaum's singing that still leave something to be desired, that would merely be to echo the old saying that 'nothing beneath the sun is perfect'. But that the sun does not warm many singers as accomplished as Mme Grünbaum, is a conviction to which I will testify with wholehearted warmth.

99. Introduction to Weigl's *Das Waisenhaus*

Written: Dresden, 31 May and 1 June 1817.
Published: DAZ, no. 133, 4 June 1817.　　　　*Signed:* Carl Maria von Weber.
Reprinted: HHS; MMW; KSS.

Das Waisenhaus was first performed at the Kärntnerthortheater, Vienna, in 1808. The text was by *Georg Friedrich Treitschke. A. Löwenberg, *Annals of Opera*, 3rd edn (London, 1978), suggests that the subject was lifted from Franz Moll's text for Stanislaus Spindler's opera with the same title (1807). One of *Weigl's most popular works, it was praised for its expressive connexion between text and music (*AMZ* XI (1808), 124–6, where a synopsis is given). A number of subsequent *AMZ* reviews, of performances in different cities, also praise the work. Weber reused some of the introduction to his essay on *Die Jugend Peters des Grossen* (above, No. 56). The production, in the summer season at the Linkesche Bad, was not a success and played to half-empty houses. The cast included Mme Mieksch (Therese), *Eduard Genast (Director of Orphanage), *Georg Wilhelmi (Colonel von Sternberg), Herr Zwich (Sturm), Mlle Schubert (Louise) and *Julie Zucker (Gustav). Weigl had accepted the post of Kapellmeister at Dresden in 1807, but negotiations then fell through and the post went to Morlacchi.

On Wednesday 4 June there will be given the first performance on our stage of *Das Waisenhaus*, opera in two acts by Treitschke, music by Joseph Weigl. Composed to a German text in 1808 in and for Vienna, it succeeded so well there that it may be said, with its successor *Die Schweizerfamilie*,[1] to have initiated a short vogue for 'grief and pain' operas. Apart from these two works, however, the emotional artificiality of the genre ensured that it was short-lived, and it came to an end with Weigl's own two-act opera *Der Bergsturz*.[2]

[1]　Vienna, 1809. Weigl's most famous work, translated into many languages.
[2]　Vienna, 1812. The opera is based on an incident when all the members of a family of Goldau, near Rigi, were killed by a landslide as they were setting off to marry their daughter.

It is always attractive to observe how an artist and his public mutually shape, educate and guide each other. A single successful, widely appreciated work will not only spawn imitators and mere copies; it also inclines the author himself to continue in the vein which has brought him success, and to prefer the means which have once proved effective to the risk involved in new attempts to win the elusive applause of his contemporaries.[3] This explains the fact that even in the case of exceptional masters such as Winter it is always a single work that makes their reputation.

Although Joseph Weigl's earlier works were marked by an exceptional quantity of tender and pleasing melodic ideas, not to speak of flawless technical correctness, the operas mentioned above seem to belong to a single period of his career. They are certainly quite different in style and approach from the works which first made his reputation, of which I will only mention *La Principessa d'Amalfi*[4] and chiefly – apart from much charming and melodious ballet music – *L'amor marinaro*.[5] His opera *Die Uniform*[6] seems to belong to this same group, though less obviously; and only *Das Waisenhaus* and *Die Schweizerfamilie* possess the tender, scrupulous and skilful gift of depiction which has endeared his work to the public.

His manner of writing is typical of the Viennese school, founded on the solid qualities and strict attention to detail learnt from the examples of Haydn and Mozart. Notable characteristics of his music include his preference for uneven rhythms, his violin writing in the top reaches of the instrument and his concern with making each musical number as self-sufficient as possible melodically, so as to fulfil the scenic demands of a work in this way rather than by rigid adherence to dramatic truth in the declamation. This may well have arisen from the ballet music of which he wrote so much. His talent seems not to have been well suited to serious drama, and his *Hadrian*[7] does not bear the hallmark of that grandeur demanded by the theme, and for that reason made no great stir in the musical world. On the other hand, he has written some dignified and masterly oratorios.

Joseph Weigl was born in 1765 in Vienna[8] and first studied according to Albrechtsberger's method and under Salieri's direction. He visited Italy, where he had some success as a composer; but the

3   Weber repeats this paragraph, up to this point, from No. 56 above.
4   Vienna, 1794. Weigl's first real success, described by Haydn as a masterpiece.
5   Vienna, 1797. Popular in Germany as *Der Korsar*.
6   Vienna, 1805; from an Italian libretto of 1798.
7   Vienna, 1807.
8   Actually Eisenstadt (Kismarton) in 1766.

greater part of his life has been spent in Vienna, where he holds the posts of Royal and Imperial Kapellmeister and director of the Opera. He has written very little chamber music, but it is worth mentioning that he is an outstandingly fine conductor of works with which he feels in sympathy.[9]

[9]   Mozart relinquished the conducting of *Figaro* and *Don Giovanni* to Weigl after a couple of performances.

100. Introduction to Cherubini's *Lodoiska*

Written: Dresden, 13 July 1817.
Published: DAZ, No. 173, 21 July 1817.   *Signed:* Carl Maria von Weber.
Reprinted: HHS; MMW; KSS.

Lodoiska was first performed at the Théâtre Feydeau, Paris, in 1791. The text was by C. F. Fillette-Loraux. In the translation by C. F. Herklots it became very popular in Germany – rather more so than in France, where *Rodolphe Kreutzer's setting, of the same year, was preferred. At Dresden, it was Weber's next production after *Das Waisenhaus* and Solié's *Le Secret* (a work he did not write about); and it rivalled the lavishness of *Raoul Barbe-bleue* (see above, No. 96), the costumes alone costing 300 thaler. The title role was sung by *Eugenie von Schüler-Biedenfeld; the other parts were taken by Frl Hunt (from the Italian Opera) (Lisinska), *Johann Bergmann (Floresky), Herr Metzner (Farbel), *Eduard Genast (Dourlinski), *Friedrich Hellwig, Herr Hoecker (Talmà) and *Georg Wilhelmi (Lisikan). The performance exposed the lack of qualifications of the soloists the young German Opera possessed when it came to a work on the scale of *Lodoiska*. Weber was forced to agree: 'As far as orchestra and chorus are concerned, everything went really so well that one could wish for no more. But the singers let it down – poor Bergmann was dreadful' (letter to his wife Caroline, 6 August 1817). Praising the orchestra and Weber's direction, the *DAZ* added that 'the realization of the sung roles could not be compared with them' (No. 203, 25 August 1817); the *AMZ* enthusiastically agreed with the praise for Weber, but concluded, 'Not even the greatest general can win battles with weak, largely unarmed troops' (*AMZ* xix (1817), 650).

On Thursday 24 July there will be given the first performance in the Königliches Hoftheater of *Lodoiska*, grand opera in three acts, with music by *Cherubini, one of the few really great artistic figures today, a classical master and discoverer of new and individual paths, whose reputation in musical history will never be dimmed. The inclination of his temperament, like that of Mozart and Beethoven – though each in a wholly individual way – coincides with that most common at the present time, namely the Romantic. A serious composer, often to the point of gloomy brooding; always choosing the most sharply defined means, hence his glowing palette; laconic and lively; sometimes apparently brusque; throwing out ideas which in fact have a close inner connexion and when presented with their full harmonic flavour are the distinguishing feature of this composer and explain the depth of his musical character, which, in the vast contours and masses conjured up by his imagination, still takes full account of every apparent detail: that is Cherubini.

It is thus that many, unable to obtain a full conspectus of a work by Cherubini, are often tempted to mistake a part for the whole, and so go astray, failing to recognize the composer's intention or only guessing part of it. This is commonest among that unhappy class of music-lovers, the complacent semi-connoisseurs. The unprejudiced music-lover, on the other hand, will be immediately gripped, even if some of Cherubini's methods appear to him alien or arbitrary. He may even shake his head over them and almost rebuke himself for allowing his feelings to get the better of him in such a strange manner, against all those rules of musical propriety which he thinks he has learnt from the familiar operatic repertory.

All Cherubini's music has a dash of melancholy; and even his most humorous and light-hearted melodies always conceal something touching. His method of working makes it impossible to say that this or that work is 'well orchestrated' – an expression that is in any case very one-sided and appears to make a quite unwarrantable division of a work into two halves. The true master sees in a flash all the potentials of an idea the moment it occurs to him. No more than a painter does he envisage a naked body that he then decks out with clothes and jewels. Not that beneath the heavy folds of a garment he is not aware of the anatomical details that cause those folds; but the whole picture must be seen *as a whole*, or the public will be aware of no more than a half-creature – a dummy or lay-figure in costume, and not a living human being.

In Cherubini this amalgamation of all means to a single unified end has often earned him – though no doubt unfairly – the charge of lacking melody; and it cannot be denied that he often subordinates what are generally accepted as the individual singer's melodic privileges to the melody of the whole musical number. This is not, perhaps, always to be recommended to other composers in its totality; but in Cherubini's case it is largely excusable (even in arias, where it would seem least pardonable) by the fact that he was writing for French singers, or screechers, who seek the expression of feeling more in the intensification of the declamatory style by means of the orchestra, whereas Italian singers rely on their own voices and powers of expression and the Germans (Mozart) attempt to combine both methods.

The above observation is founded on various of Cherubini's works. The most passionate of these are written entirely in the style described above, which is that closest to his heart and to his natural instincts. The first of this kind was in fact *Lodoiska* (Paris, 1791), followed by the superlatively fine *Eliza* (1794) and *Medea* (1797). In quite a different vein and endearing itself to all listeners was *Les Deux journées* – the universally popular *Water-carrier*.[1] Both varieties were combined in *Faniska*[2] (Vienna, 1806), although I have often felt that the composer did some violence to his own inspiration in order to conform with the somewhat effete taste of the Viennese public.

His genius would probably have taken a different direction – while certainly remaining wholly individual – had he stayed in his native Italy, where he was born (in 1760) and studied, chiefly with Sarti. Certainly his early stage works, beginning with *Quinto Fabio* (1780) are quite different from those written from the time of *Lodoiska* onwards, though they are marked by the same deep seriousness. The influence of Haydn and Mozart on Cherubini made him strike out on a new path, for true geniuses are always inspired by what they admire not to imitate but to innovate. Cherubini's last works, *Pygmalion*[3] and *Les Abencérages*,[4] are not yet familiar in Germany. In the chamber style he has written a number of cantatas and a Grand Mass in three parts, and he is said to have completed a four-part Mass.[5] As one of the inspectors of the Paris Conservatoire he has displayed great zeal in the furtherance of music and has maintained the standards worthy of a real artist.

He lives quietly in his family circle, and his way of life corresponds to that of the true artist, who can only devote himself single-mindedly to his art by cultivating the tranquillity of mind which comes from a clear conscience.

[1]   Paris, 1800; very popular in Germany in several translations, especially by Heinrich Schmieder as *Der Wasserträger* (1801); see above, No. 21.

[2]   *Faniska* was Cherubini's only German opera, written to an Italian text and translated by Joseph Sonnleithner.

[3]   *Pimmalione* was produced in Paris in 1809.

[4]   Paris, 1813; not performed in Germany until 1828, translated by Carl Herklots and with the music revised by Spontini.

[5]   Weber is probably referring to the Mass in F (1809) and the Mass in C (1816).

101. Buschmann's Terpodion

Written: Dresden, 28 August 1817.
Published: DAZ, No. 210, 2 September 1817.

Signed: Carl Maria von Weber.

Reprinted: MMW; KSS.

The Terpodion, or Labesang, was one of many contemporary attempts at developing a sustaining piano. It was invented by Johann David Buschmann in 1816, and improved by his sons in 1832. Like the earlier Clavicylinder, and Buschmann's own Uranion of 1810, it depended upon the pressing of tuned bars against a revolving cylinder by means of a keyboard. In the Terpodion, the friction cylinder was made of wood, coated with rosin, and was revolved by means of a pedal. Buschmann toured Germany with his brother, a singer and pianist, to publicize it. But despite this, and Weber's advocacy (which was no doubt encouraged by his old friendship with the Duke of Gotha), the instrument never caught on. Though he had written a piece for the harmonichord (the Adagio and Rondo, J115), Weber was not tempted by the Terpodion. For another technical description, see *AMZ* xx (1818), 608–9. The name was presumably derived from the Greek τέρπω = I please or delight.

This is the name given by the Duke of Gotha, a great lover and patron of the arts, to a new instrument whose invention the world owes very largely to his interest and active support. The name itself is both suitable and sensible. The music-lovers of Dresden will soon have the pleasure of hearing this instrument in a concert given by its inventor and builder, Johann David Buschmann of Friedrichroda bei Gotha, who has already won the approval and congratulations of our noble monarch and his family.

Herr Buschmann has devoted twelve years' work to producing a keyboard instrument with a range of five and a half octaves. The sound is produced by vibrating wooden pins, which are set in motion by friction. The result is admirable, the method by which it is produced being for the time a secret. The quality of the sound resembles that of the harmonica, which exploits the same principle, but it is greatly superior in range, volume (especially the handsome bass notes) and purity and fullness of tone. Note-values, *crescendo* and *diminuendo* and volume of sound are determined by the pressure, or simple resting, of the fingers on the keyboard. In some parts of its range, the tone of the Terpodion resembles exactly the natural notes of a number of wind instruments. The instrument is naturally best suited to solemn *legato* music, though the really amazing lightness of finger pressure required makes quick-moving passages perfectly possible. This feature, added to its convenient shape and unfailing correctness of pitch, give the Terpodion a marked advantage over all other inventions of this kind that I have known, not excluding the beautiful harmonichord invented by our admirable fellow citizen Herr Kaufmann.

102. Introduction to Catel's *Les Aubergistes de qualité*

Written: Dresden, 22 September 1817.
Published: DAZ, No. 230, 25 September 1817.

Signed: Carl Maria von Weber.

Reprinted: HHS; MMW; KSS.

Charles-Simon Catel's *Les Aubergistes de qualité* was produced at the Opéra-Comique, Paris, in 1812. The text was by Victor Étienne de Jouy. Though only a *succès d'estime*, according to F. Hellouin and J. Picard, *Catel* (Paris, 1910), it became popular as *Die vornehmen Wirte* in translations by Joseph Sonnleithner and *F. K. Hiemer. Pauline was sung by Luigia Sandrini-Caravoglia; it was her first role in German, a language of which she had a very imperfect command, though the *AMZ* commented that it was better than that of some Germans (*AMZ* xix (1817), 755–6). The cast also included *Johann Bergmann (Villeroi), *Georg Wilhelmi (Marquis), *Friedrich Burmeister (Governor), Herr Metzner (Host), *Emilie Zucker (Hostess), *Julie Zucker (Daughter), *Eduard Genast (Charlot), *Christian Geiling (Dutreillage) and Heinrich Bösenberg (Registrar). Décor and costumes were of the period of Louis XIV. The *DAZ* found it 'perhaps the purest and most accomplished performance the German Opera has yet given us' (No. 238, 4 October 1817).

On Thursday 25 September the first performance in the Königliches Hoftheater will take place of *Die vornehmen Wirte*, an opera in three acts taken from the French, with music by Catel.

This is certainly one of the most delightful contributions of the French stage, with text and music equally amusing. This operatic genre is chiefly distinguished by the verbal wit characteristic of the French; and although it would no doubt be impossible to spend a pleasant evening in company, and even perhaps earn some reputation for wit, without eventually saying something amusing, yet no one is likely to dispute the French claim to an absolute superiority in such 'conversation' operas.

The combination of wit such as this with Italian comic expressiveness and emotional warmth has rarely been so successfully achieved as in this piece of Catel's; and apart from Boieldieu and Méhul there can be few such classical masters of this style as Catel. A gift for heartfelt melody, an indefatigable vitality, skilfully planned orchestration, complete technical assurance and a telling power of expression are characteristic of Catel's work; and all these are to be found equally displayed in two admirably contrasted works – his serious grand opera *Sémiramis*[1] (1801) and his gay Italian comedy *Les Aubergistes de qualité*. These are his only two operas that are well known in Germany – the latter hardly familiar except in Vienna and Prague, the former more universally performed. His studies in musical theory have prevented him from devoting himself more to the drama. On the other hand, he is the author of a *Traité d'harmonie* (1802) used by the Conservatoire, and also of a number of instrumental works, patriotic songs etc.

Born in Paris in 1770,[2] he studied with Gossec and held a post as lecturer in harmony at the Conservatoire. For some considerable time he seems unfortunately to have written nothing for the stage. Finally, I cannot deny myself the pleasure of introducing to the public Mme Sandrini, a member of the cast in this German-language performance, and of recommending the really admirable diligence with which she has studied to overcome the difficulties which our language presents to the foreigner. I value this all the more because, important as the role is in itself, it is not one of the great showpieces of the repertory. Thus it is that to true art-lovers everything contributes with increasing delight to the final total effect.

[1]   Paris, 1802; performed in Germany in *Ignaz Castelli's translation.
[2]   Actually 1773.

103. Reply to Adolf Müllner's criticisms of Brunhilde's song in *König Yngurd*

Written: While travelling, completed Mannheim, 12 November 1817.
Published: ?
Reprinted: HHS, MMW (both inaccurate); KSS.

Adolf Müllner (1774–1829) was a lawyer and actor who made a name as a writer of *Schicksalstragödien*; he later edited the literary supplement of Cotta's *Morgenblatt für gebildete Stände*, and wrote what is regarded as the first German detective story. For the production of his *König Yngurd* (1817) in Dresden, Weber was asked by the Berlin Intendant, Count Brühl, to compose incidental music (J214). He wrote ten short numbers for brass and drums on the night of 12–13 April, adding an eleventh on 23 April – possibly No. 11, the unaccompanied song for the mad Brunhilde – for the Berlin production. He prefaced this song with a note suggesting that what he had in mind was a pioneering version of *Sprechgesang*:

The melody of this little song is only an indication, in so far as a melodic shape can be. It indicates the musical outlines or boundaries within which the actress should move; so it goes without saying that the piece should not be, in the normal sense, sung. It is above all left to the actress to express it in her own way, according to this musical indication. It would perhaps be best to allow the music to predominate starting at Θ, or certainly at ⊕.

The song drew objections from Müllner for its allegedly poor word-setting, though these do not seem (despite a reference in Jähns) to have appeared in print. Müllner's criticism (printed in full in HHS, MMW and KSS) first queried the accentuation of the passage at 'will ich sein, immer bei ihm, ewig treu ihm':

> It seems to me that here the geometrical [*sic*] relationship of the notes to each other (their duration) does not accord with the prosody, and suits the melody but not the declamation, which should here be guided by the music. The prosody has: 'will ich sein – immer bei ihm, ewig treu ihm'. But the notes have: 'will ich sein – immer bei ihm, ewig treu ihm'. In that way *ich* and *ihm* are presented as the main ideas, and the mode of utterance expresses the meaning 'I shall be his tombstone, ever with *him*, ever true to *him*', instead of the correct 'His *tombstone* shall I be, ever *with* him, ever *true* to him.' Moreover, if the actress speaks the *bei* and *treu* as short syllables, the spondee feminine rhyme will wrongly become masculine, *ihm* rhyming with *ihm*. On the other hand, I think this excellent:

Mut – ter,   Mut – ter   singt!

> Here seems to me the place where speech must pass into song. The sign Θ seems to me placed too soon, after eight bars. But perhaps the famous composer will correct my views according to the principles of his art, in which I am but a layman.

Müllner's autograph (in D-Bds) ends here; but another hand has added other criticisms. After some general observations about the different emphases music can give to poetry, this insists that all music can do is arouse feeling. It continues:

> Above all, it seems to me to be too little known or considered that all musical relationships of notes, sounds and keys are geometrically proportioned (like the fractions 1/2, 1/4, 1/8, 1/16 etc.), while relationships of syllables, stresses and modulations of speech are arithmetical, that is to say are differences expressed as, for instance, $a/a - x$, $a - x + y$, etc. Thus music cannot completely accompany the metrical flow of the verse, when delivered in good, expressive recitation, since it has for its accompaniment of the syllabic quantities only fractions with a common denominator of 2 (1/3 or 1/5 notes are not possible), while the speaker grades the proportions of the syllables much more subtly and unem-

phatically. But these proportions cannot be ignored, and what in speech is in the ratio of $1:1+x$ must not be $1:1/x$ in music.

The article concludes by allowing the composer the right of repetition, provided that this is artistically done. Weber paid a call on Müllner at Weissenfels, while on his honeymoon trip, and presumably received these criticisms. He wrote to Hinrich Lichtenstein to say, 'In Weissenfels I made the acquaintance of that Napoleon of the theatre, Müllner, with whom I spent a very interesting day' (letter of 14 May 1817). Many years later, Müllner recalled this in a letter to *Theodor Hell: 'He was one of the few composers who can *think*, and our lengthy discussion on the possible unification of contemporary music with poetry, especially dramatic poetry, gave me great pleasure' (letter of 3 March 1828).

In my opinion the first and most sacred duty of a song-writer is to observe the maximum of fidelity to the prosody of the text that he is setting. There may be cases – more particularly in elaborate pieces, less frequently in the Lied – where the absolutely correct stressing of individual syllables can be sacrificed to the inner character of the melody as a whole; but these are not our concern here.

The most frequent cause of embarrassment to a composer is the poet's failure to make the stress in a line coincide with the metric quantity of the syllables. Music can only accentuate any such divorce between voice and verse, structure and declamation; for the constituent elements of musical rhythm are tied to a far more precise movement in time than even the most conscientious reciter could ever achieve without becoming ludicrously pedantic. In return for this, however, music has far better aids and ways round problems than speech, in the important means of higher and lower pitch, for the rhythmically strong beat in the bar often bears at least similar weight and effectiveness – and therefore equal importance – to that of the higher pitch which follows it. Furthermore it is actually the function of melody to communicate the interior life expressed by the word, and to give it clear prominence. In so doing there is always a serious risk of damaging the bloom of the melody by a pedantic insistence on correctness. Deciding which is to predominate, music or poetry, is the great rock on which many good vessels have come to grief.

Applying these principles to the melodic passages alluded to by Herr Müllner, I came to the conclusion that the most deep-lying cause of Brunhilde's madness is to be found in her love for her son, which is also the inspiration of her song. It is all a question of him and her, and of *her* love for *him*; and hence my throwing into relief and emphasizing by pitch and accent every word referring to this love. The chief point seemed to be that she will be his tombstone and remain unfailingly faithful to his memory – hence the same note and stress on

sein   Lei – chen–stein will   ich   sein.

That I was mistaken was explained to me by the poet himself, although I cannot honestly say that I am fully convinced that my occasional encroaching on the rights of individual syllables was not justified by the benefits accruing to the piece as a whole. But I accept his judgement and merely allow myself to quote a few examples of my altering the melody to suit the poet's sense. I shall be interested to know whether he does not find such alterations almost painful, for the very good reason that what in speech is no more than the proper emphasizing of a word can sound downright harsh when music adds further emphasis.

If space allowed, I could give many other examples of the same kind. I entirely agree that the element of song should not be emphasized before the word *Mutter*; but I am particularly pleased that the famous poet has no objection to the repetitions at the end, because I set particular store by this privilege of music, monstrously abused though it has often been. And of this I shall hope to say more in my [*Ton*]*Künstlersleben*.

In this reply requested by Herr Müllner, I have only one excuse for attributing almost as many rights to a melodic reference as to a real song; and that lies in the nature of music and in my wish at least to show the author of *Yngurd* the care with which I have attended to every one of his demands.

The significance of a melody can be not merely altered, but completely destroyed, by accentuation and gait, so that the listener cannot possibly guess the sense intended by the composer. If a poem is badly recited, on the other hand, an attentive listener can always identify the speaker's mistakes and correct them mentally.

Mathematically speaking, musical notation is more precise than ordinary writing in denoting the rhythmical motion of the beats that make up the bar. But any mistake in the basic rhythm of a piece can easily obliterate, as far as the listener is concerned, all that has gone before. Just because (quite rightly, according to Müllner) music can only arouse feelings, movement is even more important, more sacred, in music than in poetry. The character of a piece of music is determined by its rhythmic movement, in the wider or narrower sense (tempo and metre); melody and harmony correspond to colour and form. Any music that attempts to be more than the language of emotion exceeds its function and is thus, by its very nature, bad. *Exempla sunt odiosa* – to give examples would be invidious. In the same way, music fails in its function if it deforms or destroys the sense of any text to which it is set. Since I myself have, according to the poet, not been successful in maintaining this absolute fidelity to his intentions, over *treu ihm* and *bei ihm*, all that I can do is repeat my willingness not to insist on my – in his opinion false – point of view, but to leave all further judgements to my readers.

It may be worth observing that it was not my intention to exploit the actual tonal beauty of these passages, as is made clear by the observations which I have added to the melody. I have also in this article used examples chosen by Herr Müllner, employing the same notes but altering them to his choice of length and accentuation. Even so I do not seem to have succeeded in satisfying him.

In order to obtain the greatest possible clarity, I once again quote the passages adapted as nearly as possible to Herr Müllner's ideas. According to Herr Müllner:

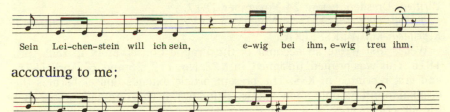

Sein   Lei–chen–stein will ich sein,   e–wig   bei   ihm, e–wig   treu ihm.

according to me;

Every artist who makes a profound study of his subject (and it is only of such that I am speaking, not the great majority) will be more or less familiar with the mathematical and geometrical relationships that occur in musical theory. It is not true that the relationships between notes, sounds and keys give only the so-called fractions 1/2, 1/4, 1/8, 1/16 etc. It is quite untrue that music denoting the length of syllables only has fractions whose denominator is 2 – for in that case there would be no 1/3 or 1/5. To prove this I give the following short instances.

Concerning notes (it will be parts of a bar that Herr Müllner means). In a bar of 3/8, the quaver and within this the semiquaver triplet etc., and the 5/4 bar: this is not counting melodies in five-bar sections. And of course the innumerable relationships within the bar that arise from syncopations of different kinds.

Concerning sounds: the creation of a sound by the stopping of a string gives e.g. the simplest triad – CGE – by means of the figures 1 1/3, 1/5. Concerning keys or tonal relationships – these develop from the formation of scales and individual sounds. In their proper purity these are proportionate, as for example 1/30 (E), 1/32 (F), or 1/24 (C), 1/25 (C sharp). I too am quite convinced that the speaking voice is capable of far subtler, less emphatic gradation in the comparative duration and modulation of individual syllables – that is to say, in the present state of musical practice. If on the other hand we include in our province non-harmonic tonal relationships or the way in which in all probability the ancients sang their poems, it may well be that there would not be much to choose between the one and the other. As regards the composer's right of repetition, there is an old proverb that the best and sharpest knife is a menace in an unskilled hand, though it can be used for magnificent carving and shaping.

104. The Prague Conservatory

Written: Dresden, before 24 November 1817.
Published: DAZ, No. 281, 24 November 1817.   *Unsigned.*
Reprinted: MMW; KSS; LKA.

Weber first wrote an account of the Prague Conservatory in mid-April 1816. This was printed, unsigned, in *KPZ*, No. 117, 26 and 27 April 1816, and first reprinted in KSS. The present article extends and elaborates the original, omitting only a few points, as follows. It was originally noted that the subscribers appointed a Board which consisted of a Director, a Supervisor and Business Manager, a Bursar and four Governors. It was noted that 'as much theory of music is taught as is necessary for the moderately talented boy to become a sound ensemble player, and for the musical genius to acquire the necessary resources to enable him to leave the school as a fully-fledged virtuoso'. The list of subjects is slightly different: in the original, logic and history are included, Italian language is substituted for French, while subjects omitted are literature, biology, and German and Italian prosody and versification. It was also emphasized that it was a 'fundamental principle of the institute to train the young not only as practical musicians but as exceptional human beings'. For the best and fullest history of the conservatory, see BKP.

Towards the end of the last century music was more devotedly fostered, and flourished more brilliantly, in Bohemia than in any other part of the Holy Roman Empire. In those days every one of a hundred monasteries would be a seed-bed for musicians; every nobleman had his private orchestra; Bohemian musicians were in great demand abroad; and Mozart himself was happiest when writing for the Prague Orchestra and the Prague public. Indeed, that public may proudly claim to have been the first to recognize and acknowledge the genius of that immortal musician. Bohemia was the homeland of Gluck, Benda, Dussek, Wranitzky, Gyrowetz and a host of others who enjoyed no mean positions in the musical pantheon. The whole country seemed to be devoted to music, and every bright summer night the streets echoed to the sound of serenades and nocturnes. These happy days passed: outstanding artists became rarer, instrumental performers less enthusiastic. But even though Bohemia lost something of its earlier reputation, the decay of our art was not so marked that we did not still produce a large number of excellent individual musicians; and it only needed a joint effort and the proper stimulus to bring about a new flowering of music.

Here was a people richly endowed by nature with musical talent and able to count among its children many heroes of the art, still possessing even in its decline musicians who, in other circumstances, might prove richly productive. And the thought that such a people should more or less lose such advantages seemed so monstrous to a number of the nobility that they founded an association with the admirable purpose of supporting the art in its decline. This excellent Society for the Promotion of Music in Bohemia came into being in March 1810 and in that same year founded the Prague Conservatory of Music. At the head of the enterprise, as its protector, stood the Governor of Bohemia, Count von Kolowrat; and any Bohemian patriot may read with pleasure the names of the noblest families in the kingdom among the list of supporters – the Prince-Archbishop; the Princes Auersperg, Clary, Colloredo-Mansfeld, Dietrichstein, Kinsky, Lobkowitz, Rohan, Schwarzenberg, Sinzendorf, Taxis, Thun, Trautmannsdorf and Wind-ischgrätz; the Counts von Althan, Bucquoi, Canal, Cavriani, Clam-Gallas and Clam-Martinitz, Colloredo, Czernin, Desfoues, Dohalsky, Firmian, Harrach, Hartig, Kinsky, Klebelsberg, Kolowrat, Lazansky, Ledebour, Millesimo, Nostitz, Pachta, Rey, Salm, Schlick, Schönborn, Stadion, Stampach, Sternberg, Swerts, Szapary, Thun, Waldstein, Windischgrätz, Wratislaw, Wrbna and Wrtby; the Lord Abbots of Strahof and Ossegg; and the Barons von Hildprandt, Kotz and Zesner. A Committee of Direction was elected consisting of Count Johann von Nostitz as President and Counts Clam-Gallas, Klebelsberg, Nostitz (Friedrich), Pachta, Schönborn and Wrtby as his Board.

This institution has prospered and perfectly fulfilled the intention of its founders, whose subscriptions maintain it. Every member has the right to put forward the names of potential students with some preliminary musical knowledge, and the Society elects them by a majority vote. Each student must complete a six-year course of training, three years in the first class and three in the second. The Directors meet as often as circumstances demand and make their decisions on each point in the agenda. These decisions are then signed and sealed. Every winter the Directors invite all members who are in Prague to a general meeting, at which a report is read on the progress and management of the institution and its financial position. Instrumental music forms the most important part of the curriculum, since the original object was to train skilled performers; and for two hours every day specially engaged teachers, in separate rooms, give instruction in each of the instruments included in a full orchestra. All students also have a daily singing lesson of one hour, devoted to singing as an essential part of any musical education. Some months ago a special class for six women singers was also initiated. The theory of music, in all its branches, also forms part of the curriculum.

The organization of the teaching is the responsibility of the Director, a musician who enjoys the highest reputation both at home and abroad – *Kapellmeister Friedrich Dionys Weber. It is to his unceasing efforts that the conservatory owes the very high reputation that it already enjoys after only six years of existence; and he also lectures on the theory of music. In addition to their musical studies students also receive instruction in the most relevant of the humanities – German and French language, mathematics, geography, natural history, German and Italian prosody and metrics, aesthetics and mythology. They are also given religious instruction.

The system by which young men are formed into artists depends on a carefully graded progress from the easy to the difficult, and on an unbroken connexion between theoretical knowledge and practical skill. Students must give proof of both in public examinations (after Easter and before the autumn holiday); each one must perform the difficult task of playing without accompaniment, and then these youthful talents are combined in a full ensemble to delight and impress listeners and connoisseurs.

Every three years there is an intake of thirty-nine pupils, which brings the numbers up to seventy-eight. These are divided, according to subjects, into two classes, each of which contains thirteen violinists, thirteen viola players, three cellists, three double bass players and four players of each of the wind instruments. No pupil may play more than one instrument, except the string players who, if their physique permits, may also study the trumpet and the trombone. After three years the lower class moves into the higher and begins attending orchestral rehearsals. These increase in number in proportion as the private lessons decrease; and in them the Director rehearses the students in the performance of major orchestral and solo works.

In order to ensure a high standard of order and discipline in the institution certain rules and prohibitions are prescribed. After finishing the six-year course students leave; and those who have done well in all subjects receive from the Director a diploma which serves as a recommendation or pass. Thanks to the singing class mentioned above, and to the circumstance that many of the previous year's leavers will have joined the theatre orchestra, there is a close association between conservatory and theatre, and this can only benefit both parties.

The conservatory generally gives three 'musical academies' or concerts every Lent, and these are great occasions for all lovers of instrumental music in the highest sense of the term.

105. Remarks in reply to Letter C on the performance of *La Vestale*

Written: Dresden, 23 January 1818.
Published: DAZ, No. 22, 27 January 1818.   *Signed:* Carl Maria von Weber.
Reprinted: MMW (slightly inaccurate); KSS; LKA.

For the production of Spontini's *La Vestale* on 14 January 1818, Weber repeated the experiment he had initiated with the royal wedding cantata *L'accoglienza* of reseating the orchestra. Originally trumpets and percussion were on the extreme right, in the space under the King's box; they could hardly be seen by the conductor, who sat at the piano in the middle of the orchestra with a cello and bass reading the continuo over his shoulders. Before him were scattered most of the remaining instruments, with trombones among the violins and violas, and with woodwind and others on the far left. Weber set the upper strings on his right, the wind and brass on his left, keeping the lower strings behind him and moving his desk forward to the prompter's box (a position that enabled him to control stage as well as orchestra, and that was favoured in Dresden into the 1890s under Ernst Schuch). In the excitement of the wedding festivities, the innovation passed off unnoticed, but at *La Vestale* the King was upset by the noise of the brass, now no longer muffled beneath his feet. On 21 January Weber received instructions through Count Einsiedel to restore the old arrangement; and two days later there appeared in the *DAZ* a review of the production which attacked the new orchestral placing, partly on the grounds that the trombones were now between the audience and the quieter instruments, and which praised the female chorus at the expense of the male chorus as Weber had trained it (No. 19, 23 January 1818). This was signed C, a pseudonym of Therese aus dem Winkel; it was an abbreviation of Comala, heroine of the epic poem by 'Ossian', described by James Macpherson in a footnote to his original edition of 1762 as 'the maid of the pleasant brow'. C was a journalist, amateur harpist and painter, and a member of the so-called Dichtertee or Liederkreis in which Dresden artists and dilettantes used to gather. Though she had helped in the arrangements for Weber's Dresden concert in 1812, her vigorous espousal of the cause of Italian opera in the city set her in opposition to Weber (as his opening remarks make clear). This was not diminished by Weber's observing in public, 'It's a shame that she has a serious disease: she can't hold her ink.' This witticism he later incorporated in a verse epigram attacking 'Letter C' (No. 118 in KSS). She replied to the *DAZ* article in hurt tones, accusing Weber of personal malice (a charge against which he was defended in an editorial footnote), and declaring that she was hereby taking leave of her pen (No. 28, 3 February 1818). The cast of *La Vestale* included Luigia Sandrini-Caravoglia in the title role, *Eugenie von Schüler-Biedenfeld (High Priestess) and Caroline Benelli (Licinius). The *AMZ* praised the orchestra as the best ever (*AMZ* xx (1818), 136).

Enthusiasm is a fine thing, and something particularly dear to artists. I can honour an enthusiast even when he is carried away by a clear southern night and every imaginable flowery scent and surrounds his plaything with the most purple colours. But when this tender little plant – often regarded from abroad with admiring glances – is transplanted here, is given an amicable reception by all right-minded and well-educated folk and proceeds to increase and multiply in this rich soil so that it comes to believe that its every breath is truth and perfection simply because it encounters no opposition – then I feel obliged to enter the lists in the cause of truth, and, with my visor open according to my regular custom, throw down my challenge.

I can only hope that I shall be calmly received and that my sincere goodwill towards Letter C will be reciprocated with the same credence, despite the fact that we choose almost directly opposite methods. I am all the more confident of encountering such good-will because the praise in what I have to say far outweighs the blame; and it is therefore all the more obvious that I am not writing from personal pique but in defence of truth.

It is an old tradition that before judging a matter one should first understand it. Is this really the case with Letter C??? Do you remember what Förster[1] wrote about the classicism of that revered and blazing genius Spontini? 'One work delights by its spirit: pure shapeliness in another. But in the classical style, form and content are one.' Letter C's appreciative recognition of the singers' merits is no more than a debt owed to truth: I offer my warm thanks for that accorded to the women's chorus and myself. The choruses in this opera are, as the subject demands, mostly for women's voices, and these put the

---

[1]   Karl Förster (1784–1841) was a Dresden teacher, poet, historian and translator (especially of Petrarch). Weber set several of his verses, and consulted him over revisions to the ending of *Euranthe*.

male-voice choruses in the shade,[2] though in general the proportion
between the voices is good. Earlier in Dresden there was no women's
chorus at all, and this explains the prominent place which these
choruses assumed in the recent production, the reverse of what
normally happens. Both on the earlier occasion and again in this last
performance the male chorus, especially the basses, lacked the fullness
and strength which only the actual physical power of a mature male
voice can command. This weakness will diminish in the course of time.
That it could not do so sooner was due to the fact that there was a
new intake of Kreuzschule pupils only every six months: a wider choice
will henceforth be available.

In connexion with the weakness of the male chorus, Letter C made
an observation, but offered no explanation of the origin or reason of
the fault. It was in fact the *women's chorus* that came in *late*, and was
thus responsible for the same thing happening in the men's chorus
which follows immediately.[3] The actual responsibility for this false
entry of the women's chorus is something that I am forbidden to
disclose by that respect and forbearance shown by every true critic
(though not, of course, by mere cavillers) towards any involuntary
mistake. No generalizations, whether complimentary or the reverse,
serve any real purpose; and unmerited blame can at most impel one
set of individuals to bring up, in self-defence, matters not meant for
public discussion, or to attack another group. For instance, should the
choruses in fact have hesitated?

The seating of the orchestra will depend entirely on the nature of
the work performed, the main object being that no instrument should
fail to be heard and that the conductor should have an equally good
view of stage and orchestra and be able, in his turn, to be clearly seen
by everyone taking part. Effects must be calculated bearing in mind
the whole body of the house. The rows immediately behind the
orchestra come off worst in all theatres, but no artistic institution can
take into consideration the same niceties as are observed at a social
gathering. Would Letter C have preferred the trumpets and 'Turkish
music' to be so concealed under the arches that they could hear and
see nothing? and thus inevitably miss the beat, as I have often heard
happen? Should the important cello figure, whose effect Spontini prized
so highly, really be played by a single instrument, with the player
bobbing up and down beneath the conductor's arm in order to catch

[2]   Whereas it is the opposite in *Cortez*. (Weber's footnote.)
[3]   The second performance was flawless in this respect, and in the third the
intonation was sometimes uncertain. (Weber's footnote.)

a glimpse of his music? The days are gone when the bass line in an Italian opera would contentedly bed down on the same note for eight or ten bars and after innumerable rehearsals was known by heart, so that it could safely be played from the score with the continuo player acting politely as page-turner or leaving even that to the leader. Such things have no place, or at best an uncertain one, in our music-making in Germany and France, and now only rarely in Italy. Still, it would be a lengthy business to justify what in fact needs no justification; and what has been said here, has been said out of respect for something which is a matter for public opinion and was in fact done in accordance with my convictions, my acoustical and other observations over the years.

There is one final thing that I should like to ask, and that is, why has Letter C expended ink exclusively on the Italian productions at the Königliches Hoftheater? A one-sided enthusiasm is a dangerous thing, which almost invariably tells against its object: and Art is a good mother, who *treats each child with the same love and the same severity*. A solid, well-founded judgement is generous and in no way lays suspicions of partisan feeling on management, public or editor. If the latter likes to publish individual panegyrics, then the panegyrist must disclose his identity.

106. Autobiographical sketch

Written: Dresden, 14 March 1818.
Printed: HHS (very inaccurate); MMW; KSS; LKA.

Weber wrote this sketch for Amadeus Wendt (1783–1836), professor of philosophy in Göttingen and a well-known writer on music and aesthetics. A warm friend of Weber's, he rewrote the text of the *Jubel-Cantate* as *Ernte-Cantate* and gave *Euryanthe* its first, enthusiastic review in the Berlin *Allgemeine musikalische Zeitung*. He was in Dresden in the first half of March 1818, and attended the première of the E flat Mass. It is not known for what purpose Wendt intended the sketch, which was not published. Its faults of memory, omissions and special pleading (for instance, on behalf of his father) make it an unreliable biographical source.

I was born on 18 December 1786[1] at Eutin in Holstein, and was given the most thorough education, with special preference shown to the fine arts, since my father was himself an excellent violinist. My family's withdrawn manner of life, the regular society of cultivated adults and

---

[1] In the register of the Eutin Landeskirche, Weber's baptismal date is given as 20 November 1786, implying a birth-date of 18 or 19 November.

the scrupulous care with which I was kept from the rough company of my contemporaries early taught me to live predominantly in the world of my own imagination and to seek in it my interests and my happiness. My time was chiefly devoted to painting and music. I was successful in several branches of the former – painting in oils, miniatures and pastel and having some skill in engraving. But imperceptibly my interest in painting dwindled and was finally ousted by music almost before I was aware of it. It was a fancy of my father's to change his place of residence with some frequency; and the constant change of teachers that this necessitated was a drawback, though one that was later more than made up for by the stimulus it gave to my individual powers and the need to draw on my own mental resources and industry. I owe my firm grounding and my achieving a powerful, well-articulated and well-characterized piano style and the equal training of both hands, to the excellent Heuschkel[2] in Hildburghausen (1796–7), a strict and assiduous teacher. As soon as my father saw the gradual budding of my talent, he made every sacrifice to further its development. He took me to Michael Haydn in Salzburg; but Haydn was a serious man too far removed from my childish condition for me to learn much from him, and that little involved a considerable effort. It was at Salzburg, in 1798, that my father encouraged me by having my first works published – Six fughettas, which were kindly reviewed in the musical press.[3] At the end of 1798 I went to Munich, where I studied singing with Valesi[4] and composition with the present court organist, Kalcher.[5] It is to Kalcher's clear, well-ordered and scrupulous teaching that I am indebted for my mastery and ease in the handling of academic forms, more particularly four-part *a cappella* writing. Such things must become second nature to any composer who wishes to express himself and his ideas clearly, just as prosody and metre must become second nature to a poet. I finished my studies with an industry that never flagged.

A preference for the dramatic began to become unmistakable in my musical individuality, and under the eyes of my master I wrote an opera entitled *Die Macht der Liebe und des Weins*, a grand Mass, several pianoforte sonatas, variations, string trios, songs etc., all of which were

---

[2]   Johann Peter Heuschkel (1773–1853), oboist, organist, composer and teacher.
[3]   J1–6, reviewed *AMZ* I (1798), 32 by Z***.
[4]   John Evangelist Wallishauser (Valesi) (1735–1811), singer and teacher.
[5]   Johann Neopmuk Kalcher (1766–1826), organist and composer. Weber dedicated the Six Variations (J7) to him.

later destroyed in a fire. The lively ambition of youth, always anxious to adopt anything that is new and attracts attention, prompted the idea of stealing Sennefelder's[6] thunder. He had just invented the process of lithography, and I believed that in fact I had made the same discovery and had even devised a better method than his. My desire to exploit this on a large scale took us to Freiberg, where all the materials needed were most easily to be had. The scale of the enterprise and the purely mechanical, soul-destroying work involved soon caused me to abandon the scheme, and I returned with redoubled enthusiasm to composition. I set Ritter von Steinberg's *Das Waldmädchen*, and the opera was performed in November, 1800. It was later given further afield than I could have wished (fourteen performances in Vienna, translated into Czech for Prague and successful in St Petersburg),[7] since it is a very immature work with no more than occasional glimpses of inventiveness. In fact Act 2 was written in ten days – one of the many regrettable consequences of the effect on a young mind of those impressive stories told of the great masters, whose example always stimulates imitation. In just the same way, an article that I read in the *Musikzeitung*,[8] spurred me on to write in an entirely new way, and revive the use of old, forgotten instruments etc. Family business having taken me to Salzburg, I there put my new plans into action and wrote the opera *Peter Schmoll und sein Nachbarn*. That was in 1801. The novelties in this score delighted my old master Michael Haydn, who wrote an unusually laudatory notice of the work, which is printed in Gerber's *Tonkünstlers-Lexikon*.[9] This opera was given in Augsburg, but naturally had no great success. I later rewrote the overture, which I published with Gombart. In 1802 my father and I made a musical tour to Leipzig, Hamburg and Holstein, during which I made a collection of theoretical works which I studied with great diligence. Unfortunately a doctor of medicine[10] overthrew all my fine theories by a volley of questions – why this? why that? and so forth – overwhelming me with doubts; and it was only gradually that I found my feet again and was able to compose in my own way, according to a system which is well founded in both nature and philosophy. My aim was to penetrate to the heart of all that the old masters had recommended and established, and to construct a complete system on those principles. I

---

6   Aloys Senefelder (1771–1824), inventor of lithography.
7   No records survive of Prague or St Petersburg performances.
8   *AMZ*.
9   *Neues historisch-biographisches Lexicon der Tonkünstler* (Leipzig, 1812–14).
10   Dr Joseph Munding, of Augsburg.

was overcome by a longing for the musical life of Vienna, and for the first time made my appearance there. It was in the company of leading Viennese musicians, including the unforgettable 'Papa' Haydn, that I met the *Abbé Vogler, who showed that willingness to help all serious efforts which is characteristic of all really great men, opening the treasure-house of his knowledge for my benefit with the most selfless generosity.

Only myself and a few others had the opportunity of observing at close quarters the profundity of that great soul, that inexhaustible store of learning and ardent recognition of all that is good – coupled with great shrewdness in assessing it – and he inspired an undying reverence in us. As for the dross and the eccentricities that upbringing, social position, enmities and misunderstandings had mingled with this precious metal, surrounding it and apparently adulterating its quality – these we came to accept as wholly minor details, easy to overlook or even to find natural.

If only I could succeed in drawing a clear portrait of this rare psychological phenomenon in the arts, something worthy of the man himself and a lesson to students of music! On Vogler's advice, but not without some considerable sacrifice on my part, I wrote no major works for the next two years, but devoted almost all my time to a thorough study of different works by the great masters. Under his guidance I analysed their structure, the development of their ideas and the means employed in each case; and I then attempted to match these and to form a clear conception of them in my own mind and in isolated studies. Nothing of mine was published during this period, except a few sets of variations and the vocal score of Vogler's opera Samori.

With my appointment as director of music at Breslau new possibilities of gaining orchestral experience came my way. In Breslau I built up a new orchestra and chorus, revised my earlier works and composed the opera Rübezahl, for which Professor Rhode[11] wrote the greater part of the libretto. My official duties left me little time for composition; but I did have time to digest the many different ideas and artistic principles that I had, as it were, swallowed perhaps too hastily, and so gradually to develop my own musical individuality.

In 1806 the art-loving Prince Eugen of Württemberg invited me to his court at Carlsruhe in Silesia, and there I composed two symphonies, several concertos and pieces for wind band. Neither the charming little theatre at Carlsruhe nor the fine orchestra survived the war. I embarked on a musical tour at a time when circumstances could hardly

[11]   Johann Gottlieb Rhode, director of the Breslau theatre.

have been more unfavourable. For a time I abandoned practical music-making and found a home with Duke Ludwig of Württemberg at Stuttgart. Stimulated by the encouragement of the excellent *Danzi, I wrote my opera *Silvana*, on *Hiemer's new version of my earlier *Waldmädchen*; *Der erste Ton*; overtures; rewrote some earlier choral pieces; and also composed some pianoforte pieces. This lasted until 1810, when I returned to practical music-making and embarked on another tour. At this point I think I may reckon to have reached artistic maturity; and all that has followed, and what is still to come, may be regarded as the rounding-off of sharp corners and the gradual clarification and increased understanding of basic principles no longer subject to change.

I travelled all over Germany; and the warmth with which my efforts were received, whether as performer or composer, and the seriousness that marked even violent differences of opinion or hostile attacks, stimulated me to exert all my powers and all the idealism of an unshakable determination – the faculties that alone consecrate a man to the true priesthood of art. My operas were given in Frankfurt, Munich, Berlin etc. and my concerts attracted the public. I met the Abbé Vogler once again, a short time before his death, and saw how he devoted himself to two brilliant pupils, *Meyerbeer and *Gänsbacher. More mature now and better able to discriminate, I could still join these two young men and profit from Vogler's deep experience. It was then that I wrote the opera *Abu Hassan* (Darmstadt, 1810). I only saw Vogler once more, in Vienna, and found him full of enthusiasm for my work. Peace to his ashes!

From 1813 to 1816 I directed the Opera in Prague, after completely reorganizing it. I lived now entirely for music, in the conviction that my true vocation lay in cultivating and furthering the cause of that art. My object in Prague once attained, and having achieved all that was feasible in the restricting circumstances of a privately run institution, I resigned my position there, knowing that all my successor needed was to be a scrupulous guardian.

Once again I sallied out into the world, content to wait for it to be made clear to me where my sphere of influence was to be. I received various flattering offers; but it was only the challenge of initiating a German Opera in Dresden that finally captured my imagination. And so I gave myself with enthusiasm and industry to my new task; and if I am one day to have an inscription on my tombstone, it could well run thus – 'Here lies a man who was always honest and selfless in his dealings with his fellow men and with the art he loved.'

107. Reply to criticism of a song in *Das Nachtlager von Granada*

Written: Dresden, 19 March 1818.
Published: *Zeitung für die elegante Welt*, No. 61, 28 March 1818.

Reprinted: KSS.   *Signed*: Carl Maria von Weber.

For Friedrich Kind's drama *Das Nachtlager in Granada*, first performed in Dresden on 22 January 1818, Weber wrote in January 1818 a song, 'Leise weht es' (J223). This is sung by the shepherdess Gabriele, with guitar accompaniment. The melody is based on a genuine Spanish tune, as Kind relates: 'My friend Prof. Hasse brought from his journey to Spain folk music of various kinds for my *Almanack*, which included pieces of music, and this I showed to Weber and placed at his disposal' (F. Kind, *Freischützbuch* (Leipzig, 1843)). In the same number of the *Zeitung* in which Weber wrote, Kind and Carl Böttiger (director of the Dresden Museum) also replied to the attack on the play by a certain K, who has not been identified.

In No. 46 of *Die Zeitung für die elegante Welt* a certain Herr K, writing from Dresden, attempted with almost malicious delight, yet apparent nonchalance, to give a damaging and garbled account of Kind's *Das Nachtlager von Granada* and of its performance. In fact he showed no mean skill in achieving his object, by failing to mention some point, by skating round another or by emphasizing a third. All these points, though favourable in themselves, were so combined as to appear quite the reverse. It is my concern here only to furnish evidence for my point of view of what Herr K calls 'the exquisite little song in which the highly trained shepherd girl even treats us to a difficult trill'. I am sorry for Herr K's sake that Spanish shepherds – or rather Spaniards in general – sing in a different way from what he imagines. The melody in question is in fact a Spanish folksong, as is the ballad (see Ursinus).[1] The vocal apparatus of Italians and Spaniards has a natural flexibility, which makes their style of singing quite unlike ours; and effects that can only be achieved by a German voice if it has been trained come quite naturally to them. It is for this reason that passage-work-like figures of several notes often occur in Italian and Spanish songs on single syllables; and in fact almost every seguidilla begins and ends with a trill.

What, then, was it that prompted Herr K's rebukes? can it have been ignorance, or was it plain malice? Unfortunately it seems to have been the latter.

[1] August Friedrich Ursinus (1764–1805) published several collections of foreign songs.

108. *The Mudfish* – a humoresque

Written: Dresden, 12 April and 1 May 1818.
Printed: HHS; MMW; KSS.

On his arrival in Dresden, Weber was invited to join the so-called Dichtertee, later renamed Liederkreis, at which artists and amateurs of all kinds would gather and read their works. It met under the protection of the Minister, Count Nostitz (who wrote under the name of Arthur von Nordstern), and its leader was Friedrich Kind. The members included the writer Eduard Gehe (librettist of *Spohr's Jessonda*), Therese aus dem Winkel (see above, No. 105), Carl Böttiger (director of the Dresden Museum and an archaeologist, drama critic and author) and Helmina von Chezy. Tieck refused to join what he contemptuously referred to as 'The Incense Institute', and its 'cliquish exclusiveness, mutual admiration and humdrum attitudes' have been categorized by H. A. Kruger in his *Pseudoromantik: Friedrich Kind und der Dresden Liederkreis* (Leipzig, 1904). One of the group's pastimes was for the ladies to choose various random words which would be disposed by lot among the men as chapter-titles for a novel. Each would then have to write his chapter, in order. Weber drew the word *Schlammbeizger*, in modern German *Schlammbeisser*, 'mudfish'. This is an eel-like fish which lives in pools that often dry up in summer, when it can utter a whistling noise. It gives warning of changes in the weather, especially of an approaching storm, by alterations in its appearance; and for this reason it was often kept in a glass jar as a weather prophet – *Wetterkundige*, or in the dialect word used by Weber, *Wettergundel*. He also uses an Eastern European name for it, *Knurrpietsche*. Its nearest English equivalent is the loach, sometimes known in Germany as a *Wetterfisch*. Weber read his 'humoresque' to the Liederkreis on 2 May 1818. *Theodor Hell, another member, had previously drawn the work *Sinngrün* (*Mimosa pudica*, a delicate plant notable for its characteristic of folding up if touched in the hours of daylight). He regarded this as a much easier option than Weber's word, and eventually published his chapter in *Urania*; the complete novel was never published.

No, it was really too much to bear and I was overwhelmed with despair. Little wonder if I had become aware of the full significance of my name, and in every fibre of my being! Filled with the blackest misery, I crept into my room, pulled my old frieze coat over the poky windows and abandoned myself to gloomy brooding in the dark. In what a black cauldron the fates had brewed the ingredients of my life! and what perverse malice had made them throw into the mixture so many wild love-potions, so that love affairs of every kind seemed to have become the law and guiding-line of my whole existence! Macbeth's witches' cauldron was surely no more hideous than mine! and yet, in strangest contradiction to my actual experience, something told me that round that cauldron stood none but gentle and benign figures of women who, like the twelve signs of the zodiac, betokened some major disaster, not without a malicious delight as they devised and added a number of oddities to the brew to see how it would all ferment and what would be the final outcome. Yes, yes, I exclaimed, that weaver's apprentice[1] was quite right when he sturdily maintained against all opposition that every human being is allotted a certain number of foolish actions and that he must work through this number; and that therefore every such action is in fact a matter for congratulation, since it means one step nearer the goal. This idea took firm hold of me, and I leapt up in delight, shouting 'Well, thank God, I can't be far wrong as I've already committed foolish actions enough, and heaven grant that their number tallies happily with that of the zodiac signs.'

To the future, then, I could look forward with content, but the present prospect seemed all the worse. But was there anything strange in that? After all, what invisible power kept me in this wretched Göttingen? It suddenly struck me that there I was, well and truly turned down by my beloved, still sitting in that wretched hole with nothing to do and no prospects. I must get away at all costs. Very good, but where? and how? That was the question. I suffered from an almost complete lack of the only wherewithal effective with postillions and hotel-keepers, the contents of the wig-box having been reduced to a minimum by Levi Meyer's old clothes shop and my tavern debts. I was too proud to go home to the flesh-pots of the chemist's. Anna Mörner, whom I could certainly help with training young Laplanders, was far too far away. Pistorius had left the university long ago, and I could certainly expect nothing more of my former patrons – in any case it was only the eighth and ninth who had given me anything, though some had made vague promises earlier on. In fact the look-out was black, and I saw in myself clear signs of all the symptoms of that moral sickness that has given Germany so many actors. That is to say, I was no use for any serious, settled course of studies and had nothing to lose. In my head, moreover, was an untidy library of multifarious and ill-digested things which could only produce poems such as 'Die Sinnpflanze' in moments of unintelligible brain-fever, when it seemed as though some higher principle outside myself spoke through me.

Without thinking, I began to look at the sides of the last packet of snuff I could call my own. It was a page from the *Hamburger Unparteiischer Korrespondent*, with an article from London, in which I read the following. 'Apart from war, art is today the only path to fortune; and proud Britain values and rewards artists more highly than

---

[1]   *Webergeselle.*

any other nation. Clementi has made a huge fortune here, and only recently the charming Catalani earned £2,000 in a single concert. It is of course undeniable that the combination of that imperious voice and the charms and graces of such a magnificent figure...'. The rest of the sentence had disappeared beneath the shopkeeper's glue, but the sparks of art, Hamburg and Catalani had already fired my spirit to a decision.[2]

An elder brother of my father's was a town musician in Hamburg, where he led a pleasant and comfortable existence. He and my father had quarrelled and he never took any notice of us, while his name was only very occasionally mentioned at home, and then in connexion with the oddest traits. It was to him that I now planned to go; the town musician was to be the first step on the ladder that I was to climb. Hamburg marks were to be converted by my talent into English pounds – thousands of them – and then I should just like to see the look on the face of my only love, for whom I felt such an indescribable sense of longing. My reputation would precede me – the wonderful singer and composer, whose works were only just beginning to show his full artistic stature. Without disclosing my identity, full of love and respect I would accompany her in one of my songs and, forgetful of all around me, I would embark on a magnificent improvisation – she would be carried away by her enthusiasm, would recognize me by the originality of my music and would sink, finally conquered and fascinated, into the arms of her *Zipperlein*.[3]

I had reached such a pitch of excitement that every moment seemed wasted until I could put my plan into execution.

All my books were rushed to the second-hand bookseller's, where they were (as students say) flogged, and the wig collection found a new master (and purchaser) at the hairdresser's. My good old trunk and every one of my belongings, including underclothes etc., were all converted into cash. I only kept my zither – and I could in all honesty say to anyone who asked me *omnia mea mecum porto*, or in other words, 'all I have is what I stand up in'. I put letters for my dear Manichees[4] on the table, giving the address of my uncle in Hamburg; and just as the first evening star was twinkling, I slung my zither over my

---

[2]   These were the years of Angelica Catalani's greatest European triumphs, and she had indeed some years previously, in 1807, been paid £2,000 for a festival appearance in England.

[3]   A rheumatic or gouty pain – here a highly ironic term of endearment.

[4]   Nineteenth-century student slang for duns, from a pun on Manes (founder of Manichaeanism) and *Mahner*, someone who issues a *Mahnung* or demand for payment.

shoulder, cocked my cap over one ear and off I went – a real troubadour, a modest little flower 'humbly bent and known to none, 'twas a dear little violet'.[5] Standing in the doorway I took a last look at the empty room, which used to contain such a heap of odd belongings: and there on the stove I saw, with a pang, the glass containing my old friend the weather prophet. He had come into my hands through a strange adventure at a literary tea party, an affair in which I had innocently become involved. He came from hands very dear to me – the clever, dainty, good-humoured, godless hands of Miss Amalie. I could not leave the mudfish in the lurch and, come what may, he could not spoil life for me on my travels. 'Come on, then, *Knurrpietsche* or *Wettergundel*,' I said, 'you shall tell me every day what's brewing and I'll take you as a sort of model in fact, for I feel a kinship between us already. You are a tough customer, and so am I – or I should not have come to life again after Chapter 5.[6] Like you, I lack a float to bring me to the surface and hitherto have stayed firmly on the bottom. My springtime is just about to begin and I mean now to raise myself, like you, from the mud of disorder to the heights of art. Heaven only grant that I do not become the prey of the reviewers, who threaten my existence as pike threaten yours. No more teachers are going to hook me. If things turn out badly and I find the art world too stormy, even if death finally marinates me, I shall imitate your example and depart this life like a swan, with a trill or at least a good *sostenuto* note. Life has only poured salt and ashes on my head without washing off the mud of neediness.'

No reader of my story will be surprised to hear that I was in a highly nervous condition, that everyday life inspired me with nothing but loathing and that I sought solitude in order to give free rein to my artistic imagination. I avoided towns and their inhabitants and found myself drawn rather to the countryman's quiet cottage, where I hoped to learn from the birds' twittering the secret of natural singing. How bitterly I regretted never having pursued my studies of anatomy far enough to obtain an accurate knowledge of the vocal organs, or having never joined an amateur orchestra rather than acquiring the art of versification! Yet in fact even such an orchestra would have offended my new sensibilities, which rejected instrumental music entirely, including harmony and the rest. The human voice! that it was which alone fascinated me. Alas! I myself had no voice, only an unbelievably firm faith in some miracle of nature which would give me one. And

[5]   From Goethe's 'Das Veilchen', set by Mozart.
[6]   Of the Liederkreis novel of composite authorship.

this same exalted sentimental mood showed itself in odd contradiction to the often exhausting experiences of my wandering artist's life, with its adventures, its nights spent in haylofts and other humble circumstances, which should obviously have kept my feet well on the ground. But no, it seems always to have been part of my character to be attracted to the exact reverse of what necessity and probability dictate. It must certainly have been a strange sight – or rather sound – for passers-by to hear me intoning hymns of praise to the divine Catalani, not worrying about any inconvenience of text but simply (like her) using the first high-sounding Italian word that came into my head. This of course gave the widest scope to my imagination, and I floated happily along in a sea of sound. Lines of trees were scales in both hands, every brook was a virtuoso passage, the smoke from every chimney a grandiose cadenza, and as for flowers – I could smell every key and hear every scent;[7] and on top of it all I felt the need, so deeply implanted in my nature, to attach myself to some other sentient being. And so what could be more natural than that, as my admiration for Catalani grew daily stronger, I should end by communicating my tender feelings to my mudfish?

Do not laugh, gentle reader (or listener), but rather pity the morbid excitability which attempted to express gratitude by attaching itself to the only living creature near at hand. How often he warned me of coming storms, how friendly was the gleam of his black eyes! Just so, I thought, must be Catalani's glance! And it is only too true that one is most attached to those who make one suffer; for it was no joke to carry the smooth glass bowl under one's arm on a hot day or a rough road; and all that I got in return was an occasional peasant meal in payment for my meteorological prophecies. And so I developed a kind of confidence in my fish and had high hopes of the reception that my garden-loving uncle in Hamburg would give him. Then that wretched stamped metal, that we call money, barred the very entrance to my paradise. I was in a wineshop in Harburg, taking some refreshment before crossing the water to Hamburg, when my last gold piece escaped through a treacherous hole in my pocket. There I sat, in the greatest embarrassment, at my wits' end and staring straight in front of me. Nor should I have noticed the only other customer repeatedly going to the window to look at the weather, had it not been for the sudden sound of a girl's charming voice from the half-open door, saying 'It's quite clear up the Elbe, father. You can safely tell the men to get ready.' 'Yes,' he replied, 'but how the devil can I be certain? I don't know my bearings hereabouts.'

[7]   Cf. below, No. 125, *Tonkünstlers Leben*, p. 319.

I raised my eyes and saw a tall, thin man with unattractive, twisted features whose rough and sly character denoted a roving and unscrupulous existence – perhaps a soldier or a sailor. 'If anyone could tell me what tomorrow's weather will be like,' he said with a coarse oath, 'I'd willingly put twenty marks in his pocket!' 'Done!' I cried. The man turned to me in amazement, and the owner of the charming voice came in from outside, curious but friendly. How her glance struck me! Catalani's must have just that same friendliness. 'Done!' I said again. 'I will stake my own existence for tomorrow's being stormy, and for good weather after that – on condition that you pay for my drinks in the meantime and then take me to my relations in Hamburg – for I take it that you must be a boatman?' 'Not exactly, sir! I'm a fireworks man who wants to display his skill first here and then in Hamburg itself. For that of course I need good weather, and I am certainly prepared to satisfy the demands of anyone who will undertake to guarantee the next few days' weather – yes, and I'll keep him company too. But what guarantee of your skill can you have to offer? It's not difficult to hire a carriage, and after a few days good living our jolly Herr Student would in all probability continue his journey.'

I was offended by this and, trusting in my mudfish, I repeated with some heat that, should I prove wrong in my prophecy, I would pledge myself to stay with him until my uncle came to bail me out. The fireworks man replied to this with a mocking grin, adding 'Well, you don't look a bad sort, you're strong and healthy.' And with that he called in from the next room a number of his tobacco-chewing mates, men of much the same kind as himself, to act as witnesses to the bargain. Then, with an odiously friendly grin, he handed me over to the nice girl, observing that if my skill proved genuine, it would be no bad thing, and if I lost my wager, seafaring folk would have no objection. Unhappily I failed to understand the deep import of these few words and was delighted to have solved the most pressing of my immediate problems. Katharina's lively eyes contributed not a little to my high spirits, and I asked her on the spot if I might make a slight rearrangement of the letters of her name, and so bring her still nearer to my ideal. She was a dark girl and free in her manners, and she consented with a laugh to my calling her Katharani.

My lodging was decent enough. Next day's bad weather was a triumph for me and was celebrated in the evening by a punch party, only spoiled for me by the loss of my last object of value – a watch – during the course of some friendly game. That, however, worried me very little, and Katharani's Catalani-voice, coupled with the hopes based on the mudfish and my uncle, kept me on my feet.

The devil of ambition caused me to conceal the mudfish and his talents, so that I need not share the glory of my meteorological prophesying; and so the little rogue Katharani had undertaken to look after both my knapsack and the fish. On the sly, however, I kept an even sharper watch on *Knurrpietsche*'s movements; and since his unusual immobility promised an unbroken spell of fine weather, I had no hesitation in deciding the day for the fireworks display.

The fulfilment of my first prophecy had inspired confidence, and every imaginable preparation was now set in hand. Among my rather raffish-looking companions there was a good deal of drinking in anticipation of a good day's business, and the drinks were chalked up against each man's name. I often felt ill at ease in this unattractive company, and it was only Katharani's eyes and voice that made life tolerable – especially when I learnt that she had heard Catalani, though I must admit that her description of the occasion was not couched in quite the language of a connoisseur.

At last the fateful day broke. At first the sky clouded over, as did my fireworks men's brows. Despite some sarcastic comments, I alone remained cheerful, for whenever I could steal a glance at my fish, he was absolutely motionless. I therefore urged my companions to continue their arrangements for the display. The day grew darker and darker. The public collected and the seats were all occupied, when suddenly a violent storm of rain destroyed all the preparations and drenched the onlookers, who angrily demanded their money back. The box-office, however, had already been dismantled, to escape the rain, and the angry crowd attacked the fireworks men with curses and shouts. They did not fail to take these out on me, and with interest. I was hurled to the ground, overwhelmed with blows and abuse and finally dragged off under cover of darkness to a wretched hovel by the Elbe, where I was pushed into a sort of cellar and, as I could hear, the door was bolted.

For a while I lay there unconscious. When at length I collected my wits, I could not understand by what right I had been so maltreated or what would happen next. Over my head some kind of celebration seemed to be in progress and there was dancing. The damp of my clothes and the place in which I found myself were becoming every moment more unbearable, when I heard Katharina's kindly little voice outside the door.

'My heart aches for you, young gentleman, but there is nothing I can do to help you. From the outset they had their eyes on you, and you delivered yourself into the hands of the press-gang when you made that unconsidered wager and repeated it before witnesses. Nothing can save you now, and you will be shipped to the colonies with the first boat that leaves. Well, many have made their fortunes there and should you be as fortunate as they, remember the assistance I gave you!' 'O mudfish, you monster!' I exclaimed in my despair. 'It is to you that I owe this terrible turn in my affairs.' 'What?' asked Katharina, 'the fish is dead, you know.' 'Dead?' I burst out. 'Yes,' she interrupted, 'and yet I took such care of it! I even gave it the best, clearest spring water the day after you came here.' 'Oh!' I cried. 'That is what killed him, and no wonder he lay so still, if he was dead.' 'Aha!' laughed my siren from outside the cellar door, 'So it was a weather fish, was it? how could you put your trust in such an animal?' 'Well, I did not really trust him myself,' I replied, 'but I was asked to look after him, and I can at least claim to have done my best for him. However, ingratitude is the reward one meets most often in this world; and it may well be that what I did for the fish will earn me the curses of my future patron, who will have to rescue me from this desperate plight, though how I do not know. Mudfish, you float over me like a heavy fate, and here I lie in the mud, as wet as you and entangled by my blind adoration for Catalani!' Deep night closed round me and I could hear the false Katharani[8] giggling as she left me. With a sigh of resignation I abandoned myself passively to my fate. 'Death looses all ties; fare thee well, mudfish!'

[8]   In 1818 Bäuerle produced in Vienna his satire *Die falsche Catalani* with a comic actor as the soprano, in travesty, and this quickly became very popular in Dresden.

109. Introduction to Mozart's *Die Entführung aus dem Serail*

Written: Dresden, 11 June 1818.
Published: DAZ, No. 142, 16 June 1818.   *Signed:* Carl Maria von Weber.
Reprinted: HHS, MMW (both misdated); KSS; LKA.

The lack of a sound ensemble of soloists forced on Weber several makeshift solutions during 1818. For the production of *Weigl's *Die Schweizerfamilie* on 22 May he was obliged to use an Italian, Sandrini, and a chorus member in the principal roles; for *Entführung* he similarly had to draw on substitutes. Constanze was sung by Mlle Hähnel, another chorister. The *AMZ* was distinctly reserved about the technique and acting of a singer with no solo experience (*AMZ* xx (1818), 527–8); the *DAZ*, which reviewed the second performance on 20 June, was more indulgent, observing that 'Up-and-coming young artists are not, strictly speaking, an object of criticism, more something to be noticed', but remarking upon her promising performance of 'Martern aller Arten' (No. 155, 1 July 1818). Belmonte was sung by *Friedrich Gerstäcker, Osmin by a mediocre character bass, Herr Toussaint, replacing Metzner, and Blondchen by *Julie Zucker, with the Pasha Selim played by the distinguished actor Friedrich Werdy. At the revival at Easter 1819 there was a new cast; Weber was ill, and the direction was slack.

On Wednesday 17 June 1818 Mozart's magnificent opera *Die Entführung aus dem Serail* will have its first performance in the Hoftheater.

There can perhaps be no more important concern for the music-lover than to observe the development of the great figures who dominate and shape the age in which they live; and this development is seen most clearly and strikingly in the chronology of their important works. Mozart was of course solemnly initiated into the secrets of his art while he was still a child. He devoted himself to rigorous studies and his creative gifts were of the highest order. But even he needed time for these elements to work and cease fermenting before he could achieve the clarity that characterizes this opera.

There is a strange kind of popular legend that this is Mozart's first opera, though it is in fact his fourteenth.[1] But here, as always in commonly received opinions, there is a genuine grain of truth – something implanted by the unknown supernatural powers that work in men's judgements. In his earlier *Idomeneo* (Munich, 1780)[2] we seem to find all the colours familiar from Mozart's later works, displayed as it were on a palette; and the weight of knowledge begins to struggle with the genius's delight in liberty. In the same way *Entführung* (Vienna, 1782) marks the victory of youth in all its freshness, though we catch glimpses of a delight in harmonic mastery and in the profusion – even excess – of a youthful and high-spirited intoxication with creation. A good example is Constanze's big aria ('Martern aller Arten'), which the composer himself seems later to have pruned. And so in a sense *Entführung* is indeed Mozart's first opera, in that it marks the first stage in that artistic condition which the world honours, marvels at and names after him 'Mozartian perfection'.

Particularly remarkable in *Entführung* are the total grasp of dramatic truth and the delineation of character by declamation, combined with passages in which the composer has not quite freed himself from the past in matters of form and melodic cut. It was only later that he

---

[1]   Weber is presumably including dramatic works of varying kinds in this reckoning.
[2]   Actually 1781.

achieved that exclusive conviction, the virile strength and presence of mind that were wholly dedicated to dramatic truth (*Figaro*, Vienna, 1786; *Don Giovanni*, *Zauberflöte*, *Titus* etc.). My own artistic taste is particularly attracted by the gaiety and spendthrift youthfulness and warmth of *Entführung*, the almost virginal sensibility of the music. It is as though Mozart had here expressed the very essence of every human being's youthful happiness, something that can never be recaptured and whose charms are inextricably connected with its weaknesses. I would even go so far as to say that in *Entführung* Mozart's artistic experience reached its full maturity and that what came later was experience of the world. Operas like *Figaro* and *Don Giovanni* justified his contemporaries in expecting further similar works from him; but with the best will in the world he could never have repeated *Entführung*.

It is the wish of our welcome guest and fellow citizen, the tenor Gerstäcker, to sing the part of Belmonte that has brought the opera to our theatre, where it is also providing the occasion for the first appearance of a youthful talent of our own. Mlle Hähnel, a member of the chorus, will be singing the part of Constanze; and I feel sure that I can happily rely on the friendly sympathy of the Dresden public in recommending her natural nervousness to their indulgence and her outstanding natural gifts to their notice.

In the same connexion it gives me great pleasure to point out that the opera chorus, which has hardly been in existence for nine months, is thus already fulfilling one of its functions as a seed-bed for the opera. Determined and knowledgeable artists are in fact already producing singers who justify the hope of gradually being able to use our own native talent to form singers whom other opera houses, who depend on chance and shifting reputation, can only match by great expenditure of money.

I should perhaps add, in connexion with *Entführung*, that the high tessitura of Constanze's music lies outside what is normally considered the soprano range. I make this point for the benefit of the minority who only approve of what is in any case inevitable and yet are obliged in the end to admit that it would be most unjust if, for example, the bass X held it against the tenor Y that he, X, was not also a tenor. Each artist is allotted his own individual sphere by providential natural gifts and by the composer's works. I should like this to be considered as an additional ground for indulgence or recommendation – if either are necessary – for Mlle Hähnel's performance.

110. Friedrich Fesca and criticism

Written: Hosterwitz, 22 and 23 July 1818.
Published: AMZ xx (1818), 581–91.   *Signed:* Carl Maria v. Weber.
Reprinted: HHS, MMW (both inaccurate); KSS, LKA.

Friedrich Fesca (1789–1826) was a violinist and composer who worked chiefly in Kassel and Carlsruhe: he was to die in the same year as Weber, also of tuberculosis. Weber's article was stimulated by a misunderstanding that had arisen between him and Fesca, who had written to him reproaching him with not having troubled to review a set of quartets in the *AMZ*. Weber tried to clear this up in a long letter (2 July 1818; in the Foreword to HHS this is published with the addressee anonymous, while in MMW *Ferdinand Fränzl is given as the addressee; Fesca was correctly identified by Kaiser, who prints the text in KSS, No. 132). Weber intended the present article to make amends to Fesca in the form of a statement of his critical attitudes, as well as providing a review of the quartets. He sent it to *Rochlitz with a covering letter, saying 'Enclosed is something for the *AMZ* which I'd like to ask you to publish as soon as possible – to calm down Fesca...I feel myself particularly required to say it as I'm as much advocate as judge, and take my stand before the public in both roles' (letter of 24 July 1818). Fesca was duly pacified.

The best method of introducing what I have to say appears to be a sort of self-accusation. In this I am aware that I am alluding to an experience common among my colleagues and something which, if openly discussed, may well reverse a number of precipitately formed opinions. Even if the result is not openly acknowledged, there is good hope that it may be privately pondered.

It is some two years since I was attracted by the search for mastery – something that becomes daily rarer – to be found in Herr Fesca's work, and undertook a detailed discussion of his quartets and quintets. These fine works were deserving of all the attention which I bestowed on them, and I was delighted by the prospect of drawing the attention of the musical world to such really deserving and beautiful creations and thereby doing the art some service.

Anyone who shares my dislike of the superficiality which has for some time characterized much critical writing, and does not feel qualified to bestow praise or blame on a work without quoting chapter and verse, will know that such scrupulous criticism is not a matter of a few hours or days. On the contrary, it presupposes an acquaintance with the work concerned so detailed and accurate that the very discussion itself leaves on the reader's mind a picture so clear that it may be called a perfect reflection. Lack of space, paucity of musical illustrations and all the other drawbacks inseparable from publication in a journal only increase the amount of time and care needed for such a project. I wonder how many writers have been happy enough always to light exactly on the point that seems most necessary and useful for a discussion, and to confine their time and their labour within those limits. For myself, I must admit that this has very seldom been granted to me. I was either distracted by other professional duties or I was repeatedly interrupted, so that work of the kind I had in mind became impossible. And so in the end I have had the same experience as with my best friends. In conversation with everyday acquaintances one can manage with a limited number of social and aesthetic expressions, which prove sufficient for the purpose. But with those who are nearer and dearer to one it is different. Half measures will not do where the affections are more deeply engaged; and if we cannot devote to them as much as we should like, we are overwhelmed by a feeling of having withheld from them something to which they have a just claim. A gulf opens between us, a feeling of embarrassment that almost spoils our relationship and we are eventually compelled to abandon the undertaking rather than continue with it at a level beneath that which we have set ourselves. Of course this is all wrong, but so it is; and let him who is conscious of his innocence throw the first stone.

I know hardly a single composer living today who is not in some way discontented with the attention that his works receive, even if it is only in quantity. The majority of them may well have right on their side. But have not editors also reason to complain about composers and critics, if they can prove that on their own side there has been no lack of invitations, commissions and requests of all sorts?

So if healthy and well-balanced men sometimes find it hard to keep within bounds, is it to be wondered at if a camp-follower or the occasional pusher gets the upper hand, throws his weight about in the judge's chair and has an exaggerated opinion of himself, if he can behave so badly with impunity? Of course it is painful for a true friend of the arts to see the sacred office of proclaiming the truth, and revealing to every master and disciple his inmost self, in unworthy hands which mostly do harm and rob criticism of the attention and respect which are its due. But are not decent people often embittered by their experience of criticism? There are far too many little men ready to echo the claim *anch'io son pittore!*,[1] men who react to any judgement of their abilities that appears not to confirm their dreams of greatness with a host of objections, contradictions and quibbles which disgrace

---

[1] 'And I, too, am a painter!' – traditionally exclaimed by Correggio in amazement before Raphael's *Santa Cecilia* in Bologna.

the whole business of criticism in the eyes of decent folk, who cannot devote all their time to this branch – or rather sub-species – of the arts. Such nobodies as these are just the people who are all agog to know who has attacked them, so that they may establish by their own dwarfish standards the true stature of their opponent. Certainly there is much to be said both for and against anonymous criticism, and everything depends on the circumstances of each individual case.

For myself, there are two reasons why I sign all my critical writings, on principle. In the first place I am myself a performer and therefore unwilling to pass an unqualified judgement on my colleagues: mine is no more than the conviction of a single individual. Secondly my own circumstances make me take into account the yapping of a lot of weaklings who always imagine the critic to be a man who has the right to indulge his malice, let his little stock of courage fail, or else use his influence to promote a work – all under the protection of the judge's robes. I believe that there is much to be said in favour of anonymity. You have only to ask yourself whether an anonymous criticism is not more representative of popular opinion (or, in other words, of pure unprejudiced truth), always provided that it is scrupulous in thoroughness and benevolent in attitude. Signed criticism is almost impossible to dissociate from subsidiary ideas that involuntarily throng the reader's mind in connexion with the writer. This is particularly true of unfavourable judgements, which are almost inevitably associated with personal prejudice, whereas one is ready to accept a favourable opinion from any source.

All this amounts to the fact that, in practice, one should accept without too much anxiety whatever fate or chance may bring in the way of criticism; that composers should not be unduly downcast if every critic does not spring to their defence; and that editors – and particularly editors of critical journals – should carefully follow the artistic movements of the day and do all they can to sweeten and smooth the rough task of those few critics who practise their profession with devotion and insight. Finally, the critics themselves should do their work with care and discrimination, never losing sight of what will further the progress of the art and exercising in their judgements a benevolent severity such as that which characterizes an affectionate friend or father.

When all is said and done, we may be thankful for the fact that an unseen fate hangs over all works of art, and undeserved praise can do no more to rescue a house-fly from death and oblivion than a poisonous sting can destroy a genuine inner life. Every work bears within itself the germ of its own life and death, and time is the only true tester of worth. I have been doubly comforted by this reflection since I have myself experienced the fact that one may have the best and most selfless desire to promote some cause and yet be obliged by an improbable chain of circumstances to wait a very long time before one can defend it before the public.

Finding myself too short of time to complete a full discussion of Herr Fesca's quartets, I recently returned the scores which I had requested so that some other critic might be entrusted with the work. Nevertheless I think it my pleasant duty to give Herr Fesca at least a proof of my high opinion of all that is good and beautiful by publishing the notes that I made as I went through his works.

The branch of music that Herr Fesca has particularly favoured (quartets etc.) is itself an indication that he belongs to the happy few who have made a serious study of the innermost substance of the art, and that in an age too often given over to superficialities. In chamber music it is not possible to rely on a few flattering ideas and brilliant passages. Those who enjoy this solid fare are already accustomed to what is both nutritious and piquant, may indeed very well be spoiled by the greatness and sublimity of Mozart's and Haydn's contributions to the genre. And so any composer who does not want to sink back into obscurity and oblivion the moment he makes his appearance must produce something really solid, the product of deep thought and feeling. I do not mean by this to imply that other musical genres do not make similar demands on the composer: but in the quartet, this musical concentrate, the statement of any idea is confined to its minimum essential constituent parts, the four voices. They can only win our attention by the nature of their relationship to each other, whereas in symphonies etc. comparatively insignificant melodies can be made effective and ornamental by skilful orchestration and the charms of variety. In quartets mere noise can never masquerade as strength; and any awkwardness of the composer in the interweaving or melodic design of the middle parts or in the relation of independent melodies to the design of the whole is as clear as daylight. Pure four-part writing corresponds to the nude in painting.

Herr Fesca is in complete control of what he undertakes to express. His models, in the best sense, were Haydn and Mozart, as they should be to any true artist, on the principle that all progress in art is stimulated by contact with another artist who stimulates not imitation but new invention. His style and his choice of melody are marked by sensibility and a certain tender amalgamation of the feelings and this, combined with strength which is by no means lacking, gives his music a very individual charm. Herr Fesca can be gay, even witty, but it is impossible to miss the predominating gravity in the later realization of his ideas. He is scrupulous in detail and his music recalls *Spohr by the piquancy of its harmony, though Herr Fesca never loses himself in Spohr's noble melancholy. His modulations are almost as brusque as Beethoven's; but he is by nature too gentle to seize the listener unexpectedly, as Beethoven does, and suddenly hold him in his giant fist over the edge of a precipice. The distinguishing feature of his art is a certain intelligent discretion which, added to depth of feeling, avoids dryness and produces an unusually happy relationship between the conception of the whole and its constituent parts. The development of his ideas is clear and well diversified, the four parts are independent; and if occasionally the president (the first violin) is given something more brilliant to perform, this is never carried to such a point that the three other instruments are reduced to menial status.

To the best of my belief, Herr Fesca has hitherto written only quartets, quintets and a symphony, which I do not know although it was most favourably reviewed in these pages.[2] I can quite understand his preference for these forms, which seem to correspond so exactly with his musical nature. All the same, it may not be wholly advisable to confine oneself exclusively to a single genre, which may – and in the end indeed must – lead to mannerisms.

Genius is something universal, and whoever possesses it can exercise it in any and every form. External impressions or stimuli cause a composer to embark on one path or another, and it is certainly true that his first steps on any other, later chosen path will be uncertain and nervous enough, perhaps, to cause any but the most persevering to lose heart. The path of his original choice was so easy and familiar, and he knew all its pitfalls so well. But with a little gentle pressure one's invention can work just as easily in the new form, and on returning to the old will bring fresh flowers. Vocal composition in particular is something that no composer should disdain. The human voice brings dramatic truth to life, and although from vocal to instrumental music is only a single step, the journey in the other direction is considerably longer. It is as though Nature wanted to have her revenge on any composer who did not pay his first respects to the instrument that she has provided. Chamber music belongs essentially to the circle of serious-minded domestic pleasures, but vocal music enlarges the view and introduces the listener to a wider panorama. Exclusive cultivation

---

[2]   Fesca had actually written a number of works in other forms by 1818.

of string quartets may easily lead, through its complications and limitation of space, to miniature painting, and thence it is only a single step to scrupulosity and over-refinement, the retailing of pettifogging detail.

I am too convinced of Herr Fesca's exceptional talents and really admirable knowledge not to ask him to apply his gifts to this other genre. There is a kind of noble and modest mistrusting of one's own powers which seems to me probably to form part of Herr Fesca's temperament. But anyone who can be so conscious of his own industry and perseverance and has such gifts as he, has nothing to fear and can therefore boldly diversify his productions, at the same time guarding against the danger of the opposite extreme.

111. Introduction to J. P. S. Schmidt's *Das Fischermädchen*

Written: Dresden, 2 December 1818.
Published: DAZ, No. 288, 3 December 1818. *Signed:* Carl Marie von Weber.
Reprinted: HHS; MMW (misdated); KSS.

Johann Philipp Samuel Schmidt (1779–1853) was a Berlin lawyer and amateur musician, a friend of Weber's, who also wrote music criticism for the *Haude- und Spenersche Zeitung*. His dozen *Singspiele* include *Feodora* (1812), *Die Alpenhütte* (1816) and *Der Kyffhäuser* (1817) (all one-act). *Das Fischermädchen, oder Hass und Liebe* was first performed in Leipzig on 5 August 1818, then in Berlin on 25 November 1818; the Dresden performance was in fact given on 5 December, with *The Magic Flute* on the 6th. It was not reviewed in the *DAZ*, but there was a brief report in *AMZ* xx (1818), 871. The cast included *Johanna Eunicke (Florentine), Beschort (Anselmo), Ludwig Rebenstein (Fernando), Blume (Franzesko) and Wauer (Balandrino).

Das Fischermädchen, a one-act opera by *Theodor Körner, with music by J. P. Schmidt of Berlin, is being given here for the first time on 6 December.

Herr Schmidt exhibits a praiseworthy intention to write in a solid and individual manner, and a number of small operas by him have been well received in Berlin and elsewhere, for instance *Feodora*, *Die Alpenhütte*, *Der Kyffhäuser-Berg* and others. His efforts are all the more praiseworthy because he is in fact an amateur, and at the present time such ideals as his are increasingly neglected even by so-called professional artists. His music suggests a preference for a highly seasoned style, with the rich orchestration and swiftly changing harmonies characteristic of modern composers. At the same time he is scrupulous in observing correct prosody, subtle expression and delineation of character. Herr Schmidt has devoted himself almost exclusively to dramatic music. He has written a number of cantatas but few purely orchestral works.

112. Controversy in the *Allgemeine musikalische Zeitung*

Written: Dresden, 11 December 1818.
Published: AMZ xx (1818), 877–80.
Signed: Carl Maria von Weber, königl. sächs. Kapellmeister und Director der königl. deutschen Oper.
Reprinted: MMW (inaccurate); KSS.

As the dispute with Letter C showed (see above, No. 105), Weber's reforms were by no means universally popular in a city that had long shown reluctance to be disturbed by novel ideas; he was, moreover, beset with problems in achieving his desired standards. Always a lively controversialist, he was stung into action by unfavourable comments on his productions of Isouard's *Joconde* and Mozart's *The Magic Flute* in *AMZ* xx (1818), 837–41. The latter performance was attacked for including an inexperienced Queen of Night in Frau Metzner (wife of the bass and chorus-master; she failed to produce the top Fs with which she had been credited) and a set of evidently inadequate Three Ladies, as well as other shortcomings:'The informed public, who can judge how good the performance of even this kind of opera was, given the means at the disposal of the company, were astonished at the insight, the expertise, the tireless care with which Herr Kapellmeister von Weber achieved it.' The criticism was by one A.C.H. (he has not been identified, though Weber seems to have known who he was), and evidently caused considerable shock, not least because Dresden was accustomed to the very indulgent reviews of the *DAZ*. As a result of the controversy, the *AMZ* critic was replaced by Carl von Miltitz (1780–1845), a court chamberlain and a composer, who contented himself with half-yearly reports of a factual nature. Privately, Weber was under no illusions as to the quality of his ensemble: 'Our men are all right, especially while we have *Gerstäcker; but we completely lack an outstanding German female singer, and the general absence of real talent is very striking' (letter to *G. F. Treitschke, 29 January 1820).

Every town has its own arbiters of artistic merit, some working openly and others anonymously. Local artists – or rather art-workers – are not usually content with these judges; and this is natural, if one takes into account the sensitivity which is a part – and indeed a necessary part – of the artistic temperament. If criticism is sincere, however, and allied to superior knowledge, it is beneficial; and, after all, it may be a long time before a patient actually feels grateful for the bitter draught that the doctor has administered with the best intentions.

Dresden has both its critics and its malcontents, and on my arrival here the latter lost no time in warning me against the former. I kept my mouth shut for almost two years, in order to see who was in the right. I was in fact on many occasions obliged to bite back a feeling of wounded pride, in the knowledge that bickering of this kind was greatly enjoyed by the outside world, though it seemed to me pointless and unworthy of the art. The conclusions that I eventually reached were the following. The Dresden faculty contains many really admirable critics, with an outstanding knowledge of harmony, history, drama and other departments of aesthetics. It follows from this that their observations have the moderation and the appearance of sincerity needed to inspire confidence and trust among the wider public unacquainted with local conditions. In fact much of the criticism published has been of such solid worth and so much to the point that I fancy very few towns could furnish the *AMZ* with correspondents of equal quality.

The question remains, however, whether such criticism is prompted by a desire to further the cause of music or by private interest – the former, possibly, only in so far as it does not conflict with the latter! Still, in all fairness, what skill and what ingenuity are displayed – with a single exception. One may say that truth is never directly flouted; but it may on occasion be conveniently forgotten. Alternatively what does not suit the writer's book may be alluded to in such a graciously condescending way that any uninformed reader cannot possibly attach any importance to the matter concerned.

Any article about Dresden will furnish an example of this sort of thing, and our local critics can hardly expect me to quote them chapter and verse and yet refuse this to interested members of the public. What I have said here will be clear enough to any Dresdener; and for foreigners it may provide a point of view from which they can judge such notices as seem in some strange way to change colour in proportion to the closeness or distance of the individual parties – as is particularly the case with the German Opera, which is unpopular with both the box-office and the critical bureau. *Habeat sibi*! each man to his own! Personally I can never be grateful enough to that bureau and its unfailingly flattering references to my activities. In this way it has given me a wonderful freedom of action without the smallest hint of personal offence; and the immediate cause of my finally breaking my silence is to be found in the notices of the operas *Joconde* and *Die Zauberflöte* in No. xlvii of the universally respected *AMZ*.

To say the very least, it was somewhat thoughtless to write of my 'achieving such a performance with the means at the disposal of the German Opera'. I will not fall into the same trap as the critic and draw upon the considerable material available for making comparisons – how, for example, *Die Zauberflöte* could have been better cast here, whether perhaps other artists are 'in a position to transcend their natural gifts' – nor will I seek to praise one set of individuals by crying down another. No, I have too much respect for art, for my colleagues of whatever nationality, and before all else, for the gracious protection under which our artistic institutions thrive.

The foundation of a German Opera is an accomplished fact, and with powerful support and encouragement from above the structure itself will be built. If at the present moment the work is not as far advanced as its builders could wish, the reason lies in circumstances that do not at present permit of any improvement. Singers such as *Mme Grünbaum, Gerstäcker, *Weixelbaum etc., who had already half consented to join the company, have withdrawn, not through any failure to recognize their merits or over any dispute about their salaries, but for other reasons of which I must not breathe even a whisper here. It may be said in passing that our resources compare very favourably with those of other theatres, including many that have a great reputation. With the approval of the court and the warm support of a large section of the public, there will be a discreet and unpretentious improvement in these resources and, in conjunction with help from other quarters, they will enable a temple to be built that is not unworthy of the art.

What an encouragement it would be to all those concerned in the enterprise – performers and public alike – if a body of men as richly gifted as the Dresden critics would tread the straight and narrow path of untainted truth! Let them consider how any other action on their part can only lead to bitterness and to the revelation of the misdirected praise for which they have been responsible. If they continue in the same way, their praise and their blame will be equally disregarded, and in fact they will fail in their chief object, should all that they have taken such pains to commend come hopelessly to grief as soon as it faces competition elsewhere.

Editorial Note

We are accepting the above communication from Kapellmeister von Weber in the same unprejudiced and uncommitted spirit as that in which we have accepted the notices of our Dresden correspondent. In fact we have not even shown this letter to our correspondent, as is normally the practice in such journals as ours. We hope to be justified in acting thus, in the eyes of both readers and participants, by the fact that Herr von Weber allows our correspondent 'great powers, significant technical knowledge, a moderation that inspires confidence and trust and also a number of firmly based and relevant judgements'. It must also be manifest to everyone that, since we are not on the spot and do not know local and personal conditions that may play a part in the matter, we are incapable of fully understanding (not to speak of rejecting), altering or suppressing anything. As far as Herr von Weber's observations are concerned, his name is universally respected and he has pledged himself to provide the necessary evidence to whomever may request it.

Reply to Weber's observations from the Dresden correspondent under attack.[1]

Dresden. Having read Kapellmeister Carl Maria von Weber's observations on our critical judgements of both the German and Italian companies, which were made with the strictest regard for truth and absolute lack of prejudice, we should like to reply in a few words. We are grateful to him for the respect which he shows for our knowledge and penetration in matters concerning both music and the theatre, and for our part we have always acknowledged the same faculties in him.

The chief point at issue is that those who are not Dresdeners are being placed in the position of judges as to whether our notices are conceived with the interests of the art in view or whether they are inspired by private interest. We can in fact assure both the Kapellmeister and our readers that our criticisms have no other inspiration but love of truth and the desire to employ our powers of reason and discernment for the benefit of art and artists. The 'critical bureau', as he likes to call it, can only reply that it has always been most indulgent in its criticisms, despite the fact that it would have had plenty of opportunity to expose to readers outside Dresden facts easy to ascertain – and in fact ascertained – by every artist and connoisseur in Dresden.

[1]   *AMZ* xxi (1819), 90–1.

Is there in fact anything that is not honest and yet moderate in tone in the notices of *Joconde* and *Die Zauberflöte?* Herr von Weber is only too aware of the answer, for so much could have been said that was not. And it may be said in passing that, with the deepest respect to him and his office, we shall not allow ourselves to be dictated to in writing our notices, and hope indeed that we shall not take to quarrelling among ourselves. This could be of no interest to our readers and would constitute an exhibition concerning individuals only and merely providing outsiders with amusement.

We respect the building that has been begun, and shall respect it more when it has achieved some degree of accomplishment, for which at present sound materials are lacking. Apollo and Thalia can allow no place of honour on Parnassus to those among whom dedication to art is lacking.

Your correspondent,

A.C.H.

Weber replied with a letter (17 February 1819) that was published in the *AMZ*, Intelligenz-Blatt ii (March), as follows:

Two contradictory contributions have been presented to the judgement of the public (see 1818, No. LI, col. 877 and 1819, No. VI, col. 90). In which contributor will you, my art-loving readers, repose greater trust and confidence? I believe it will be the one who openly and unveiledly summons his opponent before your seat of judgement without fear of a false verdict. In this connexion I should like to express my thanks to Herr A.C.H. for not requiring me to produce evidence of his prejudice, as this could have an adverse influence on the future artistic career of several people; and it will certainly be a great pleasure not to be forced into such an action. I certainly have no intention of dictating to the gentleman – truth will see to that – but I shall most certainly answer him if ever it seems necessary. However, I too hope that we shall have no quarrelling among ourselves, and with that I declare the matter closed.

113. Meyerbeer, *Emma di Resburgo* and *Alimelek*

Written: Dresden, 18 January 1820.
Published: DAZ, Nos. 17 and 18, 21 and 22 January 1820.
                                                    Signed: Carl Maria von Weber.
Reprinted: HHS; MMW (misdated); KSS; LKA.

Alimelek was the title under which *Wirth und Gast* was often performed (see above, Nos. 50 and 51). *Emma di Resburgo*, to a text by Gaetano Rossi, was first produced at the Teatro San Benedetto, Venice, on 26 June 1819; its first performance in Germany was in Dresden on 29 January 1820, by the Italian company under Weber's direction. Camille Mieksch sang Edmund; in the title role was Friederike Funk, who had been engaged in 1816 but sent at Royal expense for further training to Italy. Her voice and manner were found 'highly appropriate', and the orchestra 'excellent and flawless' (*DAZ*, No. 39, 17 February 1820): the journal agreed with Weber that the work was too Italianate. 'It was a great success. Almost every number was applauded. This is very rare with our generally very frosty public; but it's caught Rossini fever, and *Meyerbeer has paid homage to this fashionable nonsense almost to excess. I've said a few words on the subject in the *Abend-Zeitung*' (letter to *G. F. Treitschke, 29 January 1820). 'My heart bleeds to see how a German artist, gifted with his own powers of creation, turns into an imitator because of the wretched applause of the masses. Is instant applause really so hard – I won't say to despise, but at least not to regard as all-important? Do read my article in the *Abend-Zeitung* if you get the chance. But I particularly ask you that all this should be for your ears alone, for the sake of his good parents and in the hope that Meyerbeer will return from this aberration' (letter to Hinrich Lichtenstein, 27 January 1820).

Anyone who follows events in the world of the arts, and the failures and successes of works in the theatres of Germany, will be forced to the gloomy conclusion that such things depend for the most part entirely on chance. Performance itself often depends on a reputation which has been won fortuitously, or on whether a particular theatre happens at that moment to possess exactly the forces needed in order to give every element of the work in question its due importance.

Where in any case will you find a theatrical management which is free to make its plans entirely according to aesthetic principles, and with no influence from above or below, from within the theatre or without? Here it is, perhaps, that we should seek the solution of the apparent puzzle in one and the same work meeting such totally different receptions, enthusiastic applause in one place and absolute failure in another. How fortunate, on the other hand, is the composer in France or Italy who is alone responsible for the success of his works – provided that popular success is his main object – since he has only to play his cards cleverly and employ all the forces at his disposal. Supposing, though, that he has won his laurels in one country and now wishes to earn an international reputation by having his works performed abroad, who will guarantee that it will be his best works that are chosen for performance, those that are most characteristic of him and belong to his best period? The answer once again is – chance, good luck. And the composer Meyerbeer should be grateful to both for the coinciding of a number of factors which have between them brought about the almost simultaneous performances of two of his operas.

Next week we shall be hearing the following works of his: *Emma di Resburgo*, *opera seria* (in Italian) and *Alimelek*, comic opera (in German). These are two totally dissimilar gems from his richly varied treasury, and it is to be hoped that they will earn him the applause of the lovers of Italian and German opera and also that of the real connoisseur, who occupies a position between the two parties and honours true merit wherever he finds it, guided only by the composer's own principles.

Herr Meyerbeer, who comes from Berlin, was a child prodigy as a pianist, and further study has brought him so far in this field that he may be considered one of the leading pianists, if not the leading pianist, of the day. He has not been obliged to earn his own living and has devoted himself entirely to music, of which he has made a profound study. Apart from his own researches he is chiefly indebted for his musical education to his two years' study with the late *Abbé Vogler. These two years provided him with a grounding in literature and foreign languages such as all artists should be given whose intentions are serious. During this period of his life he wrote an oratorio entitled *Gott und die Natur* (written in Darmstadt and performed in Berlin in May 1811).[1] This is an excellent work, passionately felt and full of profound harmonic beauties and contrapuntal ingenuity, by no means lacking melodic charm, though chiefly marked by characteristics acquired in his studies. In rather the same vein he wrote a grand serious opera – *Jephta*, with libretto also by *Schreiber – for Munich.[2] If some connoisseurs complained that this suffered from a certain heterogeneousness of style, the explanation lay in the composer's

---

[1]   See above, No. 19.
[2]   Meyerbeer's first opera, *Jephthas Gelübde*, was first performed in Munich in 1812.

anxiety to give his singers full satisfaction. In conjunction with the extraordinary wealth of harmonic invention, particularly in the choruses, this suggested a kind of split personality in which inner conviction was at odds with the desire to please.

As early as 1813 His Royal Highness the Grand Duke of Darmstadt, on his own initiative, appointed Meyerbeer to a post as chamber composer to the court, in recognition of his gifts. His next work was an opera written for Stuttgart, *Alimelek*, later rewritten for Vienna and particularly successful in Prague; and having travelled all over Germany, the young composer went to complete his educational experience first to France and thence to Italy. There his *Romilda e Costanza* was given successfully in Padua, and more recently Venice welcomed his *Emma di Resburgo* with an enthusiasm to which the public prints bear witness. In accordance with the composer's own wish this will be the first opera in the series here. But I should like first to say something about the earlier of his operas, *Alimelek*.

The story of the awakened sleeper, from the *Thousand and One Nights*, is an attractive one, amusing and racy; and *Herr Wohlbrück (at that time in Leipzig) brought to the libretto an excellent knowledge of the theatre, a lively temperament and a good sense of what a composer needs. Meyerbeer's unity of design and delineation of character are masterly, and there are clear evidences of his profound study of music and drama in the skill with which he combines independent melodic forms. The whole score shows an active and lively imagination, the action always moves swiftly and without digressions, and only those points are emphasized which are best suited to dramatic representation. The prosody is excellent, the melodies attractive and often luxuriant, and there are many rich and novel harmonic ideas. There are also a number of surprising instrumental combinations, so delicately organized that they demand almost as much skill in performance as a string quartet. This may well be the most characteristic feature of all, and it stamps the work as unmistakably German.

On the other hand *Emma di Resburgo* bears all the marks of its country of origin and of those predominating tastes. I think that the composer's chief aim in this work was to please and to show that he could handle any form he chose with complete ease and mastery. There must be something very seriously wrong with the artistic digestion of the Italian public if a genius so potentially self-sufficient and independent as Meyerbeer has recognized the necessity not only of serving them with the ripest and most luscious fruit, but of sugaring it with all the modish devices. It goes without saying that *Emma di Resburgo* shows all the qualities of Meyerbeer's genius described above – in so far as there is a place for them – and that the observer will be amazed to find such totally different ideals in two works by the same composer. Personally I can think of no case that is comparable. Herr Meyerbeer, therefore, has shown us his versatility as well as his potential originality, and left us in no doubt of the fact that he is capable of doing whatever he pleases. If the present writer may be allowed to express a wish, it is this – that having studied the various branches of music and the emotional character of the various nations among which music flourishes, and having tested his strength as well as the flexibility of his gifts, he will now return to his German homeland and join that small band of true art-lovers who are working to create a German national opera. We are more than willing to learn from foreigners; but what we learn we wish to hand on with the stamp of our own vision of truth and our own personality, It is thus that we can hope eventually to assert our true place among the art-producing countries of Europe and build a truly German opera on the unshakable foundations laid by Mozart.

The publication of this article once more brought to the boil the simmering rivalry between the Italian and German parties, and led to a vigorous press controversy. The rival Dresden *Literarischer Merkur* published the following rejoinder (which Kaiser, in KSS, attributes to Therese aus dem Winkel).

Remarks on the article by Herr Carl Maria von Weber, Kapellmeister to the Saxon Court and director of the German Opera, in Nos. 17 and 18 of the Abend-Zeitung.

As soon as Herr Kapellmeister C. M. v. Weber came to Dresden, he showed his dissatisfaction with the musical taste of the Dresden public (although Dresden has for many years been the home of true connoisseurs and outstanding composers and performers) by attempting, as he had done earlier in Prague, to guide the judgement of audiences and to persuade them in advance that the only works that merited praise and admiration were those which enjoyed his approval and protection. Only his favourites were to be honoured. For this reason he has not hesitated now, when *Emma di Resburgo* was to be the first of Meyerbeer's operas to be given here, to try to prejudice the public in favour of this composer. On this occasion his embarrassment was obvious. For it appeared all the more difficult to exalt his friend Herr M.'s German genius, as Herr C. M. von Weber wished to do, owing to the impossibility of obtaining such an absolute ascendancy over his listeners' ears and intelligences that they were unable to distinguish the composer's genuine property from the borrowed jewellery with which it was adorned. Let us see how Herr C.M.v.W set to work. *Emma*, he must have said to himself, was written in Italy and it is therefore easy to persuade the Dresden public that Meyerbeer was seeking to please only the Italian public and that he was prepared to accommodate his noble genius to their depraved taste, in order to demonstrate that he could excel in every form of music. The only difficulty lies in the fact that there are a number of answers to this charge. In the first place this so-called depraved taste can hardly be quite as bad as Herr C.M.v.W. makes out, since the German stomach suffers from the same derangement, the most general applause greeting similar forms, as the Dresden reception of *Emma* made abundantly clear. On the other hand, if Meyerbeer shared Herr C. M. von Weber's views and was prompted by ambition, he should not have shown such absolute indifference in dyeing his pure pearls to match their surroundings like any chameleon. If a creative genius lowered himself to cater for Italian taste, which prefers the select herbs and spices of a heavy diet, he could at least serve up fresh ones in original combinations, even though the dishes might be insubstantial.

But this is not at all what Meyerbeer has done, for all his vaunted genius. He has stolen Rossini's happiest ideas, which are sure to please everywhere, combined them with delightful and glittering ideas taken from other masters new and old, and given what is undoubtedly a very ingenious patchwork the name of original invention. *Emma* had a most enthusiastic reception in Venice, partly thanks to the Italian's characteristic desire to be fair and amicable towards foreigners, and partly thanks to the local principle of giving kindly encouragement to all youthful talent and warm acknowledgement to foreign artists ambitious to learn and to excel. But if Herr C.M.v.W. had not invented such an ingenious excuse – insisting that it was a mark of unusual genius in Meyerbeer to be able, if he wished, to follow the present Italian fashion for saccharine sweetness – it would certainly have been difficult for him to excuse the composer's use of many familiar musical phrases that are so faithfully and cleverly copied that they could easily be mistaken for the originals.

It is lucky for us that Haydn, Mozart, Gluck, Piccinni, Cimarosa, Paisiello, Naumann, Schuster etc. did not possess this same versatility but each was great and original in his own style; their works have been acknowledged in every country as classics and will always remain so. Had these great lights of artistic genius imitated each other, we should now have only one kind of music and its originator would be still disputed. The true genius is not afflicted by a passion for popularity; he neither over-refines not imitates, but is a man of feeling who is a creator and well disposed towards his colleagues in every branch of the arts. In *Emma* the only musical originality is to be found in the pretensions by which the composer thinks that he can deceive the public. The frequent modulations would be effective were Meyerbeer the first to use them. The too frequent pauses and almost uninterrupted use of pizzicato (which deforms the string's natural tone) are reprehensible means of seeking favour with the public and cannot be called either novel or beautiful.

But it was by no means Herr C.M.v.W's intention simply to praise the music of this opera, and he was really concerned to draw attention to Meyerbeer's mistake in deliberately condescending from the heights of his genius. What in fact lay much closer to the writer's heart was to praise Meyerbeer's German opera *Alimelek* as a masterpiece of the first water. We are only acquainted with the music of this opera through a similar essay inserted by Herr C.M.v.W. in the *Prager Zeitung*;[3] and we therefore refrain from any judgement for the present. Meanwhile we recall having read in the Leipzig *Musikalische Zeitung* of 1814 about a Viennese performance of Meyerbeer's *Die zwei Califen*, which was also based on the *Thousand and One Nights* and had a libretto by Herr Wohlbrück. This opera, as can be seen from the article which followed, met the same fate as it had shortly before had in Stuttgart, where it was given under another title. Herr C.M.v.W's hints suggest that *Alimelek* is probably the same work under still another title:[4] However that may be, we should like to express the wish that Herr C.M.v.W will after all model himself on such great men as Haydn, Mozart, Cimarosa, Paisiello etc., who were recognized and honoured all over Europe and at the same time lived in perfect harmony with each other, respecting and acknowledging each other's merits. It is to be hoped that he will imitate their great qualities and their selfless, disinterested enthusiasm for music, and not permit himself bitter outbursts against other nations or arrogate to himself the right to try to correct and guide the judgement of a public whose taste has been formed by music of the highest standards in every field. He is doing his friend a real disservice with the connoisseurs, for excessive praise in one quarter and malicious irony employed against others demand that critical standards be raised. Anyone who maintains that Italy today has only one Rossini must at least confess that Mozart has found no successor in Germany! The classical composers of the past formed their audiences' tastes by their works, not their words. Let Herr C.M.v.W. do likewise. Let him endear himself as an opera composer in his own country and abroad, make himself master of the public's ears and heart and guide their sense of appreciation by his works, and then we will acknowledge him willingly as an Aristarchus.[5]

Since this letter is no more than an open expression of views held by many others beside ourselves and is not in any way prompted by personal hostility to a man whose personality and gifts we value, there is no necessity to give our names. Should Herr C.M.v.W. wish to make our closer acquaintance, on the other hand, we are always ready to discuss with him personally every point made in this letter.

Weber returned this salvo with a broadside. The following article was written on 15 February 1820 and published in the *Literarischer Merkur*, No. 14, 17 February 1820.

Personal attacks of any kind, even when more bitterly contrived and more amusingly expressed than those of the author of these remarks,

---

[3]   See above, No. 50.
[4]   *Wirth und Gast* was given, in revised form as *Die beiden Kalifen*, in Vienna on 20 October 1814.
[5]   Aristarchus of Samothrace, the proverbially severe critic and grammarian of the second century BC.

would not impel me to take up my pen in self-defence, had it not been for the astonishing audacity with which he has set down a number of gross falsehoods, and with a confidence of tone that reveals only too clearly his desire to win over public opinion by this show of force. Such a farrago of truth and falsehood as this, based on partial statements and total concealments, demands a thorough sifting before the highest court recognized by the artist, that of the public sitting in judgement.

First comes the following gross untruth or deliberate misrepresentation of my good intentions: 'As soon as Herr v. W. came to Dresden, he showed his dissatisfaction with the musical taste of the Dresden public by attempting, as he had done earlier in Prague, to guide the judgement of audiences and to persuade them in advance that the only works that merited praise and admiration were those which enjoyed his approval and protection.' Is that really what I did? If so, I must have exercised a truly supernatural power over people's minds. But I think that what the author must have been meaning was that this was my *intention* – for had I in fact succeeded, the author too would have been convinced and would never have made his remarks, thereby sparing me the trouble of replying.

What a gross twisting, or simply forgetting, of what I wrote a fortnight after my arrival in Dresden – a space of time in which nobody could learn to judge the taste of any public or be content or discontent with it (see *Abend-Zeitung*, No. 25, 1817).[6] How is it possible to find evidence for such presumption in the aforementioned article? I should like to repeat here the gist of what I then wrote, and let the unprejudiced reader judge. This is how I began.

To the art-loving citizens of Dresden

The amiable foresight and proven love of the arts of their gracious monarch have provided the inhabitants of Dresden with a handsome enrichment of their lives in the form of a new German Opera now being founded; and it seems as though a valuable and perhaps necessary contribution to the success of this undertaking might be made by the individual in charge of the institution, if he were to try to explain the nature, method and circumstances of the whole operation. [...][7] Those entrusted with the management and organization of this public treasure-house have therefore a duty to tell the public what it can expect and hope for, and to what extent the success of such

---

[6]   See above, No. 88.
[7]   The square brackets indicate passages of Weber's original text (see above, No. 88) that he omits here.

an undertaking depends on their benevolent reception and indulgence.[...]
No people has been so slow and so uncertain as the German in determining
its own specific art forms. Both the Italians and the French have evolved a
form of opera in which they move freely and naturally. This is not true of
the Germans, whose peculiarity it has been to adopt what seems best in other
schools, after much study and steady development; but the matter goes deeper
with them. Whereas other nations concern themselves chiefly with the
sensuous satisfaction of isolated moments, the German demands a self-
sufficient work of art, in which all the parts make up a beautiful and unified
whole. [...] What we can achieve with our present forces I can only commend
to the indulgence and benevolence of the critical public. Later, when the
company is stronger, we shall be able to make more effective use of the talent
we already possess and place it in the most advantageous light; and not until
then shall we be able to initiate a planned policy in the choice of operas to
be performed, varying them according to their musical and dramatic character
and thus giving the public the best of every period and country with the same
eye to quality of performance in every case. In order to demonstrate this wish
to music-lovers, the first performance of any new work will be preceded by
notes such as the following. Thereby I shall at least demonstrate my desire
to further the good cause so far as in me lies; and I hope that I may express
the hope that the public will understand this.

After that followed the Musico-Dramatic Articles, which represented
an attempt to assist music-lovers in their appreciation of operas new
to the Dresden Königliches Theater, by means of historical notes and
suggestions. I wrote:[8]

Of course a really good work eventually establishes itself and becomes
popular by its repeated appeals to human feeling. The effect, however, is quite
different if such feeling is, as it were, prepared for the enjoyment to come.

It is the same in all departments of life. Does not everyone seek to be
introduced into a social circle by someone who is already a member of it, and
does not the introducer seek in a few words to communicate to that circle
his friend's nature? From the cradle to the grave we rely on friends who take
on themselves the duties of godparents. May I, then, also be allowed to
recommend the works committed to my care, as they appear, to those whose
service, entertainment and improvement these works are dedicated?

Of course, there is one danger against which I must be especially on my
guard. I mean that in informing the public of the chief characteristics of my
protégé, his artistic career and that of his creator, I must not present what
is only a point of view – one meant to facilitate the proper evaluation of a
work – as though it were anticipating a judgement. That would be to affront
the most precious right of public opinion. To have recognized this danger is
already half-way towards avoiding it, as my efforts will show. Nevertheless,
I feel that here too I must count on your indulgence towards what may well
amount to excessive zeal in the good cause. The artist's enthusiasm, which

[8]   See above, No. 49.

one is so anxious to share with the rest of the world, may indeed on occasion lead me to overstep the bounds of plain reporting. [...]

Not every plant flourishes in every situation: what will blossom in one climate may wither in another. Careful tending will at least prevent malformation, and in my efforts to cultivate what is good I shall not be led astray by the opinions of partisans who have no individual opinions and are only comparatively well qualified to judge. Experience teaches us that public opinion, taken in the round, is almost always right.

The next charge preferred against me by the author of these remarks runs thus: 'Only his favourites (those of Herr C. M. v. Weber) are to be honoured.' Where have I said that? or implied it? Could it be gathered from the works that I have so far had the means and the opportunity to produce? Then let us just cast our eyes over the list, in order to acquaint ourselves with my partisanship and my foibles. Méhul, Fischer, Grétry, *Weigl, *Cherubini, Catel, Boieldieu, Isouard, Mozart, Dittersdorf, Schmidt, Dalayrac, Spontini, Himmel, Solié, *Fränzl etc. Well, that is not a bad list and I should have no reason to be ashamed of my favourites, who belong to a number of sufficiently different categories. Or did I perhaps not expend the same amount of time and trouble on the production of Rossini's *Elisabetta* and *L'Italiana in Algeri* as on other operas? No, I certainly respect all good work whatever its national source. In fact I always try, when judging any opera, to put myself in the position of the composer, and so to do him justice. But no artist must be supposed to have a blind adoration for any one *genre*, and still less to go back on his own views and his belief in what he is convinced is nearest the truth or has in fact achieved it. And there is only one truth.

What the author of the remarks says about Haydn, Mozart etc. is after my own heart and I most willingly subscribe to it. But he totally misunderstands me (it seems to be one of his hobbies) if he believes that I rate Herr Meyerbeer so highly because he can write as he does. No, I must say quite frankly that I have been deeply disappointed that he should *wish* to write as he does, nor do I think that this is the only way to win popularity in Italy. For who will be foolish enough to maintain that in the very cradle of true singing and ardent feeling there are not men of real taste among the better and more educated sort, just as there are in Vienna, Dresden, Munich, Berlin and so on? This is not to deny that the majority in Italy, as in the towns mentioned above, always prefer a fireworks display to a picture by Raphael. Who fails to enjoy the lively play of ideas and the piquant melodies in Rossini? But who can be so dazzled by these that he is ready to grant

Rossini's works dramatic truth? or does the author of the remarks consider that this need not concern a dramatic composer? If so, he is paying a very back-handed compliment to the Italian masters of an older generation, such as Paisiello, Cimarosa etc.

But where am I getting to? The author of these remarks has no desire to exchange opinions and to talk for art's sake: I am simply not to talk about such things. Indeed, may it be that one should no longer dare even to hint that present-day Italian taste is degenerate? Yet that was all that I did, and the author of the remarks has only to read the Italian papers themselves and other German journals. But I think that I shall not so easily be silenced in this way.

If his essay can be said to contain a main idea, it is simply to form among the public a party hostile to my views; and then of course woe to you, poor *Alimelek*, of whom our author has so much to say – and not to say! He can hardly have read my article in the *Prager Zeitung*; or if he read it, he is very wrong to reveal what I wrote there. Since, however, he is so pat with his quotations from the Leipzig *Musikalische Zeitung* and seems to know it so well, why I wonder does he not quote the essay that I wrote in that very paper on *Alimelek* (it appeared after the first three performances of that opera in Prague, and these took place on 22, 24 and 30 October in the year 1815)? Probably because what I wrote on that occasion gave no grounds for remarks that now serve his purpose. I shall therefore have to go so far as to help him with his quotations; and I can only hope that he will kindly accept my offer, as he is not likely to find me coming to his assistance again.

It (the opera *Alimelek*) was given at the Theater an der Wien,[9] where it was a failure – or rather, a number of unfortunate circumstances limited the performances to a single one, so that the public had no opportunity to acquaint themselves with it. Without saying too much about that particular performance of a difficult work, which is full of the finest and most varied nuances and demands little less than the ensemble expected of a quartet, I should like to make a few general remarks. The part of Alimelek was written for the singer *Herr Ehlers, who was however prevented from appearing by unavoidable circumstances and replaced by *Herr Forti. The melodic lines were altered, and thereby deprived of their original charm; whole numbers were transposed; and – without any reflection on Herr Forti's artistry – the whole conception of the title role, carefully tailored to fit Herr Ehlers's personality (so popular with the Viennese public), was very largely lost. *Mlle Buchwieser was not well that evening and proved unable to perform her role

---

9   Actually the Kärntnerthortheater, as Weber correctly gave in his original
     article (above, No. 50).

with the power which has made her such a favourite with the public, who even went so far as to give audible expression to their disappointment.

Accidents of this kind are quite enough to cause the temporary failure of a work of art, whose life and success hangs on such fragile threads, leaving aside a host of other minor circumstances which may prove unfavourable.

Of course the opera *Alimelek* is identical with *Die zwei Kalifen*, given in Vienna, and *Wirt und Gast*, given in Stuttgart. For the latter performance Meyerbeer delivered the music piecemeal and the production was prepared in a few days. Things did not go as they should and the opera was not a success, though it cannot be called a failure either. But what do such verdicts really mean, either for or against a work? *Tancredi*, for instance, which the Viennese found fascinating, left Dresden and Berlin absolutely cold. How *Alimelek* will fare here nobody can tell. There are plainly attempts to prejudice the public against it. Perhaps the author of the remarks will grant, though, that it needs considerable conviction to give an opera that has failed in Vienna in the sister-town of Prague, immediately afterwards? That it was successful proves that I was not wrong in trusting to the just sentiments of the Prague public, who were not to be hurried into making up their minds. In any case I am very far from considering *Alimelek* a perfect work (how many such works are there?), but it certainly provides evidence of the composer's individuality and inventiveness.

But what is the author of the remarks really after? Praising the virtues of Italian music at the expense of his own countrymen's? For he appears, in spite of some passages in his writing, to be in fact a German. The Italians as a nation are just as worthy of respect as any other, but 'in spite of their desire to be fair and amicable towards foreigners' they have hissed a good number of them – Himmel, for instance – yet extended their indulgence towards Meyerbeer to giving *Emma* more than seventy performances (according to the *Wiener Theaterzeitung*). How are we to explain that, since according to our author *Emma* is a botched-together piece of patchwork?

But now enough has been said to express my deep respect for all that concerns publicity and, from first to last, too much if only the author of the remarks and myself were concerned. I must therefore ask him to be so good as to forgive me if I feel absolutely no call to discuss each of his points with him by word of mouth. Knowing his *views* as I do, I have absolutely no desire to know his *appearance*.

I only feel obliged to add the sad observation that it must be painful indeed for a German artist to see how grossly misunderstood and misrepresented (even to the point of personal lampooning) are all his efforts, undertaken from the purest motives, in aid of the good cause. For me to attempt to estimate the talents that God may have given me would be an outrage against the bestowal of gifts by the giver of all good things. The world will allot them their proper place. My duty has been simply to employ all my industry, study and tireless efforts to develop as far as possible what has been entrusted to my charge. I console myself with the thought that I have indeed done this to the best of my powers, persevering and sparing no effort, and shall continue to do so with full conviction, paying respectful attention to every genuine censure and treating all merely captious criticism with the contempt that it deserves.

Postscript

The foregoing document had already been sent to the press when I found in the latest issue of the *Allgemeine musikalische Zeitung* an ally as welcome as he is unexpected, and one whose competence our author would certainly be most unlikely to dispute. This is no less a person than Rossini himself. While he was in Milan, a local critic complained that 'Italian operatic music today is totally destitute of vigour, seeking only to flatter the ear and attempting to dispel the resulting apathy of the listener by the mechanical noise of the orchestra.' Rossini's reply to this was simplicity itself. 'Believe me,' he said, 'it is a waste of time writing music of any higher quality for Italian audiences: they simply go to sleep.'[10]

C. M. v. Weber

Editorial postscript

Our readers are now in possession of enough material to clarify their own views on the fundamental subject under discussion, which is one that can leave no music-lover cold. And since nothing could be further from our wishes than to allow our pages to be used for purely polemical purposes, without any foreseeable profit to either art or knowledge, we must now consider this discussion closed as far as we are concerned.

It was, however, too much to hope that other journals would ignore such a controversy. The Berlin *Freimüthiger*, No. 39, 24 February 1820, published excerpts, prefacing them with a comment by the editor, Dr August Kuhn.

[10]   *AMZ*, XXII (1820), 78.

A very interesting argument about the development of German opera and whether it should be purely national has broken out in Dresden, hitherto the home of exclusively Italian opera. The admirable C. Maria von Weber is the leader of those who want German nationality, that is to say, German thoroughness; we see ranged against him the Italians, who prefer tinkling as the material for thoughtful music.

Alarmed by this extension of the controversy, which he now wanted to see closed, Weber caused the *DAZ* to publish a disclaimer to the effect that while permission had been given for excerpts to be republished (in the event, without acknowledgement to the *DAZ*), neither he nor the editor had the slightest foreknowledge of Kuhn's introductory remarks. It seems to have had the effect of quietening down the controversy, at any rate publicly; though there is perhaps an echo in the report of a performance of *Emma di Resburgo* in Frankfurt, in which the correspondent deplores the departure of *Spohr and observes that Meyerbeer's native German talent has been lost 'in the marshes of *Rossinismus*' (*AMZ* xxii (1820), 857), contradicting another *AMZ* report insisting that the accusations of Rossini-ism in *Emma* were groundless (*AMZ* xxii (1820), 442–3).

114. Introduction to Poissl's *Der Wettkampf zu Olympia*

Written: Dresden, 13 March 1820.
Published: DAZ, No. 64, 16 March 1820.   *Signed:* Carl Maria von Weber.
Reprinted: HHS; MMW; KSS.

*Poissl's *Der Wettkampf zu Olympia*, to a text by the composer after Metastasio's *L'Olimpiade*, was a grand opera, usually in three acts, first produced in Munich on 21 April 1815. It was also given in Stuttgart (1815), Darmstadt (1816) and Weimar (1819), where Poissl was favourably compared to Rossini (*AMZ* xxi (1819), 655–7). The Dresden performance was not reviewed in the *DAZ*. The dates of the other operas by Poissl mentioned by Weber are *Ottaviano in Sicilia* (1812), *Aucassin und Nicolette* (1813), *Athalia* (1814), *Dir wie mir* (1816), *Nittetis* (1817) and *Issipile* (1818); Poissl also wrote an overture and nine numbers for Nasolini's *Merope* (1812). In writing this introduction, Weber made use of some phrases from his introduction to *Athalia* (above, No. 76).

On Thursday 16 March 1820 will be given the first performance in the Königliches Theater of *Der Wettkampf zu Olympia*, a grand opera in two acts, freely adapted in verse from Metastasio and set to music by Baron von Poissl, Royal Bavarian Chamberlain, Knight Commander of the Grand Ducal Order of Merit of Hesse, Knight of the Order of St George.

The exact nature of so-called 'grand' opera has been much discussed, and hitherto no firm conclusion has been reached on the basic principles which determine the matter. I will content myself therefore with the present generally accepted meaning of the adjective 'grand', namely an opera in which the musical numbers are connected by a continuous *recitativo accompagnato*, fully orchestrated – in fact a scene where music holds court, surrounded by her courtiers who are in perpetual activity. Associated with this idea is the subject matter of such a work, which must also have something grandiose about it. Generally grandeur of this kind is understood to mean a subject borrowed from classical antiquity, either Greek or Roman. These ideas are not only connected with the basic principles of French classical tragedy but are derived directly from those principles since, to the best of my knowledge, it is the French who are responsible for this 'grand' opera, in which Gluck has excelled all other masters up to the present time.

We in Germany do not possess many original examples of this kind, and at the present time the fashion for the Romantic makes further compositions of this sort improbable. Apart from Herr von Mosel's admirably conceived operas *Salem* and *Cyrus*,[1] given in Vienna, and some other essays of the same kind, Herr von Poissl has particularly favoured the genre and won recognition and applause with a number of successful works.

He has devoted both his time and his energies to the art. Private study and the friendly advice of the excellent *Kapellmeister Danzi have assisted him in his development. A scholarly approach and a gift for poetry gave him a notable advantage in his search for artistic excellence. He had already written several works for the stage and for small instrumental combinations when he was fired to devote himself entirely to dramatic music by the unique reception accorded in Munich to his opera *Ottaviano in Sicilia*. There followed in quick succession, thus revealing his uninterrupted industry, after *Ottaviano*, *Der Wettkampf zu Olympia*, *Athalia*, *Aucassin und Nicolette*, more than half of the opera *Merope*, *Nittetis*, a comic opera *Dir wie mir*, *Issipile* etc. In addition to a scrupulous attention to prosody, a rich harmonic palette and apt and varied instrumentation, Baron Poissl's music is remarkable for its fluent and clearly defined melodies, which have the virtue of being extremely singable as well as tender in character. The absence of this cantabile quality is something often held against German composers,

---

[1]   Ignaz von Mosel (1772–1844) was the author of three operas for Vienna: *Die Feuerprobe* (1811), *Salem* (1813) and *Cyrus und Astyages* (1818). He was a vigorous opponent of the Viennese fashion for Rossini. One report found *Salem* eclectic but effective, and influenced by Gluck (*AMZ* xv (1813), 367).

not without good reason. He is said to be engaged at present on a grand Italian opera.[2]

> [2] Poissl's *La rappresaglia*, an *opera seria* in two acts to a text by Romani, was produced in Munich on 7 April 1820.

115. Introduction to Carl Ludwig Hellwig's
Die Bergknappen

Written: Dresden, 21 April 1820.
Published: DAZ, No. 98, 25 April 1820.   *Signed:* Carl Maria von Weber.
Reprinted: HHS; MMW; KSS; LKA.

Die Bergknappen was the first of *Hellwig's two operas, a 'Romantic Opera' in two acts to a text by *Theodor Körner. This performance, in Dresden on 27 April 1820, was its first. His other opera, *Don Silvio di Rosalba*, was not produced (though some sources mention a Berlin production in 1825). A laconic review in the *DAZ* commented 'The text is successful in regard to diction, the music sensitive and judicious. The opera was received with enthusiasm' (No. 111, 10 May 1820).

Opera composers in Germany are given so little encouragement of any sort that it is something of a surprise to find any prepared to undertake a task that demands more time, effort and exhausting experience than any other branch of the art. Both the public and the directors of opera houses recognize this, and each lays the blame on the other. Perhaps both should take their respective shares?

In Italy a whole season (*stagione*) may be filled with repetitions of two or three operas, and so the management is delighted to concentrate all its powers and resources, with excellent results. In France the situation is slightly different, but the results of a successful work are equally influential and widely spread. In both countries, however – and this remains their great advantage – the appearance of a new opera is a national event. The excitement both before and after the performance raises the composer to a position in which he can appreciate the significance of his own effort and thus cannot feel anything but greatly encouraged or – should his work be a failure – deeply depressed. An enthusiastic reception, coupled with a due reward of honour, beckons him forward and ensures him a livelihood as a composer.

There is a demand for novelty in Germany! That is already a great thing. If a new work is good, so much the better; if it is bad, well, not every work can be good. Such coolness and moderation, whether it be in praise or in blame, does nothing to feed the fires of ambition in an artist; and the decline of public interest in subsequent repetitions of the work robs the management of the means – and indeed the desire – to encourage and reward the composer properly.

I must break off here, for this subject – the passion for novelty – would take me too far afield if I were to touch on even the most closely related theme, e.g. what all but impossible feats the public demands of German operatic singers, who have to alternate between Italian *bel canto*, the dramatic style of the lighter French opera and the emotional seriousness and correct style of singing demanded by German music. All these have to be combined in a single individual.

I am coming to the point of the foregoing effusion, and it is this – that the chief virtue of the German artist is his genuine enthusiasm for his art for its own sake. Of course he may have first to assure his own livelihood by some other gainful employment.[1] For even supposing he writes a successful work for the theatre, what can he expect in Germany? Some half-dozen theatres reward him with double the copying expenses, while the rest manage it still more cheaply; and he can achieve success of this sort only after his work has succeeded in some important theatre. Otherwise, no theatrical establishment will take the risk. The few exceptions to this rule hardly count. And so the poor composer who feels the impulse shuts himself into his garret, hoping for the best, and stakes his industry, his nights' sleep, his heart's blood and his most anxious and teasing hopes on...what? on seeing his hitherto well-earned musical reputation ruined, perhaps for years, by a performance which is subject to a host of accidental misfortunes. All the same he sets to work because he feels an inner compulsion, and leaves the rest to heaven.

The opera *Die Bergknappen* will have its first performance here in the Königliches Theater on 27 April 1820. The libretto is by Theodor Körner and the work is absolutely unpretentious and clearly a labour of love. Herr Ludwig Hellwig, who is the composer, is a brother of our excellent stage director. He was born in 1773 at Kunnersdorf bei Wriezen, on the Oder, and went at the age of thirteen to study music in Berlin. He studied harmony under the late *Gürrlich, and his entering the Singakademie in his twentieth year determined the actual direction of his musical activities, which is very clear in the present work, where the choruses and ensembles are particularly important. He himself is the first to acknowledge his great indebtedness to this great institute and its worthy director, Herr Zelter.[2]

---

[1] Hellwig was for some years obliged to earn his living in a dye-works.
[2] Carl Friedrich Zelter (1758–1832) was famous as the founder of the Berlin Singakademie.

Herr Hellwig is the possessor of a fine voice and has rightly achieved a respected position as a teacher of singing. A study of the works of the greatest masters, and later contrapuntal studies with Abraham Schneider,[3] have given him skill and clarity in part-writing and thematic development. His solo and polyphonic songs have won a sympathetic hearing and he has written a Requiem, a psalm-setting[4] and other works for the Singakademie, as well as an opera, *Don Silvio di Rosalba*, which he never wanted performed, and a number of independent arias with orchestral accompaniment etc. The confidence inspired by his learning and enthusiasm may be judged by the fact that the director of the Singakadamie generally leaves Herr Hellwig as his deputy in his absence; and recently public opinion has expressed itself in his favour by his appointment as director of music at Berlin Cathedral.

> [3]   George Abraham Schneider (1770–1839) was an oboist, conductor and composer who worked in Berlin.
> [4]   Hellwig's Requiem was his Op. 9 (1809); the psalm-setting to which Weber refers was probably that of Psalm 145 (1805) for the centenary of the consecration of the French church in Berlin.

116. Introduction to Marschner's *Heinrich IV und d'Aubigné*

Written: Dresden, 7 or 8 July 1820.
Published: DAZ, No. 164, 11 July 1820.   *Signed:* Carl Maria von Weber.
Reprinted: HHS; MMW; KSS; LKA.

Heinrich IV und d'Aubigné was the third of Marschner's operas. He had made some reputation with an earlier work in Pressburg, where a local doctor and artistic dilettante, August Hornbostel, provided him with librettos. These were published under Hornbostel's pen-name, Heinrich Alberti, which Weber attaches to the Kapellmeister of the joint theatres of Pressburg and Baden, August Eckschlager. Weber set his 'Maienblümchen' (J117) in 1811. Marschner was only twenty-three when he sent the score to Weber, who immediately accepted it. However, when a year had gone by without a production, Marschner travelled to Dresden to seek Weber out and press the cause of his opera. The performance was then scheduled for 12 July 1820, but was postponed by a week to 19 July. The *DAZ*, which did not review it, mentions a performance at the Linkesche Bad on 23 July.

His first appearance before the public is a unique and solemn occasion for any composer. How much depends upon it! and how easily failure can mislead him and damage his career! He may well be able to count on his hearers' indulgence as an innovator, but against this must be set the more damaging fact of the public's indifference towards an unknown name and their careless and superficial manner of judging a work. This is particularly true of any artist who feels urged to tread an individual path, on which he will inevitably at first find passages of rough going where he has not yet been able to order things to suit his purpose. The great advantage of a reputation already made lies in the confident expectation of something outstanding, something worthy to be compared with former achievements; and in the fact that the public is prepared to take the trouble to balance any unusual features against their existing favourable opinion, and to understand their object.

Not every composer earns the right to make his first bow to a Dresden audience. It is a genuinely national event that I have to announce. Heinrich Marschner, who was born at Zittau in 1794,[1] is the composer of the opera *Heinrich der Vierte und d'Aubigné*, which will have its first performance at the Königliches Theater on 12 July 1820. It will be a delight to observe our compatriot's lively and original invention, his fluent melodic gift and rich, studied style. I will even go so far as to prophesy that such a passionate concern with dramatic truth combined with such a profound emotional nature will produce a dramatic composer worthy of our highest respect.

Marschner entered the Zittau Gymnasium and Singchor at the age of eight.[2] He was soon giving concerts, and even at this tender age he was such an enthusiastic admirer of the great German masterpieces that he would often hurry home from the concert hall to try to write something similar himself – only unfortunately he did not have the chance to study elementary harmony. When Hering[3] went to Zittau, he gave the knowledge-starved boy some lessons, though not many, and it was on his own reading of books and scores that Marschner largely depended. In 1813 he visited Prague and Leipzig and he acknowledges the part played in his musical development by listening to performances of great works and to the kindness of our excellent *Schicht. His ideas became gradually more clearly defined, the shadowy images were transferred to the full light of consciousness. A number of sonatas, cantatas, songs etc., which he wrote here, appeared in the Leipzig music shops; but what attracted him most was opera, and particularly Mozart's genius. At the beginning of 1816 he went to

---

[1] Actually 1795.
[2] Actually nine, in 1804.
[3] Karl Gottlieb Hering (1766–1853) was a famous teacher and theorist.

Vienna, and a little later he was offered a post by Count Johann Zichy at Pressburg. This gave him the leisure needed for major compositions. Where was he to find a libretto? Desperately anxious to try his wings on a first flight, he made a version of *Titus* based on the German translation appended to the Leipzig edition, and naturally enough he has refused to show the result to anyone. In November 1816 he composed *Der Kyffhäuserberg* in one act, and finally in 1817 he was given the libretto of *Heinrich* by Heinrich Alberti (this, I fancy, was the pen-name of the poet Eckschlager, who made quite a name for himself, especially in Bavaria). In 1818 he wrote the serious opera *Saidar*, by the same poet, and this was received enthusiastically at Pressburg; and it is to be hoped that next winter the public will be given an opportunity to form an opinion of their fellow countryman's achievements in the very different fields of 'conversation' and serious opera.

117. Johann Gänsbacher

Written: Dresden, early March 1821.
Published: DAZ, No. 63, 14 March 1821.   *Unsigned.*
Reprinted: KSS.

This appreciation of *Gänsbacher appeared anonymously in the *DAZ* under the heading 'Reports from Correspondents', and dated Innsbruck, February 1821. It was first attributed to Weber by Kaiser, in KSS, on the evidence of a letter to Gänsbacher: 'Your letter of 22 February, which I received on the 28th, gave me great pleasure. I would have answered by return of post if I hadn't wanted to give you similar pleasure. Enclosed is printed evidence that it's the greatest possible joy to me if I can say something about you to the world' (letter of 28 March 1821).

The Empress Marie Louise[1] has presented the composer J. B. Gänsbacher with a diamond ring bearing her initials in acknowledgement of a divertissement for piano duet[2] which he has dedicated to her. Nothing but the encouragement and praise bestowed on his earlier works by this noble connoisseur of the art could have emboldened so modest an artist to dedicate a work directly to her. On this occasion I should like to say a little more about this exceptional man, who lives quietly in his native Tyrol, almost entirely divorced from the activities of the rest of the musical world. He makes a large contribution to the

---

[1]   The Empress Marie Louise, daughter of Francis I of Austria, and Napoleon's second wife, had withdrawn to Austrian territories on her husband's abdication in 1814.
[2]   Divertissement in E flat (Op. 29).

performance and appreciation of music, and is an active supporter of the visibly flourishing Music Society in Innsbruck, of which he is in fact the founder. He has all the true Tyrolean sense of loyalty and patriotism, and he showed himself ready to sacrifice everything in the hour of danger. He is in fact our musical *Körner. When brave and loyal hearts were needed, he gave up his pleasant life and his career, hung his lyre on the wall and took up the sword[3] in defence of his native mountains and his Emperor. He distinguished himself on many occasions and won the gold medal of the Order of Merit. When the loyal Tyrolean detachments were attached to the Imperial Jaeger Regiment, Gänsbacher stayed on as Oberleutnant and organized the regimental band, thereby laying the foundation of the Innsbruck Orchestra. Anyone who knows Gänsbacher's music, which is dominated by charming melodies, tender and original invention and a dreaming, introspective quality, may find it hard to imagine him as a dashing Tyrolean sharpshooter perched aloft on his mountain heights. But his is indeed a case of virile strength amalgamating with deep feeling, something that goes far to explain his predilection for church music (as well as admirable German and Italian songs and several instrumental chamber works) and the erudition and profound feeling that mark his Masses and cantatas.

His years in Vienna and Prague, his journeys abroad and the time spent at Darmstadt in the company of *Vogler, *Meyerbeer, *Gottfried Weber and Carl Maria von Weber taught him how to employ his talents and his capacity for hard work in forming his artistic ideals. It is only to be hoped that this modest artist will publish more. His friends admire him equally as man, composer, patriot and charming singer. A few of his lighter works have been published by Gombart (Augsburg), Schlesinger (Berlin) and Artaria (Vienna).

[3] Körner's most famous collection of war poems was *Leyer und Schwert*, which also gave its name to the selection of settings by Weber.

118. Johann Sebastian Bach

Written: Dresden, 20 April 1821.
Published: J. S. Ersch and J. G. Gruber: *Allgemeine Enzyklopädie der Wissenschaften und Kunst*, Part 7 (Leipzig, 1821).   *Signed:* Karl Maria v. Weber.
Reprinted: HHS, MMW (both inaccurate and incomplete); KSS.

Weber's contribution to Ersch and Gruber's encyclopaedia was a pioneering appreciation of Bach in 'modern' terms, eight years before Mendelssohn's famous revival of the St Matthew Passion.

Bach (Johann Sebastian), born Eisenach, 21 March 1685. From time to time Providence sends into the world heroes who seize in a mighty grasp the artistic tradition that has passed comfortably from master to pupil, from one generation to the next; purify and transform it; and thus shape something novel. This new art continues for many years to serve as a model, without losing its taste of novelty or its ability to shock contemporaries by its sheer power, while the heroic originator becomes the bright focal point of his age and its taste. It is generally forgotten in such cases, though quite unjustly, that these great men were at the same time also children of the age in which they lived, and that their great achievements argue the previous existence of much that was excellent.

Sebastian Bach was one of these heroic figures. He originated so much that was new and, in its way, perfect that the history of music before his day has come to seem a kind of Dark Age, and his contemporary Handel is oddly enough regarded as belonging to a different era. Sebastian Bach's individuality was, even in its austerity, in fact Romantic, truly German to its very roots, in opposition perhaps to Handel's greatness, which was rather in the antique mould. Bach's style is grandiose, sublime and rich. He achieved his effects by the most unexpected progressions in his part-writing, thereby producing long successions of unusual rhythms in the most ingenious contrapuntal combinations. The work of this sublime artist in fact resembles a Gothic cathedral dedicated to the arts, whereas all his predecessors were lesser men who lost themselves in the arid ingenuities that were the fashion, seeking the inner life of art in mere form and therefore finding nothing. It should not of course be forgotten in this connexion that in those days music was primarily written for, and commissioned by, the Church. The organist was the directing spirit, and the world of sound that is locked up in the organ for the creative artist to release was a plentiful source of the material that a composer today must look for in the rich field of the orchestra.

Sebastian Bach worked hard to achieve that complete mastery of the organ which determined the whole character of his art. This has as its most characteristic and distinguishing feature a grandeur closely associated with the fact that the organ is essentially an instrument that achieves expressiveness by effects of mass. The greatness of Bach's music in the harmonic field comes directly from his intellectual adroitness in combining the most contradictory melodic lines into a single whole.

The freedom of his part-writing combined with its strict logic naturally compelled him to discover means of making his music performable. Pianists are therefore indebted to him for a method of fingering first communicated to the world by his son Carl Philipp Emanuel Bach in his *Versuch über die wahre Art, das Klavier zu spielen*. The particular feature of this method is the use of the thumb, never properly used before by keyboard players, who for the most part made use of their four fingers. Bach was also the inventor of the so-called 'viola pomposa', since cellists of the day could not manage the figured basses in his works. This instrument was in fact an enlarged viola, with five strings and a range of a fifth (up to E) above the range of the cello. This made the performance of wide-spaced figures more practicable.[1]

Sebastian Bach founded what is commonly called a 'school'. It is hard to imagine Mozart's supreme achievements without the stages represented by Bach and Handel. The art of performing his works effectively is in fact dead, because the pleasure that they offer does not lie on the surface, and because the richness of the harmonic structure does not allow the melodic line the absolute predominance demanded by our pampered taste.

Sebastian Bach was the son of Johann Ambrosius Bach, court and town musician at Eisenach.[2] Orphaned before he was ten, he was given his first lessons by his elder brother, Johann Christoph, who was organist at Ohrdruf; and his apprenticeship was not, apparently, without its excitements, as he was obliged to study the better works of Froberger, Kerll, Pachelbel, and so on, in secret on moonlight nights. His first appointment was to a post as a treble in the choir of the Michaelisschule in Lüneburg, and from there his passion for self-improvement took him on several occasions to Hamburg, to hear the famous organist Reincken. In 1703 he was appointed court musician at Weimar and the next year he became organist at Arnstadt.[3] From this time onwards his development was swift and sustained. In 1707 he became organist at Mühlhausen, and in the following year he returned to Weimar as court organist, and later (1714) Konzertmeister. Shortly after this he was appointed Kapellmeister by the Prince of

---

[1]   Actually the violoncello piccolo: see C. Sanford Terry, *Bach's Orchestra* (London, 1932), pp. 135–41.

[2]   The family originated in Pressburg, in Hungary; its founder was a baker, Veit Bach, who left Hungary at the beginning of the seventeenth century. See Korabinsky, *Beschreibung der Stadt Pressburg 1784*, for a full family tree. (Weber's footnote.) The correct title of M. Korabinsky's book is *Beschreibung der königlichen ungarischen Haupt-, Frey- und Krönungsstadt Pressburg* (Pressburg, 1780–3).

[3]   Actually the same year, 1703.

Anhalt-Cöthen, but in 1723 he moved to Leipzig as director of music and cantor at the Thomasschule. He died in Leipzig on 28 July 1750, of a stroke. In 1736 the Duke of Weissenfels had bestowed the title of Kapellmeister on him and the King of Poland the title of Royal Polish and Electoral Saxon Court Composer.

He had eleven sons and nine daughters, all gifted and four of them outstandingly so. Wilhelm Friedemann, sometimes called the 'Halle Bach' was born at Weimar in 1710 and died at Berlin in 1784 – a solid organist, mathematician and writer of fugues. Carl Philipp Emanuel was born at Weimar in 1714 and is commonly referred to as 'the Berlin Bach'. He had leanings towards the *galant* or rococo style and was popular with the public. His greatest service to music was his publication of the book describing the perfecting of the art of keyboard playing as discovered by his father. He died at Hamburg in 1788. Johann Christoph Friedrich, 'the Bückeburg Bach', was born at Weimar[4] in 1732 and died at Bückeburg in 1795 – the nearest in taste to his brother Emanuel. Johann Christian, called 'the English Bach' or 'the Milanese Bach', was born at Leipzig in 1735 and died in 1782 in London, where he had been Kapellmeister to the Queen. He was of all the brothers the most devoted in his music to the so-called *galant* style, and for this reason he was the most popular in his lifetime and is the most completely forgotten now. The musical endowments of the Bach family are in fact of an almost incredible wealth.[5]

[4]   Actually Leipzig.
[5]   Gerber has in his original and more recent *Tonkünstler-Lexicon* alone twenty-two complete articles. (Weber's footnote.)

119. Thanks after the première of *Der Freischütz*

Written: Berlin, 19 June 1821.
Published: Vossische privilegierte Berliner Zeitung, No. 74, 21 June 1821.
                                        Signed: Carl Maria von Weber.
Reprinted: MMW (inaccurate); KSS; LKA.

The success of *Der Freischütz* at its first performance on 18 June 1821 was the more significant because of the rivalry it represented with Spontini's *Olympie*. However, despite his Dresden controversies (see above, Nos. 105, 110 and 112), Weber was anxious not to exacerbate relations with Spontini; and he was particularly concerned that he should not be thought responsible for the leaflets thrown from the gallery on the first night suggesting in verse that his shooting would hit a nobler game than an elephant (a much-publicized feature of the décor of *Olympie*):

> So lass dir's gefallen in unserm Revier,
> Hier bleiben, so rufen, so bitten wir;
> Und wenn es auch Keinem Elephanten gilt,
> Du jagst wohl nach anderem, edlerem Wild.

Matching doggerel for doggerel:

> May it please you to stay in this neck of the woods,
> We beg you, remain and deliver the goods;
> Though few are the elephants, yet your new fame
> Shall send you a-hunting for far nobler game.

The final sentence, in square brackets, appears in the MS but not in Weber's published text.

I have been so profoundly moved that I cannot refrain from expressing my deepest and most heartfelt thanks for the really extravagant kindness and indulgence with which the noble people of Berlin have greeted the performance of my opera *Der Freischütz*. From the bottom of my heart I pay tribute to the truly touching enthusiasm shown by the excellent soloists and orchestra and the indefatigable chorus, at the same time not forgetting the tasteful production by Count Brühl. I shall always bear in mind the redoubled obligation that these things impose upon me, and shall strain every fibre of my being in pursuance of greater excellence. Indeed, the more conscious I am of my high endeavour, the more acutely I am aware of the only bitter drop in my cup of happiness. I should not merit the applause of such a public could I not pay honour where honour is due. But a jest that may hardly be a pinprick to one who has made his name cannot, in the circumstances, fail to wound me more grievously than a dagger-thrust. [And in fact by comparison with elephants, my poor owls and other harmless creatures look very small.]

120. *A bourgeois family story*

Written: Dresden, 25 December 1821.
Printed: HHS; MMW; KSS.

This was the fruit of a Christmas entertainment at the Liederkreis (see above, No. 108). The women would ask the men elaborate comic questions, requiring similarly fantastic answers. This was Weber's answer to one such question.

There was once a musician who was very unhappy. He ate hardly more than a bite and allowed himself hardly sufficient time for sleep. But nobody was surprised, because he was in the same case as the robber

Jaromir.[1] Fate, that wicked fairy, had surprised him with an envelope, and since then he had been so sunk in thought that he was quite unable to think properly any more. One day, however, a thought did come into his mind and it was like this.

'Oh! why was I ever born, and why is there such a day as 7 December, which is worse than February, and what is the point of all this thinking, that's what I ask myself', he thought. Then he sat down and went on thinking. 'Well! what's done can't be undone, the question's been put, the bullet's left the barrel – well, *Freischütz*, hit the mark and help yourself! Opera-writing doesn't amount to much but answering is hard...' This musician also had a little wife, who carried his rosin and generally looked after him when he got a bit maggoty in the head – something that does sometimes happen to musicians. 'My noble lord and master' – these were his wife's words, though her thoughts as she spoke were quite different – 'do for goodness' sake tell me why you can't face your *Butterzopf*,[2] and let me share your torturing thoughts'.

Thereupon he flew into a rage and exclaimed, 'For heaven's sake stop asking, or ask about the question! Can you read? if so, read that.' And the musician's fat little wife almost trembled as he gave her a small sheet of paper, completely blank except for two short lines –

> Would musicians survive, in hell or in heaven,
> If the world were to end on December 7?

She smiled as she read, and said, 'Why are you so frightened, dear? What can happen to you? say what you like, who can prove that you are wrong? What's more, this is by no means a novel idea but comes from Shakespeare, and is in fact no more than a variation on the theme of "To be or not to be – that is the question". Yes, yes; that *is* the question – if there are musicians after the end of the world, what will they do? Just exactly what they did before, and I know very well what you'll do then'; whereupon the musician said in a strange voice, as though speaking to himself: 'The note once sounded by the Great Composer in the music of the spheres above will sound for all eternity. The string that vibrates here below will no longer tremble there; freed from the din of earth, still humming from the sounding-board of the world, that string will sound for ever and nothing shall disturb it. Amen.'

But the wife laughed to herself. 'What fellows these musicians

---

[1]   The hero of Grillparzer's 'fate tragedy' *Die Ahnfrau* (1817), who unwittingly loves his sister and kills their father.

[2]   A particularly delicious kind of cake, made as a special treat.

are – major and minor only a semitone apart,' and, 'Is that an answer, then?' she wondered.

121. Metronome markings and recommendations for *Euryanthe*

Written: Dresden, 6, 8 and 9 May 1824.
Printed: AMZ I (1848), 123–7 (with introductory note by F. W. Jähns).
Reprinted: KSS.

Weber wrote these observations in answer to a request from Aloys Präger, Kapellmeister at the Leipzig Städtisches Theater from 1821 to 1828, in connexion with a performance of *Euryanthe* in May 1824. He later circulated them to several other theatres. Although Weber had asked for them to be treated as private, Präger felt able to publish part of them after Weber's death in the Berlin *Allgemeine musikalische Zeitung*, No. 28, 11 July 1827; and the comments after the metronome markings were included by Ernst Rudorff in his Preface to the Schlesinger full score (1866), with the metronome markings incorporated into the text.

Overture. Allegro marcato, con molto fuoco: ♩. = 92 (Largo: ♩ = 52; Tempo primo assai moderato: ♩ = 88, stringendo up to the E flat theme).

ACT 1

No. 1 Introduction. Chorus: 'Dem Frieden Heil!' Dance and recitative. Moderato maestoso: ♩ = 92. Solemn Dance: ♩ = 96 (recitative).

No. 2 Romance. Adolar: 'Unter blüh'nden Mandelbäumen'. Andante con moto: ♩ = 72.

No. 3 Chorus: 'Heil Euryanth!' Recitative 'Ich trag' es nicht!' Allegro: ♩ = 116. Agitato assai: ♩. = 104 ('Des Meeres Grund': ♩ = 69).

No. 4 Scene and Chorus: 'Wohlan! Du kennest mein herrlich Eigentum'. Maestoso assai: ♩ = 50 (Allegro: 'Es gilt': ♩ = 88). Con fuoco: ♩ = 96.

No. 5 Cavatina. Euryanthe: 'Glöcklein im Tale' and recitative. Andantino: ♪ = 76. Moderato assai: recit: ♩ = 96.

No. 6 Aria. Eglantine: 'O mein Leid ist unermessen' and recitative. Agitato ma non troppo presto: ♩ = between 88 and 92 (Largo: 'Die ihr der Liebe Tränen': ♩ = 84). Presto: 'Was hab' ich getan!': ♩ = 128.

No. 7 Duet. Euryanthe, Eglantine: 'Unter ist mein Stern gegangen'. Moderato assai: ♩ = 104 ('Trost der Liebe': ♩ = 63). Allegretto grazioso: ♩ = 80.

No. 8 Scene and aria. Eglantine: 'Betörte, die an meine Liebe glaubt'. Allegro: ♩ = 160 (Tempo: 'Brust': ♩ = 100) ('O, der Gedanke': ♩ = 100). Aria: Allegro fiero: ♩ = 144 (Moderato: ♩ = 132).

No. 9 Finale. Chorus: 'Jubeltöne, Heldensöhne'. Vivace: ♩ = 138. Allegretto: ♩. = 80.

ACT 2

No. 10 Scene and aria. Lysiart: 'Wo berg' ich mich?' and recitative: 'Der Gruft entronnen'. Aria: Allegro con fuoco: 𝅗𝅥 = 92. Andante con moto I: ♩ = 66 (Allegro: ♩ = 160). Andante con moto II: ♩ = 80 (Vivace feroce: 𝅗𝅥 = 132).

No. 11 Duet. Eglantine, Lysiart: 'Komm denn, unser Leid zu rächen!' Allegro energico: ♩ = 144 (Con strepito: 𝅗𝅥 = 104).

No. 12 Aria. Adolar: 'Wehen mir Lüfte Ruh?' Larghetto non lento: ♩ = 54 (Allegro: ♩ = 120) ('O Seligkeit, dich fass ich kaum': ♩ = 144).

No. 13 Duet. Euryanthe, Adolar: 'Hin nimm die Seele mein'. Tempo of No. 12: ♩ = 144. Allegro animato: 𝅗𝅥 = 96 ('Seufzer wie': 𝅗𝅥 = 76; from the theme onwards, Tempo primo).

In this duet there is a perpetual ebb and flow of passion in all its nuances. The right interpretation depends on singer and conductor wholly agreeing in alternating between a burning ardour that gives the music its forward impetus and a meditative intensity that holds it back. I have learnt from experience that too many markings can produce a caricature of the music. Failing the ideal interpretation, it is better to plunge straight ahead than to get lost in too many nice distinctions.

No. 14 Finale. Chorus: 'Leuchtend füllt die Königshallen'. Allegro moderato. Chorus: ♩. = 84 (Poco più moto: ♩ = 60; Allegro: 𝅗𝅥 = 100; Larghetto: ♩ = 52; Con fierezza: ♩ = 100; Maestoso assai: ♩ = 66; Allegro ma non troppo: ♩ = 144; Con tutto fuoco ed energia: ♩ = 160).

ACT 3

No. 15 Introduction. Recit. and duet. Euryanthe, Adolar: 'Hier weilest du'. Adagio non lento: ♩ = 66 (Allegro: ♩ = 160; Ritenuto, two bars after 'Abgrunds Grauen': ♩ = 66; Moderato: ♩ = 88; Più moto: ♩ = 138; Agitato: 𝅗𝅥 = 96; Non tanto allegro: 𝅗𝅥 = 88; Presto: 𝅗𝅥 = 116).

No. 16 Scene. Euryanthe, Adolar: 'Schirmende Engelschar'. Molto passionato: ♩ = 152 (Poco ritenuto: ♩ = 132; Vivace: ♩ = 160).

No. 17 Scene and Cavatina. Euryanthe: 'So bin ich nun verlassen'. Largo: ♩ = 50. Cavatina: Largo: ♪ = 66 (Più moto: ♩ = 66; Allegro marcato: ♩ = 100).

No. 18 Huntsmen's Chorus: 'Die Tale dämpfen'. Allegro marcato: ♩ = 100.

No. 19 Duet and chorus. Euryanthe, King: 'Lasst mich hier in Ruh' erblassen'. Larghetto: ♪ = 100 (the last bars slightly held back).

No. 20 Aria and chorus. Euryanthe: 'Zu ihm! zu ihm! o weilet nicht!' Allegro con fuoco: ♩ = 160 (Poco ritenuto: ♩ = 144). The remarks on No. 13 also apply to this aria.

No. 21 Scene and chorus. Bertha, Adolar: 'Der Mai, der Mai'. Allegretto: ♩. = 80 (Allegro non tanto: ♩ = 132; Allegro: ♩ = 152).

No. 22 Chorus and solo. Adolar: 'Vernichte kühn das Werk der Tücke'. Allegro: ♩. = 152.

No. 23 Wedding March with scene and chorus: 'Das Frevlerpaar!' Maestoso energico ma con moto: ♩ = 63 (Allegro moderato: ♩ = 138; Largo: ♩ = 50; Più moto: ♩ = 92; Vivace: ♩ = 160; Allegro moderato: ♩ = 104; Vivace: ♩ = 152).

No. 24 Duet and chorus. Adolar, Lysiart: 'Trotze nicht, Vermessener!' Con impeto: ♩ = 100.

No. 25 Finale: 'Last ruhn das Schwert!' Maestoso con moto: ♩ = 108 (Agitato: ♩ = 96; Con furia: ♩ = 126; Moderato assai: ♩ = 92; Poco più moto: ♩ = 138; Molto passionato: ♩ = 112; Presto marcato: ♩ = 160).

I should like to add a few remarks of a general nature, which forced themselves on my attention in connexion with this work. The individuality of the singer is, in fact, what unintentionally determines the 'colour' of each role. The possessor of an agile and flexible voice will give quite a different interpretation of a role from that given by the possessor of a large and handsome tone. One will certainly be several degrees more lively than the other; yet both can give the composer satisfaction by their performances, provided that they have correctly understood the various gradations of passion that he has indicated, and reproduced them on their own individual scale. It is the conductor's business to see that the singer is not too easy-going and does not content himself with the first interpretation that suggests itself. In actual florid passages, particularly, care must be taken that the movement of a whole number is not sacrificed to this or that individual roulade. For instance, the conclusion of Eglantine's aria should be sung with fiery brilliance, and any singer who cannot achieve this would be well advised to simplify the passage rather than allow the passionate character of the whole number to suffer. In the same way a singer who cannot bring the right vengeance-breathing manner to Elvira's aria in *Das unterbrochene Opferfest* will prejudice the work less if she omits the aria altogether than if she makes it sound like an easy-going singing exercise. The most difficult task of all, generally speaking, will always be to achieve a rhythmical relationship between the voice and the orchestra, so that they are perfectly blended and the voice is set off and carried along by the orchestra, which also enhances the emotional expressiveness of the vocal line – the truth being that the natures of the two are radically opposed to each other. The double need to take breath and to articulate words imposes a certain rhythmical freedom on all singers, something which might perhaps be compared to the beating of successive waves on the shore. Instruments (especially stringed instruments) divide time into sharply defined divisions, like the ticking of a pendulum. A perfect *espressivo* is only achieved when these contradictory characteristics are successfully blended. The beat (tempo) must not resemble the tyrannical restraint of a pounding trip-hammer, but its role in the music should rather be that of the pulse in the human body. There are no slow tempos without some points at which the music demands a faster motion if it is not to give the impression of dragging. There is no Presto, similarly, that does not need the occasional contrast of a gentler motion in order to avoid the danger of damaging the means of expression by excess of zeal.

Do not for heaven's sake let any singer for a moment suppose that what I am saying here is a defence of that lunatic style of performance in which each bar is arbitrarily distorted and the listener receives the same intolerably unpleasant impression as he is given by an acrobat's contortions. The sensation of a forward impetus, or for that matter of holding back, should never give the listener an impression of hurrying, dragging or indeed anything violent in the tempo. Musical and poetic significance can only take the forms of period or phrase, depending on the intensity of expression. In a duet, for instance, two contrasting characters may well demand different characterization of their emotional natures. A good example is the duet between Licinius and the High Priest in *La Vestale*. The more unruffled the Priest's words, and the more eloquent the violent objections of Licinius, the more clearly do their two personalities stand out, and the greater the effect. Music has no means of putting all this on paper. All depends on the sensitivity of the human individual: if this is lacking, little help can be expected from the metronome, which can only guard against the most crass errors; or from the very inadequate hints which I might be tempted to insert in order to point to further depths of meaning, had I not been warned by experience. This has taught me to regard them as superfluous and useless and the source of possible misapprehensions. Let them stand, though, since they are already there! They were added simply in answer to friendly enquiries.

122. The Berlin production of *Euryanthe*

Written: Hosterwitz, 23 June 1824.
Published: DAZ, No. 153, 26 June 1824.   *Unsigned.*
Reprinted: MMW; KSS.

Count Brühl had planned to stage *Euryanthe* in Berlin in April 1824, but on hearing nothing by the middle of March Weber wrote to ask when the final rehearsal would be so that he could attend. Spontini himself wrote back with fulsome compliments and a set of elaborate excuses about certain formalities not having been fulfilled, declaring that the work was not after all being performed (letter of 27 March 1824). Not at all mollified, Weber retorted courteously but firmly, pressing Spontini to honour the understanding that *Euryanthe* would be given in Berlin. There ensued acrimonious, and in the event unsuccessful, negotiations for a properly prepared performance, to which Karl von Holtei attempted to contribute, as Weber told Hinrich Lichtenstein: 'Holtei has sent a bitter satire on Spontini to the *Abend-Zeitung* here; I've prevented its publication so as not to add fuel to the flames, especially from here' (letter of 17 May 1824). Later he added: 'I now think the time ripe to say something here about the whole story, and I'll send you the article that will appear in the *Abend-Zeitung* by the next post as I've no time to copy it today. I've withheld my name, but don't deny that I've written it and must hope that its moderation will be appreciated' (letter of 24 June 1824).

The *Abend-Zeitung* has hitherto preserved a complete silence on this much-discussed event, and has even – in accordance with the express wish of Kapellmeister von Weber – refused a number of pointed communications directed against the Generalmusikdirektor in Berlin. The paper is however now obliged to publish the facts that the composer of *Euryanthe* has felt urgently impelled to request the postponement of this opera in Berlin and that he is indebted for the fulfilling of this request to the highest authorities in the theatre, who have shown their accustomed benevolence and sense of justice. Public opinion may be better enabled to decide whether there were sufficient grounds for his coming to this decision by a consideration of the following facts.

For months the composer could obtain no definite information about the performance of his opera. Despite the most flattering letters, it was only private information and presuppositions that turned out to be true that led him to make the above-mentioned request to the General-intendant of the various Hoftheater. In an access of almost exaggerated zeal, *Euryanthe* was suddenly to be prepared in about eighteen days; and considering the difficulty and the dimensions of the work, this seemed to the composer to spell disaster, however active and well disposed those taking part might be. He now appeals to the experience of the whole Berlin public, which knows enough about the time that has been needed to prepare other grand operas to be able to judge the truth of this assertion. Even in the case of the performance being successful, there could not possibly have been more than two of them, followed by a month's interval, since Madame Seidler's[1] holiday begins on 15 July and after that Madame Schulz[2] is unavailable.

Attention should also be drawn to the fact that in spite of the proceedings of the Generalmusikdirektion (and with no reflection on the veracity of the report) and Generalmusikdirektor Spontini's clear assertion to his colleagues on the Board that *Euryanthe* 'was of course, as you know, cast in accordance with Herr von Weber's express wishes' – in fact the casting was *not* in accordance with Herr von Weber's wishes.

In these circumstances it would have been more than foolish presumption on the part of the composer of *Euryanthe* to hope for a favourable reception, more especially as he is firmly convinced that this dramatic essay can only win, and hold, the attention of the public by a thoroughly prepared performance and the proper realization of individual roles.

[1]   Caroline Seidler (1790–1812) was the daughter of the composer Anton Wranitzky. In 1816 she moved from her native Vienna to Berlin, where in 1821 she was Weber's first Agathe.
[2]   Josephine Schulz (1790–1880) was Spontini's leading soprano in Berlin, and did eventually sing Eglantine there in December 1825.

123. Two open letters to Castil-Blaze

Written: 1. Dresden, 15 December 1825; 2: Dresden, 4 January 1826.
Published: Le Corsaire, No. 925, 22 January 1826, p. 3.
                                        Signed: Ch. M. de Weber.
Reprinted: A. Jullien, *Weber à Paris en 1826* (Paris, 1877), KSS (both with minor inaccuracies).

Der Freischütz was first performed in France, at the Théâtre de l'Odéon in Paris, on 7 December 1824, as *Robin des bois, ou Les Trois balles*. The idea for this came from a vaudeville writer, Thomas Sauvage, who suggested it to the foremost adaptor of the day, the theatre writer and musician Castil-Blaze (François Henri Joseph Blaze (1784–1857)). The action was moved to Yorkshire in the time of Charles I, with Robin (Samiel) claiming as his victim Richard (Caspar) unless a substitute is found in Lord Wentworth's gamekeeper Tony (Max). The much-contracted Wolf's Glen scene, with fewer ghostly apparitions, takes place in the ruins of St Dunstan's Abbey. Robin provides three bullets, of gold, silver and lead. The plot thenceforward deviates even further from the original, but Tony ends up in the arms of his beloved, Anna (Agathe). With the Hermit and Ottokar both removed, forgiveness is abruptly granted by Reynold (Cuno): 'ton repentir désarme ma colère; viens, cher Tony, viens embrasser ton père'. The work was hissed: Castil-Blaze thereupon organized a second première, on 16 December, putting it about that they had now completely rearranged the work. So successful was this ploy that they not only had a triumph which made them a fortune, but convinced French writers, such as Adolphe Jullien, of the existence of a 'second version'. The music is weakened by cuts and by some rearrangement of the order, and there is an insertion of the duet 'Hin nimm die Seele mein' from *Euryanthe* (for a full account of the misfortunes of the work in Paris, see G. Servières, *Freischütz* (Paris, 1913)). The case is different with the pasticcio *La Forêt de Sénart, ou La Partie de chasse de Henri IV*, made for the Odéon (14 January 1826). This used some of *Euryanthe*, as well as bits of *Der Freischütz* and music by Mozart, Beethoven, Rossini, Pacini, Generali and Meyerbeer; moreover, Castil-Blaze orchestrated the work himself from a piano score. A review in the *Journal des Débats*, signed C, declared that despite the bad arrangement of the plot and the poor acting, the piece had 'a success for which credit must go to the skilful choice of the musical pieces' (*Journal des Débats*, 16 January 1826, pp. 1–3). Weber wrote in protest first privately to Castil-Blaze, and when he obtained no reply (Castil-Blaze later asserted that he had not received the letter) he sent a copy, together with a second letter, to his Paris publisher Maurice Schlesinger (see above No. 43) for publication in all (*sic*) the Paris papers. Schlesinger chose one only, *Le Corsaire*, a cultural paper subtitled 'Journal des spectacles, de la littérature, des arts, moeurs et modes'. The letters were prefixed with a note, 'M. Weber and M. Castil-Blaze. We have received the following two letters written by M. Weber to M. Castil-Blaze (we print them word for word). M. Weber is German.' In reprinting them in his *Weber à Paris en 1826*, Jullien withheld the identity of the journal in which they had appeared, saying that he did not want others to take the credit for his efforts in finding them – a gesture denounced as 'pure egoism' by Kaiser, who did not have the opportunity of visiting Paris to search for himself and who unwittingly reproduced Jullien's inaccuracies in the text.

Dresden, 15 December[1] 1825

Monsieur,

Time was when I used to look forward to making the personal acquaintance of *L'Opéra en France*[2] as one of the chief pleasures of my coming visit to Paris. This is a book to which I shall always accord the high esteem it so richly deserves. I felt quite certain that I could derive nothing but benefit from a meeting with a writer of such pure and correct principles, and looked forward to the occasion. Imagine therefore to yourself, Monsieur, after such high hopes (as I may well denote them), my profound disappointment at seeing these hopes dashed by your behaviour to me.

In the first place, you are planning an adaptation of my opera *Der Freischütz* for the French stage. I can imagine nothing more flattering or more deserving of my sincere gratitude; but you do not consider it incumbent upon you to consult the composer, or to tell him of the modifications which may indeed be inevitable for your public. You obtain a score by means which are in fact – whatever you may think – quite illegal, since my opera has been neither engraved nor published, and no theatre or music-dealer has any right of sale. Finally, the opera is staged and you continue to remain unaware of my existence, to the point of claiming the composer's rights yourself.

I am aware of all this and am daily awaiting the honour of a letter from you, Monsieur. It seems to me impossible that a man of your merits and with your artistic convictions should totally forget what one artist and gentleman owes to another; but on the contrary, I have this moment heard that you have just published the score of *Der Freischütz*. Monsieur, I am appealing to no one but you in person, and to your sense of decency – to all the noble sentiments that you have so often expressed in speaking of art and of the duties that it imposes upon us. Allow me to nourish the hope that it is nothing more than forgetfulness, common enough among artists, that has caused you to forget the composer of *Der Freischütz*, and believe me when I say that I shall

---

[1]   In *Le Corsaire* the date is given as 4 January, the editors having confused the two letters. Jullien alters this to 15 December, and vice versa. Kaiser believed that the December dating must be wrong, however, as Weber could hardly have become impatient over the lack of an answer after barely three weeks. He suggests 15th October, the date on which Weber also wrote to Pixérécourt in Paris warning him against the purchase of an unauthorized score. However, Weber mentions December in his second letter; and the post from Dresden to Paris in 1826 would not have taken more than two or three days.

[2]   Castil-Blaze, *De l'Opéra en France* (2 vols., Paris, 1820).

continue for as long as possible to regard your talents with the real esteem that they deserve.

> I have honour to be, etc.
> Ch. M. de Weber.

Dresden, 4 January[3] 1826

Monsieur,

You have not considered it necessary to reply to my letter of 15th December and I therefore find myself obliged to write to you for a second time.

I have been informed that a work containing parts of *Euryanthe* is to be given at the Théâtre de l'Odéon. I am planning to produce this work in Paris myself; I have not sold my score, and nobody in France possesses it. Perhaps you have taken the numbers you wish to use from an engraved piano score. You have no right to mutilate my music by introducing numbers with your own personal accompaniments. It was quite enough including in *Der Freischütz* a duet from *Euryanthe*, with an accompaniment which was not mine.

You force me, Monsieur, to appeal to public opinion and to state publicly in the French press that I am being robbed, not only of music which belongs exclusively to me, but of my reputation, when mutilated works are performed with my name attached to them. In order to avoid all public disputes, which benefit art no more than they benefit artists, I urgently beg of you, Monsieur, to remove immediately from the work that you have arranged any numbers of which I am the author.

I am happy to forget the wrong that has been done to me, and prepared not to mention the subject of *Der Freischütz* again. But that must be the end, Monsieur. Please leave me the hope of our being able to meet with feelings worthy of your gifts and your intelligence. I beg to remain, etc.

> Ch. M. de Weber.

Castil-Blaze replied to these two letters in the *Journal des Débats*, adding insult to injury with a flood of excuses and self-justification, pointing out that French operas were performed in German versions and affecting wounded pride at being thus treated after all he had done for Weber (*Journal des Débats*, 25 January 1826, pp. 3–4). Schlesinger, not at all mollified, returned to the attack in *Le Corsaire* with a devastating exposé of Castil-Blaze's professional morality. Pointing out that Weber had refused to hand over the rights of *Der Freischütz* in full score even to his father, Adolf Schlesinger (see above, No. 43), he suggested that even if Castil-Blaze was within French law, no one could

---

[3]   See above, n. 1.

doubt that public opinion was against him. He then revealed that when he had, at Weber's request, shown Castil-Blaze the letters before publication, Castil-Blaze had remarked, in the presence of two witnesses, 'I know that Rossini and Weber can bring a lawsuit against me and that I could lose, but as every lawsuit in France lasts at least a year according to the course it takes, I would sell my separate arias to the music dealers, I'd break the boards of my stages with the works, and as my capital doesn't consist of an estate, I'd let them take my personal property and that wouldn't pay the legal costs.' Schlesinger concluded by pointing out, 'in Germany the translations of French operas don't contravene authors' rights, and don't alter a single bar; and two of M. C. B.'s texts were not traduced but translated.' (*Le Corsaire*, No. 935, 1 February 1826, p. 3.) Weber does not seem to have met Castil-Blaze in Paris.

124. Circular letter to all theatres

Written: Dresden, January 1826.
Published: ?
Reprinted: MMW; KSS.

No record has been found of publication in Weber's lifetime. The letter was doubtless prompted by the exchanges with Castil-Blaze (above, No. 123), and was not a unique step for a composer to take (see below, n. 1); but possibly Weber had second thoughts and never sent it for publication.

Since only France and England possess any complete system of insuring against the theft of intellectual property, and dishonest copyists and unprincipled music-dealers (such as Zulehner[1] in Mainz) have been successful in persuading some of even the best-known theatrical establishments to make illegal use of my works, I find myself obliged to trouble them with the present communication. I have the honour to inform them that my opera *Oberon*, composed in the first place for London, has been prepared for performance in Germany by an excellent German translation of Hofrat Winkler's (*Theodor Hell). This can be obtained by legal methods only from me personally. I should be most grateful to receive a short acknowlegement of this notice, which is not in any way to be regarded as a commercial advertisement of the opera, since the repertory of each theatre must depend on the individual circumstances in which it finds itself.

[1]   Georg Zulehner (1770–1841) founded his publishing firm in 1802. He gave it over to his nephew in 1811, and it was sold to Schott in 1820. Though by no means unique for the period, the firm's piratical practices were notorious: on 23 October 1803 Beethoven inserted a notice in the *Wiener Zeitung* protesting against Zulehner's issue of an unauthorized collection of his music for piano and strings (see E. Anderson, ed., *The Letters of Beethoven* (London, 1961), iii, Appendix H).

This notice, with a list of the theatrical managements to which it has been sent, will be published in the newspapers with the largest readership, in order to inform the public and to serve as a warning to privateering publishers.

I have to honour to sign myself
C. M. von Weber.

125. *Tonkünstlers Leben*

Written: (the following are the dates on which Weber is known to have been working on the novel, or to have finished a section of it; chapter and page numbers refer to the text below; chapters are numbered as in KSS):

Stuttgart, 1809: ch. 4.
Stuttgart, 2 December 1809: ch. 1, first version.
Frankfurt, 10 September 1810.
Darmstadt, 24 September 1810: ch. 6, pp. 340–5.
Darmstadt, 9 October 1810.
Mannheim, 14 October 1810: ch. 6, pp. 355–7.
Heidelberg, 4 December 1810.
Darmstadt, 18 January 1811: ch. 7.
Darmstadt, 2 October 1811: ch. 6, pp. 350–1.
Darmstadt, 5 October 1811: ch. 6, pp. 352–5.
Leipzig, January 1812: ch. 3, pp. 326–8.
Gotha, 24 September 1812.
Prague, 12 June 1813: ch. 6, pp. 345–8.
Prague, 4 February 1816.
Prague, 18 February 1816.
Berlin, 24 November 1816: ch. 6, pp. 348–9.
Berlin, 2 December 1816.
Berlin, 7 December 1816: notes and jottings, pp. 360–1.
Berlin, 7 January 1817: ch. 5, pp. 336–8.
Dresden, 17 January, 1817: notes and jottings, pp. 359–60.
Dresden, 12 June 1818: ch. 6, pp. 349–50.
Dresden, 14 November 1818: notes and jottings, pp. 361–4.
Dresden, 15 February 1819: ch. 5, pp. 335–6.
Dresden, 17 February 1819: ch. 1, second version.
Dresden, 20 March 1819: ch. 5, pp. 338–40.
Dresden, 16 July 1820: ch. 3, pp. 328–30.

Part published:
Morgenblatt für gebildete Stände, No. 309, 27 December 1809: ch. 4, as 'Fragment of a musical journey, that will perhaps be published.'

Signed: Carl Marie.

Die Muse I (1821), 49–72: ch. 1, second version; ch. 3, pp. 326–30; ch. 5, pp. 333–40, as 'Fragments from *Tonkünstlers Leben*. An Arabesque by Carl Maria von Weber.'

F. Kind, ed., *W. G. Beckers Taschenbuch zum geselligen Vergnügen* (Leipzig, 1827), pp. 371–85: ch. 6, pp. 340–57, under heading *12 Dichterreliquie*, as 'Fourth Fragment from *Tonkünstlers Leben*. An Arabesque. By Carl Maria von Weber.'

Part reprinted: AMZ xxiii (1821), 198–200; A. Wendt, *Rossinis Leben und Treiben* (Leipzig, 1824); *Symphonia. Fliegende Blätter für Musiker und Musik-freunde* ii (1866); various other later part reprintings.

Reprinted: HHS; MMW; KSS; LKA.

Weber began work on *Tonkünstlers Leben* in 1809, and published one episode that year, as detailed above. A letter to *Gänsbacher from Darmstadt, dated 24 September 1810, reported that he had submitted most of his work to Cotta, editor of the *Morgenblatt*: 'to my great delight he accepted it, and it will appear this Easter with a few engravings. His firm has such literary renown that because of this alone the fortunes and the evaluation of my work in the eyes of the world are half decided.' No more, however, did appear in print until 1821, when Kind published portions in his monthly journal *Die Muse*. Weber had written to Kind from Kiel on 21 September 1820, 'It's with great pleasure that I read your words of approval for my *Künstlersleben*. I don't doubt that much in it needs organizing, and I'm very relieved to know in whose hands it is' (reprinting this letter in his *Freischützbuch* (Leipzig, 1843), Kind erroneously noted that the extract had appeared in his magazine *Die Harfe*). With that, Weber appears to have abandoned plans that had lain in his mind for twelve years. It is doubtful whether he really intended Kind, with whom he had recently finished collaborating on *Der Freischütz*, to take over the completion of the work. Ill as he then knew himself to be, and concerned as he was to devote his energies to composition and to the cause of German opera, he probably did not expect to find time to continue the novel; but his view of Kind was not so high that he would be likely to have handed over so personal a work that still needed so much doing to it. As detailed below, the first draft indicated six chapters, the second twenty-three chapters, of which synopses of chs. 4–6 are missing. Only three chapters are fairly fully worked out; several more exist in part; and there are a number of fragments that could have found various homes in the book. The musical notes at the head of some of the chapters were intended to form a *Cirkelkanon* (canon *al rovescio*), so that it would be the same forwards and backwards and thus, Weber felt, 'to some extent a picture of human life'.

The materials of *Tonkünstlers Leben* were first collected and assembled in the evidently intended order by *Theodor Hell as vol. i of HHS; this was followed by Max Maria von Weber in Part 2 of vol. iii of MMW, the volume devoted to Weber's writings. Neither made a comparison of the part reprints with the original publications, and it was left to Georg Kaiser, in KSS, to collate these and the MS to produce a definitive text in eight chapters (which do not correspond to Weber's synopses of chapters). Other reprinted texts, such as LKA, follow Kaiser, as does the present translation.

First plan

Chapter 1

Travels.   Reception in Klubstädt at Herr von X's.

Chapter 2

Town musician. Examining the girl. Course of conversation between him and her. Final hearing. Difficulties. Permit. Pass from the police. Proposed concert and ball: the most profitable. Search for musicians. The oboist refuses to come without the clarinettist, on account of his wife etc. Scruples about the orchestra's numbers, finally six flutes etc. The landlord: 'So you want to give a concert; the girl told me when she brought my beer.' Good advice. Introduction to the club. Amateur who used to play the flute.

Chapter 3

Letter to Ernsthof. A word about first youth: his first journey with father: settling down. A life giving lessons, and assiduous studies. Father's death. Urge to travel. Youthful strength and courage to persist. Reason for visiting this small place. Recounts how he saw a very interesting girl entering a carriage. Those who were seeing her off called her Emilie. Too shy to make further enquiries. Regrets this later.

Chapter 4

Concert – empty: dancing dogs etc. Departure. Post-chaise.

Chapter 5

Arrival in a large town. Feeling of loneliness and abandonment, alone among strangers. Acquaintance with Diehl.

Chapter 6

Facts about the musical workhouse.

Second plan

Chapter 1

Decision to travel.   Reception in Herr von X's house.

Chapter 2

The town musician.   Dispute about teaching methods.   Opinions of other musicians etc.: returns home exhausted in the evening and writes to his friend in Paris, whom he has not seen for years, about the disagreeableness of giving concerts.

Chapter 3

The concert.   Passing acquaintance with a charming girl just leaving.   No one at the evening concert owing to the arrival of dancing dogs.   Several musicians play for 24 kreuzer more than the dancing dogs.   The thought of Emilie inspires his playing. [Marginal note:] Acquaintance with Diehl.   Door shut.   Someone falls down the steps on top of him, picks himself up and embraces him warmly, expresses gratitude for the good fortune of falling on Felix. 'Are you mad, sir, or do you take me for a fool? Who are you?'   'I, I am nothing, but may I ask who you are?'   'I (with a sigh) am not really anything either, but people like me are generally called artists. I also have tricks of my own, e.g. making a publisher pay, and so on. If you like, we will begin with the second year of our friendship etc.'

Chapter 7

Operatic selection.   Ball.   A is taken for a prince in love with Emilie, rescues her, mistakes her for another girl.

Chapter 8

Sleepless night.

Chapter 9

A spends a couple of long, unpleasant days in a state of the wildest passion, unable now to compose – he becomes calmer, looks vaguely at his fancy dress, puts on the same coat, fumbles absentmindedly in the pocket, and finds the devil's poem to Emilie.   Sets it to music; the poet joins him; conversation about the character of the song.

Chapter 10

Some time passes before he again sees Emilie, who has been ill with shock.   Diehl tells him of his visit to the false Emilie and of the Prince's rage at the discovery, berating his assistants etc.

Chapter 11

Makes a number of acquaintances belonging to the group, meets a travelling diseur, who declaims with X accompanying.   Distorted views of the diseur, a real vagabond artist.   One of these present, a delightful old man, asks him to teach his daughter.

Chapter 12

Diehl outlines the plan for a musical penitentiary and workhouse. [Marginal note:] three epigrams and the translation of the song, 'Non far la smorfiosa'.

Chapter 13

Enters the house, finds the room empty, sits down at the piano and improvises. While he is playing the daughter of the house comes in unobserved; stands behind him and calls out when he stops playing; deeply shaken to his innermost being, he looks round and sees Emilie. Mutual embarrassment.   Eventually her parents appear and there is a magnificent evening of music, heartily enjoyed by all.   Emilie shows him works by her favourite composer, who holds first place in her affections.   The works are his own, published under another name. Emilie is enthusiastic about them, and he can hardly prevent himself from telling her that he is the composer.   He sees the Prince on parade, a handsome man.   Thinks that the Prince observes him closely.   On imagination.   Credulity.

Chapter 14

He visits the house every day.   Improvises, making frequent use of her favourite phrases, from which Emilie recognizes him as the composer;

new delight and admiration for his modesty.   Remarks on each composer's 'fingerprints'.

Chapter 15

Comes home one day to find an invitation from the Prince.   Pleasant company, and the Prince makes a friendly approach.   His mistrust of the Prince, who speaks well about the treatment of artists.

Chapter 16

He finds himself involuntarily drawn to the Prince and spends his time between Emilie and him.   He and Emilie become daily closer, but he is not yet bold enough to refer to the episode at the Redoute.   He still wears the mauve scarf next to his heart.   Emilie happens to see it, recognizes her rescuer in him and is overcome with love for him. Declaration etc.   Boring love scene.

Chapter 17

Her father and mother realize the situation and are delighted, but both want him to give up his uncertain life as an artist and find an official post.   Indecision on his part.   Attacks by the others, even Diehl, who prophesies trouble of every kind.   Unexpectedly, he receives an invitation to act as companion to the Prince.

Chapter 18

He tells Emilie of this, and when she urges him to accept it, he discloses the story of the Redoute.   Even this does not alienate the father and mother. Vanity of women, even the best, in its acutest form.   Decision to accept the Prince's offer.

Chapter 19

New circumstances.   Life at court.   Relationship of Felix and the artists reversed.   Strange opinions of the latter about him as a dilettante.

Chapter 20

The greater his dependence on Emilie, who seems in artistic matters to share his every thought and feeling, the further apart they become in their view of life.   She is full of sophistries and half-truths, and tries to justify these to herself.   He is a pure idealist, with a strong sense of justice.   Strange, uncanny feeling between them.

Chapter 21

The Prince becomes distant.   Dario, from an Italian family, is cold and distant, a mathematician who despises music; an atheist behind a masque of extreme seriousness, sometimes combined with a diabolical smoothness and ingenuity.   He attracts Felix like a rattlesnake, and always defends Felix to Diehl, who detests him.

Chapter 22

Unpleasant feelings eventually aroused in Felix.   He feels out of his true element.   His is moody and unhappy, one moment wildly excited and the next sunk in the deepest gloom, quite unable to work.   During this time he has the dream.

Chapter 23

Complicated relationship between Emilie and the Prince.   Her weak mother fosters the relationship, while the father – a gay man of the world – pays too little attention to it and takes it all too lightly.   Felix eventually decides to make a clean break and devote himself to his art again.

End.   The artist's last will and testament.

Chapter 1 (first version)   [1809]

Out into the world with you! for the world is the artist's true sphere. What good does it do you to live with a petty clique and to earn the gracious applause of a patron in return for the wretched task of setting to music his verses, which have neither wit nor feeling? What is the warm handshake of a pretty neighbour for a few dashing waltzes or the crowd's applause for a successful march at a military parade? Out! A man's spirit must find itself in the spirits of his fellow creatures. And having once delighted men of feeling by your genius and learnt in turn from them, you can return to a peaceful home and live on what you have acquired.

I quickly packed up my compositions, embraced the few acquaintances whom I could call my friends, collected some addresses in the nearby small town and set off in the modest post-chaise recommended to me by my purse. I never know whether others share my feelings when travelling post. I move in an interior world of my own and my lips are sealed. I am unable to utter a word to my fellow travellers, who must think me the worst company in the world. The thousand objects that flit past my gaze arouse as many confused feelings in me. One theme gives place to another, and while I am elaborating the most infernally involved *fugato* in my mind, a cheeky little rondo theme will dart up, only to be elbowed out by a funeral march or the like.

My arrival in the pleasant little town of X, the first halting-place on my wanderings, put a stop to all this; and still humming Pedrillo's 'Nur ein feiger Tropf versagt' from *Die Entführung*,[1] I fell asleep, full of high hopes for my coming concert.

The next morning I went to Herr von Y's, having heard much about his musical family and his influence in the town, which was said to be considerable.

'Ah! welcome!' he exclaimed as I entered. 'Delighted to make your acquaintance. I have been told great things about you. Do you know my latest sonatas?'

Myself (in some embarrassment): 'I'm afraid I don't.'

He: 'The quartet, then?'

Myself: 'I don't think so.'

He: 'Well! if you read the newspapers and have any knowledge of writing about the arts, you must certainly know my Caprices.'

Myself (very embarrassed): 'To my shame, I must confess that I did not know you were a composer.'

He: 'My dear friend, I'm sorry that, to be frank with you, since I gather that you intend to give a concert here, I must tell you here and now that you will have difficulty in bringing it off, since your name is not known. The public here is as hard to please as the Viennese, and unless you can persuade my daughter to sing with you...'

At that moment Mademoiselle entered the room, and I was indeed

[1]   Act 2, No. 13: 'Frisch zum Kampfe! Frisch zum Streite! nur ein feiger Tropf versagt!' ('only cowards are afraid').

not a little struck by her appearance, for such an opus is not to be met with every day. Imagine a diminutive creature with a huge head covered with bristling black locks and a kind of tiara. From her mouth, which resembled a breve from the time of Aretino,[2] there issued a rasping sound about as pleasing to my ear as someone scratching on a piece of glass. This tender daughter put her spidery arms round her papa's neck and he introduced me as a music student, saying 'You must sing part of that big aria for him, you know, the one that has the very high and very low notes, the one I'm so fond of.'

She looked me up and down in a patronizing way and said, clearing her throat, 'Papa, you know that I've been so *enrhumée* lately that I shall hardly be able to do as you ask' (here she produced a tiny cough). 'Heavens! You can hear for yourself how rough my voice is!' In any case, I could hardly blame the poor air which had to force a way through a throat hardly large enough to permit the passage of breath and better suited to anatomical study than to singing. However, I suppressed my first reactions and, urged on by my desire to be polite, I begged her to sing something, however small.

Women are born to yield, and our combined pleas were too much for her. She sat down negligently at the piano, struck a few heavy chords, and after a successful attempt at a chromatic scale, she croaked her way through a bravura aria by Scarlatti. I was astonished by my own good nature, and tried to look over her shoulders (one of which was perversely higher than the other) at the music. But she had only sung a few bars when she exclaimed, 'You see, it's quite impossible!' sang a few more bars, blamed her hoarseness (though she made a noise like a booming bittern) and finally after repeated interruptions, got to the end. I gave myself a mental box on the ear for not having sufficient command of my feelings to throw in at least a couple of 'Bravos!'. But fortunately in the meantime the girl's mamma had appeared, an excellently preserved copy of Xanthippe,[3] and she burst into such a storm of applause (beside which the din of a Wranitzky[4] Allegro is a mere rustling of leaves) that my remorseful 'Bravo!' was quite drowned.

---

[2] Otherwise Guido d'Arezzo (*c.* 992–1050?), the developer of modern notation.
[3] Socrates's proverbially shrewish wife.
[4] Paul Wranitzky (Pavel Vranický) (1756–1808) was a forerunner of Weber in several ways; his *Oberon* (1789) held its place in repertories until Weber's setting. He was noted for the extent of his symphonic movements, which in their energy anticipate some elements in Beethoven, and for the enlarged wind section he sometimes used.

'Yes, my daughter is quite a genius. It's astonishing what talent she possesses. Although she only began working at her music in her thirteenth year, she has often put the town musician in his place. Yes, and she also plays wonderfully well on the Strahlharmonika. Oh! do go and get it, darling, it's such a nice instrument!'

The pains of death encompassed me at the thought of this new ordeal, and all I could do was stammer that it was an instrument particularly suited to Adagio movements. 'Just so!' exclaimed Mamma. 'Adagios – that's what it's best for! Oh, do just play the "Vogelfänger".'⁵ That was really too much for me, and I burst out laughing, to the family's horror. They started whispering to each other that my musical sense must be that of a monkey, my taste absolutely wanting. So that in less than five minutes I found myself deserted by Mamma, who hurried off to the kitchen, by Papa, called away on urgent business, and by the daughter, smitten by migraine and retiring to her room. Once alone, I drew a deep breath, as though my lungs were being asked to power the bellows of the organ in Westminster Abbey, laid my finger by my nose, and found that, although not at the moment in the right mood for such visits, I would rather take the opportunity to look up the town musician and the other musicians that I needed.

Chapter 1 (second version)   [1819]

...And the hammer flew from its socket, several strings gave up the ghost with a ping – in fact, my annoyance got so much the better of me that I withdrew my hand from the keyboard, knocking over the stool and the bare manuscript paper, and started up, pacing my narrow little room with long steps, though even in my rage craftily avoiding the chests and various bits of furniture.

For months I had been plagued, worried and tortured by an uncanny something, and during the last few weeks this feeling had become intolerable. It was a vague yearning towards the shadowy distance which might ease my pain, though I never really considered how. It was a painful tension in my inner being, frustrated by the consciousness

⁵ 'Der Vogelfänger bin ich ja', Papageno's entrance aria in *The Magic Flute*.

of a high ideal, an urge to work which seemed doomed to disappointment, an irresistible inclination to work on the grandest scale and with all my faculties, coupled with an absence of all ideas and of the creative faculty itself – a chaos of shifting and worrying thoughts, so often dominating all artists and now completely dominating me.

Before this, I had known short periods when my desires, dreams and plans for the future had been conquered by the circumstances of my life or my art, but this was an attack which had the violence of mania. Life's problems seemed to weigh unbearably upon me and I longed to escape from them into the world of art; but life and art are inextricably connected, and on this occasion they combined to increase my nervous irritability. Even the piano-stool, on which I had sat hoping to compose, seemed to have turned from my last resort into an object of sinister foreboding. The composer who finds the material for his work in that way is almost always poorly endowed from birth or on the way to entrusting his spirit to the commonplace and everyday. For these hands, these accursed piano-fingers, take on a kind of life of their own after years of practice to obtain mastery, and they become unconscious tyrants and despots over the creative faculty. *They* never invent a new idea, as all novelty is inconvenient to them. Secretly and on the sly, like the manual labourers whom they resemble, they cobble together whole works out of long-familiar, routine phrases. These almost look as though they were new, and because they sound well and flatter the ears which they have, as it were, bribed in advance, they are immediately accepted and applauded.

The composer whose *inner* ear is the judge of his composition works in quite a different way. This inner ear is an amazingly able judge of musical shapes – something peculiar to the art of music and a sacred mystery which the layman cannot fathom. For with this inner ear the composer can hear whole periods, whole pieces indeed, at a single hearing, not disturbed by the small lacunae and awkwardnesses which the composer knows that he can fill out or smooth over when he comes to revise the work. It is then that he considers details in their relation to the whole and adds any finishing touches that may be needed. This 'composer's ear' demands a perfect unity, a composition with a character of its own so marked that any listener will recognize it and pick it out immediately once he has heard it. This is what a composer demands of himself and not a patchwork of sound. Once he has conceived a work as a whole image, and decided to foster and nurture it, as it were, in the womb of his mind – for good things only mature with time – he must protect it from all unsuitable nourishment or other contacts harmful to his precious child. Otherwise the wretched servants and attendants, with their workaday instruments of lead or gold, will take a delight in crowding it out of existence as it develops, damaging its head or neck, putting out an eye or severing a foot. The composer, in fact, becomes half mad with impatience and love at the spectacle of this creative chaos.

It is then that he hears the command that is still ringing in my own ears – 'Out with you! out into the world! The world is the artist's true sphere! What use to you is life in a narrow circle or the gracious applause of a versifying patron for setting his witless and heartless verses to music? What use is the warm handshake of a pretty neighbour for a few dashing waltzes, or the crowd's applause for a successful march for a military parade? Out into the world, then! A man's spirit must find itself in the spirits of his fellow creatures. And having once delighted men of feeling by your genius and learnt in turn from them you can return home to live on what you have acquired.'

I quickly packed my many compositions and few belongings, embraced the few acquaintances whom I could call friends, and went off to the neighbouring town in the modest post-chaise urgently recommended to me by my purse. It was late evening, and my travelling companions sat by me like dumb shadows. But youth and high hopes soon assured me of a peaceful night's rest whose profound mists not even the god of dreams could blow away. In the grey dawn, the hand of the grasping postillion was more effective, as he moved from one to another like a travelling offertory bag.[6]

The first rays of the sun spread their light in calm majesty over the earth. Nature's sacred *crescendo* pulsated through the brightening air and roused the spirit of devotion in my serene and tranquil imagination. In glad confidence I raised my thoughts to Him who in His fatherly goodness had bestowed on me the gift of artistic talent, which was to be the hallmark of my existence and bear witness to Him who is the author and giver of all powers. He it was who had entrusted me with this pledge of His mercy and would surely not withhold His favour from my use of it. I could rely on the purity of my intentions with an honourable self-satisfaction and even a hint of human pride, and could bear witness to the fact that I had shunned no difficult path and no effort in my attempt to develop my spirit for the benefit and delight of my fellow men.

Nature's open spaces always have an extraordinary effect on me,

---

6   As Weber's accounts in his Diary record, it was normal practice to tip the postillion a varying amount.

and one quite unlike that aroused in other spirits. Call it talent, vocation, genius or what you will, the object towards which all your faculties converge envelops your powers of contemplation in a magic circle. It is not only the corporeal eye that has its field of vision, but the eye of the soul also. You can of course shift both by changing your point of view, and happy is the man who can proceed to enlarge this vision; but you can never stand outside it. And that is not all. The colour in which an object appears is unwittingly determined by the tone of your life and feelings; and since I speak of tones, I will not deny that in my own case everything falls into musical forms.

To me, a landscape is a kind of musical performance. I have an immediate reaction to the whole before dwelling on the salient features; in a word, my experience of a landscape, oddly enough, is an event in time. It is a 'successive' pleasure. This has both its great delights and its great pains. Among the delights I count the fact that I never know the exact position of a mountain, a tree, a house or whatever it may be. This means that every time that I look at a landscape it is, so to speak, a different performance. The great pain is in travelling, for then a fine confusion begins in my soul and everything swims and eddies before my eyes. All my ideas and images whirl, criss-cross and chase each other. If I stand absolutely still and look steadily towards the horizon, the image I obtain may be compared to something similar in the related mental world of my musical imagination, and I may well be able to take it to my heart, retain its contours and develop it. But heavens above! what a mad succession of funeral marches, rondos, furiosos and pastorals somersaults through my mind when such a succession of natural beauties is unrolled before my eyes! I become more and more silent as I struggle with the all too vivid demands of my brain. I cannot remove my gaze from the shining spectacle provided by nature, it soon becomes nothing more to me than a gaudy play of colours, my ideas completely lose their musical associations and I am overcome by the circumstances of everyday life. I think about the past and dream about the future. And so woe to any chatty neighbour, particularly at the beginning of my journey, if he hopes to find another such in me. He is sadly disappointed, and so in the end am I, for my thoughts resemble nothing so much as soap-bubbles, which rise and burst and are not even worth remembering.

Chapter 2

After I had completed a *scala descendendo*, I met a group of choristers in the street just about to strike up a song. What an instrument is the human voice, the Creator's first musical gift to man! What a marvellous thing is the human throat, the model for all other instruments and the means of expressing the strongest and deepest feelings – solemn in chorus and so touching and penetrating even in the humblest performance! I therefore called a halt to my footsteps and prepared myself for the uplifting sound of a chorale, music so close to the heart of the common people! But that day I was condemned to be tortured. To my great astonishment, the singers struck up one of the latest and finest operatic arias, from *Fanchon*.[7] But they squealed away so confusedly and so out of tune that I had no scruple in turning to one of the bass singers nearby, a lanky fellow who made good use of any pauses in the music to munch a bun, which at first distracted my attention, and asked him where the town musician lived.

'The Principal lives over there on the right,' he said. 'You can't miss his house, you'll hear music from the street, he's rehearsing the Russian horn players, but it's strictly forbidden to interrupt rehearsals.' I assured him that I too felt strongly on the subject, and went off to the house.

What an infernal spectacle greeted me as I entered the room, and how anxious I felt for my own skin! The Principal was standing surrounded by eight or nine young men playing – or making as though to play – the horn. His two hands were brandishing a massive baton, with which he was beating time, stamping his feet, and also banging with both hands on the clavier in front of him, and sometimes on the heads of his players, who were performing a work which he had composed in the style of Russian horn music, in which each horn plays only a single note. To his right and left others were playing violins, clarinets, bassoons etc. regardless of each other. Each of them was performing his own piece, *fortissimo*, punctuated by exclamations from the Principal, such as 'wrong note, you booby!' 'sharp', 'flat', 'too fast!' 'careful now!' and other things of the same kind.

The young players were the first to observe my presence and did not fail to pay more attention to me than to their music. The Principal himself was unaware of me and went on conducting madly, trying to keep the performers together regardless of what notes he played on

[7] See above, No. 91.

the clavier. The score, which lay on the music-stand above the jacks, was knocked over in the free-for-all, so that all the jacks shot up in the air like rockets and caused such a general unison of laughter that there was no question of continuing the rehearsal. It was not until some time later that my worthy self was observed and I could get a word with the town musician.

Chapter 3   [1812]
Letter to —   *Leipzig, January 1812*

I have left my peaceful A and returned to the maelstrom of the great world, but find the storms and buffetings of fate easier to bear than the silent nagging of A. The warrior learns to face death by engaging in dangerous games, and I mean to try my strength in order to face even more threatening events. I have never been able to admire the much-lauded heroes and mighty martyrs of any fanaticism for their readiness to seal their lives by a final act of suicide or some other dramatic full close. Once in every man's life a tiny flame leaps up – like the focal point of a burning glass – showing him his path and giving him the opportunity to do some great deed. But it is the small, daily recurring difficulties in every life that provide the real touchstone and separate the philosopher's genuine gold from any baser metal. How often I have had occasion to observe men who seemed admirable at a distance yet proved in their narrow domestic circle so petty! At a distance they showed nothing but calm dignity, but at home they were ready to grumble or attack a loving wife merely on account of some trivial object that was not in its accustomed place. Dignified and controlled amid the ruins of a nation, but worried and put out by the wilting of a favourite flower!

Well as I knew and appreciated all this, I was still not in a position to appreciate real simplicity and repose of mind. And what life is more full of irritating little events and petty setbacks than that of the artist? He ought by rights to stand as free as a god, conscious of his strength and steeled by his art. He seems to be lord of the world until he actually sets foot in it. Then his dreams and his powers vanish and he finds himself confined within the narrow limits of everyday life.

I had hardly set foot beyond my own threshold before I found myself besieged by such petty irritations, and I was tempted to forget my earlier experiences and my determination to hold out against them, and to turn back again. It was only the memory of a few moments sweet enough to make up for years of suffering – that, and the consciousness of possessing a friend capable of understanding and sympathizing with me almost before I opened my mouth. These reminded me of the goal I had set before myself and what the outcome of all these efforts and struggles could be.

I hardly know you and your form hovers before my imagination like a protective deity in a flaming halo. I shall never forget the moment of our meeting. The elements were raging when fate sealed our mutual contract against the enmity of the mere crowd. Let me renew the memory of that time when all was lost and all was found! Let me dream again of the days when I was guided by a good mother's hand, though alas! for so few years. I was brought up with every comfort by a well-to-do father who adored me, and from my earliest youth a love of the arts was inculcated in my impressionable mind. The talents with which heaven entrusted me developed and were on the point of spoiling my character. For my father knew only the delight of sharing in my successes. He found all that I wrote wonderful and spoke of me even to strangers in the same breath as the greatest artists. This could easily have destroyed the sense of modesty innate in every human personality, had not heaven given me a guardian angel in the shape of a mother who, while reminding me of my present childish state, did nothing to suppress the spark of genius and pointed out the true path along which I should develop if I would but apply myself. The novels that I read overheated my imagination, and I matured early in a dangerous world of ideas which nevertheless had the great advantage of providing me out of a host of heroes, with models of manly virtue. In the company of my father I travelled and saw much of Europe, though it was as in a dream, for I saw everything through the eyes of another; I increased my stock of ideas, and from being a mere empiricist, I learnt to know the world of theoretical ideas. This was a new world to me and I thought that I could exhaust the whole treasure-house of human wisdom. I swallowed whole systems of philosophy, putting a blind trust in the authority attaching to great names which had won credit in the world, knew them all by heart yet in fact knew nothing.

My mother died, leaving behind her no fixed plan for my education, for her tender good sense had told her how to instil in me fundamental principles which were to form the support of my whole being.

I lived in the same place as you, and did not hate but rather despised you, since I was always being told that you, an artist like myself, playing the same instrument and treading the same path as I, spoke ungenerously of me out of envy and secretly tried to damage my career. All this I learnt from our table-companions and also from a father whose love for me was blind; and I was weak enough not to weigh this factor, so that I had a bitter resentment against you.

Then came the war, with all its horrors, and destroyed our peaceful existence. You had only just returned from a tour, covered with glory, and were on the point of continuing it, while I was tied at home by the love of a father who could not bear to live without me by his side. Our town fell into the hands of an enemy devoid of all scruples, and my belongings fell victim to the flames. I was too late to save my beloved books or – as it seemed – my own life. I was indeed given up for lost, when in fact I had escaped from the other side of the house as the enemy entered it. Hardly had I reached the safety of the street when I was told that you had returned into the flames at great danger to yourself, in order to rescue me. Then it was as though a great void opened in my breast and the portals of love were flung wide. Nothing could prevent me from doing what you had done for me, neither my father's prayers, nor the urging of the bystanders, nor the certainty of death. Through the sea of flames, with roof-beams crashing round me and blinded by smoke, I found my way to you as you searched for me: and in an ecstasy of mutual indebtedness and affection we sank into each other's arms and sealed our eternal bond amid the raging flames, at the risk every moment of becoming their prey.

[1820]

I can never properly recount how since that day you have cared and made sacrifices for me, opened up possibilities and given me the benefit of your knowledge and experience, and unhesitatingly shared with me your hardly won professional advantages. You have shown me the real nature of the world and the falsity of my dream-picture of it. You have proved to me that the man is even more important than the artist, and shown me the honour due to common everyday life and the ideas which spring from it. How shall I recall it and speak of it? If only I may be allowed to reach a point in my career honourable enough to give value to my witness to your truth, sincerity and goodness and to give you the blessed assurance of having enriched the world by a grateful artist, in the most honourable sense of the word!

Tears of sorrow come into my eyes when I remember that it was just what you felt obliged to do for me that was the inevitable cause of our swift separation. There I stood, poor and helpless, and you let me reap all that you had sown and prepared. You handed over to me that part of Germany which you were about to tour and where your name was already known and well spoken of. You provided me with the most flattering recommendations and transferred to me the favours intended for yourself. It was most unusual for one artist to send another in his place, and the interest thus aroused told in my favour, while it inspired me to do my very best in order to justify your kindness. Whom have I to thank for all this but you – you, whom I had misjudged and who nevertheless worked on my behalf with a true artist's generosity, simply because you thought that you had recognized in me a true artistic vocation. The magnitude of your sacrifice on my behalf can be gauged only by someone acquainted with the myriad details associated with an artist's tour and aware of the strange way in which an artistic reputation is made, spreading sparks which become a blaze in one region but go quite unrecognized in another. I can honestly say that I did recognize this sacrifice, and perhaps my proud acknowledgement of my indebtedness to you is the best way of expressing my gratitude.

Look, friend, there I am, engaging once again in that humble pride, or proud humility, that often raises my spirits and as often does harm to my reputation. Am I alone in this? or is it inherent in the artist's nature? I would rather that the latter were the case; for I do not yet understand myself well enough and would rather attribute any of my faults to that dark power which I recognize as holding sway over me. I can just imagine your laughing and saying that this is the easiest way to think one's own motives always beyond reproach; or would you perhaps say that in this belief I resemble a woman? Well, and are they not in actual fact all born artists in character? But my pen is running away with me, and I must return to the point of my letter. I have in the past had plenty of practical experience and learnt much theory, pondered on many remarks and discussed many subjects in my correspondence with you, who have often confirmed me in my opinions. Yet I have often had ruefully to admit that all my knowledge is fortuitous in origin, and that my education was never conducted according to any set plan. I have as a pupil in thorough-bass a damned clever doctor,[8] who wants to be able to accompany himself on the lute, and he often makes me feel quite uncomfortable with his multitudinous questions. He has no respect for the authority of great names, but always wants every point demonstrated by argument, with the result that I often find myself in a tight corner, despite all my knowledge. Every day I become more aware of the fact that we forbid one thing

---

[8]   Joseph Munding, an Augsburg doctor and amateur musician, was one of Weber's close friends. See above, No. 106.

and recommend another without giving any reasons or going on to explain the method. We say 'Bach wrote thus. Handel never wrote this. Mozart allowed himself such and such.' But if someone chances on a happy solution of a musical problem for which there is no precedent, it must at once be rejected simply because it cannot be proved that it is allowable. How lacking music is, by its very nature, in fixed points of leverage, as it were! Instinct, always instinct is the answer we give, but who can be sure that his 'instinct' is the right one? I have therefore made a firm resolution to treat art as objectively as any other subject. After all, you can say to the beginner in any other field 'First learn this, then that. One thing follows another until you are master of the subject,' Master? Well, up to a certain point at least.

Chapter 4   [1809]

Fragment of a musical journey, that will perhaps be published

Very pleased with a successful morning completing my symphony, followed by an excellent lunch, I took a quiet nap during which I dreamed that I was suddenly transported to the concert hall, where all the instruments of the orchestra were having a party, presided over by the tender-hearted and naïvely pert oboe. On the right was a group consisting of a viola d'amore, a basset-horn, a viola da gamba and a recorder, who were all bewailing the good old days. On the left was a circle round Lady Oboe, containing clarinets and flutes of different sizes and ages, with and without innumerable novel keys, while in the middle sat the courtly clavier, surrounded by a number of charming violins, all of the school of either Pleyel or Gyrowetz. The trumpets and horns were tippling in a corner, while piccolos and flageolets shrieked childish remarks to one another across the hall, which led Lady Oboe to remark that there was something distinctly like Jean Paul in their dispositions, made completely natural by the *Pestalozzi method.[9] All was merry and bright, until suddenly a sour-faced double bass, with a couple of his cello relations, burst in and attacked the conductor's

---

[9]   Jean Paul's novels were among the most widely read books of the day in Germany, being particularly admired for their ironic humour. Especially in connexion with the reference to Pestalozzi, it is possible that Weber had in mind Jean Paul's Rousseau-inspired educational novel *Die unsichtbare Loge* (1793) or his educational treatise *Levana* (1807).

stool with such violence that the clavier and all the stringed instruments present involuntarily echoed the attackers. 'No,' exclaimed the double bass, 'The devil take me if we are to have such compositions every day. I have just been at a rehearsal of one of our latest composers' symphonies. As you know, I am a fairly tough customer, but I could hardly bear it a moment longer and in another five minutes my sound-post would infallibly have collapsed and the strings of my very being snapped. If I was not made to dance about and rave like a goat and change myself into a violin – all in order to express the nonsensical ideas of this composer – may I become a dancing master's kit and earn my living by playing Müller's and Kauer's dance arrangements.'¹⁰

First Cello (mopping the sweat from his brow): '*Cher père* is quite right, and I am so *fatigué* that I cannot remember such an *échauffement* since *Cherubini's operas.'

Tutti: 'Tell us about it, go on!'

Second Cello: 'It's hardly a story that can be told or, indeed, listened to. For according to the principles instilled in me by my divine master *[Bernhard] Romberg, the symphony we have just performed is a musical monstrosity, in which no attention is paid to the nature of any instrument or the working-out of any musical idea – or indeed to anything except the desire to appear new and original. We were made to clamber up as high as the violins –'

First Cello (interrupting): '– as though we could not do it just as well as they!'

A Second Violin: 'A cobbler should stick to his last.'

Viola: 'Yes, for I am in the middle between you, and what would there be for me to do?'

First Cello: 'Oh! it's no use talking about you. You either jog along in unison with us or have a part like the violas in Cherubini's *Les Deux journées*, designed to create a feeling of uncanny excitement. Any talk of a good melodic line – '

First Oboe: 'As far as that goes, nothing can compare with me.'

First Clarinet: 'Allow us, Madame, to draw attention to our talents as well.'

First Flute: 'Oh! certainly for marches and weddings.'

First Bassoon: 'And who resembles the divine tenor voice as closely as I do?'

---

¹⁰   Despite their importance as *Singspiel* composers, *Wenzel Müller and Ferdinand Kauer earned some scorn from the Romantics as notoriously prolific: of Müller it was said that 'new operas sprout from him like mushrooms' (*AMZ* III (1801), 800).

First Horn: 'You're surely not imagining that you can combine tenderness with strength as I do?'

Clavier: 'And what's all this compared with the full harmonies that I can produce? Whereas you're all parts of a whole. I'm independent and –'

Tutti (shouting): 'Oh! hold your tongue, you can't even sustain a single note!'

First Oboe: 'You've no portamento.'

Two Flageolets: 'Mama's right there.'

Second Cello: 'You can't even produce a proper note for tuning in all this noise.'

Trumpets and Drums (interrupting *fortissimo*): 'Be quiet! We also want to make ourselves heard. What would the whole composition be like without the effect that we make? If we don't raise our voices, there's never any applause.'

Flute: 'Common people are certainly delighted by mere noise, but spiritual things need only be whispered.'

First Violin: 'And what would become of you all, if I weren't there to lead you?'

Double Bass (jumping up): 'But I maintain that it is *I* who hold you all together and you could do nothing without me.'

Tutti (shouting): 'I'm the soul of the music. It's nothing without me.'

Suddenly the *Kalkant*[11] entered the hall and the instruments crept nervously back to their places, for they were aware that it was his powerful hand that kept them together and was responsible for rehearsing. 'What', he cried, 'rebelling again, are you? Just wait, we'll soon be given Beethoven's Eroica Symphony and than I should like to see which of you can raise a limb or a key.'

'Oh! please, not that!' they all begged.

'Can't we have an Italian opera, where one gets a nap now and then?' suggested the viola.

'Fiddlesticks!' cried the Kalkant. 'You'll learn soon enough. Do you really think that in our enlightened days, when all barriers are down, a composer will forgo the giant sweep of his inspiration out of consideration for you? Heaven forfend! Nowadays there's no longer any thought of the clarity, the precision and the emotional reserve such as we find in the old masters – Gluck, Handel or Mozart. Not a bit of it. Listen to the description of the latest symphony I've just got from Vienna. First, we have a slow tempo, full of brief, disjointed ideas, none

---

[11]   An obsolete term for a bellows-treader or organ-blower, intended here as contemptuous term for a conductor.

of them having any connexion with each other, three or four notes every quarter of an hour! That's exciting! Then a hollow drum-roll and mysterious viola passages, all decked out with the right amount of silences and general pauses; eventually, when the listener has given up all hope of surviving the tension as far as the Allegro, there comes a furious tempo in which the chief aim is to prevent any principal idea from appearing, and the listener has to try to find one on his own; there's no lack of modulations; that doesn't matter, all that matters, as in *Paer's *Leonore*, is to make a chromatic run and stop on any note you like, and there's your modulation. Above all, one must shun rules, for they only cramp genius.'[12] Suddenly a string snapped on the guitar hanging over my head, and I awoke, terrified by the idea that I was on the way to becoming either a great modern composer or – a complete fool.

Thank you, friendly accompanist of my song, for your care of me. I hurried to my newly finished work, found it was not composed according to the learned *Kalkant*'s method, and went off at peace with myself and full of high expectations, to a performance of *Don Giovanni*.

Chapter 5

People had arrived early, and art and science were being discussed with great vivacity and pleasure, when Diehl burst in with a beaming face. 'Just imagine,' he said, 'in the near future we're to have *Wallenstein*[13] with no cuts, no cuts at all!' What a delight that meant for me who only knew the great eagle with his wings clipped and was now to see him rise in his full glory. 'But tell me,' he said, turning to Felix, 'how comes it that every theatre doesn't do the same?'

Felix: 'Both actors and management want to make an effect; it's the public that wants the whole work. But it's only when they're familiar with the cut version that they want the uncut. This has been true of Schiller's works and will be true of Shakespeare, Calderòn etc.'

Diehl: 'That's the wrong way round. I should have thought that the total effect could only be produced by giving the work complete.'

---

[12]   For some observations on Weber's attitude to Beethoven, and the allegation that this passage referred to him, see above, Introduction.

[13]   Schiller's vast trilogy was first performed in Weimar between 15 and 20 April 1799.

Felix: 'Of course, if you equate the "total effect" with a perfect reproduction of the poet's idea. In the first place the poet writes the work and unites all the invisible strands whose ends spring from the depths of the basic drama. In this way his poem grows into something which takes far longer to perform than what has come to be considered the normal time for a dramatic work in the theatre. So a producer with a good grasp of the whole takes hold of the text and begins to thin out the wood, losing much that is of value and may indeed seem to the author essential. In as much as the total drama is an intelligible and coherent unity, its appreciation is a matter for the audience, whose feelings must fill out the hints expressed by the poet's delicate interior organization and motivation. The listener is gripped and wants to repeat the pleasure on his own account. He wants to recall what has struck him most at each moment of the drama. He therefore reads the work in full and is delighted to find that what his own feelings have added to each scene is clearly expressed by the author, and much better than he himself could express it, and in what a shapely and pleasing form. Now he has mastered the poet. Now he wants to enjoy an uncut production. Now he feels that every cut is a lacuna or a mutilation, though at first it seemed no more than a necessary abbreviation. Now he can accustom himself to longer spells of attention than seemed possible to him before. He finds himself in a familiar garden, where at every step he expects to find a delightful flower; he looks forward to every vista that abruptly opens before him. Though everything is familiar, it still surprises him, because he knows how surprisingly it has all been created. The first time he was not sure whether he was in a garden or a maze; and it is only when he has traversed the whole, that he has a bird's-eye view of it and understands what he is being offered.'

Diehl: 'Yes, but why must he be in such a hurry? Why does he not start quietly at the beginning and review every detail in its proper place? The pity is that people who go to the theatre or any other artistic performance always wear seven-league boots!'

Felix: 'Comparisons are odious. But you surely will not deny that there is nothing sacrosanct about what is generally considered the normal length, or duration, of a play? And this is true in general of all proportions and limitations which have unconsciously and imperceptibly come to seem like natural laws. Can you yourself concentrate your attention on the course and development of a dramatic work for longer than three hours? Does not an impatient desire to know the course of the plot spoil your quiet appreciation of individual details which direct, or at least invite, that very appreciation? Don't interrupt me, but make the objection that, if this were the chief purpose of the work, you would need to see every play only once; at the end of the first performance it would have lost all interest, as one would know the outcome already.

Of course this is not in fact the chief purpose of any play, though woe befall it unless it has an interesting plot. It is not that the dry facts of the story are of such fearful importance that one would be frightened or amazed if one read them in a three-line paragraph in a newspaper. No, it is only when we learn exactly how and why an event took place as it did and affected the mentality and behaviour of those concerned – in fact when life itself is enacted before our eyes – that the writer and his work satisfy the listener's demands. When we know the exact course of the drama, every new performance should arouse our interest and gradually stir our emotions, just as on the first occasion. If this is not the case, then the author's chosen methods have failed in their purpose and his work may be a showpiece in the theatre and highly skilled in execution, but it lacks inner veracity and, therefore, lasting vitality.'

Diehl: 'I'm very keen to hear how you apply these principles to dramatic music. Which has priority there – the dramatic action or the static moment of passion, which in fact contradicts the nature of the music? By static I mean in fact – perhaps inaccurately, but simply as the antithesis of the dramatic action – the moment of passion held in suspension by the music.'

[1819]

Felix: 'You have described exactly the great rock on which operas and their composers are all too often wrecked. How hard it is for the composer to show whether he is capable of creating a work of the imagination that makes a lasting impression, or whether his work is no more than a succession of vivid but uncertain flashes of brilliance, individually attractive but leaving no lasting impression as a whole.[14]

In no art form is this latter so hard to avoid, and therefore so frequently encountered, as in opera. This is the great dividing-line between opera and straight drama. Of course when I speak of opera I am speaking of the German and French ideal, namely a self-sufficient

[14] The following four paragraphs, except for the last sentence, are repeated from Weber's review of Hoffmann's *Undine* (above, No. 87). The only significant alteration is that in his famous definition of the unified work of art, Weber here speaks of 'the kind of opera Germans and French want'; in his *Undine* review he mentions only Germans. Minor discrepancies in punctuation and sentence division have been ignored in translation.

work of art in which every feature and every contribution by the related arts are moulded together in a certain way and dissolve, to form a new world. In most cases individual numbers decide the fate of an opera. It is only rarely that such attractive individual features, which strike the listener immediately, disappear in the final impression of the work as a whole, as should ideally occur. For ideally the listener should fall in love with the whole work and only later pick out the details of which it is composed.

The very nature and inner constitution of opera – as a whole containing other wholes – has this essential drawback, which only a few heroes of the art have managed to surmount. Every musical number has its own proper architecture, which makes it an independent and organic unity; yet this should be absorbed in any study of the work as a whole. Ensembles, in particular, can and should show a number of different aspects simultaneously, a Janus-like image, whose different faces are visible at a single glance.

Herein lies the great and profound secret of music, something that can be felt but cannot be expressed in words. The ebb, the flow and all the conflicting tides of anger, love and 'the pleasure that's all but pain' are here united, where Salamander and Undine mingle and embrace one another.[15] In a word, what love is to human beings, music is to the other arts and to human beings, for it is indeed love itself, the purest and most ethereal language, myriad-faced and containing all the colours of the rainbow in every mode of feeling, uniquely true, to be understood simultaneously by human beings of a thousand different emotional complexions.

[1817]

This veracity of music's language, in whatever unexpected form it may appear, is finally victorious in asserting its rights. The fates of all eras of musical or representational art prove this completely and on many occasions. For example, nothing could seem more improbable than Gluck's works at a time when all sensibilities were overwhelmed and unmanned by the flood of Italian music, with its powerful sensuous charm. At the present time the artistic errors that threaten us are of quite a different kind, though perhaps even more dangerous. The circumstances of life today have made it inevitable that the two extremes of death and pleasure rule our lives. The horrors of war have depressed our spirits, and misery has been all too common, so that relief has been sought in the coarsest and most primitive forms in the arts.

---

[15] In the mediaeval temperaments of Paraclesus, Salamander was the spirit of fire, Undine the spirit of water.

The theatre has become little more than a peepshow in which the noble and satisfying excitement associated with true artistic pleasure has been carefully avoided, and in its stead we have been content with the titillations of trivial jokes and melodies and dazzled by pointless stage spectacle. Accustomed in everyday life to being astonished, nothing but astonishment will serve us in the theatre. Following the gradual development of a passion or a witty building-up of all the interests involved is considered exhausting, boring and – for the unobservant – unintelligible. It is a rare thing for an audience to bring to the theatre a tranquil, open mind, prepared for any kind of impression, or a mentality attuned to the subject of the play yet unprejudiced in attitude and feeling.'

'And,' exclaimed Diehl, 'just as the English National Debt is increased by individual extravagance, so musical borrowings and demands on artistic powers and means are so immoderate that it can only end in a total bankruptcy (although the debt is only to themselves)! The wealth of music produced by the recent interest in instrumental music is being monstrously misused. The luxuriant harmony and the excessively elaborate instrumentation employed in the most insignificant and most unpretentious works have reached an extraordinary pitch. Trombones are an everyday seasoning and no composer dreams of managing with less than four horns; and just as the French have made their *ragoûts* increasingly piquant, even to the point of lacerating the eater's gums, so it is with their music. They have mistaken for feeling what is in fact merely agreeable to the ear, and vice versa, and their naturally effervescent and revolutionary mentality has found expression in their music as well. They have sacrificed clarity and simplicity of harmony, just as they sacrificed the liberty of other nations, and trampling happily on the bleeding remains of the Beautiful and the Pure, have gone madly on their way.'

'Stop!' cried Felix, 'you have gone too far in your enthusiasm and fiery metaphors, and have forgotten an important truth. The famous composer to whom you referred[16] may indeed have been deafened rather than instructed by Mozart's profundity and romantic *élan*. He may indeed have been misled by Gluck's scrupulous truth of declamation and giant's strength and felt impelled to even stronger irritants owing to his hearers' blunted organs of hearing and his own desire to give every word the maximum weight that harmony and instrumentation can provide. He may have used every conceivable artificial combination and amalgamated them to a degree which makes his

16   Spontini. (Weber's MS note.)

music bizarre, but he was still true to his great genius in making each of his works absolutely individual, a real achievement wholly his own and wholly real. These works may not be immortal, since they lack the classical quality which alone confers immortality; but they will still remain the most remarkable amalgamation of the Romantic, the witty, the sincere and the disciplined to be found in the history of art.

At the present moment the danger lies rather with the sirocco of Rossini blowing from the south. His warmth will quickly disappear; for just as the bite of the tarantula makes people dance, it is not long before they sink exhausted to the ground – cured.'

At that moment the piano-tuner, who was sitting at his instrument listening to our conversation, struck up a mad tarantella and delighted the company by cleverly introducing a witty parody of 'Di tanti palpiti'.[17] With the nimbleness of a juggler, Diehl threw off his hooded brown cloak and interrupted the merriment, thundering from a chair at the company:[18]

[1819]

Hallo there! hallo there! tiddly-rum-ti-tum!
Things are looking lively here, but I'm not quite in the picture.
Are you composers of some sort? or Turks? or melody-makers?
Do you mock the art of music so, as though poor old Apollo
Had got the gout in both his hands and couldn't beat the time out?
Is it the time of orchestral plagues, with screaming flutes and beating drums?
You're not standing here with your hands in your pockets.
Hell's let loose in the notes I hear, Castel Bel Canto's fallen low,
All Italy's in the foeman's clutches, while composers merely loll at their ease,
Make mock of Nature and don't give a damn, worry about din not notes,
Prefer folly to truth, drive the listener mad, care for the honorarium
More than the honour. Music's friends sit in sackcloth and ashes,
While directors fill their pockets. Fugues are now fudged,
Students are too dense, melody's become a malady,
Classical art and all its joys are just replaced by rum-ti-tum.
What is the cause of it all? I'll tell you.
It's all on account of the sin of applauding, all the hurraying and 'bravo'-shouting
That the public loves, and a glittering passage that mounts like a rocket
Is just the magnet the box-office needs. After the scales, for better or worse
Follows the chatter, as sure as tears follow on onion-peeling, or

[17]   Tancredi's love-song in Act 1 of Rossini's *Tancredi*, a tune that swept Europe like wildfire in the wake of the opera's 1816 Vienna première.
[18]   This speech is a detailed parody, virtually line by line, of the Capuchin's sermon in Scene 8 of Schiller's *Wallensteins Lager*.

The tail comes after the donkey's head, which is a sacred rule, I've read.
There's one great commandment: thou shalt not
Belittle the old polyphony's rules –
But where is it more blasphemed against
Than in our newest compositions?
If for every pair of consecutive fifths
Or octaves found in the latest scores
The church-bells were rung in the country round,
There'd soon be a dearth of bell-ringers; or
If for each false accent that appears
From your dirty pens, there fell but a single hair from your head,
You'd all be bald overnight, though you had such a head of hair as
Absalom.
Old Handel was quite a musical swell,
And Gluck knew a thing or two as well,
Mozart, too, was quite original.
Where will you find the text that says
That they were all just ignorant fools?
Ink, I wager, is better employed on pure polyphony than on foul
Commonplaces, yes! common as dirt.
However, the man whose inkpot's full,
He's the offender with blot and blur.
There's another commandment: thou shalt not
Steal – well, that you observe most nicely,
For what you take you take quite openly.
Not a single note is safe in the stave from your vulture's claws,
No melody and no bass is safe from your German or Gallic shafts.
What does the preacher say? 'contenti
Estote!' – be content with your cake.
But does one catch the culprit, when
The trouble starts with the public, and
No one knows what goes on inside
The public's head –

Felix: 'One minute, please. Say what you like about us composers, but hands off the public!'

Diehl (jumping off his chair): 'And hands off my Rossini, too! Do you think that knowing all his innumerable weaknesses, I love him any the less? No, long live my dear young reprobate, *l'enfant chéri de la fortune!* Look how charmingly he hurries through the room, what witty glances he casts on all sides and the lovely, sweet-smelling flowers that he is placing in those ladies' laps! What does it matter if in his haste he treads on an old man's toes, knocks over a cup or indeed shatters the big looking-glass that reflects his image so flatteringly? One forgives a dashing boy like that, takes him affectionately by the arm and look – in his spirited fun he pretends to bite! Then off he goes past the school, where he makes fun of his poor comrades as they sweat away and at best are rewarded by the public with potatoes, while he munches marzipan.

The only thing that worries me is what will happen when he begins to want to be clever. Heaven send the fluttering dragon-fly a merciful flowery death before it tries to become a bee and puts everyone out by proving a wasp!'

Chapter 6   [1810]

I had just written the last note and was enjoying my careful tracing of the arabesques round the 'finis' mark.[19] In spirit I heard the whole work sounding in my ears, and a kind of absentminded reverie mixed with the satisfaction of finishing a work was enveloping me, when the door opened and in came my jolly poet. He was wearing mask and domino and took me by the sleeve with a hasty gesture of friendliness.

'Always working – it's not good for you! Come on, there's a glittering masquerade today – I mean the second one, nobody goes to the first. There'll be pretty girls, punch, music – poor in quality but enough to deafen you. The crudest remark is taken for a witticism and a mask enables one to tell women the truth for once in a while. Quick now! come on! the carriage is at the door and you've got all you need, so quick march!'

Before I had time to make up my mind, I found myself in the carriage, cloaked and hooded by my merry friend's burly hands, then led out of the carriage at the same speed, and there I was – in the shifting throng of brightly dressed forms, who on this one day had the right not to show the public their real personalities. I was soon woken from my reverie by being dug in the ribs by several pairs of dancers, and I gradually became accustomed to the hubbub.

A man wearing a mask is a different creature, and this shows that an important part is played in human life by our observation of formalities. One thinks and speaks with greater freedom with that little bit of waxed paper in front of one's face; at last the clumsy lover dares to confess his passion, the shy girl is not afraid of blushing as she believes that it is invisible, and even friends speak to each other more frankly and a nervous guest plucks up courage to try his wits on one of his hosts.

---

[19] Weber sometimes drew a pair of flourishes on either side of his signature to a piece of music.

My high-spirited companion did not fail to ogle, and even to make cutting remarks to the peasant girls, Vestal virgins, Turkish women and nuns as they passed by. I drew back a little. The crowd separated us and I found myself facing a couple of friendly-looking bats, who squeaked out to me, 'Not played the piano for a bit?' 'No' – 'Oh! we know who you are!' 'Very honoured, I'm sure!' A gardener's girl plucked my sleeve and offered me an orange – 'That's for your lovely playing a few days ago!' A devil came up to me and said 'Just compose that!' I read 'To Emilie', seized the note hastily and said 'Even at the devil's hands I respect whatever bears her name; you shall have it at the next masquerade'. A nun clung to my arm: 'The bad music must be torturing your connoisseur's ear.' Not at all, my dear! What does torture me is that no one will talk to an artist about anything except his art – something he does not want to discuss but to feel. And sick of being recognized by almost every mask, I retired to my box.

Soon, however, an extraordinary procession of people drew me back into the hall. A large crowd of masks entered by the wide-open doors, the oddest and craziest caricatures and apparitions, large and small, and dressed in the most varying shapes and costumes. The band stopped, and Hanswurst[20] asked the public for their attention while he spouted a long, declamatory, melopoetical, allegorical set of verses, and out stepped a creature of frosty appearance in a chequered garment with a card bearing the word 'Impartiality' stuck on its forehead, with 'Zeal for art' on its mouth and a music catalogue, full of slips of paper marking places, over its heart. It stuffed a cutting into its pocket which I immediately recognized as taken from a certain journal, and then prepared to declaim the following prologue.

Prologue

Most honoured and art-loving public, we
Have always been most anxious to impress
On you that it is not for gain that we
Perform for you. Yes, and the notices,
Quite impartial in every way,
Make it clear that it's purely from love
That we practise our art, and it's not unknown
For us to lose money thereby. Yet we

[20]   Though he makes his first appearance in the early sixteenth century (Luther wrote a pamphlet *Wider Hansworst* (1541)), the character became most popular in the eighteenth century as the idle, gluttonous, gross fool of low comedy, in general more a figure of misrule than the comic compère of Weber's skit.

Shall never cease to do our best
To give new proofs of our zeal. Each year
We undertake one major work,
Though nowadays it is dangerous
To take the risk of a novel score.
But what we say is, 'Long live composers!'
Our present piece we offer now
With neither praise not blame, the work
If it has any worth will speak for itself;
And what we'd like to make quite clear
Is that this is for mutual benefit,
To all concerned, or so we hope.
The most convincing proof of this
Is the handsome paper and very low price.

Hanswurst (*jumping up*):

Allow me to say a few words to conclude.
Here there's no need for the unities;
Grand opera is what we're bringing you now,
With every sort of effect combined.
The soprano will gargle seductively,
The heroic tenor move you by raving,
The fool with his adages make you laugh,
The orchestra will rage and bluster,
The ballerina show her calves,
The leader'll delight you by his fiddling,
The producer impress you with lightning and thunder
In order to win your favour – yes!
And if this doesn't shake you to your foundations
We still have something up our sleeve,
Horses and camels by the score,
No animal's proof 'gainst our love of art.
In short, by every means that men
Of genius have ever imagined, we trust
By every golden, glittering ploy
To make sure you enjoy yourselves
(The great tendency of the times);
For even without knowing what it all means,
When you go to sup after the theatre
And your mouths are full of art and food,
You declare, this or that girl was prettily turned out,
The patter was neatly mouthed,
But the whole wasn't properly understood
And so back you have to go again.

After Hanswurst had bowed and withdrawn, Italian Grand Opera appeared – a tall, gaunt, transparent figure with a featureless face which changed little whether representing hero, swain or barbarian, and was always marked by an extraordinary saccharine look. She wore a thin gown with a train, nondescript in colour and covered with little glittering stones, which attracted the spectators' attention. As she appeared there was a noise in the orchestra in order to silence the audience. In Italy this is called the overture.[21] Then she began to sing:

Scena

Recit. Oh! Dio...addio...
Arioso. Oh! non pianger, mio bene...
   Ti lascio, idol mio...oimè!
Allegro. Già la tromba...suona...
(*colla parte*) Per te morir io voglio... (*più stretto*) o felicità!

(On the 'tà' there is a trill lasting ten bars; this is wildly applauded by the audience.)

Duetto

Caro!...cara!...(*a due*) sorte amara...

(Because of the 'a's' of 'amara' there are the prettiest passages in thirds.)

Allegro. 'Oh! barbaro tormento...

(Nobody listened, but a connoisseur shouted 'Bravo!' and the whole audience followed suit *fortissimo*.)

Hanswurst (*enters, in ecstasy*):

No, nothing's so sweet as a sweet melody!
That is the mark of genius alone,
The truly pure, the noble, the great
Releasing itself in a flood of sound,
A delight that's given to every man,
Be he tailor or cook, he can understand;
In all these arias and duets
One has the impression of having heard
Them in a host of other places.
Ear and heart are filled with rapture,
One almost wants to die oneself
When one hears the hero's dying aria,
Of course, I admit that German composers
Won't hear a word of praise about
Our poor opera – *opera seria*'s

---

[21] There is perhaps here a retort to Schaul's *Briefe über den Geschmack in der Musik*, reviewed by Weber the year before this satire was written (see above, No. 2).

Quite their bugbear. They maintain
Characterization's wanting there.
All the Italians care about
Is the singer's voice, they say, that voice
That we all adore, and they have a lot
Of other objections too. We're lucky
To have a more varied work today.
The finest aria's sung by the Emperor,
And the prima donna is hoarse with rage
Because it's not she that's singing. The poor
Composer is almost in despair
At the thought of seeing his finest work
Unperformed, and so he has
To agree to a little rewriting here
And there, in order to save from cutting
His best numbers; he doesn't complain
Of having to do more work, and passes
Whatever the prima donna wants,
But she's changed her mind – she's so sensitive!
It may be a matter of just five notes
Down for the primo basso, and up
For the seconda donna – behold!
The work's a great success and is clapped,
Nobody's noticed a spot of transposition,
And as for 'character' – that's all right.
Yes, my friends, melody, that's what's needed,
Melody makes the whole world one,
It doesn't matter whether high
Or low – in C, in G, in D,
In a prison dark or a grassy field,
Man or animal, bear or hero,
As long as it's all cantabile,
That's the way to the listeners' heart!
And so I am willing to maintain
That Italian opera is my sole
Delight, and my conclusion is
That all the rest's not worth a straw. (*Exit* Hanswurst)

French Grand Opera enters[22] – she is a well-born Parisian, and wears
the *soccus*,[23] managing with a courtly grace her long and uncomfortably
constricting Greek garment. She always has the corps de ballet by her

[22] From a parody of grand opera which appeared in 1670 in Paris itself.
(Weber's footnote; in fact it appeared in 1778, and was even performed at
the Comédie-Italienne.)

[23] The *soccus* (sock) was the low-heeled shoe worn by comic actors in Greek
and Latin drama, as opposed to the *cothurnus* for tragic actors. The mistake
is presumably deliberate.

side, and there are a number of gods lurking in the background. The action takes place between twelve o'clock and midday.

Act 1

La Princesse: Cher prince, on nous unit.
Le Prince: J'en suis ravi, princesse.
                      Peuple, chantez, dansez, montrez votre allégresse!
Chorus: Chantons, dansons, montrons notre allégresse!

Act 2

La Princesse: Amour! (*Noise of battle. The Princess faints. The Prince enters fighting and is killed.*) Cher prince!
Le Prince: Hélas!
La Princesse: Quoi?
Le Prince: J'expire!
La Princesse: O malheur!
                      Peuple, chantez, dansez, montrez votre douleur!
Chorus: Chantons, dansons, montrons notre douleur!

(*March*)

Act 3
(*Pallas appears in the clouds*)

Pallas: Pallas te rend le jour.
La Princesse: Ah quel moment!
Le Prince: Où suis-je?
                      Peuple, chantez, dansez, célébrez ce prodige!
Chorus: Dansons, chantons, célébrons ce prodige!

End

[1813]

Hanswurst (*enters truculently and speaks loudly*):

Passion's the thing, declamatory rhetoric,
All the rest is worth nothing at all.
Soaring above all the ledger-lines, look!
There fly our passion's messengers wild!
Noble bass singer, now raise up your voice,
Boldness is all, come! why not invade
The tenor's preserve, that doughty youth
Will certainly do all he can to preserve

His territory, or at most lay claim
To the alto's domain, and so it goes on!
Higher and higher! mere nature's no bar,
If you don't have a tumble, you'll soon be in flight.
The feet of the dancers will further still more
The noble emotions that have been yours.
A French heart beats anxiously, lovingly too,
At the grief that's expressed in a bold entrechat,
And the holiest friendship is clearly beheld
In the turn and the whirl of a fine pirouette.
The song and the dance, the dance and the song,
Between them alone is the highest achieved.
Drums, horns (at least four) and trombones, my good friend,
Must be found in your orchestra, and in each bar
Seven modulations at least – who'll ask 'Why?'
As long as the public is with you? Let's have
Oboes, flutes, clarinets in abundance – more than three
Times as many as three operas need.
Let the basses and fiddles rage till they smoke,
And if you find place for the big bass drum,
Set your mind at rest and bother no more,
You're famous already, you're home and dry! (*Exit quickly*)

Then there was a moment's silence. The public gradually began to get restive. Another moment's silence, and the restiveness became more marked. German Opera still refused to appear. As the noise increased, the management became really embarrassed until Hanswurst appeared, exhausted and bathed in sweat, and said:

Ladies and gentlemen, forgive me if I have no time to say concisely what I am in haste to tell you. I really fail to understand you: I don't know what impression you give me. Where is the famous patience that you have so often shown? You were always ready to wait, as long as you had been firmly promised something. I really believe that you must be imagining that you have some kind of rights. Well, just you wait a moment longer, and I believe it's right to tell you the reason you have to wait. To be quite honest, German Opera is not at all well. She suffers from nervous cramps and can't stand properly. She is surrounded by would-be helpers, but falls from one faint into another. What is more, she is so swollen by all the claims that have been made on her behalf, that she cannot get into any clothes. It is no use the arrangers trying first a French and then an Italian frock; neither seems to fit anywhere. The more sleeves and trains and fronts they sew on, the worse it becomes.

Finally some Romantic tailors have hit on the happy notion of using a native German material, and wherever possible weaving into it everything in the way of guessing and believing, contrasts and feelings that have proved effective and exciting with other nationalities. Listen, ladies and gentlemen! You can hear the thunder directly above you, and it won't be long before the storm begins. (*Exit, exhausted, muttering as he goes.*) Once you're used to being a poetical Hanswurst, that damned prose is the very devil.

(*Solemn silence, and eager expectation in the audience.*)

Agnes Bernauer. A Romantic-patriotic music drama[24]

Characters: as many as necessary.
Scene: the heart of Germany.

Scene 1. Transformation scene.
Scene 2. Agnes and Brunhilde.

Agnes: Ah! my soul is weary, woebegone and exhausted.

Brunhilde: O my lady! let not the precipitous depths of human suffering exhaust you. If you, my mistress, seize on the profane, will you, noble lady, mistake my mistaken feelings?

Agnes: Come into the castle garden. There in the murky grove of terror I am more likely to receive the necessary revelation of my fate. (*Exeunt*)

Transformation

Duke (*with companions*): Knights, follow me into the Great Hall. Before tomorrow dawns she shall give you her hand, or the otters and serpents in the castle dungeons shall follow their instincts and...you understand. (*Exit*)

Transformation

Albrecht (*entering*): Caspar, follow me!

Transformation

A Spirit appears, with warning gestures

Albrecht: Who art thou, incomprehensible being?

Spirit: I have power to do all, but hasten, noble youth, I will come to thy rescue later.

Albrecht: Rescue her, or die in the attempt!

---

[24]   Agnes Bernauer was a girl of humble birth who in 1432 secretly married Duke Albrecht III; his father, Duke Ernst of Bavaria, had her thrown from the bridge at Straubing into the Danube in a sack. A *Ritterdrama* on the subject (1781) by Joseph August Törring (1753–1826) became widely popular, and was performed in Dresden as late as 1817. Weber has barely to exaggerate the tone of the original, and indeed there was a parody, *Agnes Bernauer. Ballade. Nach einer komisch-tragischen Aufführung derselben am Rhein* (1784). See O. Brahm; 'Das deutsche Ritterdrama', *Quellen und Forschungen zur Sprach- und Culturgeschichte der germanischen Völker*, ix, 40 (Strassburg, 1880).

Two Minstrels (*entering*): One moment, noble sir, and we will recount
the tale in song.

Transformation

Finale (*A tree-covered cliff. Backstage left a castle, opposite it a vineyard,
nearer the front a hermit's cave. Left front a cave, in front of it a leaf-covered
arbour, and mid-stage two hollow trees, with an underground passage in
front of them*. Hermit (*enters, singing a prayer*). Agnes (*sings an aria
in the castle, accompanied by a chorus of grape-pickers*). Albrecht (*asleep
in the arbour, singing fragments of song in his dreams*). Kaspar (*sings
in terror a Polonaise from the hollow trees*). Brigands (*sing a wild chorus
in the cave*). Spirits (*float above* Albrecht, *protecting him*). *Noise of battle
off-stage. Distant march from the other side. Of course all this happens
simultaneously. Two thunderbolts appear from different sides of the stage
and do some damage*)
All: Ha! (*Curtain*)

Act 2

Funeral March
(Agnes *is led on to the bridge at Straubing. She hangs from a nail-head
beneath the bridge*)
Albrecht (*enters with mounted mercenaries*): (*Additional aria*)

[1816]

(*Recitative*). Come, friends, there is no time to lose, one moment's delay
   will cost her life! Swear!
Chorus: We swear!
Albrecht: What an oath!
(*Allegro*)   Over rocks and seas
          Through glittering spears
          I rescue thee,
          In honour's name,
          Let none stand in my way
          Or death's shears are his fate.
          I see thy gestures,
          And the tears in thy eyes,
          Grave, just wait a moment!
(*Arioso*)   O maiden, O floweret, so fair and so still, let none be so
          bold...
Chorus: See – the hero – see – him – rave.
Albrecht: A wondrous groaning
          Deep in me moaning,

Anxious guessings
Waves of terror,
I must in myself behold.
(*Più stretto*) But no, I haste to thy rescue.
Chorus: Hasten!
Albrecht: Thy rescuer, I haste to rescue thee!
Chorus: Yes!
Albrecht: Hasting, rescuing, thee to rescue,
             Rescuing, hasting, chains are bursting –
             (*florid passage* – 'ha–ha–ha–ha–ha–hasten')
Chorus: Victory or death!
(*They all swim through the water, the* Chancellor *impales himself on a stake.*
Albrecht *bears his beloved away in his arms. The* Duke *appears, raging*)
Albrecht (*calling*): Father!
(*The* Duke *is at once moved to pity and blesses the dripping couple*)
Final Chorus: After rain there comes the sunshine. (*The bridge is
transformed into a halo, and all ends happily*)

[1818]

Hanswurst (*enters, lost in bitter thought*):

Something is on my mind – what can it be?
My eyes are dimmed with tears of pain,
Everywhere boiling and seething, art
Seems to be bearing another art.
O, noble German fatherland,
Thou hast persecuted and banished me
To foster worse – and foreign – fools;
Say, was this a good plan? was this wise?
The English, the Spanish, Italians and French
Are inspired by a single thought and aim,
To be true to themselves and their country's name;
And thou, German art, com'st to no conclusions,
Neglecting the gods' chief gifts to thee,
Thou hast abused thine own great strength,
Noble and pure creative endeavour.
No empty aping, but bringing to life,
The very stuff of divinity.

(*The audience is becoming restive, and there are some noisy stamps and
comments*: Hanswurst had become simply a fool, useless ethics etc.
Fates, machines, trombones! *He jumps across the stage*)

Forgive me, ladies and gentlemen,
One moment!
I've had a slight disaster, which
Is common with me, I don't know why.
This sort of philosophizing is

A bad old German habit, and
Is often hard to distinguish from
Madness – I've been fool enough to come on the scene before my time;
Another ten years, and what I say
Will perhaps be better received. But please
Don't be annoyed with poor old Kasperl,
Tomorrow I'm playing the Herr von Hasperl.
I've been seized with a kind of folkishness,
You'd have been quite right if you'd howled me down.
Tomorrow then I hope for the honour
Of playing the tailor with the shears.[25]

(*Wild applause.* Hanswurst *is called back four times; he speaks about tolerance, hard work and meeting again*)

[1811]

A mad, infectious waltz then struck up. The masks lost themselves among the dancing couples, and the spectators took the chance of expressing their opinions.

'What incredible nonsense,' exclaimed a blue domino near me. 'A mass of absurdities!' said another. 'It's impossible to see what he's getting at,' said a third.

A Spaniard: 'Allow me to differ – there's a profound intelligence at work there, which I find amazingly attractive.'

Blue Domino: 'Did you really grasp what he said and understand it?'

Spaniard: 'I wouldn't go so far as to say that, but even so...'

Blue Domino: 'No, I say that it's bad – I know the author, unless I am very much mistaken, and that brain never produces anything intelligent, miserable lines...'

Hanswurst: 'Ah! blue knight, just lend me your lance...'

The Domino took to his heels.

Hanswurst: 'Aha! the critic Spiegelberg, I know him.' (*Exit*)

Meanwhile at the buffet a pretty little peasant girl went up to a Turkish woman. 'That really is sad, that you weren't there. It was such an amusing act – one of them had a very pretty frock – might be rather a bore but perfectly nice. The other made us die of laughing by the faces she made, yes, and then it got wonderfully creepy, ooh! I loved every minute of it.'

A Gypsy: 'Yes, it was really quite divine!'

'No,' exclaimed my poet, as he raised the glass of punch to his lips

---

[25] 'Ich spel' den Schneider mit der Scher': the reference is to Schneider Fips in *Kotzebue's exceedingly popular one-act *Lustspiel*, *Die gefährliche Nachbarschaft* (1806).

to drain it, 'What a lot of idiotic remarks! One man finds the whole thing silly, another quite divine, and a third "profoundly intelligent" simply because he can't understand it; and this girl here calls it "heavenly" because of a few pretty rags'.

Felix: 'Dear friend, that is the public in a nutshell, everywhere and in every age. Every man-jack thinks that in return for paying the price of a ticket he is entitled to give a judgement on matters that he doesn't understand, and has never really thought about. The work of an author's lifetime may well depend on his reaction, which depends entirely on his mood of the moment, so that on one occasion he finds a thing superb which on another he will find boring. A clumsy scene-shifter who spoils the effect of a single scene is quite enough to affect his judgement of the whole work; and this is true of all the public, whether they sit in the gallery, the boxes or the stalls.'

Diehl: 'You're quite right, my experience is the same as yours; and I have also noticed that Sunday audiences are quite different from those of any other day. The plebs come to the theatre after a good meal, when all they want is to be amused. They see something like *Das Donauweibchen*, laugh themselves silly, applaud and get some of the actors back on the stage, and lo and behold! the thing's a howling success.'

Felix: 'Then the mob of the gentry get to hear about it, want to see it, run it down, but go back to see it again; and that's the way public taste is ruined. For it is absolutely true that the public can be lured to the theatre. Give them real works of art, and in the end they will learn to pick out the best and make nice distinctions.'

Diehl: 'Between ourselves, my friend, much as I value music, your wretched operas have been responsible for a lot of harm.'

Felix: 'I admit they are hard to defend. But how often must I point out to you that justified as your complaint may be in individual cases, generally speaking...'

'Thief! stop thief! this way...no...the other way' – the cry was universal, and in the general confusion I was momentarily separated from my friend and was just pushing my way through the crowd to find him, when my arm was seized by a heavily disguised mask. 'Found, Prince.' I looked him up and down and, thinking it was a joke, was about to continue on my way when he spoke to me again. 'You must recognize me surely, or am I so unrecognizable that Your Highness does not know his humble servant – ' (and he whispered in my ear the entirely unfamiliar name 'Dario').

[1811]

Myself: 'Sir, You are mistaking me for someone else.'

Mask: 'No mistake; Your Highness came earlier than I expected, but just in time. Your Highness must make haste, it is high time and Emilie...'

'What was that? Emilie?' I exclaimed, and my imagination went madly to work, as I observed the stranger with the greatest care.

Mask: 'Yes, Emilie is entirely wrapped up in the dancing there, and at last the happy moment has come, thanks to my zeal in your service, when Your Highness can achieve the object of his desire or at least prepare the way to such an achievement.'

Myself (full of suppressed rage): 'You're a very good friend' – and as I spoke, I squeezed his hand so tightly that he must have wanted to scream.

Mask (concealing his pain): 'Yes, I can quite imagine Your Highness's passionate excitement, but make haste or my arrangements will come to nothing. As we have agreed, I have ordered Lieutenant F and Wilhelm to keep a close watch on Emilie. She is an enthusiastic dancer, and both of them are excellent dancers, too. A glass of punch, pressed on the lady, won't fail to have a certain effect and the neighbouring room has been prepared, where she can be lured on some pretext or other. One of our friends, who is an expert in such matters, has undertaken to keep the aunt's attention engaged. Your Highness appears unexpectedly in the room, the others unexpectedly withdraw. Some narcotic perfumes in the air and a Prince...what a combination! More than enough to get the better of such a flimsy creation of the brain as a woman's virtue. It cannot fail.'

I could scarcely contain myself.

'The two black Dominoes with red feathers,' continued the mask, 'are members of our party. Emilie is wearing a simple white frock with mauve ribbons – Your Highness holding the sash in his hands will be the signal of success; but now, I urgently need Your Highness's orders for, I repeat, it is high time...'

'Quite,' I returned, having in that instant made up my mind. 'It is indeed high time. Wait for me by that pillar, I will reconnoitre myself and give Wilhelm his orders!'

'I had almost forgotten the most important thing,' he called after me. 'The password for the evening is "Joy".'

'Good,' I exclaimed, and disappeared in the throng, to look for my friend Diehl. I was the prey of a host of mad, torturing feelings; a thousand conflicting plans crossed my mind. First one seemed best, then another, and in the meantime every moment was precious. Fool, said I to myself, you have only to hear Emilie's name and you fly off the handle. What evidence have you that this is your Emilie? But even supposing that it is not, what I am called upon to do is to prevent an odious prank being played, and so no more talk, but quick to action! And then by sheer good fortune up came my poet. I embraced him warmly, as though we had not met for years; and I suddenly realized clearly what must be done.

'I have something I want you to do, a deed of daring, but it must be done quickly and cleverly.'

'Excellent,' he said. 'But where? how? and when?'

I outlined the position to him in a few words and asked him to go immediately to the couple who were dancing, and whisper the password. He must take Emilie's arm at all costs, even if she resisted him, get her into the first carriage he saw and take her home, while I changed my mask and waited to see how things turned out.

'You can bring me the mauve sash as token of your mission's success and now fly! not a moment more at the risk of your friend's affection, even perhaps his life!'

Diehl: 'Don't be so worried, this is just the affair for me. You can depend on me to rescue her from the clutches of ten thousand devils.'

Away he hurried, while I changed my mask. The first moment of passion was over and I took quiet stock of myself; for my plan had been made in the twinkling of an eye, and entirely by instinct, upon which I could not rely completely.

Why did you not rescue her yourself? asked my intelligence, and my emotions answered quietly – that I was so flattered by the thought that it was *my* Emilie who was to be rescued that I could hardly have borne the certainty that I was mistaken. My imagination was then only too delighted to find another solution, which could boast the fine stamp of unselfishness. Do head and heart, then, live in perpetual enmity with each other? Are they always seeking to outdo each other, and is the right hand never to know what the left hand is doing, even when it is plain for all to see? That is a perpetual conundrum to you and every other human being!

With every sense alert, I approached Dario, who was leaning against his pillar with every sign of the most lively impatience. And in fact it seemed that matters were moving too slowly for him, so that he left his pillar and disappeared. I wandered about like a man in a dream,

anxious and fearful because my friend did not return. 'Oh! go away!'
I said crossly to an importunate Policinello determined to entertain me
with his jokes.

'Now, now, friend,' said he, 'no need to be so ill-tempered,' and
flourished the mauve sash under my nose.

'Why, it's you, in this disguise! Quick, tell me!'

'Everything in due time, brother; first, I want a glass of punch.'

We went into a side room, and after several good drinks Diehl began
to talk.

'Everything went perfectly; I gave the password and was greeted
politely. Emilie was astonished when I took her arm and began to lead
her away. She was offended when I said, "I will take you to your
carriage", cried out, and was within an ace of ruining the whole affair.
I then explained to her in a few words that there was a design on her
virtue, that an unknown nobleman (that's you, brother) had entrusted
me with the task of rescuing her in the only way possible, and would
she please, for heaven's sake, tell the coachman her address. You
should have seen the dear little creature then, in tears of happy
gratitude that made me, I confess, quite sentimental. At home, too,
when she took off her mask and looked at me with that angelic little
face of hers, stammering her thanks to me in the most touching way
when I asked for the sash – then, brother, I quite made up my mind
that if she is not your Emilie, then by your leave she shall be mine!'

'Well, go on, how was she when you left her?'

'Well, you see, hitherto it had been a fairly ordinary affair, without
much amusement. So I was bold enough to try a bit of a variation and,
as it were, work in a counter-subject.'

Myself: 'You don't mean to say that –'

He: 'Yes, just listen. When I left her, I thought of a marvellous joke.
I ran my mind through a list of my acquaintance in search of an
amiable and easy-going person, someone who did not belong to the
race of prudes and was also immediately available. I soon thought of
someone, and while I was still on Emilie's doorstep I went back and
asked her for her whole toilette.'

Myself: 'You monster! the frock she was wearing –'

He: 'Quiet, quiet, you talk like a lover, which means like a fool – in
fact, she gave me her frock and off I went with it to a certain little
friend of mine, made her put it on, gave her some instructions and told
her that there was some money to be made if she played her cards
cleverly. I took her back to the hall, entrusted her to one of the black
Dominoes, whom I told to take her to the room arranged. And just as

I had finished my little operation, the Prince himself – whom I know very well – arrived in the hall.'

Myself: 'And then?'

He: 'Oh! after that I don't know anything, except that I left my pseudo-Emilie to her fate, changed my clothes and now present myself as your humble servant.'

Myself: 'But what you have done is a monstrous, unthinking thing – after all, the girl knows you.'

He: 'Oh! don't worry your head about that. The likes of her don't often see me and when they do, it's never alone. What's more, she's only just come here and is a new acquisition of mine. All the same, I'd give something to see the face His Highness pulls when he finds himself alone not with the severe angel of virtue but with such a meek and willing little bird as I sent him in her place.'

Myself: 'However that may be, I think we ought to go now. Presumably you know Emilie's address?'

He (beating his brow): 'What a fool I am! I never thought of it again, thanks to my pretty little plan.'

Myself: 'In fact, there's absolutely no hope of ever discovering whether it really was she or not? Come on, I must have some sleep and I'm nauseated by all this gaiety and excitement.'

[1810]

I spent a sleepless night, followed by a series of dreamlike days, my mind a blank. I was a prey to that unhappy mood, common among passionate natures, whose sensation of unhappiness is caused more by their own temperaments than by external events. While others feel a quiet joy, such spirits are wrapped in exaltation. When others are merely downcast, they are consumed by grief. All their lives, their feelings and their actions are marked by extremes. And it is just this boundless, all-embracing warmth that is alone capable of understanding Schiller's 'Seid umschlungen Millionen. Diesen Kuss der ganzen Welt!',[26] but also accounts for their unhappiness, their feeling of an interior void that can never be filled.

I had recourse to music, in the hope of being able to express my feelings in sound, driven as I was by passion and heated to fever-pitch, but in vain. My mind was a chaos, my sensibilities a swift succession

---

[26] Weber had once planned a setting of these words, most famous now from Beethoven's Ninth Symphony; to Simrock he wrote, 'Among other things I'm working on Schiller's *Ode to Joy*, large, with chorus and orchestra...I regard it as the only one of Schiller's poems suitable for such extended treatment' (letter of 11 June 1811).

of births and deaths, while each new phase ended in a mood of dull, pensive vacuity of mind. And so the usual belief that a good-humoured man writes good-humoured music, the melancholy man melancholy music, was disproved in my case. In fact this belief shows an ignorance of human nature. All deep feelings are conscious, but not all find expression. Artistic creation demands a time of tranquillity of mind, when a man is capable of an individual, deliberately induced enthusiasm and can still stand outside himself, as it were, and transport himself into the object which he wishes to create.[27]

I was far from being in this condition, and it was only gradually that I regained my peace of mind. This latest sequence of events had at first seemed to bring Emilie within my grasp, but had in fact frustrated all my fairest dreams; for I was all but convinced that I should never find her again. Fate, I believed, had not created us for each other; and common sense and reflection both told me that I should gradually become less sensible of her loss and then eventually forget her. The chance sight of my fancy-dress brought back a flood of memories of her. Feeling mechanically in the pocket of the coat I had worn that evening, I found a scrap of paper which I at once recognized as the poem which the devil had given me to compose and I had promised to bring to the next masquerade. The fact that it was addressed to Emilie had been sufficient reason, but now I wanted to look more closely at its actual content. I started reading, and was delighted by the writer's charming and amiable tone. I read the poem again, and after this second reading I already had the melody clear in my mind. I hastened to commit it to paper and was busy polishing and rounding it off when I was interrupted by my friend Diehl.

'Well, thank heaven for that – you look contented and in a good humour, as you are working. Am I interrupting you?'

[27] This remark may suggest to English readers the famous definition of poetry as 'emotion recollected in tranquillity', in the Preface to the second edition of Wordsworth's and Coleridge's *Lyrical Ballads* (1800). However, the direct influence is Friedrich Wilhelm von Schelling, whose works Weber had studied in Stuttgart and whom he came to know personally in Munich in 1811. Weber's passage suggests Schelling's comments about the ego as simultaneously subjective and objective being, and about the purpose of his so-called 'transcendental idealism' – 'to proceed from the subjective as from the first and absolute and let the objective arise from it' (*System des transzendentalen Idealismus* (Tübingen, 1800)). An important element in his philosophy is the idea (one which greatly appealed to the Romantics) of spirit as the highest manifestation of Nature and inseparable from it, an idea which also coloured Weber's views about creativity. Neither Wordsworth nor Coleridge knew any Schelling in 1800, though they later read him.

Myself: 'Yes and no – in any case please stay.'

Diehl: 'This has always been a puzzle to me, and one which I wanted you to explain to me – how you carry on a conversation and compose at the same time?'

Myself: 'Yes, friend, it is almost as though Plato were right and men – or at least I – had two souls. In any case I clearly contain two "things", of which one is concerned with composition and the other with chatter. For I can talk easily and coherently about quite other subjects while I am forming and "composing" musical ideas with my whole attention. But I must admit that it has me in its grip, this composing, and I feel like someone who is being mesmerized, with my mouth speaking of matters of which I in fact know nothing whatever.'

Diehl: 'And is this true of all kinds of composition?'

Myself: 'No – at least not entirely. With the so-called strict forms, such as fugues and so on, it's harder to combine the two activities.'

Diehl: 'That's strange, as I should have thought that such things as that needed no great effort of your imagination, only a first-class knowledge of your Kirnberger, your Fux, your Wolf or whatever the brutes are called.'[28]

Myself: 'Oh! no, actually it's in abstract work such as this that one has most need of one's feelings to act as guides, so that one doesn't founder in the dry sands of boredom, misled by mere academic fluency.'

Diehl: 'Then you're not writing any fugues while you're talking so intelligently to me?'

Myself: 'You non-musicians really have got your knives into the poor fugues, haven't you? No, I've just composed a song.'

Chapter 7   [1811]

Escaping from the social round, I enter my quiet, lonely room and feel the blessed cloak of solitude round me. Here at least I can lay aside the compulsive mask with which I deliberately hide my inner being from my fellow men. I had to fight hard against circumstance to achieve this semblance of tranquillity, but not many will have divined beneath my friendly and even cheerful exterior the grief that consumes me, galling and gnawing at both mind and body.

It is only under pressure that the wave forms and the pen writes its

[28]   Among the most widely respected manuals of theory in early-nineteenth-century Germany were Johann Kirnberger's *Die Kunst des reinen Satzes* (Berlin, 1771–6), Johann Fux's *Gradus ad Parnassum* (Vienna, 1725) and, to a lesser extent, Ernst Wolf's *Musikalischer Unterricht* (Dresden, 1788).

fastest, and it is only the most unfavourable circumstances and situations that breed great men. My expectation of greatness is indeed well founded, for no mortal can boast of circumstances more odious, more depressing and more calculated to frustrate talent than mine. In everything that I have undertaken, trivial or important, fate has placed obstacles in my path; and if I have succeeded in anything, then the barriers which I have had to surmount and the difficulties which I have had to overcome have been such that they have robbed success of its sweetness. An almost punctilious insensibility to fate's blows is the only advantage gained, and together with this goes the crushing feeling that even joy is incapable of making any impression on me, now that it is inevitably accompanied by the haunting conviction that it is only in bitterness that I can experience it. From the moment of my birth my life-line has been unlike that of other men. I have no happy memories of childish illusions or the freedoms of youth. I am still young in years, but old in experience, and this is all on my own account, all due to myself and not to others. I have never been in love, because my intelligence has told me all too soon that all the women who, in my foolishness, I imagined loved me were acting from the meanest motives and merely playing with me. One pretended to love me simply because I was the only man in the town under forty, another was attracted by my uniform, and a third perhaps really believed that she loved me, simply because she felt the need of a love-affair and I happened to appear at that moment in her circle of friends. My belief in womankind, which was once a high ideal, is dead, and with it has vanished a large part of my expectation of human happiness. If I could only find one at least clever enough in her deceiving of me to make me believe her! I should be grateful to her even when I realized my mistake.

I feel that I must love: I adore women but at the same time hate and despise them. All I have known is the tender affection of brothers and sisters. My mother died early and my father loved me indulgently, so that in spite of all the love and respect I had for him, he lost my confidence. I often thought that he was weak with me, and this kind of love is never forgiven.

I thought that I had found friends. It was simply social proximity that attached them to me, and when this ceased I was forgotten. I had recourse to art, idolized great artists; and when I got to know them better, found that they were little better than myself. If masters disagree, what is the pupil to do? I should indeed have been lost, had art herself not dictated the terms of her service! And could she, my only comfort, stand before me like an enemy and, even as I embraced her, strike me to the ground in awareness of my nothingness? It is life's constricting circumstances that, like a shirt of Nessus,[29] put me at variance with myself, my friends, God and art. I achieve my own destruction by adapting myself; even as I laugh I begin to wilt, and with a witticism I condemn myself to death.

In short, the fate of humanity is pitiable, never approaching perfection, always dissatisfied and torn by inner dissensions. Man is the personification of ceaseless vacillation and activity, lacking strength, will-power and repose. There is no certainty in the momentary appearance of these things, and a proof of this is to be found in what I am writing, coming as it does from the depths of my being.

Chapter 8 (Don Juan)

The floor of the theatre was fairly full and the boxes were empty, and this proved at once, had I needed any proof, that something good was to be given. I planted myself in the middle, next to a few people who seemed to promise the least disturbance. One sat with his chin propped on the knob of his stick, looking at everything sideways and furtively, as though he had no right to be there. If some bespectacled young gentleman passed, he concealed his regret and astonishment by deep sighs, while his whole appearance, including his clothes, suggested a bravura aria of Leo's[30] time and showed me that he must be fifty years my senior. My other neighbour had very marked features, sparkling eyes and a black wig. He must have spent some time in Italy, as he became impatient for the work to begin and muttered a number of oaths and prayers to himself, only at the end revealing himself as a good German by uttering a hearty 'Kreuzdonnerwetter!'

Marginal notes to a preparatory sketch of Tonkünstlers Leben
[1817]

Pebble. Rounded by the waves until halted by the moss of love.

Facts about the musical workhouse. An article in the *Sachsenspiegel* on wandering musicians: musicians not to be tolerated in decent society.

---

[29]   The shirt, poisoned by the blood of a centaur slain by Hercules, which in turn tormented him to the point of self-immolation when he put it on.

[30]   Leonardo Leo (1694–1744).

Acquaintance with Diehl. Door banged: someone falls downstairs on top of him, picks himself up quickly, embraces him warmly, and expresses gratitude for the good fortune of falling on Felix. 'Are you mad, sir, or do you take me for a fool? Who are you?' 'I am nothing, but may I ask who you are?' I, with a sigh: 'I am not really anything either, but people like me are generally called artists. I also have tricks of my own, such as making a publisher pay and so on. If you like, we'll begin with the second year of our friendship' etc.

Kapellmeister Strich, who strikes out everything.

Hissing from the floor of the Prague theatre.

Criticizing listeners, whose ears eventually become sort of skeleton tools, by means of which everything they hear is immediately robbed of its bloom and thoroughly ransacked with a view to later transformation, if necessary, into toothpicks, enthusiastically appreciated or – if necessary – subjected to personal 'arrangement'.

Italian cadenzas, a scaffolding on which the singer can hang his best jewellery, wearing whatever he likes. Black scaffolding at an illumination.

Diehl sketches plan for musical prison and workhouse.

A chapter headed by musical notes, ♩ ♩ etc. which eventually, when the author reviews his life, become a choral cadence after having first appeared as a canon *al rovescio*, i.e. reading the same both ways.

I find my style highly coloured and – because its intention is to give an exhaustive account – slightly precious and bombastic. However I cannot divorce myself from it, however much I may respect and be deeply devoted to the clarity of a Goethe, a Schlegel or a Tieck. Perhaps it may be my very musicality that accounts for it. The many descriptive adjectives in a language closely resemble the instrumentation of a musical idea. 1 am conscious of being able to reproduce such an idea with just as much clarity as I conceived it, though this is very seldom true of ideas which I wish to express in words.

The hardest thing to bear is the congratulation of fools: being hissed requires much less patience than being applauded by the ignorant, whose ears one feels like boxing. Anyone who has learnt to swallow such applause is well on the road to self-deception and worldly wisdom, and I offer him my congratulations.

[1816]

The specification of certain historical and artistic periods according to universally similar forms and usages in everyday life and in the arts. These can be reduced almost to individual bars, lines and ceremonies, e.g. the first period, pre-Luther. Sharp outline in draughtsmanship, for that reason approaching caricature. Everything archaic marked by a certain stiffness, sincerity, pedantry-like farthingales. The same is true of dances. Old furniture, angular, wooden and spiky, resembles jigs, sarabandes etc. as opposed to the latest dances which are orgiastic, voluptuous, bold.

Second epoch, Sebastian Bach. Artificiality. Circular, mirror and *al rovescio* canons. Long ritornellos, long sleeves; angular tables and furniture, artificially ornamented. Angular part-writing and stiffness, no melody. Eye-music. Poems without rhyme. Quartet on the open strings. Old forms grandiose, e.g. Bach's *Magnificat*. Like old church-towers. Short period with Gessner etc., Pleyel and, at least in part, Haydn. Apparent unintelligibility of Klopstock and Mozart.

Third period. Fast-moving wars, fast tempos. Old and new conception of the Allegro overlap each other. Mysticism and Romanticism in poetry and music. Comedy. Example: Isegrim.[31]

Thoughts and notes for the novel

Separation of theory and practice. The latter must be innate and part of education, as part of nature and life. Later, when a man's intelligence is in any case more mature, he can make judgements, evaluate and move with greater circumspection.

[1818]

It really is a strange thing in life that one behaves so badly to one's nearest and dearest, for with anyone else, and in any other matter, one is scrupulous to answer by return of post. If this experience were confined to you and me, I should find it inexplicable and unpardonable: but since I have the same experience with other of my closest friends, and they with me, I think I can perhaps guess the explanation. In dealing with people who are complete, or virtual, strangers, one makes use of accepted social forms, confining oneself strictly to the matter in hand; no more is required of one. But it is different with a friend. One's affection forbids any half measures and one wants him to share one's life and interests, one's joys and sorrows. Nothing, we feel, that concerns us is too small to interest him, and we should like to share every experience with him at the end of every day. The greater the distance that separates us, the rarer our correspondence. And should

---

[31] Originally the name of a hero in the sagas, Isegrim became the name for the wolf in animal stories, as in *Reynard the Fox*; hence it was applied to violent, rapacious characters.

circumstances have prevented us from informing each other of our life and experience for some considerable time, we have the unsatisfactory feeling of having concealed something from him, something impossible or difficult to retrieve – and so an apparent rift can form and be a grief to both parties.

From Goethe's *Die Wahlverwandtschaften*: 'There is no surer way of retiring from the world than through art, which also provides the surest way of attaching oneself to the world.'[32]

An apparently disconnected flight of imagination, that seems to be a *Phantasiestück* rather than a movement obeying the normal rules of musical composition, if it is to be worth anything, can be attempted only by quite outstanding geniuses – men who create a world which is only apparently chaotic and really has an inner coherence that is absolutely sincere in feeling, if only one can tune one's own feelings to the same pitch. In music, on the other hand, there is already so much that is vague in expression and so much remains for the individual listener to supply from his own feelings, that such a sympathy is at best possible only to individual spirits who are in complete harmony with each other – I mean that sympathetic understanding of precisely *this* emotional development taking place in precisely *this* manner, finding precisely *these* contrasts necessary and *this* sense true. The mark of the true master, nevertheless, is to exercise an absolute control over his own and his listeners' feelings, and to reproduce with tenacious veracity his own emotional experience, making no use of any other means than the colours and shadings best calculated to create immediately in the listener a picture perfect in every detail.

True stories are often the most improbable and, if told in fictional form, would be declared quite mad. It is a strange characteristic of human life to avoid the obvious and so give truth the hallmark of fiction. In fact one could almost say that not everything that has actually taken place is true: or that there are things which have in fact taken place but which when recounted become lies.

The gift of anything unique or rare attains its importance by its resemblance to a lovers' secret. This may well be an open secret to the rest of the world, but possesses for the two concerned the magic veil which is the distinctive mark of a secret between lovers.

What an effective passage! Look! The modulation in the next three or four bars – it may even be in a single bar – is taken and placed as it were in spirits of wine. How it has been arrived at, why it must have exactly that effect and no other because of the place it occupies – no

[32]   From Part II, ch. 5 (one of the maxims in Ottilie's journal).

one considers such things. You might as well cut a single nose or felicitous light-effect from a canvas and display it as a rarity. The art lies not so much in the passage itself as in its context.

Harmful effect on young minds (and undesirable imitation) of stories of great masters as quick workers.[33]

Truth is the unchanging divine ray, only breaking through the soul's clouds and giving the prism of the imagination its different colours.

Vanity and self-love in women assert their rights whatever the circumstances may be. Flatter them when and where you will, even in the most melancholy circumstances, and they will inhale with delight the proffered incense.

Malicious people (especially German composers) are always ready to say nasty things about Italian opera. They maintain, for instance, that even the best Italian composers are unable to depict character in music. But this is all rather exaggerated; after all, the ear is always flattered, melody is always the first consideration. It is true that in this particular opera the prima donna had the misfortune of being hoarse; the famous composer, to save his best numbers, transposed her aria so that the primo basso could sing it, while the seconda donna took over the primo basso's aria in exchange – and all this without a soul noticing anything amiss with the characterization. But after all, that is the beauty of real music, that it is delightful whoever sings it and whatever key it may be in – it is always real music. Universality and an Italian aria fit everything, and for that reason I maintain that Italian music has primacy.

Composer's routine. Thoughts (or the soul) are like an additional limb of the body and have to be fed and educated in order to follow a certain course. A theatre composer is therefore just as well qualified to write good symphonies as vice versa. One's first experiment in a new genre is always the most difficult; it is easy to fall into mere imitation. After the first experience of shaping one's ideas according to a new model, all is well; that is why Haydn is so great a symphonist etc. All melodies automatically take on this character, this pattern. Genius is universal and whoever possesses it can do anything – the form it takes is a matter of chance or circumstance. It is not possible to excel at the same time in all styles and genres, that is why composers devote themselves to different genres at different times in their careers; all good operas have points of resemblance.

---

[33]   Cf. above, No. 106.

Catalogue of favourite works

The Creation for one flute.

The Battle of Austerlitz for two guitars.

The Seasons for two little flageolets, arranged by A. E. Müller[34] of Leipzig.

Musical Bouquet, a monthly journal for cultured amateurs, to be played for private enjoyment on the clavier or fortepiano. Included are the finale of *Don Giovanni* Act 1, with fingering, arranged for solo voice.

Bürger's *Lenore* and Schiller's *Die Kindesmörderin*[35] arranged to well known folk-tunes.

A decoration is a patent, pinned to the wearer's chest, ensuring that his every remark will be answered by a deep bow.

Only a note of deep harmonic affinity makes a string vibrate, waking its inner life though still untouched, and this closely related note, if sounded too loudly, can shatter a glass. Thus it is with the human heart, which sounds in harmony if the right note be struck, and can in the same way be shattered.

Amateurishness. 'I particularly admire a player's treatment of *piano* and *forte*: as soon as I have learnt my piece, I can't wait to show how well I can do it.'

Italian music – orchestration. Oboi coi flauti, flauti coi violini. Fagotto col basso. Violino secondo col primo. Viola col basso. Voice ad libitum, violins follow voice.

---

[34]   August Eberhard Müller (1767–1817), cantor of St Thomas's, Leipzig; his works included an *Elementarbuch für Flöten-Spieler* (Leipzig, n.d.).

[35]   Both ballads were exceedingly popular in their day.

Biographical glossary

Allram, Joseph (1778–1835). He made his début in Prague in 1798, remaining at the Landestheater until 1834. He was especially popular in *buffo* roles. In *Wenzel Müller's day he sang in many of Raimund's pieces for which Müller wrote the music; in Weber's, he generally sang secondary bass roles. His wife Marie (born Illner) sang soubrette roles but also appeared as Donna Elvira, and as Marzelline (*Fidelio*). Weber noted that she was 'also excellent in older roles...proved herself good at everything, and also appears in drama' (Notizen-Buch). In 1816 Weber wrote her a comic poem (KSS, No. 102).

Allram, Marie *see* Allram, Joseph

Berger, Ludwig (b. 1782). A tenor and an accomplished guitarist; he knew Weber in Stuttgart, Mannheim (1809–10) and Carlsruhe (1812–13). He composed a set of *Deutsche Lieder*, and was the dedicatee of the six songs Weber published with Simrock, later numbered Op. 15.

Bergmann, Johann Gottfried (1795–1831). He studied at the Dresden Kreuzschule and with Mieksch, becoming principal tenor in the German company in 1816. Though he had quite a sonorous voice, especially in the middle register, he had weak high notes and sang roughly and forcefully. His slight stature and lack of acting ability further made him little more than a stopgap when Weber was in need of a leading tenor.

Berner, Friedrich Wilhelm (1780–1827). Berner was organist of St Elisabeth's Church in Breslau on Weber's arrival in 1804; he was also a fine pianist, and clarinettist in the theatre orchestra. It was Berner, arriving to look over the *Rübezahl* music one evening, who discovered Weber unconscious from having accidentally drunk from a bottle containing engraving acid. His works, largely choral, include an *Abschiedschor an meinem Freund Weber* (1806).

Biedenfeld, Eugenie von Schüler *see* Schüler-Biedenfeld, Eugenie von

Bocklet, Carl Maria von (1801–81). He studied the violin with *F. W. Pixis, the piano with Závora and composition with *Dionys Weber. Soon after settling in Vienna as first violin in the Theater an der Wien he abandoned the violin for the piano. He was admired as a pianist by Beethoven, and became close friends with Schubert, who dedicated the D major Piano Sonata (D850) to him; he also gave the first performance of several of Schubert's works, including the 'Wanderer' Fantasia.

Böhler, Christine (1798–1860). She first appeared as a child actress, then made her soprano début in Frankfurt in 1814; she also appeared as a pianist. She sang in Prague 1815–17, together with her mother. In his notes on the

Prague principals in his Notizen-Buch, Weber marks against her name, 'Boys' parts, Benjamin [in Méhul's *Joseph*], Adolf in [*Paer's] *Camilla*, and young girls.' She also sang Mozart's Barbarina, Servilia and Dorabella. She then abandoned opera and studied acting with Sophie Schröder. In 1817–18 she was in Leipzig, where she married the bass *Eduard Genast in 1820. They then moved to Weimar. Goethe wrote a poem to her, 'Treu wünsch' ich dir' (1822). Her name was wrongly transcribed from Weber's handwriting by *Theodor Hell in HHS as 'Böders', and this was copied by subsequent editors of Weber's writings.

Brandt, Caroline (1794–1852). Weber's wife was born in Bonn, the daughter of a tenor and violinist in the Electoral Chapel. She made her first appearance aged eight, and her youth was spent in various German companies. Her first regular engagement was at Frankfurt in 1810, where she became popular in *jeune naïve* roles in drama and opera. She made a successful Prague début on 1 January 1812 as Cinderella (the title role in Isouard's *Aschenbrödel*), a role she was to repeat many times. Bäuerle's *Wiener Allgemeine Theaterzeitung* described her as 'one of the most charming actresses and singers in naïve-humorous roles the German stage has known. Everything she does on the stage is of indescribable neatness and precision. It is a pity that her figure is so small, for she could also do much in tragic roles.' Weber, on engaging her, noted that she was good in 'simple, gay and so-called *Spielrollen*; also acts a lot in plays' (Notizen-Buch). After many difficulties, Weber married her in Dresden on 4 November 1817, 'the most important event of my life' (Diary). Though she settled into the role of wife and mother, with some initial restlessness but apparently few regrets for the stage, she was able to offer professional advice to her husband: for instance, it was on her suggestion that the original first scene of *Der Freischütz* was dropped in favour of the more effective opening on the village shooting match. In her long widowhood she cared attentively and providently for the two children, and preserved all Weber's possessions and papers – including the Diary he had asked her to destroy (perhaps for fear of distressing her with some candid references to love affairs he had had before he met her).

Brizzi, Antonio (b. between 1760 and 1770, d. 1852). Born in Bologna, he had his first great success in Venice in *Zingarelli's *Giulietta e Romeo* in 1796. In Dresden in 1806 he was admired by Napoleon, and engaged together with his wife, Francesca Riccardi. He became very popular in Vienna and Munich. He had a range of over two octaves, and was admired especially in sentimental roles.

Buchwieser, Kathinka [Katharina] (1788?–1828). She was especially popular as a singer and actress of soubrette and *Fein-Koketten* roles at the time of the Congress of Vienna, later marrying Count Laszny von Fokusfodva. Some sources give her birth-date as 1798, but she was reported to be fifteen in 1803 (*AMZ* XVII (1815), 581–9), suggesting the more probable birth-date of 1788.

She began her career in about 1809, and was admired by the young Eichendorff in 1811. In 1815 she was said to have been ill and to have left the stage (*AMZ* XVII (1815), 724), but other reports indicate that she made some appearances until 1817.

Burmeister, Friedrich (1771–1851). He pursued a busy career as a travelling actor and singer before settling in Dresden in 1811. His forte was comedy, and he was praised by Tieck for his Fool in *King Lear*. Though he sang second tenor roles when needed, he was essentially an actor of subtle comic gifts.

Cartellieri, Casimir Antonio (1772–1807). He was born in Danzig, the son of two singers, Giuseppe Cartellieri and Elisabeth Böhm. After studying with Albrechtsberger and Salieri, he became Kapellmeister to Prince Lobkowitz. His works include operas (among them *Rübezahl* (1801)) and concert music.

Castelli, Ignaz Franz (1781–1862). Castelli's *Memoiren meines Lebens* (Vienna and Prague, 1861) give a vivid picture of his life in the Viennese theatre in the first half of the nineteenth century. As a young man he had worked in a travelling company, and he contributed large numbers of theatre pieces to the repertory: his collected works run to sixteen volumes. He wrote the libretto for Schubert's opera *Die Verschworenen*; and Weber composed two songs for his play *Diana von Poitiers*, 'Ein König' (J195) and another now lost, also setting Castelli's poem 'Wunsch und Entsagung'. Castelli in turn wrote his 'Schlummerlied' with a melody of Weber's in mind (a male-voice chorus, J285).

Cherubini, Luigi (1760–1842). Berlioz's disobliging portrait of Cherubini in his *Mémoires* is not one that would have been recognized by many of the other Romantics, for whom he was an heroic father figure. If neither represents the whole truth, he was certainly a powerful influence on the emergent Romantic opera. His operas first began to feature prominently in German repertories in the first decade of the nineteenth century, when French opera made a great advance in Germany, in particular the works of Cherubini, Méhul and *Paer. Cherubini's *Démophoon, Lodoiska, Faniska, Les Deux journées, Eliza* and *Médée* were all popular. Weber greatly admired them: he produced *Les Deux journées* (as *Der Wasserträger*) in Prague and *Faniska* in both Prague and Dresden. *Les Deux journées* had a distinct influence on him (see No. 21), and the use of natural forces as a functional element in the drama, also remarkable in Méhul, clearly impressed him in *Faniska, Eliza* and *Lodoiska*. The latter's villain, Dourlinski, is an ancestor of the vengeful baritone or bass villains of Romantic opera such as Pizarro in *Fidelio* (Beethoven was another great admirer, and beneficiary, of Cherubini) and Weber's Caspar.

Clement, Franz (1780–1842). He made a reputation as a violinist while still a child, and after travelling widely (including to England, where he played in concerts with Haydn) he became conductor of the recently founded Theater an der Wien in 1802. His playing impressed Beethoven, who wrote his violin concerto 'par Clemenza pour Clement'; and his feats of musicianship, which included transcribing whole works from memory, won the admiration of Weber and *Spohr. Weber described his style as 'Old school, but precise.' Later, he was able to take over the conducting of the Prague orchestra when Weber was ill or absent.

Czegka, Anna (1782–1850). Born Auernhammer, she sang under her married name in various forms such as Czeska, Čejka, Čejková, etc. She joined Weber's company at the beginning of 1816, and was then one of the senior singers in a predominantly youthful company. In his Notizen-Buch, he describes her as a character soprano, perhaps at the lower end of the soprano range and with a mezzo quality in her voice, to judge by his comments and by the roles she took: Oscar Teuber describes her as an alto (*Geschichte des Prager Theaters* (Prague, 1883–5)). Her roles included Mozart's Sextus as well as the Countess. The commission that presented *Liebich with objections to Weber's régime (see No. 52) observed that she was 'useful for male soprano roles, but as a singer she would startle the dead back to life'. She was a skilled pianist, and a notable teacher at the conservatory 1817–22, 1839. Her most famous pupil was Henriette Sontag. She moved to Dresden in 1824, returning to Prague in 1826. She also composed some songs. See Weber's review of her concert, No. 54.

Danzi, Franz (1763–1827). 'A popular little man with a round head and sharp, clever eyes that always seemed good-humoured' (MMW I, p. 143), Danzi was one of the most important early influences on Weber. Arriving in Stuttgart as court Kapellmeister in 1807, he immediately befriended the younger man and set about recalling him from his dissolute habits to a sense of vocation as a composer. He greatly encouraged, and took an interest in, the composition of *Silvana*. Danzi's operas are precursors of Weber's own in their care for the role of the orchestra and their Romantic feeling. They include *Der Kuss* (Munich, 1789), *El Bondokani* (Munich, 1802) and *Iphigenia in Aulis* (Munich, 1807). His greatest success, however, was with another work, *Die Mitternachtstunde* (Munich, 1798), which was hailed as 'one of the best original German comic operas' by the *AMZ* (IV (1801), 188–90). The aria 'Der Schutzgeist, der Liebende', from *Der Quasimann* (Munich, 1789), became popular, in part through Danzi's use of it for variations in the first movement of his String Quartet, Op. 6, no. 1, in his Third Potpourri for clarinet and orchestra, and in a keyboard concerto; and Weber liked it enough to use it in the Grand Potpourri (J64) as the subject of the final rondo (see MMW I, p. 142). The Andante theme in J64, also used in the Variations (J94) and attached to Danzi's pseudonym Rapunzel in the Musical Letter (J60), may be by Danzi but has not been identified. Danzi gave Weber letters of introduction to the Mannheim group of musicians who were to become his close friends and the nucleus of the Harmonischer Verein. Some of Weber's letters to Danzi are reprinted in E. Reipschläger, *Schubaur, Danzi und Poissl als Opernkomponisten* (Berlin, 1811).

Dickhut, Christian (dates unknown). A horn virtuoso, he also played the cello and guitar, and wrote music for his instruments. In 1812 he invented a sprung tuning slide to temper notes while playing; this was described in an article by *Gottfried Weber, 'Wichtige Verbesserung des Horns', *AMZ* xiv (1812), 759–64. He was in Mannheim in this year, as a guitarist according to D. Prat, *Diccionario de guitarristas* (Buenos Aires, n.d.).

Dusch, Alexander von (1789–1876). When Weber arrived in Mannheim in 1810, Dusch was a law student at nearby Heidelberg. He quickly formed a close friendship with Weber, and together with *Gottfried Weber (who had married his sister Augusta) they took pleasure in wandering the countryside singing folksongs to Carl Maria's guitar accompaniment. At Stift Neuburg in 1810, he overheard Weber humming melodies that (he told F. W. Jähns in a letter in 1860) he later recognized in *Oberon*; and it was on this occasion that they first read the Apel and Laun *Gespensterbuch*, out of which Dusch began preparing a libretto for Weber on *Der Freischütz*. He became a member of the Harmonischer Verein, under the pseudonym The Unknown. An enthusiastic amateur cellist, he was the dedicatee of Weber's Variations for cello (J94), written in eight hours chiefly out of music previously used in the Grand Potpourri of 1808 (J64) and No. 3 of the Six Pieces for Piano Duet (J83): their technique suggests that he was competent, but no virtuoso. He wrote the text of the song 'Des Künstlers Abschied' (J105) in his room on 8 December 1810, which Weber forthwith set to guitar accompaniment. Dusch also told Jähns that it was to mark their own imminent parting; and indeed they did not meet again. Dusch later became a Minister of State in Baden, and made a reputation with his historical and ecclesiastical writings.

Duvernoy, Frédéric (1765–1838). He was one of the first horn players to break the tradition of dividing performers into *cor-alte* or *cor-basse*. Specializing as he did in the middle register, he developed the new category of *cor-mixte*. He was one of the original staff of the Conservatoire appointed in An III (1795), and became a famous figure in Paris: for the première of Spontini's *La Vestale* in 1807, the playbills gave his name greater size and prominence than that of any other artist. He composed much music for the horn, including twelve concertos. FétisB is unusual in having some reservations about his playing, still more about his compositions.

Ehlers, Wilhelm (1774–1845). Self-taught as a tenor, he sang on various German stages (including Weimar, under Goethe), before moving to Vienna in 1813. He continued to sing all over Germany, subsequently becoming director of the theatres at Frankfurt (1831) and Mainz (1835). He also composed songs, including Goethe settings which he would sing to the poet to his own guitar accompaniment.

Eunicke, Johanna (1800–56). The daughter of the tenor Friedrich Eunicke (1764–1844) by his second marriage, to the soubrette Therese Schwachhofer (b. 1774), she made her début in Berlin as Susanna (*Figaro*). Among her most famous roles were Fanchon, Olivier (*Jean de Paris*) and Zerlina. She was Weber's first Aennchen in Berlin in 1821. Though she overstrained her voice early in her career, she continued successfully on the stage as an actress until 1825, when she retired in order to marry.

Farník, Václav (1770–1838). The most distinguished Czech clarinettist of his generation, he taught at the Prague Conservatory from its foundation and was still on the register in 1832. He was in Count Pachta's band in 1796, as 'Herr Wenzel', and was praised as 'a very gifted and outstanding clarinettist' (BKP), and as an artist 'whose playing is marvelled at by all connoisseurs' (DKB, where his date of birth is given as 1765).

Fischer, Antonie von (d. 1851). Antonie von Peierl (Peyerl) married the architect Karl von Fischer, who built the Munich Hof- und Nationaltheater, and sang as Frau von Fischer in Munich 1805–23. Among her most famous roles was Gluck's Iphigenia, in which a drawing of her exists; she also sang Julia in *La Vestale*, the Countess in *Les Deux journées*, the Princess in *Jean de Paris* and much else. The reviews in the *Dramatischer Briefwechsel* by 'Jakob Klaubauf' (the librarian T. E. Reischel) praise her 'silver voice' and repeatedly describe her Mozart performances (Susanna and Pamina) as *sehr brav*.

Flerx, Josefa   *see* Flerx, Karl

Flerx, Karl (d. 1816). He was a dancer and comic actor who became very popular at the Munich Hoftheater. In 1810 he married the soprano Josefa Lang (1791–1862), who also sang as Flerx-Lang. She was the first Fatime in *Abu Hassan* in Munich in 1811: 'A fiery artist', according to Weber.

Forti, Anton (1790–1859). Born in Vienna, he spent most of his life there. He sang some tenor roles, including Weber's Max, but made his real reputation as a baritone: he was the first Lysiart in *Euryanthe* in 1823, a famous Figaro, Don Giovanni and Pizarro, and was even able to sing Sarastro. He won first prize in a State Lottery in 1833 and retired, though he did occasionally return to the stage. He was still making some appearances in 1841, especially in French opera.

Fränzl, Ferdinand (1770–1833). Son of the violinist Ignaz Fränzl (see above, No. 59), he first appeared in public as a violinist at the age of seven. He played in the Mannheim Orchestra, and then became a famous travelling virtuoso. He studied composition in Strasbourg with F. X. Richter and Ignaz Pleyel, and in Bologna with Padre Martini. He became court Kapellmeister and director of the Munich Opera in 1806. Weber came to know him in 1811, and they remained friends. His best-known opera, *Carlo Fioras* (1810), was a popular Munich repertory piece, and Weber gave it in Prague in 1813. He wrote a new finale for Méhul's *Joseph* when Weber produced it in Dresden. See Weber's review of his Prague concert, above, No. 59.

Frey, M. (d. 1832). He became court Kapellmeister in Mannheim, and was described by Schilling as being admired as a man no less than as a musician: FétisB calls him an able violinist. His operas include *Der Kyffhäuserberg* and a one-act setting of Goethe's *Jery und Bätely* which was very favourably reviewed on its first performance, in Mannheim in 1815 (*AMZ* XVII (1815), 772–5).

Fröhlich, Joseph (1780–1862). Weber met the renowned teacher in Würzburg in 1811, and hoped (without success) to recruit him for the Harmonischer Verein. Fröhlich was later to carry out Weber's plan for a life of *Vogler (*Biographie des grossen Tonkünstlers Abt Georg Joseph Vogler* (Würzburg, 1845)).

Gänsbacher, Johann (1778–1844). Weber first met Gänsbacher in Vienna, where they were fellow pupils of *Vogler and soon friends. Gänsbacher had already won distinction at the age of eighteen as a soldier in the Tyrolean War of Liberation, selling his violin to buy his equipment and then winning a medal for gallantry. He was close to Weber in Mannheim, Darmstadt and Heidelberg, joining the Harmonischer Verein (as 'Triole') and playing in Weber's concerts; and together with *Gottfried Weber and *Meyerbeer he was one of the group of Vogler's favourite pupils in Darmstadt. He wrote two solos in the cantata they composed for Vogler's birthday, to words by Weber; and Weber translated the Italian words of his setting of 'L'amerò sarò costante' into German. He was helpful in paving Weber's way in Prague; and Weber in turn hoped to secure him as Kapellmeister in Dresden in 1823, being forestalled by Gänsbacher's meanwhile accepting the post of organist of St Stephen's, Vienna. His Autobiography gives a vivid picture of the contemporary scene (unpublished but quoted substantially in various works, e.g. A. Schmidt, *Denksteine* (Vienna, 1848)). See above, No. 117.

Geiling, Christian Traugott (1772–1860). An actor of wide experience, he settled in Dresden in 1817, playing low comedy roles, caricatures and minor roles. He normally sang bass, but was also required to alternate parts with the tenors *Geyer and *Wilhelmi as necessary. He delivered his music in a kind of speech-song, and was said to depict his parts not so much with pencil strokes as with a broom.

Genast, Eduard (1797–1866). The son of Goethe's stage director Anton Genast, he learnt his craft in the Weimar Theatre. Here, though by his own account he lacked the necessary low notes, he made his début as Osmin. Moving to Stuttgart, he studied further, and sang in many cities including Dresden, where Weber engaged him as first bass. He has left a vivid and entertaining account of his theatrical life in *Aus Weimars klassischer und nachklassischer Zeit: Aus dem Tagebuch eines alten Schauspielers* (4 vols., Leipzig, 1862–6; 5th edn, Stuttgart, 1905). See Böhler, Christine.

Gerstäcker, Friedrich (1788–1825). Having sung as a boy in the Kreuzschule in Dresden, he worked in various opera companies, including Seconda's, touring widely. He joined Weber's company in 1820, leaving over a salary dispute in the same year. Weber remained on cordial terms with him, and gave him careful advice: 'Above all, my dear friend, take care of your precious health, and trust in the natural resonance of your voice. Your enthusiasm sometimes leads you to want to use perhaps too much force. This gives the listener a sense of strain...So treat your voice like a colt and give it daily some quite careful schooling and lungeing. You'll laugh and say, a Kapellmeister can't write two lines without lecturing. But *it comes from the heart*, as I'm fond of you...' (letter of 27 April 1821). Gerstäcker was the father of the traveller and adventure novelist Friedrich Gerstäcker (1816–72).

Geyer, Ludwig (1780–1821). Best known to posterity as Wagner's stepfather, Geyer played a useful part as an actor and *buffo* tenor in Weber's Dresden company. He was an expert and versatile performer, useful for his ability to handle different kinds of role efficiently, among them 'humorous and genuine knights, Jews and pedants'; these he is said to have acted in an exaggerated fashion. As the author of a number of minor pieces for the theatre, he was valuable for his skill in arranging and adapting plays.

Giuliani, Mauro (1781–1828). He was in Vienna by 1806, where he established himself as the most successful and popular guitar virtuoso of the day, winning the friendship and approval of Beethoven. He was said to play 'with rare charm, fluency and power' (*AMZ* ix (1806–7), 89). Travelling as far afield as England and Russia, he made a European reputation, while his numerous compositions helped to develop the technical resources of the guitar and give it new status as a serious instrument.

Grünbaum, Johann Christian   *see* Grünbaum, Therese

Grünbaum, Therese (1797–1876). She was the daughter of *Wenzel Müller by his first marriage to the singer Magdalena Reiningthal. She made her first stage appearance as a child, for instance as Lili in *Das Donauweibchen*. In 1807 she moved to Prague when her father took up his appointment at the Opera. In 1813 she married the tenor Johann Christian Grünbaum (1785–1870), whom Weber described as co-principal with *Stöger in Prague and an artist always willing to help out at moments of need (Notizen-Buch). This was the year in which Weber engaged her for his theatre in Prague, where she already had a high reputation. Weber refers to 'the marvellous talent of this great singer' (letter to *Franz Danzi, 24 May 1816). She sang Amazily (to her husband's Cortez) in Weber's first Prague production, *Fernand Cortez* (9 September 1813), and many other leading roles. She moved to Vienna in 1816 (her last Prague appearance was in September), where she was hailed as 'the German Catalani', but made guest appearances in May and June 1817 in Dresden. Weber tried to secure her for his Dresden company; he wrote

Eglantine in *Euryanthe* for her. She retired from the Vienna Court Opera in 1828, and settled in Berlin. Her 'heavenly art' was celebrated in a sonnet by Friedrich Schott (*DAZ*, No. 111, 9 May 1817). Her daughter Caroline Grünbaum (1814–68) made her début in Vienna in 1829. After successes in different cities, she joined the Berlin Königstädtertheater in 1832. She retired in 1844. See above, Nos. 63 and 98.

Gürrlich, Joseph August (1761–1817). Had the Berlin Court Opera at which he was appointed Kapellmeister in 1816 not burnt down, Weber would have succeeded him on his death in the following year. He was respected as a bass player and a teacher, and wrote a number of operas and much other music.

Harlas, Helene (1785–1818). Put into a convent at fifteen, she emerged after only a year and then studied singing with such success that she was engaged for the Munich court after three years. She retired upon her marriage, but when this proved unsuccessful she reappeared. Her roles included Constanze, and *Poissl wrote several of his operas for her. She was one of the few true German sopranos of her day (a visit to Venice when she was at the height of her fame was a failure). She often sang in concerts with the clarinettist Bärmann, and Weber wrote for her his concert aria 'Non paventar, mia vita' (J181). She was regularly singled out for approval in the columns of the *AMZ*, e.g. a review praising her strong middle register and her expressive qualities, while having reservations about her upper register (*AMZ* XIX (1818), 597). The *AMZ* also published a sympathetic obituary of her, commending her for paying more attention to expression and declamation than to roulades (*AMZ* XXI (1819), 3–6).

Häser, Charlotte (1784–1871). The three children of the Leipzig music director Johann Georg Häser (1729–1809) were August Ferdinand (1779–1844), chorus-master in Weimar in 1817 and also a composer; Christian Wilhelm (1781–1867), a successful bass who sang in Prague from 1804 to 1809, moving by way of Breslau and Vienna to Stuttgart (1814–44); and, the most famous of the family, the soprano Charlotte. After a career as a concert singer, she went to the Italian Opera in Dresden (1803–6), then travelled widely and had an unprecedented success (for a German singer) in Italy, where she was hailed as *la divina tedesca*. She was one of the first women to sing men's roles. She was admired for the absence of unnecessary decoration in her singing, and her clarity and simplicity (e.g. *AMZ* XIX (1812), 303–4) – qualities greatly prized by German Romantic critics.

Häser, Christian Wilhelm   *see* Häser, Charlotte

Hause [House], **Wenzel** [Václav] (1764–1847). Originally a violinist in Prince Lobkowitz's band, he joined the orchestra of the Stavov Theatre and turned to the double bass in 1815. He became one of the first virtuosos on the instrument, and its first professor at the Prague Conservatory (1811–45). He published a well-known *Contrabassschule* (1828), which was translated into French and German, and several sets of important studies that are still used by students. Evidently an easy-going man, he was later reproached for allowing his pupils to practice in gloves in cold weather.

Heigel, Max (1752–1811). For thirty-one years an actor at the Munich Hoftheater, Heigel was also a poet and the author of a song in *Kotzebue's *Der arme Minnesinger* set by Weber (J113). Weber recruited him for the Harmonischer Verein; and was bitterly disappointed when the Trauermusik (J116) which he had written for Heigel's funeral was replaced by Winter's Requiem, 'through the carelessness and sloppiness of Heigel's son' (Diary, 20 June 1811). He was responsible for the translation of Dalayrac's *Léhéman* as *Makdonald* (see above, No. 24).

Hell, Theodor (1775–1856). This was the pseudonym of Carl Gottlieb Theodor Winkler, archivist in Dresden and later a director of the Hoftheater. He translated from French, Portuguese (the first German version of Camões's *Lusiads*) and English: he made the singing translation of *Oberon*. He was editor of the *DAZ* from 1817 to 1843, and edited the first comprehensive collection of Weber's writings (HHS).

Hellwig, Carl Friedrich Ludwig (1773–1838). Having studied various instruments and subjects, he was taken into the Berlin Singakademie by Zelter, becoming assistant director in 1803. For the Liedertafel, which he joined on its foundation in 1809, he wrote many songs. He became Berlin court and cathedral organist in 1813. He was a close friend of Weber, who added a note recording some of the above appointments and others to Hellwig's MS autobiographical sketch (1820). Apart from church music and songs, he wrote two operas, *Die Bergknappen* (1820: see above, No. 115) and *Don Silvio di Rosalba* (unproduced). He made a number of important piano arrangements of famous scores, by Bach, Handel and Gluck among others (see above, No. 40); he was one of the first arrangers to include instrumental indications. He was the brother of the stage director *Friedrich Hellwig.

Hellwig, Friedrich (1782–1825). As stage director of the Dresden German Opera, he was one of Weber's most important collaborators. Though not a producer in anything like the modern sense of the term, and for all his evident intelligence not gifted with a very powerful imagination, he was an experienced man of the theatre and a sound craftsman. He sang bass roles until his increasing duties as a director enabled him to free himself from a task to which he was not ideally suited. Weber described him as 'a thoroughly good, sound, diligent man, but easily wounded and got down if he himself feels he can't bring something off as he would wish and would recognize as his ideal' (letter of 27 June 1817).

Hermstedt, Johann (1778–1841). It was in Gotha in 1808 that his clarinet playing first impressed *Spohr, who wrote much music for him. He had modelled his style on the singers and violinists he had heard as a military bandsman in Dresden, which did not prevent Weber from suggesting that the study of some outstanding singers would benefit him (see above, No. 42). Spohr referred to his 'extraordinary technique, brilliance of tone and purity of intonation' (*Selbstbiographie*). Despite this praise in print, Weber was more reserved privately, referring to his 'thick, somewhat hollow tone. Masters fearful difficulties, but not always elegantly, often against the nature of the instrument...fine phrasing as well, but has appropriated many violinists' tricks which occasionally come off. But he lacks Bärmann's complete evenness of tone from top to bottom and divinely tasteful phrasing' (Diary, 27 September 1812). Hermstedt requested a concerto from Weber, which he reluctantly promised: 'this was small satisfaction to me' (Diary, 28 September 1812). Weber further noted in his Diary for 4 February 1815 that he was writing a concerto for Hermstedt. This never saw the light of day; but it is possible that the Grand Duo Concertant (J204), written between 5 July and 8 November 1815, began life in this way, as material for a concerto. It is the only one of Weber's clarinet works that does not bear a dedication to Bärmann, whom, as a close friend, he might not have wanted to upset with a dedication to a powerful rival.

Hiemer, Franz Karl (1768–1822). Poet, officer, painter, actor and court official, also making a reputation as a dramatist and librettist, Hiemer was one of the dilettante soldiers of fortune to whom Weber was drawn particularly in his early years. Hiemer rearranged the text of Weber's opera *Das Waldmädchen* as *Silvana*, though it needed a cajoling verse-letter from Weber to persuade him to finish it (reprinted in KSS); and he also wrote the libretto of *Abu Hassan*. Weber set two of his poems as guitar songs, 'Die Schäferstunde' (J91) and the popular *Wiegenlied* 'Schlaf, Herzenssöhnchen' (J96). Hiemer also translated many operas for Stuttgart, including works by Boieldieu, Catel, Dalayrac, Méhul, Della Maria, Martín y Soler, Generali, Niccolini, Nasolini, Rossini and *Zingarelli. He also made a version of Thomas d'Hèle's text for Grétry's *Le Jugement de Midas* as *Apollos Wettgesang* for Sutor (Stuttgart, 1808).

Hoffmann, E. T. A. (1776–1822). It was in 1811, during Hoffmann's time as director of the Bamberg Nationaltheater, that he and Weber first met. Though they never became close friends, they had a considerable if wary respect for one another. Weber greatly admired Hoffmann's originality and was intrigued by his cultivation of the weirder aspects of Romanticism, both in his stories and in the grotesque personal aura he affected. He was also an enthusiastic admirer of *Undine*, about which he wrote one of his most famous articles (above, No. 87). However, he was distressed by Hoffmann's attitude at the time of the *Freischütz* première, when he found himself mocked, and possibly attacked in print. The authorship of the anonymous articles that appeared in the *Vossische Zeitung*, which gave the work a distinctly cool reception and made fun of some of its features, has generally been attributed to Hoffmann; though this is painstakingly challenged in W. Kron, *Die angebliche Freischütz-Kritiken E. T. A. Hoffmanns* (Munich, 1957). Hoffmann was the translator of Spontini's *Olympie*, the rival work in Berlin, and did in conversation use Spontini as a stick with which to beat Weber.

Hummel, Jan Nepomuk (1778–1837). One of the great pianist-composers of his day, he exercised a considerable influence on Weber. Hinrich Lichtenstein asserted that Weber was the superior improviser to 'greater (or rather, more accomplished) pianists like Hummel and Kalkbrenner, with whom, however little they may have meant it, there always seemed a desire to please' (memoir prefacing E. Rudorff, ed., *Briefe von Carl Maria von Weber an Hinrich Lichtenstein* (Brunswick, 1900)). Hummel was probably the inspiration for much in Weber's technique, and his suite of *Tänze für den Apollosaal* (1808) is a clear ancestor of Weber's *Aufforderung zum Tanze* (J260) in its use of a sequence of dances for a piano concert work. The two knew and respected one another, and maintained contact after their Prague meeting during Weber's Dresden years. It was Hummel who recommended Julius Benedict to Weber as pupil.

Januš [Janusch], **Michal** [Michael] (dates unknown). Weber secured him as first flute in the Prague Opera Orchestra, though the Notizen-Buch records that he left after three months – possibly the ill-health mentioned in Weber's review of his concert with *Sellner (above, No. 55) was connected with this. He published a number of exercises and other pieces for flute, including a sonata with guitar, and possibly some religious music.

Kainz, Josef (1773–1855). He sang in Vienna before being summoned by *Liebich to Prague, where he became one of the mainstays of the Opera. His roles included Don Giovanni, Almaviva and Pizarro, as well as many in the French repertory; he was also the first Faust in *Spohr's opera. He made a name as an exceptionally musical singer and generous colleague, who could step into an ill singer's shoes at the shortest notice; he also helped on the administrative side in times of need. His wife Katharina (born Schröffel; 1767) was a pupil of Valesi; she was also an admired violinist and pianist. Their daughter Marianne (1800–66) sang in Prague until 1819; she then travelled in Italy, where she was one of the first German sopranos to have a success. By her first husband Konstantin Holland she had a daughter, Marie (1833–74), who was a soprano.

Kainz, Katharina   *see* Kainz, Josef

Kainz, Marianne   *see* Kainz, Josef

Kalivoda [Kalliwoda], **Jan Křtitel Václav** [Johann Wenzel] (1801–66). After studying with *Dionys Weber and with *Pixis at the Prague Conservatory

(1811–17), he joined Weber's orchestra at the Opera. One of the most important Czech violinists of his day, he also composed much music, not only for his instrument. This includes seven symphonies – Schumann gave the Fifth a very respectful review – and an opera, *Blanda* (1847), to a text by Weber's old *Freischütz* collaborator Friedrich Kind.

Körner, Theodor (1791–1813). His death in August 1813 in a skirmish near Gadebusch made him instantly a national hero, and his poems, usually sentimental, exhortatory or both, won him the exaggerated temporary fame that has been the lot of other fallen soldier-poets. Weber set several of his poems in the three volumes characteristically entitled *Leyer und Schwert*.

Kotzebue, August von (1761–1819). One of the most popular playwrights of the day, he led an adventurous life that included periods in Russia in the diplomatic service, as theatre director, and briefly as Siberian convict. His fluently written plays, sometimes shamelessly plagiarized, made him famous throughout Europe as a Romantic for middle-brows. Some were popular in England, one of them featuring as *Lovers' Vows* in Jane Austen's *Mansfield Park*. His murder by the student Karl Sand, on suspicion of acting as a right-wing political agent, gave Metternich the excuse for the repression of much liberal activity, especially in student societies.

Kreutzer, Conradin (1780–1849). It was the success of his *Libussa* in Vienna at the end of 1822 that established Kreutzer as Kapellmeister of the Kärntnerthortheater. He took over in *Euryanthe* at the fourth performance from Weber, who noted that it had gone 'really well' (Diary, 1 November 1823). However, he also exacted cuts in the work amounting to 352 bars; though publicly courteous about this, Weber privately referred to the score as now being *zersetzt* ('disintegrated').

Kreutzer, Rodolphe (1766–1831). One of the most famous violinists of his day, and remembered now chiefly for his studies and as the dedicatee of Beethoven's Op. 47 Sonata, he was also a prolific composer. His operas include a *Lodoiska* (1791) written in rivalry to *Cherubini. He composed a large amount of music for his instrument, including nineteen concertos.

Lang, Regina (1789–1827). The daughter of the soprano Sabine Hitzelberger, who had married the Munich court violinist Theobald Lang, she was a popular member of the Opera and greatly impressed Napoleon on his visit in 1805. She retired in November 1811, six months after Weber admired her in Isouard's *Cendrillon*: the performance of Myrrha in *Das unterbrochene Opferfest* noticed in No. 29 above must have been virtually her last.

Liebich, Johann Karl (1773–1816). He began his career as an actor while still very young, and toured with the Roland Theatre Company until 1787. Settling in Prague, he was much admired in comic roles (e.g. by Tieck) and for his gifts as an extemporizer: he was one of the last major exponents of the old *Stegreifkomödie*, or improvised comedy. In 1806 he became director of the theatre, swiftly raising it to a position of international renown 'by means of his honest, amiable personality, round which his whole company willingly revolved, each cheerfully determined to do everything in his power. A melting smile from Liebich was worth more than the tyranny of a self-willed despot...' (O. Teuber, *Geschichte des Prager Theaters* (Prague, 1883–5)). His contract was extended in 1812, and in 1813 he engaged Weber as director of the Opera. By now suffering from crippling attacks of kidney stone, and in constant pain, he was unable to maintain such direct control. He did, however, make a few stage appearances under Weber, for instance in the title role of *Fränzl's Carlo Fioras* on 19 December 1813. He married the actress Johanna Wimmer in 1803; after his death she married the tenor *J. A. Stöger.

Meyerbeer, Giacomo (born Jakob Liebmann Meyer Beer) (1791–1864). Weber first met the eighteen-year-old Jakob Beer in Darmstadt in 1810, where they were fellow pupils of the *Abbé Vogler. They became close friends, and even collaborated (with *Gänsbacher) on a cantata for Vogler's birthday (in which Therese Beer sang – out of tune, Weber complained) (see above, No. 8). Meyerbeer joined the Harmonischer Verein, and wrote articles for it under the pseudonyms Philodikaios and Julius Billig. He later lost interest in its affairs; and he and Weber drifted apart because of their differing ambitions, Weber finding Meyerbeer's too personal for the good of the cause of German opera so close to his own heart. Weber remained on warm terms with Meyerbeer's kindly parents, the wealthy banker Herz Beer and his intellectually inclined wife Amalie; when in Berlin, he often stayed in their Charlottenburg house (including for the première of *Der Freischütz*). However, his scruples made him refuse their gift of a pair of silver candlesticks when he produced Meyerbeer's *Emma di Resburgo* and *Alimelek* in Dresden on 26 January and 22 February 1810, perhaps partly because of his hostile comments. Weber was also friendly with the other Beer children, Heinrich (who inherited the Berlin house), Therese, Hans and the astronomer Wilhelm.

After Weber's death, Meyerbeer loyally supported his widow Caroline, helping her with advice and giving the proceeds of a production of *Euryanthe* to the committee which Wagner organized for the return to Dresden of Weber's remains from London. Meyerbeer also took over the *Drei Pintos* sketches, hoping to complete them; but he was dismayed by the slimness of the material and what he saw as the feebleness of the text. He hesitated long over the material, to Caroline's frustration, and even discussed with Wilhelm the possibility of a new libretto by Charlotte Birch-Pfeiffer based on *Zschokke's *Blondin von Namur*. But by the time of her death in 1852, Caroline had still failed to get anything definite out of Meyerbeer, who eventually returned the material to the Weber family, unused.

Mittermayer [Mittermaier], **Georg** (1783–1858). He studied under Winter and made his début in the Munich Opera in 1806, being especially successful in *Paer's and Rossini's tenor roles. He sang the title role in the first performance of *Abu Hassan*.

Moscheles, Ignaz (1794–1870). Moscheles's career was just beginning when Weber wrote his account of the Carlsbad concert (see above, No. 79), and during the next ten years he won a European reputation as one of the greatest virtuosos of the age. On his marriage to Charlotte Embden he settled in London, where he was one of the circle of musicians who surrounded Weber during his last illness. Moscheles's account of Weber's last days and death (in C. Moscheles, ed., *Aus Moscheles Leben* (Leipzig, 1872–3)) somewhat exaggerates the role he played in the events. He notated from memory the piano part of Weber's last song, 'From Chindara's Warbling Fount' (J308), which the composer played but was too weak to write down.

Muck, Joseph Alois (b. 1761). He took to the stage at the age of twenty, after studying literature and philosophy. In 1789 he joined the Munich Opera, where his fine bass voice made him one of its most valuable members. Weber greatly admired him, especially for his performance as the first Omar in *Abu Hassan*.

Müller, Wenzel (1767–1835). His professional career began when he was appointed conductor of the Brünn theatre at the age of sixteen. In 1786 he moved to Vienna, where he spent the rest of his life, apart from the years 1807–13, when he was in Prague. Though a competent theatre musician who developed the German and Czech *Singspiel* repertory to some extent, he did not make a great mark in Prague, and Weber was appointed his successor in the hope that the decline in standards could be halted. Part of his motive in accepting the Prague post seems to have been the wish to be near his daughter *Therese (Grünbaum). Of his 250-odd stage works, the most famous were *Kaspar der Fagottist* (1791), *Das neue Sontagskind* (1793), *Die Schwestern von Prag* (1794), and the series of highly popular Viennese *Zauberpossen* and other comedies to texts by Bäuerle, Meisl and especially Raimund (e.g. *Alpenkönig und Menschenfeind*).

Nägeli, Hans Georg (1773–1836). Nägeli's renown as a teacher and publisher stood high among the Romantics; and it was with the idea of studying his *Pestalozzian theories that Weber went to see him in Zürich in 1811. He also hoped to recruit Nägeli for the Harmonischer Verein, and to persuade him to publish its projected journal – without success. His Diary for 30 August 1811 records that he visited Nägeli's singing school and played there; he found Nägeli's compositions featureless, but greatly enjoyed the exchange of views they had.

Naumann, Johann Gottlieb (1741–1801). The most important Dresden opera composer between Hasse and Weber, Naumann wrote a vast amount of music for the Saxon court. Though he composed operas in Danish and Swedish during one of his visits to Scandinavia, he kept to Italian opera in Dresden.

Paer, Ferdinando (1771–1839). His career took him to Vienna, where he had a great success with *Camilla* (1799), and then in 1801 to Dresden as Kapellmeister. He stayed there until 1806, composing *Sargino* and *Leonore* (to the plot used by Beethoven); he then moved to Paris. His works remained very popular in Germany, especially in Dresden: in 1812 the *AMZ* remarked on the fact that no new Paer opera was being given (*AMZ* XIV (1812), 468).

Pestalozzi, Johann Heinrich (1746–1827). In 1811 Weber made a trip to Switzerland partly with the object of studying Pestalozzi's educational ideas. In common with many of the Romantics, he was drawn to a theory based on the Rousseau-inspired idea of instruction taking human nature as its starting-point, with observation of the natural world playing a key part as a principle. He failed to meet Pestalozzi, but was disappointed in the standard of singing in the institute run by *Nägeli along Pestalozzian lines.

Pixis, Friedrich Wilhelm (1786–1842). The son of the composer Friedrich Wilhelm Pixis and brother of the pianist-composer Johann Peter Pixis (1788–1864), he toured Germany with them as a violinist. From 1806 to 1810 he was in Vienna, then moved to Prague as teacher at the new conservatory and Kapellmeister at the theatre. For Weber's reviews of one of his concerts and one of Johann Peter's, see above, Nos. 57 and 78.

Poissl, Johann Nepomuk von (1783–1865). He was the son of a court chamberlain, and studied music with *Danzi and *Vogler, through them becoming a friend of Weber. In 1823 he was appointed Second Intendant at Munich, where he held posts until 1848. His operas were mostly Italian in subject and to some extent in manner; they also belong to early German Romanticism in certain stylistic aspects, including some use of motif (e.g. in *Athalia*), and in their continuous composition. Poissl was also the first German composer consistently to write his own librettos (in five cases, after Metastasio). His work was praised with reservations in the *AMZ*: a characteristic review, of *Aucassin und Nicolette* (1813), declared that the music was 'pleasing, flattering to the ear, intelligible, singable and well scored, but lacking in any special inventive gift' (*AMZ* XV (1813), 419). Of his thirteen operas, the most successful were *Ottaviano in Sicilia* (1812), *Aucassin und Nicolette* (1813), *Athalia* (1814 – his most celebrated work; see above, No. 76), *Der Wettkampf zu Olympia* (1815) and *Nittetis* (1817).

Ritter, Peter (1763–1846). As a former pupil of *Vogler, Ritter naturally attracted Weber's interest. He was a fine cellist as well as a composer, and played in the Mannheim Orchestra from 1784 before becoming Kapellmeister in 1803. Some of his twenty-one operas and *Singspiele*, which were quite popular in their day, suggest his adherence to the earlier Mannheim school. The most successful was *Der Eremit auf Formentara* (Mannheim, 1788). The *AMZ* complained that his *Kotzebue *Singspiel*, *Feodora* (Mannheim, 1812), had among other defects an overture of 'too much liveliness and too little

Romanticism' (*AMZ* xiv (1812), 349). His *Die lustigen Weiber von Windsor* (Mannheim, 1794) is an early Falstaff opera, though not (as is sometimes stated) the first.

Rochlitz (Johann) Friedrich (1769–1842). One of Weber's earliest admirers, Rochlitz published a favourable review of the Six Fughettas (J1–6) in the second number of the *AMZ* (i (1798), 32); and thereafter he remained a steadfastly loyal supporter. His championship of the cause of German opera was one close to Weber's heart; and as well as contributing regularly to Rochlitz's *AMZ*, Weber wrote him many letters in which are discussed matters of artistic interest to them in their campaign. Rochlitz provided the words which Weber set for *Der erste Ton* (J58), the Hymn *In seiner Ordnung schafft der Herr* (J154) and the song 'Es stürmt auf der Flur' (J161). Weber's Fourth Piano Sonata (J287) is dedicated to him.

Rode, Pierre (1774–1830). His European fame as a violin virtuoso, which extended from Spain to Russia, made a great mark in Germany. Beethoven finished his G major Sonata for Rode, though he had reservations about the performance; and *Spohr modelled his style on Rode's, though he latterly shared in the general disappointment felt at the decline in Rode's powers. He wrote thirteen violin concertos, many sets of variations, and a set of twenty-four Caprices that were long popular among violinists.

Romberg, Andreas (1767–1821). He was a cousin and close friend of *Bernhard Romberg, with whom he toured widely as a violinist. After a successful period in Hamburg (1802–15), he became Kapellmeister in Gotha in succession to *Spohr, who praised him as 'an accomplished and thoughtful artist' while finding his violin playing 'indescribably cold and dry' (*Selbstbiographie*).

Romberg, Bernhard (1767–1841). He was a cousin and close friend of *Andreas Romberg, and was the founder of a whole school of German cellists. The two cousins toured widely together, even reaching Russia in 1812 (and being forced to flee the burning of Moscow). Later, when Spontini's appointment as Kapellmeister in Berlin dashed Romberg's hopes of the post, he resumed his wandering life.

Schicht, Johann Gottfried (1753–1823). He succeeded J. A. Hiller as conductor of the Leipzig Gewandhaus concerts in 1785, and became cantor of St Thomas's in 1810. His many works are mostly church music. His pupils included Marschner and Reissiger.

Schmalz, Amalie (1771–1848). After studying with *Naumann in Dresden, she returned to her native Berlin in 1790. She remained here throughout her career, apart from a brief period in Rome, 1808–10. Her most famous roles included Spontini's Vestale, which she sang at the Berlin première in 1811.

Her voice had a range of three octaves, from G to G in alt, and was clear and resonant.

Schnepf, Joseph (dates unknown). He was a baritone who sang in Prague (though not in Weber's company), later becoming supervisor of singing studies at the conservatory, 1819–38.

Schönberger, Marianne (1785–1882). Born in Mannheim, she was the daughter of an Italian bass player named Marconi and a German mother. She made her first stage appearance aged nine (according to EBL). She developed a strong contralto voice; this was greatly admired by *Cherubini, who engaged her for the Vienna Opera. Intrigues forced her out of Vienna, and she spent the greater part of her career as a travelling virtuoso. She married the landscape painter Lorenz Schönberger (1768–1847). Her farewell performance was in Mannheim as Titus on 2 January 1834; she then withdrew into private life, first to Amsterdam, then in 1842 to Mainz, and finally in 1847 to Darmstadt. Her career had lasted almost sixty years, and she died only a few days short of her ninety-seventh birthday. *Gottfried Weber praised the strength and beauty of her voice, and other reports extolled her fine tone and masterly acting (e.g. *AMZ* xx (1818), 301), though some found her tone too powerful and her manner heavy (*AMZ* xvi (1814), 316). It was largely the scarcity of good tenors, still being lamented by *Rochlitz in 1818 (*AMZ* xx (1818), 301), coupled with the lack of good contralto roles mentioned by Weber, that encouraged her to make a speciality of singing tenor roles (untransposed) – at the suggestion of her husband, according to one report (*Rheinische Correspondenz*, No. 56, 25 February 1810).

Schreiber, Aloys (1763–1841). After working as a schoolmaster and a drama critic, he became professor of aesthetics in Heidelberg. He wrote the text of Meyerbeer's oratorio *Gott und die Natur* (see above, No. 19), and was the author of many novels, plays, essays, historical and topographical works, etc.

Schüler-Biedenfeld, Eugenie von (b. 1783). An Italian, born Bonasegla, she studied in Italy and sang in Vienna and throughout Germany. She married a Baden Government Councillor, Karl Ferdinand von Schüler-Biedenfeld, author of books on many topics, including a study – somewhat garrulous but useful for its views on contemporary opera – entitled *Die komische Oper* (Leipzig, 1848). Her efficient Italian training was let down by her ungainly appearance and the awkwardness of her acting, and she was unpopular with the public. She sang only three roles with Weber, *Cherubini's Lodoiska, Hofrätin Döring in Solié's *Le Secret* and the High Priestess in *La Vestale*.

Sellner, Joseph (1787–1843). He joined an Austrian regiment in 1805, and later directed a band in Hungary. After playing as principal oboe in the Pest Theatre, he was invited by Weber to Prague, where he also studied composition with Tomašek. He was a versatile and talented musician, who played a number of instruments (including, Weber's Notizen-Buch records, the guitar: see above, Nos. 55 and 82). He returned to Vienna in 1817, where he became a famous teacher. His *Theoretischpraktische Oboen-Schule* (Vienna, 1825), which was translated into French and Italian, remained for many years a standard work. He also published some compositions, chiefly for oboe. His thirteen-key oboe was the most advanced instrument of its day, and was a model for many years to come (illustration in P. Bate; *The Oboe* (London, 1956), where he is described as 'the father of the modern German oboe'). FétisB describes his style as 'at once elegant and expressive'. The construction of his oboe, and the tradition he helped to found, suggest a broader, softer style than the more brilliant, incisive French manner. See Weber's review of his concert with *Michal Januš, above, No. 55.

Siebert, Franz (dates unknown). The principal bass at the Prague Opera, he was one of the busiest and most versatile artists in Weber's company. His roles included Mozart's Leporello, Figaro and Publius, Rocco (*Fidelio*), and many leading parts in works by Méhul, *Cherubini, Spontini, *Paer, Dalayrac, etc. See Weber's review of one of his concerts, above, No. 53.

Spohr, Louis (1784–1859). Spohr first met Weber in Stuttgart in 1807, and was by his own account somewhat dismissive of his *Rübezahl*. Later they became friends, especially during Weber's visit to Gotha in 1812. Spohr had been Kapellmeister since 1805, and was on the point of departure. In 1806 he married the harpist Dorette Scheidler (1787–1834). Weber produced Spohr's *Faust* in 1816 (see above, No. 80) and admired a good deal in his music, though not without reservations: he found *The Last Judgement* 'very lengthy and studied, pointlessly modulated and constructed entirely on Mozartian ideas' (Diary, 16 September 1812), but praised the G minor Quartet as 'very beautiful and well composed, plenty of flow and unity' (Diary, 27 September 1812). Spohr rather cautiously returned the compliments, suggesting that the success of *Der Freischütz* was because of Weber's gift in writing for the masses. He had himself abandoned a *Freischütz* (to a libretto with a tragic ending) on learning of Weber's plans. It was at Weber's recommendation that Spohr was appointed to Kassel in 1822, as he gratefully acknowledged in his *Selbstbiographie* (Kassel and Göttingen, 1860–1).

Stöger, Johann August (1791–1861). He changed his family name of Althaller to Stöger on abandoning the Church for the stage. He had a great success as a tenor first in Vienna, then in Brno and Olomouc, before he attracted the attention of *Liebich in Prague. However, he did not join the company until 1816, on Liebich's death, when he worked as administrator. He left Prague in 1821, though he married Liebich's widow Johanna in the following year; he then became a very successful theatre director in Vienna before returning to Prague, where he helped to restore the theatre's standards from the decline into which they had fallen in the wake of Weber's departure.

Stümer, Johann Heinrich (1789–1857). The son of a village cantor, he studied with Righini and made his début as Belmonte in Berlin in 1811. He had a vast repertory that included sacred music as well as all the main tenor roles in Berlin: he sang the Evangelist in Mendelssohn's 1829 revival of Bach's St Matthew Passion. He appeared in Dresden as a guest, but Weber failed to secure him as a member of the company. He sang Max in *Der Freischütz* ninety-six times between 1821 and 1830, and Huon in *Oberon* in 1828.

Tochtermann, Philipp Jakob (1775–1833). One of the most successful character tenors of his day in Munich, he first studied under *Danzi before making his début in Mannheim in 1797. He moved to Munich in 1799, where he remained throughout his career. He became producer in 1799, court singer in 1802, and director of the Opera in 1817. He was no less admired for his fine voice than for the intelligence of his acting. His most famous role was Simeon in Méhul's *Joseph*.

Tollmann, Johann (1775–1829). A violinist in the Munich Court Orchestra, he moved to Basel in 1805 as director of the Amateur Concerts.

Treitschke, Georg Friedrich (1776–1842). From about 1800 he was in Vienna, working in various theatres as director and librettist. He is most famous for the operatic projects on which he worked with Beethoven, above all the revision of Sonnleithner's text of *Fidelio* for the second revival in 1814. He also wrote texts for a number of other composers, especially *Weigl. Weber knew him well and corresponded with him.

Vitásek [Witasek, Wittaschek, Wittassek], **Jan Nepomuk** [Johann August] (1771–1839). From 1814 he was director of music at Prague Cathedral. He composed much music, in a style that did not go beyond a basically Mozartian idiom. His most famous work was the opera *David* (Prague, 1810).

Vogler, Abbé **Georg Joseph** (1749–1814). Vogler's reputation as an organist, composer, theorist and travelling virtuoso was at its height when Weber first met him, in Vienna in 1803. Much impressed by Vogler's flamboyant personality, Weber was ready to overlook the strong element of charlatanry that went with Vogler's undoubted gifts. He made the vocal score of Vogler's opera *Samori* (J39: a task he found little better than drudgery). It was Vogler who first drew Weber's attention to folksong, and who secured him his first post, as Kapellmeister in Breslau in 1804. Later, in Darmstadt in 1810, Weber, *Meyerbeer, *Gänsbacher and *Gottfried Weber formed a group of Vogler's favourite pupils. A very real affection existed between them and their teacher: they planned and wrote a birthday ode for him (see above, No. 8), and Weber intended to write a biography of him, though this never progressed further than two articles (above, Nos. 7 and 77).

Weber, Bernard Anselm (1766–1821). Like his namesakes (but not relations) *Gottfried and Carl Maria, Weber was a pupil of *Vogler, and toured with him.

He became Kapellmeister in Berlin in 1793, remaining powerful and effective until in 1818 illness compelled him gradually to withdraw from his duties. Though committed to German opera, and the composer of some quite successful works, he behaved jealously towards Carl Maria over *Silvana*, in part because he seems to have feared being supplanted in his post by a younger and more talented rival. Carl Maria reviewed his *Deodata* in Munich courteously (see above No. 25).

Weber, (Friedrich) Dionys [Diviš] (1766–1842). Like Carl Maria (to whom he was no relation), he studied with *Vogler. He was a composer, especially of dance music, a celebrated teacher, and from 1811 director of the newly founded Prague Conservatory. He was not warmly disposed towards Carl Maria, whose musical tastes were hardly to the liking of a man who could not follow Beethoven beyond the Second Symphony and next to Mozart admired Lindpaintner: this is on the evidence of Wagner (in *Mein Leben* (Munich, 1911)), who nevertheless managed to secure a performance of his own C major Symphony under Weber's 'dry and terribly noisy baton'.

Weber, Gottfried (1779–1839). When Carl Maria von Weber was expelled from Stuttgart in 1810, it was in the house of his namesake (but not relation) Gottfried that lodging was found for his father Franz Anton. Gottfried's influence gained a hearing for Carl Maria in the town, and their close friendship resulted in the formation of the Harmonischer Verein. Gottfried was secretary, treasurer and archivist, and contributed essays under the pseudonyms G. Giusto and Julius Billig (one he shared with *Meyerbeer). A famous theorist, he was regarded by *Vogler as the most learned of the talented group of pupils that included Meyerbeer, Carl Maria and *Gänsbacher. Together with Gottfried's brother-in-law *Alexander von Dusch, the two Webers spent much time wandering about the countryside singing and playing (to Carl Maria's guitar accompaniment) the folksongs that were then a novel Romantic thrill, tinged with Rousseauist delight in the virtues of simple peasants and their art. Carl Maria had reservations about Gottfried's Chronometer, a primitive metronome consisting of a pendulum with calibrated knots on the string, since he resisted judging and maintaining tempo by mechanical means. Carl Maria's First Symphony was dedicated to Gottfried, and Gottfried dedicated his Op. 15 Piano Sonata to Carl Maria: his request for a performance was answered musically, with sly reference to its chromatic nature, in the canon 'Die Sonate soll ich spielen' (J89). Carl Maria's letters to Gottfried are valuable for the information they contain about contemporary musical life.

Weigl, Joseph (1766–1846). His numerous operas were popular especially in Vienna. The most successful of them, *Die Schweizerfamilie* (1809), conquered virtually every German stage, and others which had long careers included *Die Uniform* (1798), *L'amor marinaro* (*Der Korsar, oder Die Liebe unter den Seeleuten*, 1797) and *Das Waisenhaus* (1808). See Weber's essay on the latter, above,

No. 99, and on *Die Jugend Peters des Grossen*, above, No. 56. He was nearly appointed to the Italian Opera in Dresden in 1807, a post that would have made him Weber's opposite number from 1817 onwards; it went instead to Morlacchi.

Weixelbaum, Georg (b. 1780). Abandoning theological studies, he first studied the violin and then took to the stage, where he became one of the most successful German tenors of the day. He also composed an opera, *Berthold der Zaeringer*. The *AMZ* described him as having a fine voice and a good technique, his chief fault being his tendency to sentimental interpretations and roles (*AMZ* XIII (1811), 411–12). His wife Josephine (born Marchetti-Fantozzi, 1786) was taken from Naples to Berlin by her mother at the age of nine and set to study music. She made her début in Dresden at sixteen, moving two years later to Munich and becoming principal soprano at the Opera in 1805. She married Weixelbaum in 1809.

Weixelbaum, Josephine   *see* Weixelbaum, Georg.

Wenzel, Jan (1762–1831). Abandoning the Church for music, he became a famous piano and singing teacher in Prague. He was also organist of St Vitus's Cathedral for forty years, from 1791. He made the first piano arrangements of Mozart's symphonies, and published some piano music of his own. He was said to play Mozart, Clementi and Koželuh 'with a swift, lively and marvellous dexterity' (DKB). See Weber's review of his concert, above, No. 73.

Westenholz, Friedrich (1778–1840). A distinguished oboist, he was one of eight children of the composer Carl von Westenholz (1736–89) and the singer and pianist Eleonore Fritscher (1759–1838). She also composed, and her works, like her son's, were published by Schlesinger. Friedrich's sinfonia concertante for flute and oboe was his Op. 6: see above, No. 5, for Weber's review of a performance by *Sellner and *Januš.

Wilhelmi, Georg (b. 1787). He joined *Liebich's company in Prague as an actor and singer, taking secondary roles such as the Commandant in *Les Deux journées*. He was then engaged as an actor in Dresden in 1817, for 'young lovers and intriguers, also *bons vivants*', and in the absence of a leading tenor was obliged to sing second tenor roles. He had a powerful voice of limited range: in *Joseph* he 'shouted and sang out of tune, lacking as he did a sound technique' (*AMZ* XIX (1817), 34), though *Theodor Hell praised him as 'powerful and pleasant; he is well trained and has unusual fluency' (*DAZ*, No. 34, 8 February 1817).

Wohlbrück, Johann Gottfried (1770–1822). Born in Berlin, he made his début as an actor in Kassel in 1789. He was in Riga in 1796–8, playing a few character roles. After other engagements, he moved to Munich in 1810, leaving in 1817 to become director of the Leipzig Stadttheater. He was much praised for his character acting in the Iffland school. His writings include a five-act play, *Das Gelübde* (Hamburg, 1802), as well as *Kampf und Sieg* for Weber. His wife was a contralto who specialized in comic roles. They had several children: Gustav Friedrich became a well-known character actor; Ludwig August was also a character actor who, after a colourful career in Germany, fled to Turkey and was killed when caught breaking into a harem; Marianne was a soprano who had been a successful Queen of Night (though she did not please Weber), and who later married Heinrich Marschner; and Wilhelm August wrote the text for Marschner's *Der Vampyr*. Another daughter was a soprano whom Weber had heard as Joas in *Poissl's *Athalia* in Munich in 1814.

Wurm, Ferdinand (Albert Aloys) (1783–1834). A popular *buffo* tenor, actor and dancer, he made his first appearance as Hanswurst in various travelling companies before accepting an engagement in Warsaw in 1801. He moved to Würzburg in 1804, and then joined the Berlin Nationaltheater in 1809, making his début as Tamino. One of his most famous parts was Lorenz in *Das Hausgesinde* (see above No. 90); his success led to the work being given a hundred times in less than two years. He left Berlin in 1815.

Zingarelli, Niccolò Antonio (1752–1836). Though his highly successful and prolific career took place almost entirely in Italy, his fame extended to Germany, where a good many of his operas, particularly the comic ones, became popular at the Italian Court Operas.

Zschokke, Heinrich (1771–1848). Though of German birth, he spent most of his career in Switzerland, especially in Aarau (where Weber missed seeing him on a visit to try to recruit him for the Harmonischer Verein). His historical novels modelled on Scott excited the interest of his fellow Romantics; and perhaps the success of his first important work, a sensational novel about secret societies, *Die schwarzen Brüder* (1791–5), also made Weber think of him as a potential member of the Verein.

Zucker, Emilie   *see* Zucker, Julie.

Zucker, Julie (1800–25). The daughter of the actor and singer Eleonora Zucker and granddaughter of the actor Heinrich Bösenberg, she first played children's roles in the Italian Opera in Dresden, also appearing in plays. She joined the German Opera on 10 March 1817. Having matured into a useful and talented member of the company, she made a success of Aennchen in *Der Freischütz*. She married the first horn of the orchestra, August Haase, in 1819. By 1818 she had become the leading soubrette of the German Opera, and a very popular artist, with a small but lively and true voice. She was praised for her 'exceptional sprightliness, tenderness and charm' (*DAZ*, No. 234, 30 September 1823). Illness forced her to retire in 1824, and she died when not yet twenty-five. She often appeared with her elder sister Emilie, who was normally cast in elderly comic roles.

Index

This index lists all references to persons; an exception is made in the case of the list of Bohemian nobles who supported the foundation of the Prague Conservatory, which may be found on p. 245. Works are indexed under their composer or author. Page references in bold type are to an essay by Weber on the subject. *denotes an entry in the Biographical Glossary (pp. 365–87).

389